D1384687

Ring of Ice

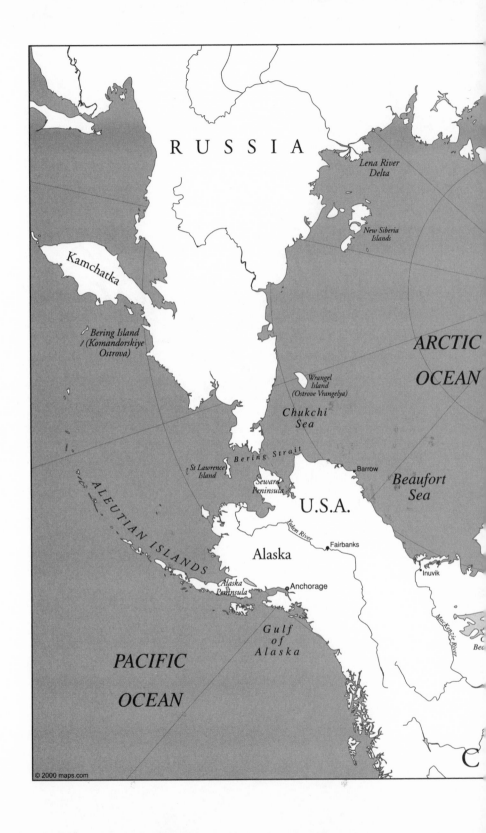

RUSSIA

Lena River Delta

New Siberia Islands

Kamchatka

Bering Island (Komandorskiye Ostrova)

Wrangel Island (Ostrove Vrangelya)

ARCTIC

OCEAN

Chukchi Sea

Bering Strait

St Lawrence Island

Barrow

Beaufort Sea

Seward Peninsula

U.S.A.

Yukon River

Fairbanks

ALEUTIAN ISLANDS

Alaska

Inuvik

Alaska Peninsula

Anchorage

MacKenzie River

Bea

PACIFIC

Gulf of Alaska

OCEAN

C

NORWAY

Norwegian Sea

Franz Josef Land

Spitsbergen (Svalbard)

60°

70°

80°

Greenland Sea

ICELAND

North Pole

Denmark Strait

GREENLAND

Arctic Circle

Thule (Qaanaaq)

Upernavik

JEEN

ABETH

ANDS

Ellesmere Island

Baffin Bay

Godthab (Nuuk)

Davis Strait

Devon Island

rry Channel

Somerset Island

Prince of Wales Island

Baffin Island

Boothia Peninsula

King William Island

Igloolik

Pelly Bay

Foxe Basin

Labrador Sea

Frobisher Bay

Hudson Strait

Barren Grounds

Cape Wolstenholme

Hudson Bay

N A D A

ATLANTIC OCEAN

Ring of Ice

True Tales of Adventure, Exploration,
and Arctic Life

Edited by **Peter Stark**

The Lyons Press

Designed by Compset, Inc.

Printed in the United States of America

10 9 8 7 6 5 4 3 2 1

Library of Congress Cataloging-in-Publication Data

Ring of ice: true tales of adventure, exploration, and Arctic life / edited by Peter Stark.
    p. cm.
    Includes bibliographical references.
    ISBN 1-55821-537-9 (hc)
    1. Arctic regions—Discovery and exploration.   2. Arctic regions—Descrip-tion and travel.   3. Arctic peoples—Social life and customs.   I. Stark, Peter, 1954–

    G608   .R52 2000
    998—dc21   00-025546

"Bering Wrecks His Ship in Siberia and Steller Has the Last Laugh" reprinted from *George Wilhelm Steller: Journal of a Voyage with Bering, 1741–1742*, edited and with an introduction by O. W. Frost; translated by Margritt A. Engel with the permission of the publishers, Stanford University Press. Copyright © 1988 by the Board of Trustees of the Leland Stanford Junior University.

"Amundsen Answers, 'Yes.'" reprinted from *Roald Amundsen: My Life as an Explorer* by Roald Amundsen. Used by permission of Doubleday, a division of Random House, Inc.

"The Story of Comock the Eskimo" reprinted from *The Story of Comock the Es-kimo* as told to Robert Flaherty and edited by Edmund Carpenter with permis-sion of Edmund Carpenter.

"Kabloona: A Visit to Father Henry's Ice Cave" reprinted with permission of the Estate of Gontran de Poncins and the Watkins/Loomis Agency.

*To the Peoples
of the Arctic*

$\mathcal{C}$ontents

Contents of Poetry

xii   Contents

Acknowledgments

I'd like to thank for their help in suggesting material for this anthology librarian Phil Cronenwett of the Special Collections department at Dartmouth College that oversees the Stefansson collection of Arctic exploration literature; Marvin Falk of the Alaskan Polar Region Department, Rasmuson Library, University of Alaska, Fairbanks; Frank Soos and Jim Rupert of the University of Alaska, Fairbanks, writing program; Kenneth Mikko, editor of *N66*, literary magazine of the Barents Region; Murray Morgan; Barry Lopez; Mark Watkins; and Seth Kantner. Also very helpful were the staffs at the Suzzallo Library of the University of Washington, Seattle; the library of the Arctic Institute of North America at the University of Calgary; Mansfield Library at the University of Montana; and the Missoula Public Library. Special thanks go to Jane Ragsdale who did a diligent and thorough job in helping research the earliest exploration literature. Peter Burford was instrumental in the conception and early stage of this project. The editorial staff at The Lyons Press has been a delight to work with throughout, in particular Bryan Oettel and Becky Koh, who did much to bring shape and strength to its overall design.

My deep thanks to my wife, Amy, and our two small children, Molly and Skyler, who didn't mind (usually) as I hauled milk crates of photocopies and dusty old volumes—and sometimes the entire photocopy machine—on our family travels and through our daily life, and when I periodically disappeared into the Arctic of my imagination for hours at a time. Lastly, my everlasting gratitude to the peoples of the Arctic; without them, the world would be much poorer in spirit.

The lands around my dwelling
Are more beautiful
From the day
When it is given me to see
Faces I have never seen before.
All is more beautiful,
All is more beautiful,
And life is Thankfulness.
These guests of mine
Make my house grand.

—Takornâq (Iglulik Eskimo woman)

Sun and Moon

THE MOON SLEPT with many women, but did not get pleasure from any of them. Then he decided to sleep with his pretty little sister, the Sun. He covered his face with ashes and slipped into her sleeping skins. Afterwards she said:

"Whoever you are, do it again . . ."

And so they did it again, all night long.

In the morning, the Sun learned the identity of her lover. Now she became quite upset. "You will never do this awful thing to me again, Brother," she said.

"Oh no? I am the stronger."

She picked up an *ulu* and cut off her breasts. Then she mixed her own urine and blood in a dish with the breasts and made *akutaq*. This she gave to her brother, saying: "Here, eat this if you want to see how I taste!" Then she dashed out of the house. The Moon paused to eat the breasts, and then went after her.

And still he pursues his sister, even today, to get her for his mate. But she is faster and always keeps well ahead of him. Thus, owing to the Moon's lust, does night follow day.

—Arctic legend

$\mathcal{I}$ntroduction

Through the nineteenth century, Arctic explorers believed that they needed only to smash their ships through a ring of ice, circling the top of the globe like some giant frosted doughnut, and they'd break out into a warm, open polar sea. From there they'd tack easily on soft breezes to the North Pole and thence to the wealthy coasts of the Orient. Hundreds of adventurers were crushed in their ships by ice, killed off by scurvy and starvation and frozen to death on ice floes before the others realized that what covered the top of the world was ice, ice, and more ice—something that the Inuit inhabitants of the region, of course, knew all along.

Over the last two centuries, scores of expeditions have penetrated far into the High Arctic and brought back knowledge that has begun to fill this vast hole in the European imagination. Yet still the Arctic remains a great blank spot in the Southern mind, a negation rather than an affirmation, a kind of vast white death.

The aim of this anthology is to add life and color to this monochromatic landscape. There are stories beyond number from the Arctic, stories of the people and animals who have managed for thousands of years to live there, and stories of the Southern explorers who attempted—and inevitably failed—to "conquer" with brute force the unyielding snow and ice and tundra. The stories, to me at least, are stunning in their courage and forbearance and, at times, ignorance and arrogance. Most of all, they're stunning in their sheer human drama, for the hardships of the Arctic, perhaps more than of any other inhabited environment on earth, heighten the joy and deepen the suffering of being alive.

The exploration of the Arctic is, as much as anything, a story of wrecks, and starvation, and thwarted hopes of the Europeans (I include Americans in this term). Slowly, only over hundreds of years did they begin to grasp that their vaunted navies and armies and their know-how, which had conquered and colonized much of Africa, Asia, and the Americas, were utterly powerless before the brutal cold and crushing plates of ice that slide inexorably about the top of the world. Unlike those warm continents nearer the Equator, here in the Arctic the natives weren't the threat: The natives were the saviors, rescuing the ice-trapped Europeans from starvation, scurvy, and exposure with warm huts and freshly killed game. For all their violence, there is a gentle side to the stories from the Arctic, for all the tragedy, something tender.

I've chosen to let the story of the Arctic's exploration by Europeans form the "backbone" of the anthology. Though Greeks and Vikings and other adventurers had visited the Arctic centuries earlier, I begin this anthology with the approach of the nineteenth century, when "Arctic fever" began to sweep Europe and America. Framing this story of exploration, and interspersed throughout it, are Inuit poems and legends, as well as accounts of Inuit life. These show some of the warmth of a people who inhabit the planet's coldest regions. At times, the juxtaposition of the Inuit poems and legends with the explorers' journals points up the vast gaps between the two cultures—for example, between the goal-oriented, Christian-fueled, march-til-you-drop-no-matter-what-the-obstacle Europeans and the infinite patience and humility of the Inuit who can wait . . . wait . . . wait . . . until the moment, or the ice conditions, or the wind are just right to travel, to hunt, to build an igloo and sleep. One also sees the common humanity shared by these two wildly different groups—the simple, ecstatic joy of feasting after long deprivation versus the bottomless grief at the loss of a child or a beloved shipmate.

I've chosen, in the most unscientific way, both the European and Inuit excerpts that tell this story of the Arctic. My major criteria have been to select excerpts that 1) make compelling reading; 2) take place above treeline (only one of the many possible definitions of "Arctic"); 3) contribute to the sense of overall story; and 4) represent as many distinct voices as possible. Mostly I've chosen by my gut—the approaching-middle-age gut of someone who has a deep affection for the Arctic and its people, who has read and written much about it and traveled with Inuit hunters by dogsled, camping on the sea ice and sharing boiled seal intestines and raw liver and narwhal skin, but who remains unequivocally an outsider, a Southerner. Out of the thousands of excerpts I could have chosen in an infinite variety of combinations, this anthology represents only one version—only one person's version—of the Arctic.

Most, but not all, of the excerpts concern the Arctic of North America or Greenland and relatively few the Scandinavian or Siberian Arctic. There are many reasons for this: the availability of materials in English; the intensity of exploration in the American and Greenlandic Arctic in the nineteenth century; and the range of the Inuit (Eskimo) culture, which reaches from Greenland across North America to eastern Siberia but does not stretch across most of Siberia or Europe. Much good writing has come out of Alaska, and the state has its own body of literature and even its own anthologies. However, relatively little of that work is included here as most of it is set well below "treeline."

I've chosen to precede each of the excerpts with an Inuit poem to serve as a kind of counterpoint to the explorers' accounts. To me, the traditional Inuit poetry is the most eloquent expression of a people's perception of their world and the values they worked out in order to survive the incredible rigors of the Arctic. The poems emphasize the Inuit ethic of sharing, egalitarianism, and incessant hunting, as well as the simple joys and fears of life. This is particularly poignant in contrast to the accounts of the explorers, in which the theme is more often the drive, drive, drive to ram one's way through the ice toward some abstract geographical goal, often with disastrous results. But we also see in the poems the psychological strain, caused by living day in and day out in the harsh environment, in the form of murders, jealousies, and the sudden explosion of anger.

I've tried to match each poem with an explorer's excerpt on the basis of subject matter and tone. Thus (to cite one of the less obvious examples) the Inuit "poems of derision" about jealousy complement the bitter Cook-Peary controversy over who was the first to reach the North Pole. Almost all of the poems were originally collected early in the twentieth century by Knud Rasmussen; most are taken from Tom Lowenstein's fine rendering of these poems into English in his *Eskimo Poems from Canada and Greenland*. The Inuit legends are from Lawrence Millman's collection of stories from across the Arctic, *A Kayak Full of Ghosts*.

A final note about "graphic" material: Readers may find some excerpts in this anthology gruesome, violent, sexual, and, to some at least, promiscuous and obscene. I've made no effort to cull or soften this material, as some earlier collections have, and in fact have taken care to include it. One of the fascinations about life in the Arctic is how profoundly elemental it is due to the very sparseness of the landscape and harshness of the climate. There is no doubt about where one stands in the food chain: One kills and eats other beings in order to survive. In times of famine those other beings might be other humans, even kin, who themselves have died of starvation. Likewise, in a world of ice that gives up little easily, sexuality, like an abundance of food, is a pleasure to be savored, although the urge sometimes goes awry.

—PETER STARK
Missoula, Montana

The Uncertain Life
To be spoken when suddenly in mortal danger

See, great earth,
these heaps
of pale bones in the wind!

They crumble in the air
of the wide world,
in the wide world's air,
pale, wind-dried bones,
decaying in the air!

—Padloq (Iglulik Eskimo man)

What is the Earth?

THREE FRIENDS WERE curious about the size and shape of the earth. They were so curious that they decided to go exploring. They had traveled for three days and two nights when they came to an enormous ice-house. "Let's go in," one of the friends said. And so they went into the house, which seemed to be without end. They followed the walls in order not to get lost. Where was the passage through which they'd entered? They walked for days, for months, for years. At last they grew very weary. It was all they could do to crawl now. Then two of the friends could no longer crawl and they sat down and died. The third friend managed to find the exit-passage. His kayak was exactly where he'd left it. He came back to his people as a very old man. And he told them: "The earth is simply a very big ice-house."

Then he died too.

—Arctic legend

BOOK I

The Search for the Northwest Passage

From the time Columbus and his contemporaries discovered that an entire continent stood in the way of the hope for a cheap, quick passage to the riches of the Orient, European explorers set out to find a route to all that wealth that led over the top of North America—the fabled Northwest Passage. At the same time, others probed over the top of Russia and Siberia in search of the Northeast Passage. The search for the Northwest Passage continued through the nineteenth century—first out of hope, then, long after it had been shown to be virtually worthless as a navigation route, out of fierce national pride. Among those who tried to negotiate it and failed were men like Sir John Franklin, who with his two ships and 128 men utterly vanished in the attempt. Not until 1906 did a boat finally navigate its entire length—Roald Amundsen, in the tiny *Gjoa*, who spent three years poking along it. Instead of monetary riches, what the search for the Passage gave to the world was a wealth of geographical information, including the exploration and mapping of much of the North American Arctic, not to mention a richness of drama and determination equaled in few other realms of human endeavor.

Charm for Good Weather

Ija-ija,
a furious storm
surrounds me,
   ija-ija!
But quiet and glossy
lies the sea,
   ija-ija!
The spirit of the air
smooths my path,
   ija-ija!
I paddle on
in quiet water,
out of danger.
   Ija-ija!

—East Greenland Eskimos

Steller Has the Last Laugh

BY GEORG WILHELM STELLER (GERMAN, 1741)

A Danish navigator in Russian employ, Vitus Bering had sailed north in 1725 along the Siberian coast and through the strait that now bears his name and determined that land did not connect Asia and America. In 1741, after spending ten years in the building of ships and other preparations in Siberia, he sailed again for North America to explore its commercial possibilities. The voyage was a calamity of misjudgments, according to the writings of his cabin mate, Georg Wilhelm Steller. These accrued in a final climactic disaster on the return home to Russia's Kamchatka coast when Bering's scurvy-ridden ship piled onto a barren island, and, shipwrecked, Bering himself perished.

Steller, the expedition's German-born scientist, records in contemptuous undertones how he was ridiculed by the ship's officers and sailors for his botanizing and curiosity, and laughed at whenever he suggested an alternate way of doing something. The expedition had gone awry from the start. After building two ships in Kamchatka and crossing the North Pacific, the *St. Peter*, separated from her sister ship, reached the American coastline late in the summer season. To Steller's disgust, the expedition's leaders were chafing to hurry back to Russia before winter closed in, although the original plan had been to overwinter in America. The *St. Peter*

5

put in very briefly at Kayak Island and Cape St. Elias in today's
Gulf of Alaska. Steller landed by small boat for a frenzied ten
hours of exploration and collecting until the ship's officers sent a
message to Steller on shore telling him, quite literally, to get his ass
back onboard or they'd sail home without him.

Still, Steller managed to learn or infer a great deal from those
ten hours—he speculated, for example, that the natives (who were
identified many years later as Chugach Eskimo) had originally
come from Kamchatka because he saw in an abandoned camp how
they prepared an infusion of sweet grass exactly like the natives in
Siberia. He had another chance for more exploration when the ship
stopped for water on an island off the Alaskan Peninsula. On this
homeward voyage Steller was accorded a bittersweet revenge for the
abuses he'd suffered. The *St. Peter* staggered back across the Pacific
through autumn storms with its crew dying one by one of scurvy
and too weak to set the sails properly. (Steller treated them as best
he could with grasses he'd learned were antiscorbutics.) Desperate
to make landfall, the party's leaders mistook a remote and unknown
island—henceforth known as Bering Island—as a familiar section
of the Kamchatka coastline. While they tried to decide whether this
was in fact the mainland, a storm cast the ship over the island's reef
and eventually broke her to pieces. The Bering party found itself
shipwrecked on an inaccessible island with winter coming on.

Bering quickly died of scurvy. Steller became a de facto leader
and supervised the construction of the underground winter huts
that saved their lives. The survivors hunted the abundant game on
the island, its fresh meat curing their ailment. With the coming of
spring, they busied themselves in constructing a small boat from
the salvaged timbers of their wrecked ship. That summer, packed
in so tightly they could not turn over as they slept, Steller and the
last survivors of the Bering expedition—forty-six of the original
seventy-eight men—sailed home to the Russian mainland.

The first excerpt begins as the party spots land after their
scurvy-plagued, storm-battered crossing of the Pacific toward
home. It follows the wreck of the *St. Peter* and the building of un-

derground huts in which to spend the winter on the uninhabited island where they've washed up. The second excerpt picks up the following summer as the party constructs a boat out of the timber of
the ruined ship and sets off again toward Kamchatka.

How great and extraordinary was the joy of everyone over this sight is
indescribable. The half-dead crawled out to see it. From our hearts we
thanked God for his favor. The very sick Captain-Commander was
himself not a little cheered, and everyone spoke about how he intended
to take care of his health and to take a rest after suffering such terrible
hardships. Cups of brandy, here and there secretly concealed, were
produced to sustain the pleasure. We heard trumpeted forth with the
voice of a herald the coolly spoken words, "If there had been a thousand navigators, they could not have hit it within a hair's breadth like
this in their reckoning. We are not even half a mile off."

Sketches of Avacha were taken in hand. The land was found to
agree completely with the sketches: Isopa, Cape Shipunski, the mouth
of the harbor, and the lighthouse were pointed out. Although they
could have known according to the reckoning that we were at the very
least at 55 degrees and regardless of the fact that Avacha was still two
degrees farther south, the course was set toward the north because they
saw a cape they called Shipunski.

When we had sailed around the imagined Isopa, which was the outermost point of the first island, and were in the inlet between the first
and second island, whose channel we could not yet see to regard them
as islands, it happened that the noon sun prompted an observation, according to which we were between 55 and 56 degrees, north latitude;
consequently, we began to doubt, not unreasonably, that this was the
region around Avacha. They endeavored to go back around the south-
east end of the first island, which we had considered to be Isopa, but in
vain, though they tried, tacking, until evening. Toward evening we
turned to the north to get away from the land because we expected a
storm, which indeed turned up in the night.

Since the sails remained standing on the mast and topmast as they
had stood during the day, not bound up, and could not be taken in by

the weak remnant of men in the rising storm in the middle of the night, the shrouds of the mainmast were torn to pieces by the mighty force of the wind and the sails so that in the morning, after the restless and stormy night had changed into a most pleasant day and weather, we did not dare to carry as much sail as we could and needed to carry.

Therefore, on November 6, Master Khitrov, having previously brought the Lieutenant to his point of view and persuaded the subordinate officers and ordinary seamen, proposed that the Captain-Commander, in consideration of the late time, the bad weather, the ruined shrouds, the useless mast, the distance to Avacha, and the small number of sick and feeble sailors and soldiers, should hold a council in which it would be resolved to go ashore in a bay before us in the west where a harbor was conjectured to be at a distance of six miles as determined by the naked eye. And this was then also brought about in the following way: the Captain-Commander insisted that we should attempt to reach the port since we had already borne and hazarded so much and even now had still six barrels of water and could use the foremast and proceed with the lower sail. Both officers argued against his opinion and insisted on going ashore in the bay, having won over the subordinate officers and crew to this plan, who consented to it and were willing to put their signatures to the decision if, as unknowledgeable individuals, they could be assured positively that this land was Kamchatka. If it was not, they would be willing to risk the utmost and work to their last hour.

Nevertheless, some people, by smooth as well as harsh words, were made to sign against their will because—Master Khitrov professing that if this were not Kamchatka, he would let his head be chopped off—the matter now depended on a very few.

Then the Captain-Commander ordered the adjutant, at that time reduced in rank to sailor, presently Lieutenant Ovtsin, to express his opinion. But when he concurred in the Captain-Commander's opinion, the two officers answered: "Out! Shut up, you dog, you son of a bitch!" So he had to leave the council.

At last, according to rank, my turn came also. But reflecting on Ovtsin's example, I answered: "I have not been consulted about anything from the start, and my advice will not be taken if it is not just as you want it. Besides, the gentlemen themselves say I am no seaman, so I would rather say nothing."

Then I was asked if I would not at least, as a credible person (which I was now for the first time considered), add a written statement attesting to the sickness and miserable condition of the crew, which in good conscience I agreed to do.

And thus it was decided to enter the bay and land there, but from there to send for posthorses for the transport of the crew to Nishnei. Although the site contradicted the opinion that this could be Kamchatka because the mainland of Kamchatka lies northeast-southwest from Cape Chukchi to Lopatka, whereas Bering's Island lies northwest-southeast, still hope remained that it could be one of the Kamchatkan capes, most of which lie in the aforesaid direction. Although the land seemed too large for a cape and none on Kamchatka is known to surpass Shipunski, which is 15 miles long, this island could at least be estimated at 25 miles by eyesight, and, besides, other points of land extended from it way out to sea so that by all rights it could be considered rather a land apart than a cape. Although it could and should be decided from all this that it neither was nor could be the land of Kamchatka or a cape, and, besides, no one on our ship professed to know it, the false notion from the first expedition reassured everyone that no island could be found this close to Kamchatka at this latitude, where exploration had been undertaken at sea for fifty miles to the east.

Therefore we sailed into the bay straight to shore without further concern about anything.

When toward four o'clock in the evening we got so close to land that we were but a mile away yet for three hours no officer had appeared on deck (as customary in all dangerous circumstances) and they all were gently and sweetly asleep, I went to the Captain-Commander and asked that he might please order that at least one of the officers be at his watch to look for a spot where we could drop anchor because it appeared that they intended to drift ashore without further precaution. Whereupon both were called on deck but did not show any greater care than to order holding straight for the shore.

When later, toward sunset, we had gotten within two versts of shore, they began to lower the lead and advanced a verst closer, where finally at nine fathoms they dropped anchor. By now it was nighttime but very bright from the moonlight, when after the lapse of a half-hour such a heavy surf came up at this place that the ship was tossed back and forth like a ball, on the point of hitting bottom, and the anchor rope broke so that we could think of nothing but the ship's being smashed to pieces on the bottom. The confusion became still greater because of the constant breaking of the waves, the cries and lamentations, so that we knew neither who should give orders nor who was being ordered. All they did, terrified and gripped by fear of death, was to shout that the anchor should be cut and a new one thrown into the surf.

When they had lost two anchors in half a quarter-hour, the present Lieutenant Ovtsin with the then-boatswain came at last and forbade the casting of any more anchors because it was to no avail as long as we were tossed hither and yon between the waves on the reef, but they advised rather to let the ship float. When we were across the reefs and surf, the aforesaid men who kept their wits and could make reasonable decisions let the last anchor drop, and we were situated between the surf and the shore as in a calm lake, suddenly calm and free of all fear of being stranded.

How strange were the positions held and how wise the speeches made during this time can be concluded from the fact that some, while in obvious danger to their lives, could not keep from laughing. One asked, "Is the water very salty?" as if death were sweeter in sweet water. Another cried out to encourage the men: "Oh, we are all done for! O God, our ship! A disaster has befallen our ship!" And God now revealed the resolute hearts that had been bursting with courage before!

The biggest speechmaker and adviser in all things kept himself hidden until others, with God's help, had found counsel. Then he, too, started to encourage the men that they should not be afraid. But he was pale as a corpse in his resoluteness.

In this confusion, once again a bit of folly occurred. Although we had carried with us for some days several dead soldiers and the dead trumpeter to bury them ashore, they were now flung without ceremony head over heels into the sea since some superstitious persons, at the start of the terror, considered the dead as the cause of the rising sea.

All through the night, it was very pleasant and bright.

On November 7, we again had a very pleasant bright day and northwest winds.

This morning I packed up as much of my baggage as I could get together, and because now I clearly saw that our ship could not hold beyond the first severe storm, when it must be driven either into the sea or on shore and broken into pieces, I went ashore first, together with Plenisner, my cossack, and several sick men.

We were not yet on the beach when something struck us as strange, namely, some sea otters came from shore toward us into the sea, which some of us at first from a distance took for bears, others for wolverines, but afterwards got to know only too well.

As soon as I was ashore, Plenisner went hunting with a shotgun, but I reconnoitered the natural environment, and, when I had made various observations, returned toward evening to the sick, where we also found the Lieutenant very weak and faint. We treated ourselves to tea, whereby I said to the Lieutenant, "God knows if this is Kamchatka."

But he answered me: "What else would it be? We will soon send for posthorses. But we will let the ship be brought by cossacks to the mouth of the Kamchatka River. We can always raise the anchors. The first priority is that we save the men."

During this time Plenisner came, related what he had observed, and brought a half-dozen ptarmigans, which he sent to the Captain-Commander with the Lieutenant to invigorate him through this fresh food. I, however, sent him some nasturtium plants and brooklime for a salad.

Meanwhile, two cossacks and a cannoneer came who had killed two sea otters and two seals, news that appeared quite extraordinary to us, and we reproached them for having taken the pelts and not bringing the meat in for our refreshment. Whereupon they fetched a seal because it appeared to them better to eat than the sea otter.

When it was evening, I cooked a few ptarmigan as a soup and ate it with Plenisner, young Waxell, and my cossack. During this time, Plenisner made a hut of driftwood and an old sail. Under it we slept overnight together with the sick.

On November 8, we enjoyed pleasant weather once more.

This morning Plenisner and I made an agreement that he should shoot birds while I was to look for other things that would be usable as food, but toward noon we should meet one another at this place.

At first I went with my cossack to the east along the beach, gathered various natural specimens, and chased a sea otter, whereas my cossack shot eight blue foxes whose numbers and fatness and also the fact that they were not at all shy surprised me extraordinarily. And since I saw at the same time on the beach many manatees, which I had never seen before—nor could I even know what kind of an animal it was since half of it was constantly under water—and since my cossack, to the question whether this was not the *plevun* or *makoai* of the Kamchadals (about which I had gathered only verbal information), answered that this animal existed nowhere on Kamchatka, and since at the same time I did not notice the slightest tree or shrub, I came to doubt that this could possibly be Kamchatka, but was perhaps an island, in which opinion the sea clouds over in the south confirmed me still more, that this land was not wide and accordingly was an island everywhere surrounded by water.

Toward noon I came to our hut. After I had eaten there with Plenisner, we both decided to go with our cossack to the west along the beach and look around for woods or timber. But we did not find the least bit. On the other hand, we saw several sea otters and killed some blue foxes and ptarmigans, and on our way home we sat down by a small stream, treated ourselves to tea, and thanked God from the heart that we had sufficient water and firm ground again, whereby we reflected on everything—on what strange things had happened to us, and on the unjust proceedings of various men.

Today an attempt was made by bringing out the anchors, large and small, as many as we had, to make the ship as secure as possible, and the ship did not come ashore.

In the evening as we sat around a campfire, having eaten our meal, a blue fox came and before our very eyes took away two ptarmigans—the first instance of so many future tricks and thefts.

Through the following words, I encouraged my sick and feeble cossack and thereby made a start of our future comradeship, since he regarded me as the cause of his misfortune and reproached me for my curiosity, which had brought me in this misery: "Cheer up!" I said. "God will help. Even if this is not our country, we still have hope of getting there. You will not die of hunger. If you cannot work and wait on me, I will wait on you. I know your honest heart and what you have done for me. Everything I have is yours also. Just ask and I will share with you half of all I have until God helps."

But he said: "Good enough. I will serve your majesty with pleasure. But you have brought me into this misery. Who forced you to go with these people? Could you not have enjoyed the good life on the Bolshaia River?"

I laughed heartily at his candor and said: "Thank God, we are both alive. If I have dragged you into this misery, then you have also, with God's help, a faithful friend and benefactor in me. My intentions were good, Thoma. So let yours be good also. After all, you do not know what could have happened to you at home."

Meanwhile, I let this conversation serve to concern myself about how we could shelter ourselves against winter by building a hut, if this country should not be Kamchatka but an island. In the evening, therefore, I began to discuss with Plenisner that we should build a hut in any case, and, no matter how circumstances might turn out, we would stand by each other in word and deed as good friends. Even though he did not want to agree with my opinion that this was an island, he pretended to, in order not to depress me, and consented to my proposal to build a hut.

On November 9, the wind was easterly, the weather rather tolerable.

In the morning we went out to scout for a site and to gather wood, and we surveyed the spot where we later built and the whole command spent the winter and put up their dwellings. However, we spent altogether too much time killing foxes, of which Plenisner and I killed 60 in a day, partly slaying them with an ax, partly stabbing them with a lakut *palma*.

Toward evening we went back to our old hut, where we encountered more sick who had been brought ashore.

On November 10, the wind was easterly, the weather clear before noon, overcast in the afternoon, and in the night the wind blew a lot of snow around.

We carried all our baggage a verst away to the site that we had selected the day before for building a dwelling. During this time, a number of sick were brought ashore from the ship, among them also the Captain-Commander, who spent this evening and night under a tent. Together with others I was with him, and I was amazed at his composure and strange contentment.

He asked what I thought of this land.

I replied, "It does not look like Kamchatka to me." I explained that the abundance and tame self-possession of the animals alone clearly indicated that it must be a sparsely inhabited or entirely uninhabited land. Nonetheless, it could not be far from Katchatka, since the land plants I had observed here were precisely the same in number, species, and size as in Kamchatka, whereas, on the other hand, the most peculiar plants discovered in America were not to be found here in similar locales. Besides, I had found a poplar window shutter with cross moldings brought some years ago at high tide and washed over with sand at the place where we later built our huts. I showed it and at the same time drew attention to the fact that it was certainly Russian workmanship and undoubtedly from the *ambars* erected at the mouth of the Kamchatka River, and it might well be that this was Cape Kronotski, which, by all sensible reasons and experience—though reliable information was wanting—was the most likely place. But still I did not refrain from expressing the doubts I had about it because of another experience. I showed a piece of a fox trap I had found the first day on the beach, in which, instead of iron teeth, there were *zubki,* or teeth, of a shell that authors call Entale. I mentioned not having any information that this shell was found on Kamchatka, and I had not seen any either. Rather, it was to be supposed that it had drifted here from America and that this invention had been attached for lack of iron, since through trade in Kamchatka iron teeth and pins could be found in abundance among all Kamchadals, and I had not received any word of such an invention in spite of all my inquiries. At the same time I also disclosed my view with regard to the unknown sea animal, the manatee, and the character of the sea clouds opposite in the south.

Whereupon he replied, "The ship probably cannot be saved. May God spare us our longboat!"

Toward evening, after we had eaten with the Captain-Commander the ptarmigans that Plenisner had shot during the day, the assistant surgeon Betge and I came to an agreement: that if he liked, he could stay with us, for which he thanked me. And thus our company was four men strong.

So we walked to our new homesite, sat by a campfire, and over a cup of tea discussed how we would put our plan into effect. To that end, we erected a small hut, which I covered with my two overcoats and an old blanket. We covered the cracks on the sides with dead foxes that we had killed that day and had lying about in heaps. Then we went to bed.

But Betge went to the Captain-Commander.

About midnight a violent wind arose that brought a lot of snow with it, blew off our roof, and chased Plenisner, my cossack, and me from our beds.

We ran all along the seashore in the night, gathered driftwood together, brought it to a pit like a grave dug for two people, and decided to spend the night here. We put crosspieces of wood over the top, covered the roof with our clothes, coats, and blankets, made a fire to keep us warm, and went to sleep. God be thanked, we spent the night very well in this way.

The next day, November 11, I went to the sea and hauled up a seal, whose fat I cooked with peas and consumed with my three comrades, who during this time fabricated two shovels and started to enlarge our "grave."

In the afternoon, the Captain-Commander was carried to us on poles and had a tent of sailcloth put up on the spot that we at first picked out for our dwelling, and we treated him, as well as the other officers who came to our "grave," to tea.

Toward evening both officers went back to the ship, and Master Khitrov proposed to the Lieutenant to spend the winter aboard ship in the open sea since they would have there more warmth and comfort than ashore, where, lacking wood, they would have to endure the winter under a tent. And this proposal was accepted as very reasonable, although three days later the Master came ashore of his own volition and could not be made to go back aboard ship even under orders when he was supposed to beach the ship.

At any rate, we enlarged our dwelling in the earth by digging, and we strenuously gathered wood everywhere on the beach for its roof. Every evening we put up a light roof, and we acquired the fifth man, assistant constable Roselius, for our company. Several of the rank and file who still had some strength left also began to dig out a four-cornered "grave" in the frozen sand, and they covered it the next day with double sails to keep the sick under it.

On November 12, we worked busily on our house and saw also that others, following our example, dug out a third dwelling for themselves in the same way, which later got its name from its initiator, the boatswain Aleksei Ivanov.

That day many sick were brought from the ship, among them some who, like the cannoneer, died as soon as they came into the air, others in the boat on the crossing over like the soldier Savin Stepanov, others once on shore like the sailor Sylvester.

This afternoon for the first time with Plenisner and Betge, I went hunting or, as we afterwards called it in Siberian, on the *promysel.* We clubbed four sea otters, of which we hid half in the river which afterwards received the name Sea Otter Creek; the field on which they were killed became Sea Otter Field. The meat, together with the pelts and entrails, we carried home.

We got home at night, made various tasty dishes from the liver, kidney, heart, and meat, and dined on them with thanks and prayers that God might not deprive us of this food in the future and thereby force us to feed on the stinking carcasses of the hated foxes, which, for this reason, we did not intend to kill off but wanted only to frighten.

But already we considered the precious otter pelts as a useless burden that had lost their value, and because we did not have time to dry and prepare them, they were thrown down from one day to the next until they finally spoiled entirely, together with many other skins, and were chewed up by the foxes. On the other hand, we began to value some things more highly that formerly we had had little or no regard for, such as axes, knives, awls, needles, thread, shoelaces, shoes, shirts; stockings, poles, rope, and the like, which many a one would formerly not have deigned to pick up.

We realized that our character, knowledge, and other superior traits would in the future neither entitle us to respect and preference before others, nor be sufficient to maintain our lives. Therefore, before shame and necessity forced us, we ourselves resolved to work according to the strength we still had left and to do what we could, so as not to be laughed at later or to wait first for an order.

Thus we five Germans also entered into a community of goods among ourselves concerning the victuals we still had left and with it one household management that in the end we might not fall short. Of the others—three cossacks and the late Captain-Commander's two servants who later joined us—although not treating them as before, we nevertheless demanded that they obey when we decided something together since, after all, they got all the household goods and other necessities from us.

Meanwhile, we began to call each and all by their patronymic and first names to win over the men so that if something unfortunate should occur in the future, we could count more on their loyalty and be a jump ahead. And we soon saw that Peter Maximovich was more obliging than Petrusha had been earlier.

Besides, although we came to an agreement among ourselves this evening about how we would arrange our housekeeping in the future in case this or that misfortune occurred, since the hope of getting to Asia, so far as we were concerned, was not altogether abandoned, we discussed the unfortunate circumstances in which we all had been placed in such a short time that, setting aside the routine work belonging to everyone, we were now bound to work in a way we were not used to just to maintain a difficult life. Nonetheless, we admonished each other not to lose heart and, with the greatest possible cheerfulness and earnestness, to do everything necessary for our own happiness as well as for the welfare of others and by our efforts to support in all sincerity the strength and initiative of all the rest.

This day I took over to the Captain-Commander a young sea otter, still nursing on its mother, and recommended it to him as persuasively as possible, that he might order it to be prepared for him for lack of fresh food.

But he declared a very great aversion for it and wondered at my taste, which was adapted to the circumstances of time and place, and he preferred to refresh himself as long as possible with ptarmigan, of which he got more from our company than he could eat.

On November 13, we continued our building project and divided into three parties. The first went to work to bring the sick and provisions from the ship; others dragged home large logs four versts from Wood Creek. I and a sick cannoneer remained at home. I took over the cooking, while he constructed a sled with which to haul wood and other necessities.

And everywhere we looked on nothing but depressing and terrifying sights.

Even before they could be buried, the dead were mutilated by foxes that sniffed at and even dared to attack the sick—still alive and helpless—who were lying on the beach everywhere without cover under the open sky. One screamed because he was cold, another from hunger and thirst, as the mouths of many were in such a wretched state from scurvy that they could not eat anything on account of the great pain because the gums were swollen up like a sponge, brown-black and grown high over the teeth and covering them.

The foxes, which now turned up among us in countless numbers, became accustomed to the sight of men and, contrary to habit and nature, ever tamer, more wicked, and so malicious that they dragged apart all the baggage, ate the leather sacks, scattered the provisions, stole and dragged away from one his boots, from another his socks and trousers, gloves, coats, all of which yet lay under the open sky and for lack of ablebodied men could not be protected. They even dragged off iron and other implements that were of no use to them. There was nothing they did not sniff at and steal from, and it seemed that these evil animals would chastise us more and more in the future, as actually happened. For this punishment perhaps the popular Kamchatkan fox skins may be responsible, and thus, like the Philistines, we were to be punished, in turn, by foxes.

It also seemed that, the more we slew and the oftener we tortured them most cruelly before the eyes of others, letting them run off half-skinned, without eyes, without tails, and with feet half-roasted, the more malicious the others became and the more determined, so that they even penetrated our dwellings and dragged away everything they could get to, even iron and all kinds of gear. At the same time, they made us laugh in our greatest misery by their crafty and comical monkey tricks.

Having taken on the position of cook, I took up yet a second function, to visit the Captain-Commander now and then, and to give him a hand in one thing or another since he could now have little service from his two servants, who were sometimes not present when he asked for a drink of water.

Moreover, because we were the first who had set up housekeeping, we were able to come to the assistance of some of the weak and sick and to bring them a warm soup, and we continued in this way until they were somewhat recovered and were able to care for themselves.

This day the barracks was finished, and during the afternoon we carried in a lot of the sick. But because of the narrowness of the space, they were lying about everywhere on the ground, covered with rags and clothes. Nobody could nurse the others, and there was nothing but wailing and complaining whereby they many times called God's judgment down for revenge on the originators of their misfortune, and this sight was so pitiful and sad since one pitied the other, but no one could render suitable assistance to the other, so that even the most courageous should have lost heart.

On November 15, all the sick were finally brought ashore. We took one of them, named Boris Sand, to take care of in our dwelling. God brought him back to health within three months.

Master Khitrov begged us fervently, for God's sake, to take him into our partnership and to assign him a corner because he could not possibly lie among the ordinary seamen who day as well as night reproached him for all kinds of past affairs, accused him of all kinds of mistreatment, and let out all kinds of threats. He said he could not stand it any longer, and he would consequently have to die under the open sky. But because our dwelling was already crammed full and no one was allowed to take action on anything without the foreknowledge of the others, we were all opposed because we were all offended by him, and we refused him all hope, because he was healthy and lazy, and he alone had plunged us into this misfortune.

During the following days, our misery and the work became ever greater. All the sick were finally brought ashore, Lieutenant Waxell last of all. He was in such terrible shape from scurvy that we all gave up hope for his life. But we did not fail to rush to his and the others' assistance with household and medical help as best we could, forgetting all his previous behavior. We were now all the more interested in his recovery, being fearful that after his death, when the command would fall to Master Khitrov, by some dreaded calamity our deliverance from this place could be delayed for a very long time or not happen at all because of universal hatred and mistrust.

In spite of the Lieutenant's urgent request, we could not take him into our hut, but we promised to see to it that a special one would be built for him and several of the sick. We had our men do it, and in the meantime he had to bear being with the others in the barracks.

On this day, through three men who had been sent out, we also received the sad news (which depressed the common ranks even more and made them more difficult) that in the west they had not found any signs that this was Kamchatka—rather that human beings had never been here.

Besides, we were in daily fear that by the constant storms the ship might sail suddenly into the sea and with it all our provisions and hope of deliverance would be lost since, because of the high waves within three or four days later, we could not get to the ship any more with the boat—and because too many difficulties were encountered with Master Khitrov, who already some time ago had been ordered to beach the ship. Also, ten or twelve men, who up to now had worked beyond their capacity without relief and to the end of this month had often been obliged to go into the cold sea up to their armpits, were so exhausted that we anyway saw our impending doom to be close at hand.

Generally, want, lack of clothing, cold and dampness, weakness, sickness, impatience, and despair were daily guests.

Even a little rest was enjoyed with the secret condition that we should be strengthened by it for the even harder and more incessant work that could be foreseen far into the future. But when, toward the end of November, the packet boat was put on the beach by a storm better than human industry could perhaps have accomplished it, people started to relax.

Since now all difficulties about the dismantled ship and food were over and since also for a change we sometimes caught in our half-rotted fishnets so many fish that we were supplied for eight days from a single haul, we made progress with the help of many hands, with redoubled courage, and with the constant exertion and friendly encouragement of Lieutenant Waxell so that toward mid-July, insofar as its hull was concerned, the ship stood ready on the stocks. The rest of the time up to August 13 was spent in making rigging, spars, and masts, in blacksmithing, in the tedious burning of tar from old ropes, and in erecting a platform for launching the ship, costing all the more trouble because we were poorly supplied with wood and other materials. The wood for the platform was everywhere hauled in from distant parts of the coast; fastening down the platform was effected by putting the cannons on it.

Others built a storehouse in which to keep the materials we left behind. Still others were busy with construction of an oven and preparation of biscuit for the trip. Some prepared the barrels (which had to be made fast for the voyage) with iron hoops and ropes because such work had earlier been left undone in Okhotsk. Some reconnoitered the bottom of the sea. There was not a one wanting to be idle, nor supposed to be, the closer and dearer to each was the hope of deliverance from this island to his homeland. Although the hope of acquiring more otter pelts made some wish to spend yet another winter, they finally out of shame would not consider it.

On August 8, everything was in order and ready for the voyage. In the afternoon, we all said a prayer in which we begged God for a successful launching of the ship (which was dedicated to the holy apostle Peter and named after him), and having finished our prayer, in the name of God we began the launching.

But to our great consternation, it happened that the ship stood still and by its weight pressed down on the platform, which had been inadvertently built too low. Nevertheless, we worked with all our strength and, by using winches, raised it up so far that the mistake could be remedied by means of a few thick planks pushed in on the sides between the ship and the platform, and thereupon the ship was successfully launched. But by that time the high tide had subsided, and the final launch into the sea remained suspended until the next day when, at flood tide, the ship was successfully let into the sea.

Subsequently we worked night and day. On August 11, the mast was set in place and secured with shrouds. Next, water and provisions and everyone's baggage were loaded in.

Everyone had to declare in writing beforehand how much weight he wished to take along. Whatever exceeded the allowed weight was left behind.

While the vessel was being loaded, the carpenters were still making a small boat that could be placed on deck so that we could use it in an emergency.

Our ship's provisions consisted of 25 puds of rye flour; five barrels of salted manatee meat; two puds of peas; and one barrel of salted beef, which had been spared even in our often-urgent need on the return voyage from America. In addition, each man was given four pounds of butter. Most who had managed economically had retained so much from their small provision that, on departure, they were able to bake a half-pud of biscuit from it and take it along. Those, however, who had earlier lived too well made themselves biscuit of dried manatee meat.

On August 13, one and all, with much inner turmoil, left their dwellings for the last time and went on board the ship. It was either going to take us to the frontiers of Asia and our beloved fatherland or, after so much toil, hope, and longing, would pass judgment on our miserable pilgrimage according to the will of the Highest. When we all had boarded the ship, we realized for the first time how crowded the space was and how difficult the voyage would be for that reason. We lay one on top of the other and crawled over one another. The Lieutenant, Master Khitrov, I, and the Lieutenant's son had in the narrow cabin ultimately the best space. The other 42 men were lying in the hold, which was packed so full with water barrels, provisions, and baggage that the crew could scarcely lie between all that and the deck. At all times three men shared two places because the entire crew was divided into three watches. But because the space was still too crowded, we began to throw into the sea the pillows, bedding, and clothing that had been brought along from the shore.

The new ship was 36 feet at the keel and 42 feet from stem to stern.

In the meantime, we saw the foxes on the beach inspect our dwellings with the greatest glee and occupy them as theirs; it seemed to amaze them that no one hindered them as usual. Besides, they found so many remnants of fat and meat come to them as their share in one fell swoop, to which diversion we left them on our part from the bottom of our hearts.

On the morning of August 14, we besought God in a special prayer for his blessed help and support for a successful voyage. Then we weighed anchor. Because the west wind helped us to pass by the southeastern point of the island, we elected—although the mouth of the Kamchatka River was twice as close and our ship scarcely in condition to endure an autumn storm—nevertheless the straight course to Avacha Bay. We advanced with a slight wind to such an extent that toward noon we were in the channel between Bering's Island and the island lying parallel five miles opposite to the east, and toward evening we reached the southeast end of our island.

This afternoon we spent in high spirits since in bright and pleasant weather we passed by the island on which we knew all the mountains and valleys, whose paths we had climbed so many times with great effort to scout for our food and for other reasons and on which we had bestowed names from various circumstances and events. Thereby God's grace and mercy became manifested to all, the more brightly considering how miserably we had arrived there on November 6, had miraculously nourished ourselves on this barren island, and with amazing labor had become ever more healthy, hardened, and strengthened; and the more we gazed at the island on our farewell, the clearer appeared to us, as in a mirror, God's wonderful and loving guidance.

Late in the evening we had come so far, thank God, that we were opposite the outermost point of the island.

On Sunday, August 15, the wind was gentle before noon, and we still had the southern side of the island in sight. Toward nightfall the wind increased, and after we cut and let drift in the sea the ship's large yawl, which up to now had served us so well but now had become a hindrance to our ship, we also completely lost sight of the island, and with wind and weather being very favorable, we began now to continue the straight course to Avacha west by south.

But toward midnight we were suddenly struck by the utmost terror because our ship was all at once filling with water through an unknown leak, which incident seemed all the more dangerous since everybody was familiar with the soundness of the new ship, and since the wind was strong, space cramped, and thus everyone was in everyone else's way. Also, because the ship was so tightly loaded, it was extremely difficult to discover the cause of the leak. Moreover, the pumps, when their use was most necessary, were plugged by numerous chips left in the hold since someone had forgotten to put kettles under them. In these circumstances, the sails were immediately taken in. Some cleared the baggage out of the way and looked for the leak. Others unceasingly poured out water with the kettles. Some threw into the sea the iron cannonballs and grapeshot brought along from the shore. And so it most fortunately happened that, when the ship was lightened and the leak in the ship plugged—the leak had been meanwhile discovered by our carpenter just where he had supposed it was and turned out to be above the waterline—we saw ourselves rescued from even this danger and from our sinking. But since through this accident we had been so fortuitously warned, we did not neglect to correct the oversight and to put kettles in under the pumps in the hold. It was also observed that this leak had occurred when the ship, after the platform broke, had been raised up with winches whose upper part had been attached under the waterline, and the boards had the more easily been moved out of alignment since, to speed up construction, they had been fastened only with iron nails without a single wooden peg.

On August 16, we continued the course we had started. On Tuesday, August 17, we suddenly caught sight of the mainland of Kamchatka; we came out of the sea opposite Cape Kronotski and found ourselves hardly a mile from shore since we caught sight of it during dark, foggy weather. Nevertheless, we stuck to the plan to sail for the harbor, from which we were still approximately thirty miles distant. However, since there was either a complete calm or contrary wind the whole time along the Kamchatkan shore, we spent another nine days tacking until, finally, on August 26, after using the oars 24 hours without a break, we arrived in the night at the entrance to the bay, and on the evening of August 27 anchored in the long-sought harbor itself.

As great as was the joy of each and all over our deliverance and safe arrival, yet the contrary and unexpected news that we received from a Kamchadal at the entrance put us in a far greater agitation and a complete forgetfulness of ourselves. Everyone had considered us dead or otherwise come to grief; our property left behind had fallen into other hands and had mostly been carried off. Therefore, joy and sorrow often changed in a few moments, according to the nature of the news about general and special happenings. We were all so accustomed to misery and wretched living that, instead of other enterprises, we considered that the previous circumstances would always continue and thought we were dreaming the present ones.

The next day, after we had heartily thanked Almighty God in a common prayer for his gracious protection, our miraculous preservation, and our happy return to Asia and at the same time to each one's fatherland, the naval officers decided to go on to Okhotsk this autumn. I bade them farewell and prepared to hike the thirty miles to the Bolshaia River and to reach my own longed-for people. I arrived there safely on September 5 and joined in celebrating the high festival of the name-day of Her Majesty, our most gracious Empress.

After some weeks had passed, we received the news that, because of strong contrary winds, the ship destined for Okhotsk had returned to the harbor to pass the winter. But at Bolshaia River the news of our reaching port had not been transmitted to the galliot *Okhotsk* because of the negligence of the commander there, even though the galliot did not sail out of the river mouth to Okhotsk until the third day after receipt of the news in the *ostrog*. Because of these two incidents, we had to bear being counted among the dead eight months longer than necessary.

The Widow's Song

Why will people
have no mercy on me?
Sleep comes hard
since Maula's killer
showed no mercy.
Ijaja-ijaja.

Was the agony I felt so strange,
when I saw the man I loved
thrown on the earth
with bowed head?
Murdered by enemies,
worms have for ever
deprived him
of his homecoming.
Ijaja-ijaja.

He was not alone
in leaving me.
My little son
has vanished
to the shadow-land.
Ijaja-ijaja.

Now I'm like a beast
caught in the snare
of my hut.
Ijaja-ijaja.

Long will be my journey
on the earth.
It seems as if
I'll never get beyond
the foot-prints that I make. . . .

A worthless amulet
is all my property:
while the northern light
dances its sparkling steps
in the sky.

—Qernertoq (Copper Eskimo woman)

Samuel Hearne Witnesses a Massacre

BY SAMUEL HEARNE (BRITISH, 1771)

One of the most intrepid and successful of the early Arctic explorers, Samuel Hearne has been dubbed "the Marco Polo of the Barren Lands"—the vast, difficult region of tundra west of Hudson Bay. His résumé reads like a boy's adventure novel: He lost his father at a young age, rejected his mother's wishes that he pursue a classical education, and shipped out at age eleven as a servant boy in the Royal Navy to do battle with the French fleet. At age twenty-one he signed on with the Hudson's Bay Company, serving as mate of a sloop that traded with the Inuit along the great bay's western shore. Starting in 1769, at the age of twenty-four, he embarked on the first of three foot journeys across the unexplored Barren Grounds in search of the Coppermine River, rumored to empty into the Arctic Ocean and contain great mineral riches. He thus became one of the first Europeans to make an overland journey to what is now the Canadian shore of the Arctic Ocean; in his journal of those travels he left behind one of the most eloquent documents of Arctic exploration.

In this excerpt Hearne first encounters the Inuit who live along the Arctic Ocean near the Coppermine's mouth. The Indians who serve as Hearne's guides are traditional enemies with the Inuit, and Hearne stands by, helpless and in horror, while his companions am-

27

bush and brutally slaughter the band of unsuspecting Inuit. From that day, the waterfall on the Coppermine where the massacre occurred has been called "Bloody Falls."

Soon after our arrival at the river-side, three Indians were sent off as spies, in order to see if any Esquimaux were inhabiting the river-side between us and the sea. After walking about three-quarters of a mile by the side of the river, we put up, when most of the Indians went a hunting, and killed several musk-oxen and some deer. They were employed all the remainder of the day and night in splitting and drying the meat by the fire. As we were not then in want of provisions, and as deer and other animals were so plentiful, that each day's journey might have provided for itself, I was at a loss to account for this unusual œconomy of my companions; but was soon informed, that those preparations were made with a view to have victuals enough ready-cooked to serve us to the river's mouth, without being obliged to kill any in our way, as the report of the guns, and the smoke of the fires, would be liable to alarm the natives, if any should be near at hand, and give them an opportunity of escaping.

Early in the morning of the fifteenth, we set out, when I immediately began my survey, which I continued about ten miles down the river, till heavy rain coming on we were obliged to put up; and the place where we lay that night was the end, or edge of the woods, the whole space between it and the sea being entirely barren hills and wide open marshes. In the course of this day's survey, I found the river as full of shoals as the part which I had seen before; and in many places it was so greatly diminished in its width, that in our way we passed by two more capital falls.

Early in the morning of the sixteenth, the weather being fine and pleasant, I again proceeded with my survey, and continued it for ten miles farther down the river; but still found it the same as before, being every where full of falls and shoals. At this time (it being about noon) the three men who had been sent as spies met us on their return, and informed my companions that five tents of Esquimaux were on the west side of the river. The situation, they said, was very convenient for surprising them; and, according to their account, I judged it to be about twelve miles from the place we met the spies. When the Indians received this intelligence, no further attendance or attention was paid to my survey, but their whole thoughts were immediately engaged in planning the best method of attack, and how they might steal on the poor Esquimaux the ensuing night, and kill them all while asleep. To accomplish this bloody design more effectually, the Indians thought it necessary to cross the river as soon as possible; and, by the account of the spies, it appeared that no part was more convenient for the purpose than that where we had met them, it being there very smooth, and at a considerable distance from any fall. Accordingly, after the Indians had put all their guns, spears, targets, &c. in good order, we crossed the river, which took up some time.

When we arrived on the West side of the river, each painted the front of his target or shield; some with the figure of the Sun, others with that of the Moon, several with different kinds of birds and beasts of prey, and many with the images of imaginary beings, which, according to their silly notions, are the inhabitants of the differents elements, Earth, Sea, Air, &c.

On enquiring the reason of their doing so, I learned that each man painted his shield with the image of that being on which he relied most for success in the intended engagement. Some were contented with a single representation; while others, doubtful, as I suppose, of the quality and power of any single being, had their shields covered to the very margin with a group of hieroglyphics, quite unintelligible to every one except the painter. Indeed, from the hurry in which this business was necessarily done, the want of every colour but red and black, and the deficiency of skill in the artist, most of those paintings had more the appearance of a number of accidental blotches, than "of any thing that is on the earth, or in the water under the earth"; and though some few of them conveyed a tolerable idea of the thing intended, yet even these were many degrees worse than our country sign-paintings in England.

When this piece of superstition was completed, we began to advance toward the Esquimaux tents; but were very careful to avoid crossing any hills, or talking loud, for fear of being seen or overheard by the inhabitants; by which means the distance was not only much greater than it otherwise would have been, but, for the sake of keeping in the lowest grounds, we were obliged to walk through entire swamps of stiff marly clay, sometimes up to the knees. Our course, however, on this occasion, though very serpentine, was not altogether so remote from the river as entirely to exclude me from a view of it the whole way : on the contrary, several times (according to the situation of the ground) we advanced so near it, as to give me an opportunity of convincing myself that it was as unnavigable as it was in those parts which I had surveyed before, and which entirely corresponded with the accounts given of it by the spies.

It is perhaps worth remarking, that my crew, though an undisciplined rabble, and by no means accustomed to war or command, seemingly acted on this horrid occasion with the utmost uniformity of sentiment. There was not among them the least altercation or separate opinion; all were united in the general cause, and as ready to follow where Matonabbee led, as he appeared to be ready to lead, according to the advice of an old Copper Indian, who had joined us on our first arrival at the river where this bloody business was first proposed.

Never was reciprocity of interest more generally regarded among a number of people, than it was on the present occasion by my crew, for not one was a moment in want of any thing that another could spare; and if ever the spirit of disinterested friendship expanded the heart of a Northern Indian, it was here exhibited in the most extensive meaning of the word. Property of every kind that could be of general use now ceased to be private, and every one who had any thing which came under that description, seemed proud of an opportunity of giving it, or lending it to those who had none, or were most in want of it.

The number of my crew was so much greater than that which five tents could contain, and the warlike manner in which they were equipped so greatly superior to what could be expected of the poor Esquimaux, that no less than a total massacre of every one of them was likely to be the case, unless Providence should work a miracle for their deliverance.

The land was so situated that we walked under cover of the rocks and hills till we were within two hundred yards of the tents. There we lay in ambush for some time, watching the motions of the Esquimaux; and here the Indians would have advised me to stay till the fight was over, but to this I could by no means consent; for I considered that when the Esquimaux came to be surprised, they would try every way to escape, and if they found me alone, not knowing me from an enemy, they would probably proceed to violence against me when no person was near to assist. For this reason I determined to accompany them, telling them at the same time, that I would not have any hand in the murder they were about to commit, unless I found it necessary for my own safety. The Indians were not displeased at this proposal; one of them immediately fixed me a spear, and another lent me a broad bayonet for my protection, but at that time I could not be provided with a target; nor did I want to be encumbered with such an unnecessary piece of lumber.

While we lay in ambush, the Indians performed the last ceremonies which were thought necessary before the engagement. These chiefly consisted in painting their faces; some all black, some all red, and others with a mixture of the two; and to prevent their hair from blowing into their eyes, it was either tied before and behind, and on both sides, or else cut short all round. The next thing they considered was to make themselves as light as possible for running; which they did, by pulling off their stockings, and either cutting off the sleeves of their jackets, or rolling them up close to their armpits; and though the muskettoes at that time were so numerous as to surpass all credibility, yet some of the Indians actually pulled off their jackets and entered the lists quite naked, except their breech-cloths and shoes. Fearing I might have occasion to run with the rest, I thought it also advisable to pull off my stockings and cap, and to tie my hair as close up as possible.

By the time the Indians had made themselves thus completely frightful, it was near one o'clock in the morning of the seventeenth; when finding all the Esquimaux quiet in their tents, they rushed forth from their ambuscade, and fell on the poor unsuspecting creatures, unperceived till close at the very eves of their tents, when they soon began the bloody massacre, while I stood neuter in the rear.

In a few seconds, the horrible scene commenced; it was shocking beyond description; the poor unhappy victims were surprised in the midst of their sleep, and had neither time nor power to make any resistance; men, women, and children, in all upward of twenty, ran out of their tents stark naked, and endeavoured to make their escape; but the Indians having possession of all the landside, to no place could they fly for shelter. One alternative only remained, that of jumping into the river; but, as none of them attempted it, they all fell a sacrifice to Indian barbarity!

The shrieks and groans of the poor expiring wretches were truly dreadful; and my horror was much increased at seeing a young girl, seemingly about eighteen years of age, killed so near me, that when the first spear was stuck into her side she fell down at my feet, and twisted round my legs, so that it was with difficulty that I could disengage myself from her dying grasps. As two Indian men pursued this unfortunate victim, I solicited very hard for her life; but the murderers made no reply till they had stuck both their spears through her body, and transfixed her to the ground. They then looked me sternly in the face, and began to ridicule me, by asking if I wanted an Esquimaux wife; and paid not the smallest regard to the shrieks and agony of the poor wretch, who was twining round their spears like an eel! Indeed, after receiving much abusive language from them on the occasion, I was at length obliged to desire that they would be more expeditious in dispatching their victim out of her misery, otherwise I should be obliged, out of pity, to assist in the friendly office of putting an end to the existence of a fellow-creature who was so cruelly wounded. On this request being made, one of the Indians hastily drew his spear from the place where it was first lodged, and pierced it through her breast near the heart. The love of life, however, even in this most miserable state, was so predominant, that thought this might justly be called the most merciful act that could be done for the poor creature, it seemed to be unwelcome, for though much exhausted by pain and loss of blood, she made several efforts to ward off the friendly blow. My situation and the terror of my mind at beholding this butchery, cannot easily be conceived, much less described; though I summed up all the fortitude I was master of on the occasion, it was with difficulty that I could refrain from tears; and I am confident that my features must have feelingly expressed how sincerely I was affected at the barbarous scene I then witnessed; even at this hour I cannot reflect on the transactions of that horrid day without shedding tears.

The brutish manner in which these savages used the bodies they had so cruelly bereaved of life was so shocking, that it would be indecent to describe it; particularly their curiosity in examining, and the remarks they made, on the formation of the women; which, they pretended to say, differed materially from that of their own. For my own part I must acknowledge, that however favourable the opportunity for determining that point might have been, yet my thoughts at the time were too much agitated to admit of any such remarks; and I firmly believe, that had there actually been as much difference between them as there is said to be between the Hottentots and those of Europe, it would not have been in my power to have marked the distinction. I have reason to think, however, that there is no ground for the assertion; and really believe that the declaration of the Indians on this occasion, was utterly void of truth, and proceeded only from the implacable hatred they bore to the whole tribe of people of whom I am speaking.

When the Indians had completed the murder of the poor Esquimaux, seven other tents on the East side the river immediately engaged their attention : very luckily, however, our canoes and baggage had been left at a little distance up the river, so that they had no way of crossing to get at them. The river at this part being little more than eighty yards wide, they began firing at them from the West side. The poor Esquimaux on the opposite shore, though all up in arms, did not attempt to abandon their tents; and they were so un-acquainted with the nature of fire-arms, that when the bullets struck the ground, they ran in crowds to see what was sent them, and seemed anxious to examine all the pieces of lead which they found flattened against the rocks. At length one of the Esquimaux men was shot in the calf of his leg, which put them in great confusion. They all immediately embarked in their little canoes, and paddled to a shoal in the middle of the river, which being somewhat more than a gunshot from any part of the shore, put them out of the reach of our barbarians.

When the savages discovered that the surviving Esquimaux had gained the shore above mentioned, the Northern Indians began to plunder the tents of the deceased of all the copper utensils they could find; such as hatchets, bayonets, knives, &c. after which they assembled on the top of an adjacent high hill, and standing all in a cluster, so as to form a solid circle, with their spears erect in the air, gave many shouts of victory, constantly clashing their spears against each other, and frequently calling out *tima! tima!** by way of derision to the poor surviving Esquimaux, who were standing on the shoal almost knee-deep in water. After parading the hill for some time, it was agreed to return up the river to the place where we had left our canoes and baggage, which was about half a mile distant, and then to cross the river again and plunder the seven tents on the East side. This resolution was immediately put in force; and as ferrying across with only three or four canoes† took a considerable time, and as we

---

*Tima in the Esquimaux language is a friendly word similar to *what cheer?*

†When the fifteen Indians turned back at the Stony Mountains, they took two or three canoes with them ; some of our crew that were sent ahead as messengers had not yet returned, which occasioned the number of our canoes to be so small.

were, from the crookedness of the river and the form of the land, entirely under cover, several of the poor surviving Esquimaux, thinking
probably that we were gone about our business, and meant to trouble
them no more, had returned from the shoal to their habitations. When
we approached their tents, which we did under cover of the rocks, we
found them busily employed tying up bundles. These the Indians
seized with their usual ferocity; on which, the Esquimaux having
their canoes lying ready in the water, immediately embarked, and all
of them got safe to the former shoal, except an old man, who was so
intent on collecting his things, that the Indians coming upon him before he could reach his canoe, he fell a sacrifice to their fury : I verily
believe not less than twenty had a hand in his death, as his whole
body was like a cullender. It is here necessary to observe that the
spies when on the look-out, could not see these seven tents, though
close under them, as the bank, on which they stood, stretched over
them.

It ought to have been mentioned in its proper place, that in making
our retreat up the river, after killing the Esquimaux on the West side,
we saw an old woman sitting by the side of the water, killing salmon,
which lay at the foot of the fall as thick as a shoal of herrings. Whether
from the noise of the fall, or a natural defect in the old woman's hearing, it is hard to determine, but certain it is, she had no knowledge of
the tragical scene which had been so lately transacted at the tents,
though she was no more than two hundred yards from the place. When
we first perceived her, she seemed perfectly at ease, and was entirely
surrounded with the produce of her labour. From her manner of behaviour, and the appearance of her eyes, which were as red as blood, it is
more than probable that her sight was not very good; for she scarcely
discerned that the Indians were enemies, till they were within twice the
length of their spears of her. It was in vain that she attempted to fly, for
the wretches of my crew transfixed her to the ground in a few seconds,
and butchered her in the most savage manner. There was scarcely a
man among them who had not a thrust at her with his spear; and many
in doing this, aimed at torture, rather than immediate death, as they not

only poked out her eyes, but stabbed her in many parts very remote from those which are vital.

It may appear strange, that a person supposed to be almost blind should be employed in the business of fishing, and particularly with any degree of success; but when the multitude of fish is taken into the account, the wonder will cease. Indeed they were so numerous at the foot of the fall, that when a light pole, armed with a few spikes, which was the instrument the old woman used, was put under water, and hauled up with a jerk, it was scarcely possible to miss them. Some of my Indians tried the method, for curiosity, with the old woman's staff, and seldom got less than two at a jerk, sometimes three or four. Those fish, though very fine, and beautifully red, are but small, seldom weighing more (as near as I could judge) than six or seven pounds, and in general much less. Their numbers at this place were almost incredible, perhaps equal to any thing that is related of the salmon in Kamschatka, or any other part of the world. It does not appear that the Esquimaux have any other method of catching the fish, unless it be by spears and darts; for no appearance of nets was discovered either at their tents, or on any part of the shore. This is the case with all the Esquimaux on the West side of Hudson's Bay; spearing in Summer, and angling in Winter, are the only methods they have yet devised to catch fish, though at times their whole dependence for support is on that article.

When the Indians had plundered the seven tents of all the copper utensils, which seemed the only thing worth their notice, they threw all the tents and tent-poles into the river, destroyed a vast quantity of dried salmon, musk-oxen flesh, and other provisions; broke all the stone kettles; and, in fact, did all the mischief they possibly could to distress the poor creatures they could not murder, and who were standing on the shoal before mentioned, obliged to be woeful spectators of their great, or perhaps irreparable loss.

After the Indians had completed this piece of wantonness we sat down, and made a good meal of fresh salmon, which were as numerous at the place where we now rested, as they were on the West side of the river. When we had finished our meal, which was the first we had enjoyed for many hours, the Indians told me that they were again ready to assist me in making an end of my survey.

I Wonder Where?

Deep down, deep down inside,
you can get cold with fear.
Deep down, deep down inside,
you can get cold with fear
because you married
one who stayed a child,
who never grew.
Yet no-one wanted to be like
"The Lightly Downed",
who grew up like
an average human being,
restless and unbalanced.

Deep down, deep down inside,
you can get cold with fear.
Deep down, deep down inside,
you can get cold with fear
because game flees from you.
I wonder where?
I wonder where?
The musk oxen,
and the great inland bear,
the reindeer-herds,
all take to flight.
I wonder where?

—Netsit (Copper Eskimo man)

Franklin's First Retreat

BY JOHN FRANKLIN AND DR. JOHN RICHARDSON (BRITISH, 1820)

John Franklin—later Sir John—would become the Arctic's greatest tragic European hero when, searching for the Northwest Passage in 1845, he and his two ships and 128 men vanished. The search for Franklin became a cause celebre in Europe and America, with dozens of expeditions launched over the next fifteen years to find him—a number of them bankrolled by his widow—and countless poems and paens and pleas for search funds written on his behalf by members of a captivated public.

But despite all the breast-beating for him, Franklin was neither a very physically fit nor very clever explorer, though surely not lacking in sheer determination. Many of the mistakes that culminated in his destruction on the fatal third Franklin Expedition to the Arctic already were apparent in his two earlier expeditions. To the reader who knows Franklin's ultimate fate, his repeated decision to push on despite the contrary advice of the natives jumps out from the pages of his own journals. These dramatic journals of his first expeditions also happened to win him wide celebrity on his return to England as "the man who ate his boots."

The passages excerpted here are found in his account of the first Franklin Expedition. Franklin was then a thirty-three-year-old officer in the Royal Navy who had fought in the great battles of the Napoleonic Wars. With the French vanquished and Britain convinced of its own military prowess, the Royal Navy starting about 1817 turned its attention to staking out a Northwest Passage, expecting to make short work of it and claim the North Pole. Franklin served as second-in-command of the *Trent,* one of two ships sent north from Spitsbergen in 1818 to break through the "ring of ice," tack across that "open polar sea," and snag the North Pole. This attempt, of course, was quickly repelled by the ice.

On the strength of his duty aboard the *Trent,* Franklin was chosen to lead an overland expedition—though he had no experience on the tundra—from Great Slave Lake across the Barren Grounds to the Arctic Ocean as Samuel Hearne had done. But where Hearne had turned back south, Franklin's party was instructed to accomplish a monumental task—paddle or sail east all the way across the top of North America and map the Arctic coast. If possible, the party could meet up with the Royal Navy ships that were probing the Passage from the Atlantic side under Edward Parry.

Accompanying Franklin were Dr. John Richardson, a skilled surgeon and naturalist, and midshipmen and artists Robert Hood and George Back, plus a Scottish seaman, John Hepburn. They engaged an ever-changing number of Canadian voyageurs and Copper, Métis, and Iroquois Indians to haul the expedition's supplies on their backs and by canoe. The first excerpt describes a verbal confrontation between Captain Franklin and the Indian chief Akaitcho, who warned that the season was too far advanced for Franklin's group to head down the Coppermine to the sea. Contrary to Akaitcho's advice, Franklin pushes to go on down the Coppermine, planning to return at some later date to a winter quarters his party is building near Great Slave Lake. In the second excerpt, Franklin reaches the Arctic Ocean the following summer (having ultimately conceded to Akaitcho's advice). Pressing east along the Arctic coastline in hope of discovering the Passage, Franklin delays—until far too late, it turns out—the decision to turn back to their winter quarters at Fort Enterprise. The following excerpts show the tragic consequences of that decision.

[Aug. 25th, 1820] Akaitcho arrived with his party, and we were greatly disappointed at finding they had stored up only fifteen reindeer for us. St. Germain informed us, that having heard of the death of the chief's brother-in-law, they had spent several days in bewailing his loss, instead of hunting. We learned also, that the decease of this man had caused another party of the tribe, who had been sent by Mr. Wentzel to prepare provision for us on the banks of the Copper-Mine River, to remove to the shores of the Great Bear Lake, distant from our proposed route. Mortifying as these circumstances were, they produced less painful sensations than we experienced in the evening, by the refusal of Akaitcho to accompany us in the proposed descent of the Copper Mine River. When Mr. Wentzel, by my direction, communicated to him my intention of proceeding at once on that service, he desired a conference with me upon the subject, which being immediately granted, he began by stating, that the very attempt would be rash and dangerous, as the weather was cold, the leaves were falling, some geese had passed to the southward, and the winter would shortly set in; and that, as he considered the lives of all who went on such a journey would be forfeited, he neither would go himself, nor permit his hunters to accompany us. He said there was no wood within eleven days' march, during which time we could not have any fire, as the moss, which the Indians use in their summer excursions, would be too wet for burning, in consequence of the recent rains; that we should be forty days in descending the Copper-Mine River, six of which would be expended in getting to its banks, and that we might be blocked up by the ice in the next moon; and during the whole journey the party must experience great suffering for want of food, as the reindeer had already left the river.

He was now reminded that these statements were very different from the account he had given, both at Port Providence and on the route hither; and that up to this moment, we had been encouraged by his conversation to expect that the party might descend the Copper-

Mine River, accompanied by the Indians. He replied, that at the former place he had been unacquainted with our slow mode of traveling, and that the alteration, in his opinion, arose from the advance of winter.

We now informed him, that we were provided with instruments by which we could ascertain the state of the air and water, and that we did not imagine the winter to be so near as he supposed; however, we promised to return on discovering the first change in the season. He was also told that all the baggage being left behind, our canoes would now, of course, travel infinitely more expeditiously than anything he had hitherto witnessed. Akaitcho appeared to feel hurt, that we should continue to press the matter further, and answered with some warmth: "Well, I have said everything I can urge, to dissuade you from going on this service, on which it seems, you wish to sacrifice your own lives, as well as the Indians who might attend you: however, if after all I have said, you are determined to go, some of my young men shall join the party, because it shall not be said, that we permitted you to die alone after having brought you hither; but from the moment they embark in the canoes, I and my relatives shall lament them as dead."

We could only reply to this forcible appeal, by assuring him and the Indians who were seated around him, that we felt the most anxious solicitude for the safety of every individual, and that it was far from our intention to proceed without considering every argument for and against the proposed journey.

We next informed him, that it would be very desirable to see the river at any rate, that we might give some positive information about its situation and size, in our next letters to the great chief; and that we were very anxious to get on its banks for the purpose of observing an eclipse of the sun, which we described to him, and said would happen in a few days. He received this communication with more temper than the preceding, though he immediately assigned as a reason for his declining to go, that "the Indians must now procure a sufficient quantity of deer-skins for winter clothing for themselves, and dresses for the Canadians, who would need them if they had to travel in the winter." Finding him so averse to proceed, and feeling, at the same time, how essential his continuance with us was, not only to our future success, but even to our existence during the winter; I closed the conversation here, intending to propose to him next morning some modification of the plan, which might meet his approbation. Soon after we were gone, however, he informed Mr. Wentzel, with whom he was in the habit of speaking confidentially, that as his advice was neglected, his presence was useless, and he should, therefore, return to Fort Providence with his hunters, after he had collected some winter provision for us. Mr. Wentzel having reported this to me, the night was passed in great anxiety, and after weighing all the arguments that presented themselves to my mind, I came reluctantly to the determination of relinquishing the intention of going any distance down the river this season.

[Aug. 14th, 1821] We encamped at the end of twenty-four miles' march, on the north-west side of a bay, to which I have given the name of my friend Captain Parry, now employed in the interesting research for a North-West Passage. Drift wood had become very scarce, and we found none near the encampment; a fire, however, was not required, as we served out pemmican for supper, and the evening was unusually warm.

On the following morning the breeze was fresh, and the waves rather high. In paddling along the west side of Parry's Bay, we saw several deer, but owing to the openness of the country, the hunters could not approach them. They killed, however, two swans that were moulting, several cranes, and many grey geese. We procured also some caccawees, which were then moulting and assembled in immense flocks. In the evening, having rounded Point Beechy, and passed Hurd's Islands, we were exposed to much inconvenience and danger from a heavy rolling sea; the canoes receiving many severe blows, and shipping a good deal of water, which induced us to encamp at five P.M. opposite to Cape Croker, which we had passed on the morning of the 12th; the channel, which lay between our situation and it, being about seven miles wide. We had now reached the northern point of entrance into this sound, which I have named in honor of Lord Viscount Melville, the First Lord of the Admiralty. It is thirty miles wide from east to west, and twenty from north to south; and in coasting it we had sailed eighty-seven and a quarter geographical miles.

Shortly after the tents were pitched, Mr. Back reported from the steersmen that both canoes had sustained material injury during this day's voyage. I found upon examination that fifteen timbers of the first canoe were broken, some of them in two places, and that the second canoe was so loose in the frame that its timbers could not be bound in the usual secure manner, and consequently there was danger of its bark separating from the gunwales if exposed to a heavy sea. Distressing as were these circumstances, they gave me less pain than the discovery that our people, who had hitherto displayed, in following us through dangers and difficulties no less novel than appalling to them, a courage beyond our expectation, now felt serious apprehensions for their safety, which so possessed their minds that they were not restrained even by the presence of their officers from expressing them. Their fears, we imagined, had been principally excited by the interpreters, St. Germain and Adam, who from the outset had foreboded every calamity; and we now strongly suspected that their recent want of success in their hunting excursions, had proceeded from an intentional relaxation in their efforts to kill deer, in order that the want of provision might compel us to put a period to our voyage.

I must now mention that many concurrent circumstances had caused me, during the few last days, to meditate on the approach of this painful necessity. The strong breezes we had encountered for some days, led me to fear that the season was breaking up, and severe weather would soon ensue, which we could not sustain in a country destitute of fuel. Our stock of provision was now reduced to a quantity of pemmican only sufficient for three days' consumption, and the prospect of increasing it was not encouraging, for though reindeer were seen, they could not be easily approached on the level shores we were now coasting, besides, it was to be apprehended they would soon migrate to the south. It was evident that the time spent in exploring the Arctic and Melville Sounds, and Bathurst's Inlet, had precluded the hope of reaching Repulse Bay, which at the outset of the voyage we had fondly cherished; and it was equally obvious that as our distance from any of the trading establishments would increase as we proceeded, the hazardous traverse across the barren grounds, which we should have to make, if compelled to abandon the canoes upon any part of the coast, would become greater.

I this evening communicated to the officers my sentiments on these points, as well as respecting our return, and was happy to find that their opinions coincided with my own. We were all convinced of the necessity of putting a speedy termination to our advance, as the hope which we had cherished of meeting the Esquimaux and procuring provision from them, could now scarcely be entertained; but yet we were desirous of proceeding, until the land should be seen trending again to the eastward; that we might be satisfied of its separation from what we had conceived, in passing from Cape Barrow to Bathurst's Inlet, to be a great chain of islands. As it was necessary, however, at all events, to set a limit to our advance, I announced my determination of returning after four days examination, unless, indeed, we should previously meet the Esquimaux, and be enabled to make some arrangement for passing the winter with them. This communication was joyfully received by the men, and we hoped that the industry of our hunters being once more excited, we should be able to add to our stock of provision.

[Aug. 17th, 1821] My original intention, whenever the season should compel us to relinquish the survey, had been to return by the way of the Copper-Mine River, and, in pursuance of my arrangement with the Hook to travel to Slave Lake through the line of woods extending thither by the Great Bear and Marten Lakes, but our scanty stock of provision and the length of the voyage rendered it necessary to make for a nearer place. We had already found that the country, between Cape Barrow and the Copper-Mine River, would not supply our wants, and this it seemed probable would now be still more the case; besides, at this advanced season, we expected the frequent recurrence of gales, which would cause great detention, if not danger in proceeding along that very rocky part of the coast.

I determined, therefore, to make at once for Arctic Sound, where we had found the animals more numerous than at any other place; and entering Hood's River, to advance up that stream as far as it was navigable, and then to construct small canoes out of the materials of the larger ones, which could be carried in crossing the barren grounds to Fort Enterprize.

August 19.—We were almost beaten out of our comfortless abodes by rain during the night, and this morning the gale continued without diminution. The thermometer fell to 33°. Two men were sent with Junius to search for the deer which Augustus had killed. Junius returned in the evening bringing part of the meat, but owing to the thickness of the weather, his companions parted from him and did not make their appearance. Divine service was read. On the 20th we were presented with the most chilling prospect, the small pools of water being frozen over, the ground being covered with snow, and the thermometer at the freezing point at mid-day. Flights of geese were passing to the southward. The wind however was more moderate, having changed to the eastward. Considerable anxiety prevailing respecting Belanger and Michel, the two men who strayed from Junius yesterday, the rest were sent out to look for them. The search was successful, and they all returned in the evening. The stragglers were much fatigued, and had suffered severely from the cold, one of them having his thighs frozen, and what under our circumstances was most grievous, they had thrown away all the meat. The wind during the night returned to the northwest quarter, blew more violently than ever, and raised a very turbulent sea. The next day did not improve our condition, the snow remained on the ground, and the small pools were frozen. Our hunters were sent out, but they returned after a fatiguing day's march without having seen any animals. We made a scanty meal off a handful of pemmican, after which only half a bag remained.

The wind abated after midnight, and the surf diminished rapidly, which caused us to be on the alert at a very early hour on the 22d, but we had to wait until six A.M. for the return of Augustus, who had continued out all night on an unsuccessful pursuit of deer. It appears that he walked a few miles farther along the coast, than the party had done on the 18th, and from a sketch he drew on the sand, we were confirmed in our former opinion that the shore inclined more to the eastward beyond Point Turnagain. He also drew a river of considerable size, that discharges its waters into Walker's Bay; on the banks of which stream he saw a piece of wood, such as the Esquimaux use in producing fire, and other marks so fresh that he supposed they had recently visited the spot. We therefore left several iron materials for them. Our men, cheered by the prospect of returning, embarked with the utmost alacrity; and, paddling with unusual vigor, carried us across Riley's and Walker's Bays, a distance of twenty miles before noon, when we landed on Slate-Clay Point, as the wind had freshened too much to permit us to continue the voyage. The whole party went to hunt, but returned without success in the evening, drenched with the heavy rain which commenced soon after they had set out. Several deer were seen, but could not be approached in this naked country; and as our stock of pemmican did not admit of serving out two meals, we went dinnerless to bed.

Soon after our departure to-day, a sealed tin-case, sufficiently buoyant to float, was thrown overboard, containing a short account of our proceedings, and the position of the most conspicuous points. The wind blew off the land, the water was smooth, and as the sea is in this part more free from islands than in any other, there was every probability of its being driven off the shore into the current; which, as I have before mentioned, we suppose, from the circumstance of Mackenzie's River being the only known stream that brings down the wood we have found along the shores, to set to the eastward.

August 23.—A severe frost caused us to pass a comfortless night. At 2 P.M. we set sail, and the men voluntarily launched out to make a traverse of fifteen miles across Melville Sound, before a strong wind and heavy sea. The privation of food, under which our voyagers were then laboring, absorbed every other terror; otherwise the most powerful persuasion could not have induced them to attempt such a traverse. It was with the utmost difficulty that the canoes were kept from turning their broadsides to the waves, though we sometimes steered with all the paddles. One of them narrowly escaped being overset by this accident, happening, in mid-channel, where the waves were so high that the mast-head of our canoe was often hid from the other, though it was sailing within hail.

The traverse, however, was made; we were then near a high rocky lee shore, on which a heavy surf was beating. The wind being on the beam, the canoes drifted fast to leeward; and, on rounding a point, the recoil of the sea from the rocks was so great that they were with difficulty kept from foundering. We looked in vain for a sheltered bay to land in; but, at length, being unable to weather another point, we were obliged to put ashore on the open beach, which, fortunately, was sandy at this spot. The debarkation was effected without further injury than the splitting of the head of the second canoe, which was easily repaired.

Our encampment being near to the place where we killed the deer on the 11th, almost the whole party went out to hunt, but they returned in the evening without having seen any game. The berries, however, were ripe and plentiful, and, with the addition of some country tea, furnished a supper. There were some showers in the afternoon, and the weather was cold, the thermometer being 42°, but the evening and night were calm and fine. It may be remarked that the musquitoes disappeared when the late gales commenced.

August 24.—Embarking at three A.M., we stretched across the eastern entrance of Bathurst's Inlet, and arrived at an island, which I have named after Colonel Barry, of Newton Barry. Some deer being seen on the beach, the hunters went in pursuit of them, and succeeded in killing three females, which enabled us to save our last remaining meal of pemmican. They saw also some fresh tracks of musk oxen on the banks of a small stream, which flowed into a lake in the centre of the island. These animals must have crossed a channel, at least three miles wide, to reach the nearest of these islands. Some specimens of variegated pebbles and jasper were found here imbedded in the amygdaloidal rock.

Re-embarking at two P.M., and continuing through what was supposed to be a channel between two islands, we found our passage barred by a gravelly isthmus of only ten yards in width; the canoes and cargoes were carried across it, and we passed into Bathurst's Inlet through another similar channel, bounded on both sides by steep rocky hills. The wind then changing from S.E. to N.W. brought heavy rain, and we encamped at seven P.M., having advanced eighteen miles.

August 25.—Starting this morning with a free breeze in our favor, we soon reached that part of Barry's Island where the canoes were detained on the 2d and 3d of this month, and contrary to what we then experienced, the deer were now plentiful. The hunters killed two, and we were relieved from all apprehension of an immediate want of food. One would suppose the deer were about to retire to the main shore, from their assembling at this time in such numbers on the islands nearest the coast. Those we saw were generally females with their young, and all of them very lean.

The wind continued in the same direction until we had rounded Point Wollaston, and then changed to a quarter which enabled us to steer for Hood's River, which we ascended as high as the first rapid, and encamped. Here terminated our voyage on the Arctic sea, during which we had gone over six hundred and fifty geographical miles. Our Canadian voyagers could not restrain their expressions of joy at having turned their backs on the sea, and they passed the evening talking over their past adventures with much humor and no little exaggeration. The consideration that the most painful, and certainly the most hazardous, part of the journey was yet to come, did not depress their spirits at all. It is due to their character to mention that they displayed much courage in encountering the dangers of the sea, magnified to them by their novelty.

[Sept. 9th, 1821] Junius arrived in the afternoon, and informed us that he had seen a large herd of musk-oxen on the banks of Cracroft's River, and had wounded one of them, but it had escaped. He brought about four pounds of meat, the remains of a deer that had been devoured by the wolves. The poor fellow was much fatigued, having walked throughout the night, but as the weather was particularly favorable for our crossing the river, we could not allow him to rest. After he had taken some refreshment we proceeded to the river. The canoe being put into the water was found extremely ticklish, but it was managed with much dexterity by St. Germain, Adam, and Peltier, who ferried over one passenger at a time, causing him to lie flat in its bottom, by no means a pleasant position, owing to its leakiness, but there was no alternative. The transport of the whole party was effected by five-o'clock, and we walked about two miles further, and encamped, having come five miles and three-quarters on a south-west course. Two young alpine hares were shot by St. Germain, which, with the small piece of meat brought in by Junius, furnished the supper of the whole party. There was no *tripe de roche* here. The country had now become decidedly hilly, and was covered with snow. The lake preserved its western direction, as far as I could see from the summit of the highest mountain near the encampment. We subsequently learned from the Copper Indians, that the part at which we had crossed the river was the *Congecatha wha chaga* of Hearne, of which I had little idea at the time, not only from the difference of latitude, but also from its being so much farther east of the mouth of the Copper-Mine River, than his track is laid down. He only making one degree and three-quarters difference of longitude, and we upwards of four. Had I been aware of the fact, several days' harassing march, and a disastrous accident would have been prevented by keeping on the western side of the lake, instead of crossing the river. We were informed also, that this river is the Anatessy, or River of Strangers, and is supposed to fall into Bathurst's Inlet; but although the Indians have visited its mouth, their description was not sufficient to identify it with any of the rivers whose mouths we had seen. It probably falls in that part of the coast which was hid from our view by Goulburn's or Elliot's Islands.

September 10.—We had a cold north wind, and the atmosphere was foggy. The thermometer 18° at five A.M. In the course of our march this morning, we passed many small lakes; and the ground, becoming higher and more hilly as we receded from the river, was covered to a much greater depth with snow. This rendered walking not only extremely laborious, but also hazardous in the highest degree; for the sides of the hills, as is usual throughout the barren grounds, abounding in accumulations of large angular stones, it often happened that the men fell into the interstices with their loads on their backs, being deceived by the smooth appearance of the drifted snow. If any one had broken a limb here, his fate would have been melancholy indeed; we could neither have remained with him, nor carried him on. We halted at ten to gather *tripe de roche,* but it was so frozen, that we were quite benumbed with cold before a sufficiency could be collected even for a scanty meal. On proceeding, our men were somewhat cheered, by observing on the sandy summit of a hill, from whence the snow had been blown, the summer track of a man and afterwards by seeing several deer tracks on the snow. About noon the weather cleared up a little, and, to our great joy, we saw a herd of musk-oxen grazing in a valley below us. The party instantly halted, and the best hunters were sent out; they approached the animals with the utmost caution, no less than two hours being consumed before they got within gun-shot. In the meantime we beheld their proceedings with extreme anxiety, and many secret prayers were, doubtless, offered up for their success. At length they opened their fire, and we had the satisfaction of seeing one of the largest cows fall; another was wounded, but escaped. This success infused spirit into our starving party. To skin and cut up the animal was the work of a few minutes. The contents of its stomach were devoured upon the spot, and the raw intestines, which were next attacked, were pronounced by the most delicate amongst us to be excellent. A few willows, whose tops were seen peeping through the snow in the bottom of the valley, were quickly grubbed, the tents pitched, and supper cooked, and devoured with avidity. This was the sixth day since we had had a good meal. The *tripe de roche,* even where we got enough, only serving to allay the pangs of hunger for a short time. After supper, two of the hunters went in pursuit of the herd, but could not get near them.

We were detained all the next day by a strong southerly wind, and were much incommoded in the tents by the drift snow. The temperature was 20°. The average for the last ten days about 24.5°. We restricted ourselves to one meal to-day as we were at rest, and there was only meat remaining sufficient for the next day.

The gale had not diminished on the 12th, and, as we were fearful of its continuance for some time, we determined on going forward; our only doubt regarded the preservation of the canoe, but the men promised to pay particular attention to it, and the most careful persons were appointed to take it in charge. The snow was two feet deep, and the ground much broken, which rendered the march extremely painful. The whole party complained more of faintness and weakness than they had ever done before; their strength seemed to have been impaired by the recent supply of animal food. In the afternoon the wind abated, and the snow ceased; cheered with the change, we proceeded forward at a quicker pace, and encamped at six P.M., having come eleven miles. Our supper consumed the last of our meat.

We set out on the 13th, in thick hazy weather, and, after an hour's march, had the extreme mortification to find ourselves on the borders of a large lake, which we subsequently learned from the Indians was named Contwoy-to, or Rum Lake; neither of its extremities could be seen. As the portion which lay to the east seemed the widest, we coasted along to the westward portion in search of a crossing-place. This lake being bounded by steep and lofty hills, our march was very fatiguing. Those sides which were exposed to the sun were free from snow, and we found upon them some excellent berries. We encamped at six P.M., having come only six miles and a half. Crédit was then missing, and he did not return during the night. We supped off a single partridge and some *tripe de roche*; this unpalatable weed was now quite nauseous to the whole party, and in several it produced bowel complaints. Mr. Hood was the greatest sufferer from this cause. This evening we were extremely distressed at discovering that our improvident companions, since we left Hood's River, had thrown away three of the fishing nets, and burnt the floats; they knew we had brought them to procure subsistence for the party, when the animals should fail, and we could scarcely believe the fact of their having wilfully deprived themselves of this resource, especially when we considered that most of them had passed the greater part of their servitude in situations where the nets alone had supplied them with food. Being thus deprived of our principal resource, that of fishing, and the men evidently getting weaker every day, it became necessary to lighten their burdens of every thing except ammunition, clothing, and the instruments that were required to find our way. I, therefore, issued directions to deposit at this encampment the dipping needle, azimuth compass, magnet, a large thermometer, and a few books we had carried, having torn out of these such parts as we should require to work the observations for latitude and longitude. I also promised, as an excitement to the efforts in hunting, my gun to St. Germain, and an ample compensation to Adam, or any of the other men who should kill any animals. Mr. Hood, on this occasion, lent his gun to Michel, the Iroquois, who was very eager in the chase, and often successful.

September 14.—This morning the officers being assembled round a small fire, Perrault presented each of us with a small piece of meat which he had saved from his allowance. It was received with great thankfulness, and such an act of self-denial and kindness, being totally unexpected in a Canadian voyager, filled our eyes with tears. In directing our course to a river issuing from the lake, we met Crédit, who communicated the joyful intelligence of his having killed two deer in the morning. We instantly halted, and having shared the deer that was nearest to us, prepared breakfast. After which, the other deer was sent for, and we went down to the river, which was about three hundred yards wide, and flowed with great velocity through a broken rocky channel. Having searched for a part where the current was most smooth, the canoe was placed in the water at the head of a rapid, and St. Germain, Solomon, Belanger, and I, embarked in order to cross. We went from the shore very well, but in mid-channel the canoe became difficult to manage under our burden, as the breeze was fresh. The current drove us to the edge of the rapid, when Belanger unfortunately applied his paddle to avert the apparent danger of being forced down it, and lost his balance. The canoe was overset in consequence in the middle of the rapid. We fortunately kept hold of it, until we touched a rock where the water did not reach higher than our waists; here we kept our footing, notwithstanding the strength of the current, until the water was emptied out of the canoe. Belanger then held the canoe steady whilst St. Germain placed me in it, and afterwards embarked himself in a very dexterous manner. It was impossible, however, to embark Belanger, as the canoe would have been hurried down the rapid, the moment he should have raised his foot from the rock on which he stood. We were, therefore, compelled to leave him in his perilous situation. We had not gone twenty yards before the canoe, striking on a sudden rock, went down. The place being shallow, we were again enabled to empty it, and the third attempt brought us to the shore. In the mean time Belanger was suffering extremely, immersed to his middle in the centre of a rapid, the temperature of which was very little above the freezing point, and the upper part of his body covered with wet clothes, exposed in a temperature not much above zero, to a strong breeze. He called piteously for relief, and St. Germain on his return endeavored to embark him, but in vain. The canoe was hurried down the rapid, and when he landed he was rendered by the cold incapable of further exertion, and Adam attempted to embark Belanger, but found it impossible. An attempt was next made to carry out to him a line, made of the slings of the men's loads. This also failed, the current acting so strongly upon it, as to prevent the canoe from steering, and it was finally broken and carried down the stream. At length, when Belanger's strength seemed almost exhausted, the canoe reached him with a small cord belonging to one of the nets, and he was dragged perfectly senseless through the rapid. By the direction of Dr. Richardson, he was instantly stripped, and being rolled up in blankets, two men undressed themselves and went to bed with him; but it was some hours before he recovered his warmth and sensations. As soon as Belanger was placed in his bed, the officers immediately sent over my blankets and a person to make a fire. Augustus brought the canoe over, and in returning he was obliged to descend both the rapids, before he could get across the stream; which hazardous service he performed with the greatest coolness and judgment. It is impossible to describe my sensations as I witnessed the various unsuccessful attempts to relieve Belanger. The distance prevented my seeing distinctly what was going on, and I continued pacing up and down upon the rock on which I landed, regardless of the coldness of my drenched and stiffening garments. The canoe, in every attempt to reach him, was hurried down the rapid, and was lost to the view amongst the rocky islets, with a rapidity that seemed to threaten certain destruction; once, indeed, I fancied that I saw it overwhelmed in the waves. Such an event would have been fatal to the whole party. Separated as I was from my companions, without gun, ammunition, hatchet, or the means of making a fire, and in wet clothes, my doom would have been speedily sealed. My companions too, driven to the necessity of coasting the lake, must have sunk under the fatigue of rounding its innumerable arms and bays, which, as we have learned from the Indians, are very extensive. By the goodness of Providence, however, we were spared at that time, and some of us have been permitted to offer up our thanksgivings, in a civilized land, for the signal deliverances we then and afterwards experienced.

[Oct. 5th, 1821] Mr. Hood, who was now very feeble, and Dr. Richardson, who attached himself to him, walked together at a gentle pace in the rear of the party. I kept with the foremost men, to cause them to halt occasionally, until the stragglers came up. Resuming our march after breakfast, we followed the track of Mr. Back's party, and encamped early, as all of us were much fatigued, particularly Crédit, who having to-day carried the men's tent, it being his turn to do so, was so exhausted, that when he reached the encampment he was unable to stand. The *tripe de roche* disagreed with this man and with Vaillant, in consequence of which they were the first whose strength totally failed. We had a small quantity of this weed in the evening, and the rest of our supper was made up of scraps of roasted leather. The distance walked to-day was six miles. As Crédit was very weak in the morning, his load was reduced to little more than his personal luggage, consisting of his blanket, shoes, and gun. Previous to setting out, the whole party ate the remains of their old shoes, and whatever scraps of leather they had, to strengthen their stomachs for the fatigue of the day's journey. We left the encampment at nine, and pursued our route over a range of bleak hills. The wind having increased to a strong gale in the course of the morning, became piercingly cold, and the drift rendered it difficult for those in the rear to follow the track over the heights, whilst in the valleys, where it was sufficiently marked, from the depth of the snow, the labor of walking was proportionably great. Those in advance made as usual frequent halts, yet being unable from the severity of the weather to remain long still, they were obliged to move on before the rear could come up, and the party, of course, straggled very much.

About noon Samandrè coming up, informed us that Crédit and Vaillant could advance no further. Some willows being discovered in a valley near to us, I proposed to halt the party there whilst Dr. Richardson went back to visit them. I hoped too, that when the sufferers received the information of a fire being kindled at so short a distance, they would be cheered, and use their utmost efforts to reach it, but this proved a vain hope. The Doctor found Vaillant about a mile and a half in the rear, much exhausted with cold and fatigue. Having encouraged him to advance to the fire, after repeated solicitations he made the attempt, but fell down amongst the deep snow at every step. Leaving him in this situation, the Doctor went about half a mile farther back, to the spot where Crédit was said to have halted, and the track being nearly obliterated by the snow drift, it became unsafe for him to go further. Returning he passed Vaillant, who having moved only a few yards in his absence, had fallen down, was unable to rise, and could scarcely answer his questions. Being unable to afford him any effectual assistance, he hastened on to inform us of his situation. When J. B. Belanger had heard the melancholy account, he went immediately to aid Vaillant, and bring up his burden. Respecting Crédit, we were informed by Samandrè, that he had stopped a short distance behind Vaillant, but that his intention was to return to the encampment of the preceding evening.

When Belanger came back with Vaillant's load, he informed us that he had found him lying on his back, benumbed with cold, and incapable of being roused. The stoutest men of the party were now earnestly entreated to bring him to the fire, but they declared themselves unequal to the task; and, on the contrary, urged me to allow them to throw down their loads, and proceed to Fort Enterprize with the utmost speed. A compliance with their desire would have caused the loss of the whole party, for the men were totally ignorant of the course to be taken, and none of the officers, who could have directed the march, were sufficiently strong to keep up at the pace they would then walk; besides, even supposing them to have found their way, the strongest men would certainly have deserted the weak. Something, however, was absolutely necessary to be done, to relieve them as much as possible from their burdens, and the officers consulted on the subject. Mr. Hood and Dr. Richardson proposed to remain behind, with a single attendant, at the first place where sufficient wood and *tripe de roche* should be found for ten days' consumption; and that I should proceed as expeditiously as possible with the men to the house, and thence send them immediate relief. They strongly urged that this arrangement would contribute to the safety of the rest of the party, by relieving them from the burden of a tent, and several other articles; and that they might afford aid to Crédit, if he should unexpectedly come up. I was distressed beyond description at the thought of leaving them in such a dangerous situation, and for a long time combated their proposal; but they strenuously urged, that this step afforded the only chance of safety for the party, and I reluctantly acceded to it. The ammunition, of which we had a small barrel, was also to be left with them, and it was hoped that this deposit would be a strong inducement for the Indians to venture across the barren grounds to their aid. We communicated this resolution to the men, who were cheered at the slightest prospect of alleviation of their present miseries, and they promised with great appearance of earnestness to return to those officers, upon the first supply of food.

The party then moved on; Vaillant's blanket and other necessaries were left in the track, at the request of the Canadians, without any hope, however, of him being able to reach them. After marching until dusk without seeing a favorable place for encamping, night compelled us to take shelter under the lee of a hill, amongst some willows, with which, after many attempts, we at length made a fire. It was not sufficient, however, to warm the whole party, much less to thaw our shoes; and the weather not permitting the gathering of *tripe de roche,* we had nothing to cook.

The painful retrospection of the melancholy events of the day banished sleep, and we shuddered as we contemplated the dreadful effects of this bitterly cold night on our two companions, if still living. Some faint hopes were entertained of Crédit's surviving the storm, as he was provided with a good blanket, and had leather to eat.

The weather was mild next morning. We left the encampment at nine, and a little before noon came to a pretty extensive thicket of small willows, near which there appeared a supply of *tripe de roche* on the face of the rocks. At this place Dr. Richardson and Mr. Hood determined to remain, with John Hepburn, who volunteered to stop with them. The tent was securely pitched, a few willows collected, and the ammunition and all other articles were deposited, except each man's clothing, one tent, a sufficiency of ammunition for the journey, and the officer's journals. I had only one blanket, which was carried for me, and two pair of shoes. The offer was now made for any of the men, who felt themselves too weak to proceed, to remain with the officers, but none of them accepted it. Michel alone felt some inclination to do so. After we had united in thanksgiving and prayers to Almighty God, I separated from my companions, deeply afflicted that a train of melancholy circumstances should have demanded of me the severe trial of parting from friends in such a condition, who had become endeared to me by their constant kindness, and co-operation, and a participation of numerous sufferings. This trial I could not have been induced to undergo, but for the reasons they had so strongly urged the day before, to which my own judgment assented, and for the sanguine hope I felt of either finding a supply of provision at Fort Enterprize, or meeting the Indians in the immediate vicinity of that place, according to my arrangements with Mr. Wentzel and Akaitcho. Previously to our starting, Peltier and Benoit repeated their promises, to return to them with provision, if any should be found at the house, or to guide the Indians to them, if any were met.

Greatly as Mr. Hood was exhausted, and, indeed, incapable as he must have proved, of encountering the fatigue of our next day's journey, so that I felt his resolution to be prudent, I was sensible that his determination to remain, was mainly prompted by the disinterested and generous wish to remove impediments to the progress of the rest of the party. Dr. Richardson and Hepburn, who were both in a state of strength to keep pace with the men, beside this motive which they shared with him, were influenced in their resolution to remain; the former by the desire which had distinguished his character, throughout the expedition, of devoting himself to the succor of the weak, and the latter by the zealous attachment he had ever shewn towards his officers.

We set out without waiting to take any of the *tripe de roche,* and walked at a tolerable pace, and in an hour arrived at a fine group of pines, about a mile and a quarter from the tent. We sincerely regretted not having seen these before we had separated from our companions, as they would have been better supplied with fuel here, and there appeared to be more *tripe de roche* than where we had left them.

Descending afterwards into a more level country, we found the snow very deep, and the labor of wading through it so fatigued the whole party, that we were compelled to encamp, after a march of four miles and a half. Belanger and Michel were left far behind, and when they arrived at the encampment appeared quite exhausted. The former, bursting into tears, declared his inability to proceed with the party, and begged me to let him go back next morning to the tent, and shortly afterwards Michel made the same request. I was in hopes they might recover a little strength by the night's rest, and therefore deferred giving any permission until the morning. The sudden failure in the strength of these men cast a gloom over the rest, which I tried in vain to remove, by repeated assurances that the distance to Fort Enterprize was short, and that we should, in all probability, reach it in four days. Not being able to find any *tripe de roche,* we drank an infusion of the Labrador tea plant, *(ledum palustre,)* and ate a few morsels of burnt leather for supper. We were unable to raise the tent, and found its weight too great to carry it on; we, therefore, cut it up, and took a part of the canvas for a cover. The night was bitterly cold, and though we lay as close to each other as possible, having no shelter, we could not keep ourselves sufficiently warm to sleep. A strong gale came on after midnight, which increased the severity of the weather. In the morning Belanger and Michel renewed their request to be permitted to go back to the tent, assuring me they were still weaker than on the preceding evening, and less capable of going forward; and they urged, that the stopping at a place where there was a supply of *tripe de roche* was their only chance of preserving life; under these circumstances, I could not do otherwise than yield to their desire. I wrote a note to Dr. Richardson and Mr. Hood, informing them of the pines we had passed, and recommending their removing thither. Having found that Michel was carrying a considerable quantity of ammunition, I desired him to divide it among my party, leaving him only ten balls and a little shot, to kill any animals he might meet on his way to the tent. This man was very particular in his inquiries respecting the direction of the house, and the course we meant to pursue; he also said, that if he should be able, he would go and search for Vaillant and Crédit; and he requested my permission to take Vaillant's blanket, if he should find it, to which I agreed, and mentioned it in my notes to the officers.

Scarcely were these arrangements finished, before Perrault and Fontano were seized with a fit of dizziness, and betrayed other symptoms of extreme debility. Some tea was quickly prepared for them, and after drinking it, and eating a few morsels of burnt leather, they recovered, and expressed their desire to go forward; but the other men, alarmed at what they had just witnessed, became doubtful of their own strength, and, giving way to absolute dejection, declared their own inability to move. I now earnestly pressed upon them the necessity of continuing our journey, as the only means of saving their own lives, as well as those of our friends at the tent; and, after much entreaty, got them to set out at ten A.M.: Belanger and Michel were left at the encampment, and proposed to start shortly afterwards. By the time we had gone about two hundred yards, Perrault became again dizzy, and desired us to halt, which we did, until he, recovering, proposed to march on. Ten minutes more had hardly elapsed before he again desired us to stop, and, bursting into tears, declared he was totally exhausted, and unable to accompany us further. As the encampment was not more than a quarter of a mile distant, we proposed that he should return to it, and rejoin Belanger and Michel, whom we knew to be still there, from perceiving the smoke of a fresh fire; and because they had not made any preparation for starting when we left them. He readily acquiesced in the proposition, and having taken a friendly leave of each of us, and enjoined us to make all the haste we could in sending relief, he turned back, keeping his gun and ammunition. We watched him until he was near to the fire, and then proceeded. During these detentions, Augustus becoming impatient of the delay, had walked on, and we lost sight of him. The labor we experienced in wading through the deep snow induced us to cross a moderate sized lake, which lay in our track, but we found this operation far more harassing. As the surface of the ice was perfectly smooth, we slipt at almost every step, and were frequently blown down by the wind with such force as to shake our whole frames.

Poor Fontano was completely exhausted by the labor of making this traverse, and we made a halt until his strength was recruited, by which time the party was benumbed with cold. Proceeding again, he got on tolerably well for a little time, but being again seized with faintness and dizziness, he fell often, and at length exclaimed that he could go no further. We immediately stopped, and endeavored to encourage him to persevere, until we should find some willows, to encamp; he insisted, however, that he could not march any longer through this deep snow; and said, that if he should even reach our encampment this evening, he must be left there, provided *tripe de roche* could not be procured to recruit his strength. The poor man was overwhelmed with grief, and seemed desirous to remain at that spot. We were about two miles from the place where the other men had been left, and as the track to it was beaten, we proposed to him to return thither, as we thought it probable he would find the men still there; at any rate he would be able to get fuel to keep him warm during the night; and, on the next day, he could follow their track to the officers' tent; and, should the path be covered by the snow, the pines we had passed yesterday would guide him, as they were yet in view.

I cannot describe my anguish on the occasion of separating from another companion under circumstances so distressing. There was, however, no alternative. The extreme debility of the rest of the party, put the carrying him quite out of the question, as he himself admitted; and it was evident that the frequent delays he must occasion if he accompanied us, and did not gain strength, must have endangered the lives of the whole. By returning he had the prospect of getting to the tent where *tripe de roche* could be obtained, which agreed with him better than with any other of the party, and which he was always very assiduous in gathering. After some hesitation he determined on returning, and set out, having bid each of us farewell in the tenderest manner. We watched him with inexpressible anxiety for some time, and were rejoiced to find, though he had got on slowly, that he kept on his legs better than before. Antonio Fontano was an Italian, and had served many years in De Meuron's regiment. He had spoken to me that very morning, and after his first attack of dizziness, about his father; and had begged, that should he survive, I would take him with me to England, and put him in the way of reaching home.

The party was now reduced to five persons, Adam, Peltier, Benoit, Samandrè, and myself. Continuing the journey, we came, after an hour's walk, to some willows, and encamped under the shelter of a rock, having walked in the whole four miles and a half. We made an attempt to gather some *tripe de roche,* but could not, owing to the severity of the weather. Our supper, therefore, consisted of tea and a few morsels of leather.

Augustus did not make his appearance, but we felt no alarm at his absence, supposing he would go to the tent if he missed our track. Having fire, we procured a little sleep. Next morning the breeze was light and the weather mild, which enabled us to collect some *tripe de roche,* and to enjoy the only meal we had for four days. We derived great benefit from it, and walked with considerably more ease than yesterday. Without the strength it supplied, we should certainly have been unable to oppose the strong breeze we had in the afternoon. After walking about five miles, we came upon the borders of Marten Lake, and were rejoiced to find it frozen, so that we could continue our course straight for Fort Enterprize. We encamped at the first rapid in Winter River amidst willows and alders; but these were so frozen, and the snow fell so thick, that the men had great difficulty in making a fire. This proving insufficient to warm us, or even thaw our shoes, and having no food to prepare, we crept under our blankets. The arrival in a well known part raised the spirits of the men to a high pitch, and we kept up a cheerful conversation until sleep overpowered us. The night was very stormy, and the morning scarcely less so; but, being desirous to reach the house to-day, we commenced our journey very early. We were gratified by the sight of a large herd of reindeer on the side of the hill near the track, but our only hunter, Adam, was too feeble to pursue them. Our shoes and garments were stiffened by the frost, and we walked in great pain until we arrived at some stunted pines, at which we halted, made a good fire, and procured the refreshment of tea. The weather becoming fine in the afternoon, we continued our journey, passed the Dog-rib Rock, and encamped among a clump of pines of considerable growth, about a mile further on. Here we enjoyed the comfort of a large fire for the first time since our departure from the sea coast; but this gratification was purchased at the expense of many severe falls that we had in crossing a stony valley, to get to these pines. There was no *tripe de roche,* and we drank tea and ate some of our shoes for supper. Next morning, after taking the usual repast of tea, we proceeded to the house. Musing on what we were likely to find there, our minds were agitated between hope and fear, and, contrary to the custom we had kept up, of supporting our spirits by conversation, we went silently forward.

At length we reached Fort Enterprize, and to our infinite disappointment and grief found it a perfectly desolate habitation. There was no deposit of provision, no trace of the Indians, no letter from Mr. Wentzel to point out where the Indians might be found. It would be impossible for me to describe our sensations after entering this miserable abode, and discovering how we had been neglected; the whole party shed tears, not so much for our own fate, as for that of our friends in the rear, whose lives depended entirely on our sending immediate relief from this place.

I found a note, however, from Mr. Back, stating that he had reached the house two days ago, and was going in search of the Indians, at a part where St. Germain deemed it probable they might be found. If he was unsuccessful, he purposed walking to Fort Providence, and sending succor from thence. But he doubted whether he or his party could perform the journey to that place in their present debilitated state. It was evident that any supply that could be sent from Fort Providence would be long in reaching us, and could not be sufficient to enable us to afford any assistance to our companions behind, and that the only relief for them must be procured from the Indians. I resolved, therefore, on going also in search of them; but my companions were absolutely incapable of proceeding, and I thought, by halting two or three days they might gather a little strength, whilst the delay would afford us the chance of learning whether Mr. Back had seen the Indians.

We now looked round for the means of subsistence, and were gratified to find several deer skins, which had been thrown away during our former residence. The bones were gathered from the heap of ashes, these with the skins, and the addition of *tripe de roche,* we considered would support us tolerably well for a time. As to the house, the parchment being torn from the windows, the apartment we selected for our abode was exposed to all the rigor of the season. We endeavored to exclude the wind as much as possible, by placing loose boards against the apertures. The temperature was now between 15° and 20° below zero. We procured fuel by pulling up the flooring of the other rooms, and water for the purpose of cooking by melting the snow.

[Oct. 26th, 1821] We perceived our strength decline every day, and every exertion began to be irksome; when we were once seated the greatest effort was necessary in order to rise, and we had frequently to lift each other from our seats; but even in this pitiable condition we conversed cheerfully, being sanguine as to the speedy arrival of the Indians. We calculated indeed that they should be near the situation where they had remained last winter, our men would have reached them by this day. Having expended all the wood which we could procure from our present dwelling, without endangering its falling, Peltier began this day to pull down the partitions of the adjoining houses. Though these were only distant about twenty yards, yet the increase of labor in carrying the wood fatigued him so much, that by the evening he was exhausted. On the next day his weakness was such, especially in the arms, of which he chiefly complained, that he with difficulty lifted the hatchet; still he persevered, Samandrè and I assisting him in bringing in the wood, but our united strength could only collect sufficient to replenish the fire four times in the course of the day. As the insides of our mouths had become sore from eating the bone soup, we relinquished the use of it, and now boiled our skin, which mode of dressing we found more palatable than frying it, as we had hitherto done.

On the 29th, Peltier felt his pains more severe, and could only cut a few pieces of wood. Samandrè, who was still almost as weak, relieved him a little time, and I assisted them in carrying in the wood. We endeavored to pick some *tripe de roche,* but in vain, as it was entirely frozen. In turning up the snow, in searching for bones, I found several pieces of bark, which proved a valuable acquisition, as we were almost destitute of dry wood proper for kindling the fire. We saw a herd of reindeer sporting on the river, about half a mile from the house; they remained there a considerable time, but none of the party felt themselves sufficiently strong to go after them, nor was there one of us who could have fired a gun without resting it.

Whilst we were seated round the fire this evening, discoursing about the anticipated relief, the conversation was suddenly interrupted by Peltier's exclaiming with joy, *"Ah! le monde!"* imagining that he heard the Indians in the other room; immediately afterwards, to his bitter disappointment, Dr. Richardson and Hepburn entered, each carrying his bundle. Peltier, however, soon recovered himself enough to express his joy at their safe arrival, and his regret that their companions were not with them. When I saw them alone my own mind was instantly filled with apprehensions respecting my friend Hood, and our other companions, which were immediately confirmed by the Doctor's melancholy communication, that Mr. Hood and Michel were dead. Perrault and Fontano had neither reached the tent, nor been heard of by them. This intelligence produced a melancholy despondency in the minds of my party, and on that account the particulars were deferred until another opportunity. We were all shocked at beholding the emaciated countenances of the Doctor and Hepburn, as they strongly evidenced their extremely debilitated state. The alteration in our appearance was equally distressing to them, for since the swellings had subsided, we were little more than skin and bone. The Doctor particularly remarked the sepulchral tone of our voices, which he requested us to make more cheerful if possible, unconscious that his own partook of the same key.

Hepburn having shot a partridge, which was brought to the house, the Doctor tore out the feathers, and having held it to the fire a few minutes, divided it into seven portions. Each piece was ravenously devoured by my companions, as it was the first morsel of flesh any of us had tasted for thirty-one days, unless indeed the small gristly particles which we found occasionally adhering to the pounded bones may be termed flesh. Our spirits were revived by this small supply.

November 7.—Adam had passed a restless night, being disquieted by gloomy apprehensions of approaching death, which we tried in vain to dispel. He was so low in the morning as to be scarcely able to speak. I remained in bed by his side to cheer him as much as possible. The Doctor and Hepburn went to cut wood. They had hardly begun their labor, when they were amazed at hearing the report of a musket. They could scarcely believe that there was really any one near, until they heard a shout, and immediately espied three Indians close to the house. Adam and I heard the latter noise, and I was fearful that a part of the house had fallen upon one of my companions, a disaster which had in fact been thought not unlikely. My alarm was only momentary, Dr. Richardson came in to communicate the joyful intelligence that relief had arrived. He and myself immediately addressed thanksgiving to the throne of mercy for this deliverance, but poor Adam was in so low a state that he could scarcely comprehend the information. When the Indians entered, he attempted to rise but sank down again. But for this seasonable interposition of Providence, his existence must have terminated in a few hours, and that of the rest probably not in many days.

The Indians had left Akaitcho's encampment on the 5th November, having been sent by Mr. Back with all possible expedition, after he had arrived at their tents. They brought but a small supply of provisions, that they might travel quickly. It consisted of dried deer's meat, some fat, and a few tongues. Dr. Richardson, Hepburn, and I, eagerly devoured the food, which they imprudently presented to us, in too great abundance, and in consequence we suffered dreadfully from indigestion, and had no rest the whole night. Adam being unable to feed himself, was more judiciously treated by them, and suffered less; his spirits revived hourly. The circumstance of our eating more food than was proper in our present condition, was another striking proof of the debility of our minds. We were perfectly aware of the danger, and Dr. Richardson repeatedly cautioned us to be moderate; but he was himself unable to practise the caution he so judiciously recommended.

Boudel-kell, the youngest of the Indians, after resting about an hour, returned to Akaitcho with the intelligence of our situation, and he conveyed a note from me to Mr. Back, requesting another supply of meat as soon as possible. The two others, "Crooked-Foot and the Rat," remained to take care of us, until we should be able to move forward.

The note I received by the Indians from Mr. Back, communicated a tale of distress with regard to himself and his party, as painful as that which we had suffered.

November 8.—The Indians this morning requested us to remove to an encampment on the banks of the river, as they were unwilling to remain in the house in which the bodies of our deceased companions were lying exposed to view. We agreed to remove but the day proved too stormy, and Dr. Richardson and Hepburn having dragged the bodies to a short distance, and covered them with snow, the objections of the Indians to remain in the house were removed, and they began to clear our room of the accumulation of dirt and fragments of pounded bones. The improved state of our apartment, and the large and cheerful fires they kept up, produced in us a sensation of comfort to which we had long been strangers. In the evening they brought in a pile of dried wood, which was lying on the river side, and on which we had often cast a wishful eye, being unable to drag it up the bank. The Indians set about every thing with an activity that amazed us. Indeed, contrasted with our emaciated figures and extreme debility, their frames appeared to us gigantic, and their strength supernatural. These kind creatures next turned their attention to our personal appearance, and prevailed upon us to shave and wash ourselves. The beards of the Doctor and Hepburn had been untouched since they left the sea coast, and were become of a hideous length, and peculiarly offensive to the Indians.* The Doctor and I suffered extremely from distention, and therefore ate sparingly. Hepburn was getting better, and Adam recovered his strength with amazing rapidity.

November 9.—This morning was pleasantly fine. Crooked-Foot caught four large trout in Winter Lake, which were very much prized, especially by the Doctor and myself, who had taken a dislike to meat,

---

*The first alvine discharges after we received food, were, as Hearne remarks on a similar occasion, attended with excessive pain. Previous to the arrival of the Indians, the urinary secretion was extremely abundant, and we were obliged to rise from bed in consequence upwards of ten times in a night. This was an extreme annoyance in our reduced state. It may, perhaps, be attributed to the quantity of the country tea that we drank.

in consequence of our sufferings from repletion, which rendered us almost incapable of moving. Adam and Hepburn in a great measure escaped this. Though the night was stormy, and our apartment freely admitted the wind, we felt no inconvenience, the Indians were so very careful in covering us up, and in keeping a good fire; and our plentiful cheer gave such power of resisting the cold, that we could scarcely believe otherwise than that the season had become milder.

On the 13th, the weather was stormy, with constant snow. The Indians became desponding at the nonarrival of the supply, and would neither go to hunt nor fish. They frequently expressed their fears of some misfortune having befallen Boudel-kell; and, in the evening, went off suddenly, without apprizing us of their intention, having first given to each of us a handful of pounded meat, which they had reserved. Their departure, at first, gave rise to a suspicion of their having deserted us, not meaning to return, especially as the explanations of Adam, who appeared to be in their secret, were very unsatisfactory. At length, by interrogations, we got from him the information, that they designed to march night and day, until they should reach Akaitcho's encampment, whence they would send us aid. As we had combated their fears about Boudel-kell, they, perhaps, apprehended that we should oppose their determination, and therefore concealed it. We were now left a second time without food, and without appetites recovered, and strongly excited by recent indulgence.

On the following day the Doctor and Hepburn resumed their former occupation of collecting wood, and I was able to assist a little in bringing it into the house. Adam, whose expectation of the arrival of the Indians had been raised by the fineness of the weather, became, towards night, very desponding, and refused to eat the singed skin. The night was stormy, and there was a heavy fall of snow. The next day he became still more dejected. About eleven Hepburn, who had gone out for wood, came in with the intelligence that a party appeared upon the river. The room was instantly swept, and, in compliance with the prejudices of the Indians, every scrap of skin was carefully removed out of sight; for these simple people imagine, that burning deer-skin renders them unsuccessful in hunting. The party proved to be Crooked-Foot, Thooee-yorre, and the Fop, with the wives of the two latter dragging provisions. They were accompanied by Benoit, one of our own men.

We were rejoiced to learn, by a note from Mr. Back, dated November 11, that he and his companions had so recruited their strength that they were preparing to proceed to Fort Providence. Adam recovered his spirits on the arrival of the Indians, and even walked about the room with an appearance of strength and activity that surprised us all. As it was of consequence to get amongst the reindeer before our present supply should fail, we made preparations for quitting Fort Enterprize the next day; and, accordingly, at an early hour on the 16th, having united in thanksgiving and prayer, the whole party left the house after breakfast. Our feelings on quitting the Fort, where we had formerly enjoyed much comfort, if not happiness, and, latterly, experienced a degree of misery scarcely to be paralleled, may be more easily conceived than described. The Indians treated us with the utmost tenderness, gave us their snow-shoes and walked without themselves, keeping by our sides, that they might lift us when we fell. We descended Winter River, and, about noon, crossed the head of Round-Rock Lake, distant about three miles from the house, where we were obliged to halt, as Dr. Richardson was unable to proceed. The swellings in his limbs rendered him by much the weakest of the party. The Indians prepared our encampment, cooked for us, and fed us as if we had been children; evincing humanity that would have done honor to the most civilized people. The night was mild, and fatigue made us sleep soundly.

From this period to the 26th of November we gradually continued to improve, under the kindness and attention of our Indians. On this day we arrived in safety at the abode of our chief and companion, Akaitcho. We were received by the party assembled in the leader's tent, with looks of compassion, and profound silence, which lasted about a quarter of an hour, and by which they meant to express their condolence for our sufferings. The conversation did not begin until we had tasted food. The Chief, Akaitcho, shewed us the most friendly hospitality, and all sorts of personal attention, even to cooking for us with his own hands, an office which he never performs for himself.

Greeting to the Women of the Feasting-house

Important archery contests and ball-games were always concluded with wife-swapping, when the songs of the evening had been sung. To symbolise this festivity, the women arrived at the snow-hut carrying great gulls' feathers, held high above their heads. Here is the song with which they were received:

Women, women,
young women!
Aj, they come,
in fine new furs,
women, women,
young women!

Aj, they carry festive gulls' wings
in their fine white gloves.
See, they sway,
see, they call,
and blush with eagerness!

Women, women,
young women!
Aj-aj,
aj-aj-aj!

The edges of their long skirts
ripple as they come.
See how beautifully
they glide towards the men,
who joyfully await
rewards of victory!
Women, women,
young women!

—Orulo (Iglulik Eskimo woman)

The Crew of the Investigator Makes a Narrow Escape

BY JOHANN AUGUST MIERTSCHING (GERMAN, 1850–54)

On his second overland expedition (1826–27), John Franklin and his friend Dr. Richardson charted another huge stretch of the Arctic coastline. He returned to England a hero to marry Jane Griffin, a wealthy beauty and accomplished poet. Ambitious for her husband's career, Jane Franklin urged him to pursue more expeditions into the Arctic; but the Royal Navy's interest in finding the Northwest Passage had flagged temporarily and instead Franklin was posted to the governorship of Tasmania, then a prison colony for Britain.

Lady Franklin hated the narrow-mindedness of the colonial society and Sir John soon ran afoul of the embedded bureaucracy, whose colonial secretary declared a vendetta against him. Franklin was portrayed in the Tasmanian press as "a man in petticoats" and Lady Franklin as the woman who issued the orders to him. The feud eventually reached London, and Franklin was recalled from the colony. He returned to England in 1844, nearing age sixty, despondent, with what he felt was a badly damaged reputation.

Franklin's Arctic-explorer friends rallied around him and pushed the Admiralty to let him embark on another attempt at the Northwest Passage. Though Franklin himself admitted he was too old and plump for another overland journey, he thought life aboard ship

71

would be to his liking. Arctic fever had again swept England with the return of James Clark Ross's successful expedition to Antarctica, which pushed farther south than any expedition before. Ross's two large ships, *Erebus* and *Terror,* were quickly readied for a new Franklin expedition. In his hurried preparations, Franklin didn't bother much with plans for a relief party or a system of emergency depots and backup boats advocated by old John Ross, a veteran explorer who had survived four winters trapped in the Arctic ice.

On May 19, 1845, the *Erebus* and *Terror* sailed from Gravesend with Sir John Franklin standing on deck waving a white handkerchief to Lady Franklin and daughter Eleanor, standing on the pier. The last Europeans to see the members of the third Franklin Expedition alive were the crew of a whaler, who spotted the two ships moored to an iceberg a month later. Nothing was heard from Franklin through 1845, through all of 1846, and into early 1847, when old John Ross started to worry aloud that Franklin had already spent two winters in the Arctic and would be facing a third. As he had promised Franklin, Ross was ready to set off in search of the missing party but the Admiralty brushed him off, convinced that nothing could go wrong with an expedition so well-equipped and so determined as Franklin's.

By the next spring, in 1848, with no sign of Franklin still, the Admiralty was not so cavalier. It announced a huge prize—twenty thousand pounds—to anyone who could bring aid to the Franklin party. The government that year dispatched a three-pronged search—ships sailing into the Arctic from the west, from the east, and another party searching overland, but no sign of Franklin was found and the public took up the cause. During the next eleven years, over fifty expeditions would set out in search of the missing Franklin, many of them urged forward by Lady Franklin, who funded three of the expeditions out of her own purse. It was this massive, consuming search for Franklin that resulted in the exploration of much of the North American Arctic.

One of the search vessels was the *Investigator,* whose crew survived four winters trapped in the Arctic and would have met the same fate as Franklin's but for a miraculous bit of luck. As it was, the *Investigator*'s ever-ambitious Captain Robert McClure and his crew became the first Europeans to complete the Northwest Passage, although they did it "backwards"—from west to east—and they traveled the crux portion of it not by water but across the ice on foot while running for their lives.

The logistics are complicated, but their essence is this: In 1850 the *Investigator* was dispatched to enter the Arctic from the west—Alaska—in search of Franklin while another group of rescue ships would enter from the east. After leaving behind his sister ship, *Enterprise,* McClure and the *Investigator* probed deep into the Arctic waters that first season and, freezing the ship in for the winter near Banks Island, sighted during a sledge journey the channel that formed the final crucial link of the Northwest Passage. With the breakup of the ice the next summer, McClure tried to cross the channel, but found it choked with ice streaming down from the polar pack. He tried rounding Banks Island and approaching the channel farther north but was stopped again by the ice. With winter coming on and many harrowing escapes, McClure put into a bay on Banks Island to let the ship freeze in until the following summer.

Summer came and the Bay of Mercy, as they'd paradoxically named it, didn't thaw. The crew of the *Investigator* now spent a *third* winter in the ice. Supplies were dwindling, the men weakening with scurvy, and it was clear the end was nearing. Teams were making ready for a final desperate dash hundreds of miles for help when one spring day a black dot appeared on the ice. It was a man, Lieutenant Pim, of the *Resolute,* which had been sent out to find McClure's lost party (which, of course, was supposedly looking for Franklin's lost party). The *Resolute* was locked in the ice on the opposite side of the strait and making ready to sail out that spring. The crew of the *Investigator* dragged their scurvy-weakened bodies on deck and cheered Lieutenant Pim. They were rescued! Or so they thought. After an arduous journey across the strait, thus completing the Northwest Passage, the *Investigator* crew reached the food and relative comfort of the *Resolute.* But then *she* couldn't break out of the ice the following summer. Now the *Investigator*'s crew spent a *fourth* winter trapped in the ice aboard the *Resolute.* Finally, the aging Sir Edward Belcher, commander of the expedition to which the *Resolute* belonged and himself eager to return to his plush life back in England, gave the order to abandon not only the *Resolute,* but several other of his ships that he feared were trapped for another winter. Taking only what they could carry, all crews headed toward the *North Star,* his supply ship safely moored at Beechey Island.

These excerpts, from the aptly titled *Frozen Ships,* are the account of a young Moravian missionary, Johann August Miertsching. He had served for years among the Inuit of Labrador, spoke their language fluently, and was traveling aboard the *Investigator* as interpreter. His is a very human perspective from outside the Royal Navy. The four-year voyage and salty *Investigator* crew sorely tested his piety and patience, and he is horrified at the outset of the voyage when he realizes the kind of company he has joined. But as the *Investigator* makes one close escape from destruction after another, Miertsching records in his diary how the seeds of religious faith began to take root among the crew, and one detects the genuine affection he developed for captain and sailors.

The excerpts from Miertsching's diary open in July 1850, after the *Investigator* has made the voyage from England, around Cape Horn, and it is sailing up the northwest coast of Alaska. The excerpts that follow trace the ship's course eastward into Arctic waters and toward the thickening ice and un-Christianized Eskimo bands. In these passages, Miertsching describes how the *Investigator* was caught in the ice that first winter, Captain McClure's discovery of the Northwest Passage, and the silence of the winter cold. The last part of the excerpt concerns the *Investigator's* inability to break free of the Arctic's grip. Note that Miertsching's three diary entries excerpted here are all dated during the freeze-up of the sea in September, but in consecutive years: 1851, 1852, and 1853. Miertsching and the crew of the *Investigator* finally escaped from the Arctic on September 13, 1854, with his resolve that "never again shall I cross that line."

---

30 July (lat. 68° 57'; long. 168° 37'; temp. 44°)

Weather fine and wind very light. We were very busy writing letters. The ship *Plover* is lying near us. This ship, a twelve-gun brig, was sent from England in 1848 to Kotzebue Sound with orders to lie at anchor here as a depot for the crews of Sir John Franklin, should they make their way from east to west through the frozen seas into Bering Strait. To this ship supplies are sent annually from the Sandwich Islands, and she lies here anchored in the ice for eleven months, and for one month cruises to the northwards from Bering Strait. A great number of friendly Eskimos have gathered on the shore opposite the ship; unfortunately there is no one on the ship to use this grand opportunity of teaching them something of their creation and salvation; rather the men—and this includes high-ranking officers—behave themselves so shamelessly that here one will soon have an Anglo-Eskimo colony.

---

2 August (lat. 72° 1'; long. 166° 12'; temp. 40°)

Wind strong and fair; weather bright and cold. At 9 a.m. resounded the cry from the crow's-nest, "Ice", and in two hours we were ringed around with huge masses of ice, but sailed ever deeper therein, and the ship suffered many severe shocks. At 2 p.m. we were fixed and motionless. As far as sight extends from the crow's-nest the ice appears a solid, unbroken mass; with much toil and labour the ship was got about, and by night made her way into open water; we began now, instead of north, to steer east along the mainland shore. We saw several hundred—some, including the captain, asserted a thousand—walrus, young and old, lying on the ice; if the ship came near them at a given signal all dived and made a great commotion in the water; but they soon returned to the ice again.

---

8 August (lat. 70° 54'; long. 154° 43'; temp. 37°)

Yesterday I had another long talk on Christianity with the captain; he asserted that on a ship at sea no one could hold that form of Christianity which is observed on land: at sea a man must have spirit and not hang his head; I told him that I would gladly call myself and really *be* a Christian, and yet I held my head every whit as high as he, and among other things quoted St. Paul: "Freut euch", etc., along with other texts. He could only reply that "I was not yet a true seaman, or I would have other views; Mr. Marx, who had formerly been a lieutenant on a number of warships, had adopted my sort of land-Christianity, and had learned by experience that it did not serve on board ship; so he gave up the sea, and became a parson and writes tracts for old wives; I should have given the leaflets which I had distributed among the seamen to lost women, who would have given me more thanks than his sailors." The captain broke off the discussion and asked me to sing something; he himself handed me my guitar—I opened my hymn-book and sang the hymn, "How great a bliss to be a sheep of Jesus, and to be guided by His shepherd staff", etc.; he listened with pleasure to three verses, and then thanked me and wished me good night.

19 August (lat. 71° 32'; long. 144° 50'; temp. 33°)

Last night was sleepless and full of anxiety; I was twice thrown from my bed by the thunderous shocks of the ice. Today snow, rain, and fog, so that one can barely see for two hundred paces. Strong west wind and appalling ice. The ice grows ever heavier and the water-lanes narrower. At 11 a.m. the ship was beset and jammed amidst immovable masses of ice. The ice-masses, floating closely packed one against another, rose twelve to fifteen feet above the surface of the sea; and many are so broad that one could plant a city thereon. After three hours' hard work the ship could again be sailed back by the way we had come, but in the next half-hour of sailing we were again fast beset; again two hours' hard work; and now there was no more hope of going to the north through the ice, for all perceived the impossibility; so the captain gave up the plan; the ship was put about, yet we could not go back, but lay there quite helpless. The temper of the crew was far from pleasant: to the captain no man dared to speak.

24 August (lat. 69° 43'; long. 131° 57'; temp. 37°)

By continuous beating to windward we make a little headway; in the last two days only fifty English miles. Today at 10 a.m. as we slanted in towards the shore we saw Eskimos as usual; but some of the sailors—who, one may note, have keen eyes—insisted that they could make out a man in European dress. Thereupon the captain determined to land in person. He wrote a letter in the hope that through these people (who were sure to be in communication with the inhabitants of the Mackenzie valley) it might be forwarded to the Europeans who dwell there. The colours were hoisted on our ship. At 12 noon we quitted the ship—the captain,

Dr. Armstrong, and I, with six seamen in a boat—and pulled for the land; we saw only a few Eskimos, and these received us in no friendly manner as we disembarked; they faced us with spears, long knives, and drawn bows. Every attempt to approach the savages in friendly fashion was unsuccessful; but the captain was determined not to go back without questioning them; finally after several unavailing endeavours I managed to get within ten paces of these hostile folk, and spoke to them in a friendly tone; and finally they began to listen and ceased their horrible shrieking and howling. They bade us go away and pointed to the ship which was just then in motion. I picked up a few arrows, bore them in my hand (I was without weapons) and, approaching, gave them back; again they grew very excited, so that I thought it best to draw from my pocket a pistol loaded with blank shot and fire it in the air; this device helped; they grew somewhat quieter and began to listen to me, trembling the while all over and with a white foam on their lips; and finally they were persuaded to lay down their weapons; and the captain and the rest came forward, also without weapons, and at last we were good friends. They invited us to their fine new-built wooden homes, and gave us fowl, fish, and reindeer skins in exchange for knives, saws, etc. Their friendship was even warmer than that, already recorded, of Attua. Old Kairoluak (chief in this region) especially enjoyed himself. This man had a fine house and two tents; everywhere was order and cleanliness, such as I had never seen among Eskimos; great heaps of reindeer, bear, fox, and wolverine skins, were ready for bargaining purposes. These people have never seen Europeans before and have no traffic with the Hudson's Bay traders on the Mackenzie River, but dispose of their wares westwards where they do business with Attua. Old Kairoluak's son had recently had the misfortune to break the bone of his leg a little above the ankle, and now lay helpless and in great pain. The doctor examined him, but our stay was too short for anything to be done; and probably in a few weeks this fine young Eskimo would no longer be alive. If the Eskimos see no prospect of the speedy cure or improvement of an invalid they quickly give up hope altogether, and when the family moves to another region they leave the sick one in a lonely place where no Eskimo dogs come, set a little food by him, and thenceforth think of him no more. On a little sandhill we saw a peculiar wooden monument, and asked what it was. The people told us that strangers (*tujormints* or *kaimaraijets*) had come to this place without a boat, and had built a house of driftwood on the cape, and lived there; in time all fowl, seal, and reindeer had disappeared, and they must have been starving; then all but one of these strangers disappeared and the last—when the Eskimos came seeking the game which had vanished—was found dead on the ground, and Kairoluak had buried him there. I could not ascertain the date of this occurrence. Probably it is an old legend derived from some fight with the Indians. I would gladly have talked longer with the Eskimos about this story and about more important matters, and to tell them something of a God, their Creator and Preserver, but suddenly the captain shouted, "The ship is aground!" and bade us hurry to the boat. We had scarcely reached the ship—which was *not* aground—when a fog descended so thick that one could not see twenty paces. Deeming it his duty, the captain determined to visit the cape pointed out by the Eskimos, where the *tujormints* had built a house, in order perhaps through relics to learn more of the tragic story, but the thick fog prevented him from doing this today. It always grieves me and especially on this occasion to leave these poor people to lead their lives in heathenish ignorance without being able to impart to them something of an abiding faith. The Eskimos put to shame so many Christians in this that they go on long journeys to dispose of their wares, in order not to receive worthless stuff in exchange, but articles that are good and useful to them.

31 August (Cape Bathurst, temp. 29°)

All night we lay at anchor, and today, although the weather is fine and the wind fair, the ship remained at anchor, because the captain wished to visit the Eskimos.

We had barely got out of the boat when a swarm of Eskimos came pouring down towards us with long spears, knives, harpoons, and bows ready drawn; they let fly several arrows and set up a hideous outcry. The women were following behind them with more weapons. In his desire to avoid unpleasantness the captain kept on asking, "What is to be done? What is to be done?" I handed the captain my gun, securely fastened my

Eskimo frock, and ran as fast as I could towards them; which caused in their ranks a—to me—most disagreeable disturbance. I drew my pistol from my pocket, discharged it in the air before their eyes, and shouted to them to throw down their weapons. But they only shouted all the louder: "Shuitok, shuitok, Kalauroktuta." I took my stand before them with my pistol in my hand, unloaded—but the Eskimos did not know that, being unaware that one must load a fire-arm before discharging it—and told them that we were friends, brought gifts, and intended to do them no harm whatever; whereupon they became more quiet and peaceful; the captain came forward to join me, and finally, after much debate and giving of pledges, they laid down their weapons, but left their knives within easy reach on the ground. I marked a line on the snow between them and us which no one was to cross, and this also impressed them. They became more friendly, and finally all fear vanished, and they brought wives, children, and sucklings, and laid their little ones in our arms that we might observe them more closely. These Eskimos exchange wares with the Locheaux or Hare Indians, who dwell inland, also in a state of heathendom; whose speech the Eskimos understand, and who carry their goods to Fort Good Hope on the Mackenzie River. After the captain had ended his business—which consisted of asking the Eskimos questions—and was convinced that these people knew nothing of Sir John Franklin and his unlucky crews, he handed to the Eskimo Kenalualik the letter directed to the Hudson's Bay station, along with many gifts for himself; the man promised to do his best to attend to it. While the captain was studying the features of the country I took advantage of my freedom and entertained myself with these poor, wild, simple folk; they listened gladly to me, and asked many questions, helping me with signs when their words and expressions were unknown to me. These people also know nothing of a Divine Being on high, and have apparently never thought that the sun, moon, rocks, and water were created by anyone, and were much astonished when I told them of a great, good Spirit, Who can do whatsoever He wills, and to Whom nothing is impossible—that He dwells above the sun, moon, and stars and watches all that we do, that this Spirit has created everything, including the first men, etc., at which they stared at me in amazement, and frequently cried out in wonder. They accepted all that

I told them, but in connection with the stars old Kenalualik thus informed me: Above us is a great blue chest, the Sun's house; in daytime and through the long arctic summer the sun is not in his house, but when he goes there it becomes dark, but there are clean-cut little holes through which he can view the water and the land, and these are the stars. These Eskimos also have their own peculiar conception of the life after death. It is that there are two lands, one good, and one not good. In the good land dwells a good spirit who looks after the wild animals, that they do not disappear from the land. In the bad land dwells also a spirit who is bad and always does men harm. When an Eskimo dies, if he has in life clothed the widows and orphans and given them food, he comes into the good land where the sun shines always and where there is never rain, ice, or strong winds, but always warm weather and countless seal, reindeer, etc., and these are not wild or shy; one can catch them with one's hands. He, on the contrary, who has not had a good character in his life, comes to the bad land which is the complete opposite of the good land. While I was carrying on this, to me, most interesting conversation with these Eskimos whom I was beginning to love, the captain came and summoned me to the boat. I rose and was about to go, but my grey-headed friend, Kenalualik, held me back; he said that I should wait and tell them more, and should live with them. I replied that I could not do this, but must go with the ship to seek our friends who were lost in the ice; at which he offered me a sledge and dogs, with which I could go to the ship over the ice when the next moon disappeared and the sea was frozen; but till then I should remain with him; to which I replied that the ship might go far, and I would be unable to find it; at which he repeated his former offers, and added thereto a tent, so that I was to have sledge, dogs, and tent. I told him firmly that my *angajuga* (commander, captain) was telling me to come and that I must follow and obey. But he began once more to repeat his promises and set before me his daughter with the words "takka unna" ("take her"). In the meantime the captain came to fetch me, and he took us both by the arm and conducted us to the boat where we distributed gifts and re-embarked. To my old friend Kenalualik and his daughter—a girl of very lovely appearance, some sixteen years old—I gave double gifts, and to the latter many needles, because these are of special value.

An Eskimo woman was caught making off with our boat compass. I also missed by pocket-handkerchief, but recovered it from an Eskimo who bore a genuinely thievish appearance. To escape from the throng which was pressing upon us we took to the boat and left these poor folk lining the beach and wishing us a thousand *aksusijy* (farewells). Fifteen *kayaks* and Eskimos in their *umiaks* accompanied us to the ship where the sailors delighted them with many gifts—many were dressed from head to foot in European garb. As it was beginning to grow foggy they returned joyously to their families in their new clothes. The dialect of these people is somewhat different from that of other Eskimos along this coast; they understood me very well; but to me, especially at the first, it was difficult to understand them—they were almost unintelligible. A number of them have brown hair and blue eyes; their clothes, made skillfully out of the best skins, set off well the figures of these small but well-proportioned people. They call Cape Bathurst Nuvoak, the first or nearest island Akkunek, the next Tuppelisoak; the water between the cape and the first island they name *koruk*. The dogs of these people are of the same breed as in Labrador.

---

21 September (beset in ice; temp. 7°)

We are frozen in the ice and are being pushed along with it to the north; If only it would keep on going through Barrow Strait to Melville Island! on both sides along the shore is open water, but we cannot get there with the ship, and fast-frozen here must await helplessly what the future may bring. This evening again, as is usual on Saturday, uproarious noise and recreation; it seems as if the men must work themselves into a state of absolute exhaustion on Saturday night in order to observe Sunday with the strict repose which English custom enjoins; the noise grew too much even for the captain, and he let the men go to bed an hour early.

---

26 September (lat. 72° 45'; long. 118° 3'; temp. 3°)

Yesterday we had only a few hours of repose; we had lain down for a short while only, when we had to rise, and, cold and tired and weary, we stood the night through, and a part of the day, on deck. The blows of the ice on the ship were frightful. The gale drove the ship with the ice again northwards towards the high, rocky, 120-foot, perpendicular south side of the island, which now we have named Princess Royal Island; and in order not to be dashed against this steep mountain wall the ship, after much toil and labour, was moored with six hawsers to a great floe. We came within fifty feet of the deadly crag, and yet were again preserved. The water there was 65 feet deep. The past night was the most horrible that we have yet experienced; we have endured storms at sea when almost all the upper masts were carried away, but, appalling as a storm at sea is, everyone of us vows, "Ten hurricanes at sea are not the equal of last night"; these hours of terror I am not able to describe, and store them in my memory where they are so deeply imprinted that never in all my life will the impression be effaced, but will remind me of what I owe to my Lord and Saviour Whose grace and pity are unspeakably great. To His honour was the last drop of my blood consecrated. For seventeen hours we stood ready on the deck where each moment appeared to be our last; great massive pieces of ice three and four times the size of the ship were pushed one on top of another and under continuing pressure forced into a towering heap which would then come tumbling down with a thunderous roar. In the thick of this ice-revolution lay the ship, thrown now on one broadside, now on the other, then again heaved up out of the water, and, when the towering ice collapsed, the ship came crashing down into the sea. The ship's beams were so sprung apart that the tarred oakum was falling out of the seams; even the casks in the hold began to crack. These casks are stowed so tightly that they cannot budge with the rolling of the ship; two of them cracked, so great was the pressure on the ship. Had we seen a chance of reaching land across this surging ice-field, not a man would have remained on the ship; but neither by boat nor on foot was this possible; so we had to endure, and expect each moment to be our last; yes, so utter was the despair, when every man saw clearly that here was no hope of rescue, that in the very next moment the ship might be crushed like a nutshell, that some sailors, with neither hope nor the fear of God before their eyes, burst open the chamber where the spirits were stored, made themselves and others completely drunk and stupefied their senses, so that in this condition they might escape the agonies of death. Our helplessness and danger had reached the highest point—the ship was flung over on her broadside, and a towering ice-heap was threatening to cover her with rubble, and so in a moment to bury seventy-six [sixty-six] men in a living tomb; then spoke the mercy of God: "Thus far shalt thou go, but no further"; the commotion in the ice died away, and it lay without the least motion; we gazed at one another, and marvelled at this sudden change: one doubted whether it was fact or fantasy. The ship was lying on her side and we stood rigid, expecting a fresh outbreak of this frightful volcanic upheaval; but the good Lord held the ice in His mighty hand; it lay quiet and motionless. A strong watch was set on deck; the rest of us went, tired, limp, and drenched, to enjoy a little rest.

27 September (lat. 72° 42'; long. 118° 4'; temp. 2°)

The ice is still at rest, and the cold is binding it into a solid mass. On board amongst the crew there is a hush; the men behave as if frightened and few words are exchanged; they all seem to have suffered a shock and to have no spirit left; no work was done today; except for the strong watch on deck, all were enjoying sorely needed sleep and repose. The six anchors with which the ship had yesterday been moored to a great floe have been lost through the parting of the hawsers. As the ship is lying on her broadside and no one can walk on deck or on the ice, everyone keeps to his cabin. The ship has been pumped out; 25 inches of water stand in her.

28 September (lat. 72° 44'; long. 117° 55'; temp. 5°)

The night passed quietly and every man could have his rest out; yet must every man hold himself ready, prepared at any moment to become a homeless wanderer. The watches on the upper and lower decks have strict orders to be very alert. The wind has wholly died away; and the whole mass of ice, and naturally we with it, have been slowly drifting to the north with the ebb and flow of the tide.

All the time the ice is freezing more solidly together. The ship, which still lay on her side, was righted today, but not all the labour and machinery employed could set her upon a perfectly even keel, for she rests entirely upon ice, and cannot be trimmed as if she were afloat. Everyone worked with a diligence which surprised even the captain; all the officers were willing and carried out their duties without a word. Although it is Saturday, yet there is no singing or dancing; everything is strangely quiet. This evening I passed the time most agreeably with the captain.

---

29 September (temp. 8°)

Last night and today no movement in the ice. Since yesterday we have remained in one and the same place, four miles north of the Princess Royal Islands, six miles from the coast to the east, eight miles from that to the west. Should the ice continue to freeze together as it has done since the day before yesterday and should no fresh upheaval occur, this place will have to be named our winter quarters. No Divine Service was held today. The mood of the men is very impressive and very strange. A quiet reigns over the ship which is altogether wholesome and a little odd; each man moves, works, does his duty, and attends to his responsibilities willingly and as if with pleasure; every man is very earnest. The captain appears on deck as usual, but seldom speaks a word and that only to the first lieutenant. I dined with the captain today, read him a sermon after coffee, and we talked on various agreeable topics; he told me how he proposed tomorrow to deal with the men who had burst open the wine and rum kegs a few days before, and we talked much about that. The interior of the ship is very damp, for water has leaked in everywhere, and it is beginning also to be cold. Clothes and linen are damp and there is no way of drying them. I often feel depressed in these mournful surroundings. Lord, strengthen me and give me health and courage.

---

30 September (lat. 72° 46'; long. 118° 12'; temp. 2°)

The weather is and remains fine but cold; everything is freezing into a mass; there has been no wind for some days, and, though the ice stirs, it remains quiet in the neighbourhood of the ship. This morning came the order from the captain that no work was to be done. At 9 a.m. the crew was mustered, and after the captain had inspected the ship, he read an extract from the Articles of War relating to discipline on board ship, and the punishment by which it is enforced. While this was being read everyone stood bareheaded. After this reading the captain addressed the men in terms of vehement rebuke, set before them their disgraceful behaviour, called them a band of thieves, unworthy of the name of Englishmen, and said that he was ashamed that such base robbers, such a thievish rabble, should walk the deck of an English ship, etc., etc. He then pronounced against the offenders the punishment which they had deserved and would receive. After this severe rebuke he began to admonish the men; he set plainly before them the danger in which we had been, still were, and still would be, and showed them that all human strength and skill were ineffective in such hours of need; only Almighty Providence had through a manifest miracle saved us from certain death, etc. Even old sailors inured to danger, with weather-beaten faces, could not restrain their tears, and all to a man promised amendment and gave the captain a cheer. In the afternoon the three ringleaders were punished.

---

7 October 1850 (temp. max. 0°, min. −5°, med. 2°)

Until today, the 7th, we have had weather fine and calm but very cold; the new-frozen ice is a foot thick; although the ice is in constant movement, yet it is quite still near the ship. Yet we must always be prepared for flight in event of another convulsion in the ice. The topmasts and yards have been taken down; on the upper deck also they are working to make ready for winter. All the work is carried out willingly and cheerfully. The coarse "language of the sea" is also less indulged in. My servant and friend, Farquharson, is much troubled because the sailors cannot read and instruct themselves by means of books and tracts. The captain and his officers are now on the best of terms and the unpleasantness which formerly existed has not recurred since our departure from the Sandwich Islands. Every day I spend some most agreeable hours with the captain: he seems now to realize that he is not the good exemplary Christian which he used to think himself; for some days he has been reading his Bible morning and evening. The health of the crew is very good; now there is no one on the sick list. On every clear day the aurora borealis appears to the south-east from 7 to 11 p.m.

31 October (temp. max. −5°, min. −23°, med. −16°)

Yesterday morning at 8:30 the captain came back from his expedition, and came on board without being observed on the ice. He had left behind his crew and sledge nine miles from the ship at 10 o'clock yesterday, thinking to reach the ship by 2 p.m., but it began to snow, he lost his way and wandered the whole night and could not find the ship; he had no rest, sleep, food or drink; he was twice in danger from polar bears, but had seen them before they saw him. He fired off all his powder to draw the attention of the ship's watch, but probably was too far from the ship for this to be heard. Finally, after he had been wandering for twenty hours, the sky cleared, the sun rose, and he found himself in the midst of hummocks a half hour's walk from the ship. He came aboard more like a corpse than a living man; his limbs were stiff with cold; he could not speak a word. He was carried to his cabin, where both doctors, Armstrong and Piers, took charge of him. At midday the captain's sledge-crew came aboard in great anxiety to learn whether the captain had arrived before them. After the captain left them they had set up the tent and prepared a good meal. Soon after, snow began to fall and they thought it necessary to remain in the tent and spend the night on the ice. Now they were in excellent condition after an absence of ten days, rejoicing at the success of thier journey. On 26 October they had reached the end of the water in which we and the ship were frozen, and found themselves at the east end of the land Captain Parry had sighted thirty years before from Melville Island and had named Banks Land. To the north they saw ice only; to the east the shore of Prince Albert Land fell away: so the problem of the Northwest Passage, disputed for 300 years, was solved.

20 December (temp. max. −34°, min. −37°, med. −36°)

For several days the weather has been very pleasant; although dark and cold, for there has been no wind. As far as one can see, nothing is visible except snow and ice; no tree, bush, or stone to lend relief to the expanse of white. Nature is dead, and such a stillness reigns that one hears his watch ticking in his pocket—indeed, some assert that they can hear their hearts beat.

1 September 1851 (temp. max. 27° , min. 24° , med. 25°)

The ice is without motion and is beginning to freeze into one solid mass; the land is decked in the white of new-fallen snow. The captain spoke to the assembled crew at some length today. He reminded them of the gracious protection granted the ship and with much kindness and the deepest sincerity admonished them to keep this miraculous deliverance in mind, and not to be despondent or lose heart at the outset of another winter season: it had been his wish to bring the ship into a safe winter harbour; no one would have expected that after only four days of open sailing water to be frozen in here as early as 20 August, etc. In conclusion he said that he would do his utmost to make life happy for every one of them. The very high hummocks near the ship have been blown up and a broader road levelled to the shore.

3 September 1852

. . . The little water we saw last month is all frozen again. From hour to hour we watch and wait anxiously and hope that some disturbance will break the ice in the sea, and grant us passage at least to Melville Island: everyone has despaired of reaching England this year.

13 September [1853] (temp. max. 18° , min. 8° , med. 13°)

Continuous very cold weather and perfect calm. The new ice is 5 inches thick. Our yearning wish and best hope to reach Europe this year is crushed and extinguished for good and all. Ah! to endure a fourth winter in this life at sea is almost too much. The mood on the ship and the feeling that masters everyone as he looks forward to the immediate future is more easily imagined than described. Ah, Lord, give me patience and trust in Thee as the one Helper and Comforter in time of need.

13 September [1854] (lat. 63° 15'; long. 54°, 54')

. . . We intended to put in to Holsteinburg . . . but were prevented by the strong land wind, so we sailed away southwards and towards evening passed out of the Arctic Circle. Since the 27th of July 1850, when we crossed that line in Bering Strait, we have been in the Arctic Circle. I hope that never again shall I cross that line.

Charm for Seal Blubber

Spirit of the air,
I call, I call!
I hiccup throaty sounds
which come from my inside.
Here I stand,
and shout my songs up
by my little hut.
Spirit of the air,
I call, I call!
Send me blubber
as you used to,
send me blubber
as you used to,
send me blubber!

—Tatilgak (Copper Eskimo man)

How Dr. Hayes Learned to Love Seal Blubber

BY DR. I. I. HAYES (AMERICAN, 1854)

I n 1850, while the *Investigator* and many other British ships made their way north, the first American expedition to the Arctic was getting underway. Lady Franklin had written to President Zachary Taylor for American assistance, but Congress turned down the request to appropriate funds for a search vessel. Into the breach stepped Henry Grinnell, a wealthy New Yorker, who purchased and outfitted two ships, the *Rescue* and the *Advance,* to help in the Franklin search, manning them with Navy personnel.

On board the *Advance* as assistant surgeon was Elisha Kent Kane, the romantically minded son of a prominent Philadelphia family who had struggled all his life for his father's approval. The *Advance* returned to the United States a year later, carrying news of the discovery by various search parties of Franklin's first winter quarters on Beechey Island, though this discovery revealed nothing of where the *Erebus* and *Terror* had sailed next.

As the following year's search for Franklin geared up, Kane proposed taking the *Advance* up to Northern Greenland, on the theory that some of the Franklin party might be living with the Eskimos there. Kane, who had meanwhile started a torrid romance with a famous teenage spirit medium named Margaret Fox, was a firm believer in the notion of an "open polar sea." Like McClure pushing hard for the Northwest Passage while ostensibly engaged in the Franklin search, it seems Kane really wasn't so much interested in finding Franklin as he was in finding the North Pole.

The outcome was predictable. Kane thrust the stoutly reinforced, metal-sheathed *Advance* so far north along the Greenland coast that it froze in through the winter of 1853 to 1854, and never melted out during the following summer. Carl Petersen, a Greenlandic whaler aboard the *Advance,* was convinced that their best hope lay in sledging and sailing in small open boats the thousand miles south to the outpost of Upernavik. Though opposed to the idea, Kane gave his crew the choice of whether they wished to remain another winter aboard the ice-locked *Advance* or set south with Petersen, though he confided in his private journals the bitter resentment he held against those who left him. Nine of the crewmen elected to go, including Petersen and the ship's doctor, Isaac I. Hayes.

All manner of calamity befell the group, some of it quite comical. Winter stopped them with less than half of their journey completed, and they had to hole up in a crack in the rock that they managed to turn into a frigid hut on a gameless stretch of Greenland shore. As they weaken with starvation, the *angakok* Kalutunah (an Inuit shaman) appears at the entrance to their hut with chunks of walrus flippers and other meats. Over the next days and weeks he is followed by a stream of curious Eskimo from settlements up and down the coast. The stranded explorers cannot convince Kalutunah to take them south over the treacherous ice of Melville Bay by dogsled to Upernavik, which no one in his lifetime has attempted; Kalutunah won't even sell them a dogteam so they can attempt it themselves. They try to walk back to the *Advance,* three hundred miles north, but turn back after only eight miles, nearly dead of hunger and winter's cold. Finally, they hatch a plot: Dr. Hayes will measure a dose of opium into Kalutunah's meat stew, and when he passes out, they'll steal his dogsled and make their retreat to the *Advance.*

In his book about this failed escape to the south, *Arctic Boat Journey,* Hayes writes vividly and dramatically and at times quite amusingly. Though he regards them as "savages," Hayes, with his scientific curiosity, finds much to admire in the Eskimos' ingenuity at surviving in the Arctic and offers up some fine set pieces describing their stone winter huts shaped like "an old-fashioned clay country oven," their sled runners fashioned of bits of bone with the intricacy of a "Chinese puzzle," and their unflagging hospitality. Excerpted here is the moment in Hayes's account when the adventurers put into motion their plot to drug Kalutunah and make a dash three hundred miles in the dead of winter for the *Advance*. When the group first left the comforts of the *Advance*, they disdained the soot-caked huts of the Eskimos and the hunks of raw blubber proffered in hospitality, but now, as they retreat, starving and frozen, back toward the ship in defeat, the hapless explorers crawl humbly into the huts and gratefully gobble down the raw, dripping Eskimo fare.

I had not returned from my walk more than two hours, before three Esquimau hunters, with as many sledges, arrived from Netlik. One of them was Kalutunah. Their visit seemed to have been prompted by curiosity, for they brought nothing to trade; and they came into the hut with only two small pieces of meat, which were scarcely more than sufficient to furnish to themselves a moderate meal. One of these pieces was appropriated without ceremony to the use of our party, notwithstanding that the proceeding was protested against by the hunters, with a multitude of sullen "Na! na! na-miks!" Men in our condition were not likely to be deterred by a mere verbal negative. An equivalent for the meat was afterward given to them, and they appeared to be satisfied. Both pieces were soon cooking.

I now repeated to Kalutunah a request which had been made on previous occasions, viz: that his people should take us upon their sledges and carry us northward to the Oomeaksoak. His answer was the same as it had been hitherto. It was then proposed to him and his companions that they should hire to us their teams; but this also they declined to do. No offers which we could make seemed to produce the slightest impression upon them; and it was clear that nothing would induce them to comply with our wishes, nor even to give us any reason for their refusal. In fact they thoroughly understood our situation; and we now entertained no doubt that they had made up their minds, with a unanimity which at an earlier period seemed improbable, to abandon us to our fate and to profit by it. In this view we were confirmed by a discovery which one of our men made upon going down to their sledges. They had brought with them several large pieces of bear and walrus meat, which they were evidently determined that we should not obtain; and to insure this they had buried the pieces in the snow. For this procedure they might well have had motives which it was not for us to question; for example, provisions might be scarce at their settlement. Upon inquiring of Kalutunah if such was the case, he informed us that they had, the day before, captured a bear, three seals, and a walrus. They had, then, plenty, and could not possibly have been actuated by the necessary selfish prudence which I had in charity attributed to them.

The question to be decided became a very plain one. Here were six civilized men, who had no resort for the preservation of their lives, their usefulness, and the happiness of their families, except in the aid of sledges and teams which the savage owners obstinately refused to sell or to hire. The expectation of seizing, after we should have starved or frozen to death, our remaining effects, was the only motive of the refusal. The savages were within easy reach of their friends, and could suffer little by a short delay of their return. For their property compensation could be made after our arrival at the brig. For my own part, before attempting to negotiate with Kalutunah, I had determined that his party should not escape us in case of failure in our application to them for aid.

My comrades were not behind me in their inclinations. Indeed, it is to their credit that in so desperate an extremity, they were willing to restrain themselves from measures of a kind to give us, at the time, far less trouble than those which I suggested. Being unwilling that any unnecessary harm should come to the Esquimaux, I proposed to put them to sleep with opium; then, taking possession of their dogs and sledges, to push northward as rapidly as possible; and leaving them to awaken at their leisure, to stop for a few hours of rest among our friends at Northumberland Island; then to make directly for Cape Alexander, with the hope of getting so far the start of Kalutunah and his companions, that before they could arrive at Netlik and spread the alarm, we should be beyond their reach.

This plan met with the unanimous sanction of the party; and we prepared to put it into immediate execution.

In the way of this there were some difficulties. Our guests were manifesting great uneasiness, and a decided disinclination to remain. Many threatening glances and very few kind words had been bestowed upon them; and they were evidently beginning to feel that they were not in a safe place. It became now our first duty to reassure them; and accordingly, the angry looks gave place to friendly smiles. The old, familiar habits of our people were resumed. Many presents were given to them. I tore the remaining pictures from my "Anatomy," and the picture of the poor foot-sore boy who wanted washing, from "Copperfield," and gave them to Kalutunah for his children. Such pieces of wood as remained to us, were distributed amongst them. Each received a comb. This last they had sometimes seen us use, and they proceeded immediately to comb out their matted hair, or rather, to attempt that work; but forty years of neglect, blubber, and filth had so glued their locks together, that there was no possibility of getting a comb through them. The jests excited by these attempts to imitate our practices did more to restore confidence than anything else.

At length was reached the climax of our hospitalities. The stew which we had been preparing for our guests was ready, and was placed before them; and they were soon greedily devouring it. This proceeding was watched by us with mingled anxiety and satisfaction; for, while the pot was over the fire, I had turned into it, unobserved, the contents of a small vial of laudanum. The soup of course contained the larger part of the opium; but being small in quantity it had been made so bitter that they would not eat more than the half of it. In order to prevent either of them from getting an overdose we divided the fluid into three equal portions; and then with intense interest awaited the result, apprehensive that the narcotic had not been administered in sufficiently large quantity to insure the desired effect.

After an interval of painful watchfulness on the part of my companions, the hunters began to droop their eyelids, and asked to be allowed to lie down and sleep. We were not long in granting their wish, and never before had we manifested more kindly dispositions toward them. We assisted them in taking off their coats and boots, and then wrapped them up in our blankets, about which we were no longer fastidious.

Our guests were in a few minutes asleep; but I did not know how much of their drowsiness was due to fatigue, (for they had been hunting,) and how much to the opium; nor were we by any means assured that their sleep was sound; for they exhibited signs of restlessness which greatly alarmed us. Every movement had therefore to be conducted with the utmost circumspection.

To prepare for starting was the work of a few minutes. We were in full travelling dress, coats, boots, and mittens, and some of us wore masks; the hunters' whips were in our hands, and nothing remained to be done but to get a cup from the shelf. The moment was a critical one, for, if the sleepers should awake, our scheme must be revealed. Godfrey reached up for the desired cup, and down came the whole contents of the shelf, rattling to the ground. I saw the sleepers start; and anticipating the result, instantly sprang to the light and extinguished it with a blow of my mittened hand. As was to be expected the hunters were aroused. Kalutunah gave a grunt and inquired what was the matter. I answered him by throwing myself upon the breck, and crawling to his side, hugged him close, and cried, "Singikpok," (sleep). He laughed, muttered something which I could not understand, and without having suspected that anything was wrong, again fell asleep.

This incident convinced us that we could not much rely upon either the soundness or the long continuance of the slumbers which we had secured, and that in order to prevent our guests from getting to Netlik before we should be beyond their reach, we must resort to other expedients. They must be confined within the hut, and the possibility of their escape prevented until relief could come to them from their companions at the settlement. This could only be accomplished by carrying off their clothing.

I slipped from the side of the sleeping savage, and sought for a little package which had dropped from my hand in the excitement of extinguishing the lamp. This package contained some of my journal-entries, some scientific notes, some records respecting the Esquimaux, and other important papers, and I could ill afford to lose it; but nowhere could it be found, nor was it safe to seek long. Everything was ready; my companions were impatient to be off; the cups thrown from the shelf were scattered about the hut, endangering every movement. If the savages should detect us in the act of leaving, I knew that their fate was sealed. The risks were too great, the moment was too critical, to admit of delay. I abandoned the search.

We crawled noiselessly out of the hut, carrying with us the boots, coats, and mittens of the sleepers. Stephenson was fortunately better than he had been for weeks. I gave to him the rifle, and stationed him with it on one side of the door. I took the double-barrelled shot-gun and occupied the side opposite. All of the firearms being now under my control, it was my intention, in case the Esquimaux should discover us, to await their coming out of the hut, and, under cover of our guns, compel them to mount the sledges and drive us northward.

Mr. Sonntag went down with the other men and prepared the sledges for starting. The dogs were greatly frightened by the sudden and novel treatment to which the strangers subjected them; and it was not without much trouble that they were harnessed. Meanwhile one of the men brought up the greater portion of the meat which was found buried in the snow; and having placed it in the passage, (it was sufficient, with economy, to last the prisoners five or six days,) we tore down the snow wall in front of the hut; and, with the frozen blocks, barricaded the doorway. Sonntag cried to us that all was ready. Leaving the sentinel's post I took Stephenson by the arm, and supported him to my sledge. Mr. Sonntag and John had one, and Whipple and Godfrey the other, of the remaining two. The poor dogs, howling in terror, dashed off at the first crack of the whip, and once more Fort Desolation was at our backs.

The dogs gave us much trouble. Unaccustomed to us, or to our voices, and startled by our sudden appearance among them, they seemed to be too much frightened to submit to control; and, setting off at a furious pace, they dashed helter-skelter over the plain, some running one way, some another, their tails down, their ears up,—all uttering their peculiar wild cry, and all, seemingly possessed with the one idea of breaking away from their strange-looking drivers. My team twice took me back nearly to the hut, before I succeeded in getting any mastery of them; and, weak as I was, they had by that time nearly mastered me. Meantime John and Godfrey were having a similar contest with their respective teams, which had carried them out among the rough ice half a mile from the coast.

At length my brutes' heads were turned from the hut, and we were dashing at a ten-knot speed after the other sledges. I thought now that my trouble was over; but no sooner had I overtaken my companions than my wolfish herd flew past them; and then wheeling short around, some to the right, some to the left, they turned the sledge over backward, rolled Stephenson and myself into a snow-drift, and beat a hasty retreat. I caught the up-stander as I tumbled off, and was dragged several yards before I could regain my feet, and throw myself upon the sledge. At this moment the dogs were plunging through a ridge of hummocks. The point of one of the runners caught a block of ice. All but two of the traces snapped off; and away went the dogs back toward their narcotized masters. To secure them again was of course impossible. The two animals which remained were hastily attached, one to each of the other sledges; and leaving the third sledge jammed in the ice we continued our course.

As we proceeded the dogs became more accustomed to our voices, and we made good headway. Cape Parry was reached without further accident. Here we halted, in a cave on the southern side of the point, for the purpose of making some repairs, and refreshing ourselves with a little rest and a pot of coffee.

The cave gave us a good protection against a light wind which had sprung up during our journey. It was about forty feet in depth, and twelve in height; and being on a level with the sea it had a smooth, glassy floor. The dogs wire picketed near its mouth; and, after being fed, they huddled quietly together; and, well reconciled to their new masters, they gave themselves no more uneasiness. Godfrey had broken his whipstock in his efforts to control their refractory tempers, and John had whipped his lash half away. Without repairing these, it was impossible to proceed with the teams, and fully two hours had elapsed before we were ready to continue our journey.

I was preparing to start with Mr. Sonntag to pick a track through the hummocks which lay across the little bight into which we had come, when three men with a sledge hove in sight around a point of land, about a hundred yards from our camp. They were at once recognized as our late prisoners. They had been able to extricate from the ice the sledge which we had been forced to abandon; and, refreshed by their food and sleep, they had quickly attached our fugitive dogs and started on our trail.

Each party discovered the other at the same moment, and both were equally surprised. The Esquimaux were of course in our power; but the surest way to guard against the hostility of the tribe, in consequence of our act of aggression, seemed to be to strike terror into these men; for a savage despises nothing as much as weakness, and respects nothing as much as strength.

Seizing the rifle, I sprang over the ice-foot and ran out to meet them. Sonntag was at my side with the gun. The Esquimaux stopped when they saw us approaching, and held their ground until we came within thirty yards of them, when, halting, I brought the rifle to my shoulder and aimed toward them. They turned away and, throwing their arms wildly about their heads, called loudly to us not to shoot.—"Na-mik! na-mik! na-mik!" I lowered my rifle and beckoned to them to advance. This they did cautiously, assuring us at every step that they were friends.

By this time Whipple had come up, and each of us seized a prisoner. I took Kalutunah by the collar, and, after giving him a hearty shake, in token of my displeasure, I marched him before me to the mouth of the cave; then facing him around toward his sledge, I pointed to it with my gun; and, turning toward the north, I told him, of course chiefly by signs, that if he took the whip which lay on the snow at his feet and drove us to the Oomeaksoak, I would give him back his dogs, sledge, coat, boots, and mittens, but that if he did not do this, he and his companions should be shot forthwith; and, suiting the action to the word, I pushed him from me, and made a feint to level my gun. He sidled away a few paces, crying, "Na! na!—Na-mik! na-mik!" over and over again, as fast as his tongue could utter the words, making gestures all the time with his right hand, in imitation of driving dogs; and with his left pointing northward. It being now evident that he understood both my demand and the penalty in case of non-compliance, I rested the stock of my gun upon the ice and nodded my approval of his decision. I then beckoned him toward me, and, pointing to the dogs, sledges, &c., I gave him to understand that we would consider all those things as ours until the terms of the contract were complied with on his part. He approached with his old-fashioned familiarity, and expressed his satisfaction by an overwhelming volley of "tyma," (good or right). He was evidently convinced that the tables had turned, and that I was doing him a great favor, in negotiating instead of using the dreaded weapon.

Our prisoners were a sorry looking party. They had arrayed themselves in our blankets, cutting holes in the middle of them for their heads. If not the original inventors of the Spanish *poncho* they are none the less entitled to credit for their ingenuity. One was dressed in red, another in white, and another in blue. One of them had discovered and appropriated an old pair of discarded boots; the others had wrapped their feet in pieces of our blankets. None of them seemed to have suffered from the cold. They had been awakened by the dogs running over the roof, as we had feared would be the case. The opium did not seem to have had more than a brief effect.

The cunning fellows had found means to light the lamp; and discovering that we had taken their sledges and had abandoned the hut, they had evidently resolved not to be altogether losers by the operation; and, in a business-like manner, they had proceeded to collect whatever they could carry away. In addition to the presents which we had made them, they had upon their sledge several tin-cups and tin-plates, a spoon, an old russia cap, a part of my lost manuscript records, and some other small articles; the useful and the useless all piled together. These things had been carried under their arms until they found the sledge. They had left the hut expecting to walk to Netlik or they would doubtless have taken more.

As a proof of our disposition to trust them we restored their clothing; and as they slipped into their jumpers, and tied on their moccasins, I could not but reflect that this was a strange way to make people happy. A more grateful set of fellows I had never seen. Our plan had succeeded better than was anticipated; for they did not attempt to touch dogs, sledge, or even a whip until they were bidden.

We were soon under way; and, running around the cape, we headed in for Netlik. The time occupied in reaching it was greatly protracted in consequence of our being obliged to walk or run during at least one third of the time, in order to prevent ourselves from freezing.

We were first made aware that we approached the village by the howling of an immense pack of dogs, which grouped themselves together on the white hill-side, and set up their wild concert, that could be heard at the distance of several miles. As we neared the shore, a crowd of men, women, and children came down over the ice-foot to meet us.

The savages, to the number of about fifty, assembled around us the moment we came to a halt. Among them I recognized many familiar faces. Everybody seemed greatly surprised to see us, especially under such auspices. They were all eager for news,—why we came, and why we had been brought, seemed to be the prevailing questions.

Feeling that it was still necessary to maintain the tone of authority with which we had commenced the adventure, we met all their advances with reserve. Without giving time for an invitation, we told Kalutunah that three of us would go to each of the two huts; and, having stopped there long enough to eat and sleep, we would continue our journey. For the benefit of the assembled multitude, just so much of the Cape Parry pantomine was repeated as was necessary to draw from Kalutunah and his two companions a renewal of their pledges, with which they were no less prompt than on the previous occasion.*

Our situation required the use of whatever advantage could be drawn from the superstitious fear which the savages had of our weapons. The Esquimaux outnumbered us as eight to one; we were half dead with cold, hunger, and fatigue; we could not even feel assured that our guns were in a condition to be discharged; and with

---

*In relation to the knowledge of fire-arms, the reader will observe a great difference between the Esquimaux of Smith Strait and those mentioned in the reports of the later English Expeditions to the north coasts of America. The former had, with a few exceptions in cases where communication had been held with the whale and discovery ships about Cape York, no practical acquaintance whatever with the terrible weapons of the white men, previous to the arrival of the Advance; and although a vague account of our guns must have spread through the settlements, yet we owed our safety to the fact that the "charm" of novelty had not been dispelled before we were thrown among the savages without other protection than the threats narrated in the text.

much of our prestige destroyed by preceding events, we had good reason to doubt our ability to maintain ourselves in case of any general excitement of the people into whose midst we had been thrown.

The dogs were given in charge of the boys, and we proceeded to the village. Mr. Sonntag, taking with him John and Whipple, was conducted to the hut of the chief, while I, with Stephenson and Godfrey, was taken by Kalutunah to his own mansion.

The settlement was now greatly enlarged by the people who had come from the south; and as I walked up from the beach I observed several snow-houses grouped around the two stone hovels which constituted the permanent portion of the village. In these snow-houses the moving families which we had recently entertained in our hut at Booth Bay were temporarily sojourning.

Kalutunah, in order the better to keep out the wind, had lengthened with snow the covered entrance to his hut, so that we were obliged to crawl fully twenty feet before we emerged into the dimly lighted apartment. It was completely deserted, the inmates having gone down to meet the sledges; but they were close behind us with others drawn by curiosity, and all came pouring in until the place seemed likely to be more tightly packed than it was when I visited it in September. The discomfort which would thus be caused, and the embarrassment to be anticipated in case any hostile feeling toward us should spring up, induced me to request Kalutunah not to admit any other persons than the ordinary inmates. He hesitated, manifestly regarding my procedure as an invasion of his authority, and he looked for a moment as though he would ask "is not my house my own?" The exigence, however, appeared to justify a little forwardness on my part, which being clearly expressed with the aid of a hint towards the "boom," the intruders retired from the hut and from the passage, leaving only about a dozen persons within. Fortunately several of these were small children.

Oh the luxury of that savage den! Ten weeks before, when I visited it, it was to me the embodiment of all that was most repulsive; now it was a real "weary man's rest." Our enfeebled bodies had just been exposed during fifteen consecutive hours, in travelling between forty and fifty miles. So great was the exhaustion of one of the party that he fell from debility alone the moment he went into the cold air. We were in a fit condition to appreciate the blessings of a place where we could lie down without the certainty of freezing; and we indulged in no close criticism of our surroundings.

We received all manner of kind attentions from our host. The women pulled off our boots, mittens, coats, and stockings, and hung them up to dry. My beard was frozen fast to the fur of my coat; and it was the warm hand of Kalutunah's wife that thawed away the ice. Meats of different kinds were brought in and offered to us in the only styles known to the Esquimau *cuisine,* that is, parboiled and raw; or as Stephenson more elegantly expressed it, "cooked with fire," and "cooked with frost;" but our fatigue had destroyed our appetites, and the warmth of the hut soon so overcame us that we fell asleep in the very act of taking food from the hand of our hostess. Now that the stimulus under which we had been acting was removed, scarcely anything could have prevented us from sleeping at the end of the first half-hour of our stay in that close, warm place. The hut was warmer by 120° than the atmosphere to which we had been so long exposed.

I lay down among a promiscuous collection of half-clad and un-clad men, women, and children; and my first consciousness was of some one pulling at my feet. It was the mistress of the establishment, who had prepared for us a plentiful meal; and we were soon doing such justice to the boiled steaks of bear, and the frozen steaks of seal, as need not have shamed an Esquimau hunter. Another long nap followed this feast; another feast followed the nap; and so on alternately through greater or less stages, until we had recovered from our fatigue and were strengthened by our good fare. We then signified to Kalutunah that we were prepared to start; and in a few minutes he had everything ready for us. The stars told us that we had been resting about twenty-seven hours.

Taking leave of the good people of Netlik, we clambered down over the ice-foot, and then mounting the sledges, we followed the path among the hummocks which Kalutunah's son picked for us, until we were clear of the bay, when, waving adieu to the young Esquimaux who had followed us, we continued our journey over the frozen sea.

Song of a Dead One

Joy fills me
When daylight breaks
And the sun
Glides silently forward.

But I lie choked with fear
Greedy maggot throngs
Eat into my collarbone cavity
And tear away my eyes.

Anxiously I lie and meditate.
How choked with fear I was
When they buried me
In a snow hut on a lake.

When they sealed the door
Incomprehensible
How my soul could escape.

Greater grew my fear
When the ice split
And the crack grew thunderously
Over the heavens.

Glorious was life
In winter
But did winter bring me joy?
Worries corroded
Worries for sole-skins and boot-skins.

Glorious was life
In summer
But did summer bring me joy?
Ever I was anxious
For sleeping furs.

Glorious was life
On the sea ice.
But did that bring me joy?
Ever was I anxious
For no salmon wished to bite.

Was it so beautiful
When I stood flushed, embar-
rassed,
In the swirl of the feasthouse,
And the choir ridiculed me,
Getting stuck with my song?

Tell me, now, was life so good on
earth?
Here joy fills me
When daylight breaks
And the sun
Glides silently forward.

—Netsit (Copper Eskimo man)

The Lost Franklin Found

BY DR. JOHN RAE (BRITISH, 1854)

As Miertsching and McClure of the *Investigator* were finally making their way back to England after four years trapped in the ice, and Isaac Hayes was attempting his escape from the *Advance*, Dr. John Rae was dogsledding overland in the vicinity of the Boothia Peninsula, surveying the land and keeping an eye out for Franklin. A Hudson's Bay Company employee, Rae was an exceptionally skilled Arctic traveler. While the Royal Navy suffered with inadequate woolen garb, scurvy-inducing salt pork, unwieldy ships, and exhausting man-hauled sledges, Rae was smart enough to adopt Inuit methods of sled travel, their fur clothing, and their hunting techniques. Near Pelly Bay in spring 1854, Rae heard from a party of Inuit that a large group of white men had perished not far away some four years earlier. Rae immediately suspected that this was the remnants of the Franklin expedition. He soon collected more stories and relics to prove unequivocably that it was.

England acted with outrage over the suggestion that members of the Royal Navy could possibly engage in so depraved an act as cannibalism, as Rae had reported, and concluded that the Franklin party was massacred by hostile Eskimos. By this time, the Royal Navy, having expended many ships and resources on the search, was exhausted with it, but Lady Franklin persisted to know the final fate of her husband. She financed yet another expedition on a small yacht, the *Fox*, and put it in command of young Captain Leopold McClintock, who had explored long stretches of the Arctic coastline by man-hauled sledges during three earlier searches for Franklin.

In the spring of 1859 McClintock and party were sledging on the west coast of King William Island, to the southwest of the Boothia Peninsula. This was a good ways south of where previous expeditions had focused the search for Franklin. McClintock's party discovered the first actual evidence of the death of Franklin and his men, eleven years after the massive search for Franklin had begun: a skeleton of a man in European dress sprawled on the shore; a wooden boat mounted on a sledge in which lay two more skeletons; and a cairn containing a brief record of the Franklin Expedition up to spring 1848: The *Erebus* and *Terror* had wintered in 1845 and 1846 at Beechey Island, made substantial progress on completing the Northwest Passage the following summer (by some claims they "discovered" it), but were trapped in ice in early September 1846 off King William Island. In June the following year Franklin died, the ship remained locked in ice throughout that summer—in 1847—and now, as Captain Crozier and Senior Officer Fitzjames scribbled this note on April 25, 1848, the remaining 105 men of the third Franklin Expedition were abandoning the ships and heading south, presumably toward the trading posts around Great Slave Lake hundreds of miles away.

John Rae's interviews with the Eskimos five years earlier had already turned up many of these facts. His letter to the Admiralty fills in the ultimate fate of the Franklin Expedition, at least according to the Eskimo accounts. Note that in closing his letter Rae implies that, by using native techniques, *he*, unlike the Franklin party, didn't have any difficulty surviving the Arctic winter.

REPULSE BAY, July 29.

"SIR,—I have the honor to mention, for the information of my Lords Commissioners of the Admiralty, that during my journey over the ice and snow this spring, with the view of completing the survey of the west shore of Boothia, I met with Esquimaux in Pelly Bay, from one of whom I learned that a party of 'white men' (Kablounans) had perished from want of food some distance to the westward, and not far beyond a large river, containing many falls and rapids. Subsequently, further particulars were received, and a number of articles purchased, which places the fate of a portion, if not of all, of the then survivors of Sir John Franklin's long-lost party beyond a doubt—a fate terrible as the imagination can conceive.

"The substance of the information obtained at various times and from various sources was as follows—

"In the spring, four winters past (spring, 1850,) a party of 'white men,' amounting to about forty, were seen traveling southward over the ice and dragging a boat with them, by some Esquimaux, who were killing seals near the north shore of King Williams' Land, which is a large island. None of the party could speak the Esquimaux language intelligibly, but by signs the natives were made to understand that their ship, or ships, had been crushed by the ice, and that they were now going to where they expected to find deer to shoot. From the appearance of the men, all of whom except one officer, looked thin, they were then supposed to be getting short of provisions, and purchased a small seal from the natives. At a later date the same season, but previous to the breaking up of the ice, the bodies of some thirty persons were discovered on the continent, and five on an island near it, about a long day's journey to the N. W. of a large stream, which can be no other than Back's Great Fish River, (named by the Esquimaux Doot-ko-hi-calik,) as its description, and that of the low shore in the neighborhood of Point Ogle and Montreal Island, agree exactly with that of Sir George Back. Some of the bodies had been buried, (probably those of the first victims of famine,) some were in a tent or tents, others under the boat, which had been turned over to form a shelter, and several lay scattered about in different directions. Of those found on the island, one was supposed to have been an officer, as he had a telescope strapped over his shoulders, and his double-barreled gun lay underneath him.

"From the mutilated state of many of the corpses, and the contents of the kettles, it is evident that our wretched countrymen had been driven to the last resource—cannibalism—as a means of prolonging existence.

"There appeared to have been an abundant stock of ammunition, as the powder was emptied in a heap on the ground by the natives out of the kegs or cases containing it; and a quantity of ball and shot was found below high-water mark, having probably been left on the ice close to the beach. There must have been a number of watches, compasses, telescopes, guns, (several double-barreled,) &c., all of which appear to have been broken up, as I saw pieces of those different articles with the Esquimaux, together with some silver spoons and forks. I purchased as many as I could get. A list of the most important of these I enclose, with a rough sketch of the crests and initials on the forks and spoons. The articles themselves shall be handed over to the Secretary of the Hudson's Bay Company on my arrival in London.

"None of the Esquimaux with whom I conversed had seen the 'whites,' nor had they ever been at the place where the bodies were found, but had their information from those who had been there, and who had seen the party when traveling.

"I offer no apology for taking the liberty of addressing you, as I do so from a belief that their lordships would be desirous of being put in possession, at as early a date as possible, of any tidings, however meagre and unexpectedly obtained, regarding this painfully interesting subject.

"I may add that, by means of our guns and nets, we obtained an ample supply of provisions last autumn, and my small party passed the winter in snow-houses in comparative comfort, the skins of the deer shot affording abundant warm clothing and bedding. My spring journey was a failure, in consequence of an accumulation of obstacles, several of which my former experience in arctic traveling had not taught me to expect. I have, &c.

JOHN RAE, C.F.,
"Commanding Hudson's Bay
Company's Arctic Expedition."

Song to Spring

Winter has been long and hard, and the people of the village have suffered privation. Everyone is exhausted, and many believe that they're not going to live until spring.

Then a man goes out along the coast in a kayak, where the first open water is beginning to appear. He comes to a hillside, which he climbs so as to have a view of any openings in the ice where he can hunt seal. Weak, and faint with hunger, he labours up the hill, until he discovers a snowdrift which the warmth of the sun is loosening from the mountain. He feels such happiness that he bursts out in song:

Aja-ha   aja-ha
I was out in my kayak
making towards land.
Aja-ha   aja-ha
I came to a snow-drift
that had just begun to melt.
Aja-hai-ja   aja-hai-ja
And I knew that it was spring:
we'd lived through winter!
Aja-hai-ja   aja-hai-ja
And I was frightened
I would be too weak,
too weak
to take in all that beauty!
Aja-hai-ja
Aja-hai-ja
Aja-ha.

—East Greenland Eskimos

Tyson's Wonderful Drift

BY CAPTAIN GEORGE E. TYSON (AMERICAN, 1871)

The story of Captain Tyson and his party's half-year-long stay on a drifting ice floe remains one of the most remarkable adventures in the history of Arctic exploration. Kept fed and sheltered by two Inuit hunters, who also had their wives and children to care for, the party of sailors rode the floe from October 1872 to May 1873, straight through an Arctic winter. It drifted south some fifteen hundred miles from the waters off northern Greenland down to the shipping lanes of the North Atlantic, where it melted and shattered into ever smaller fragments as the survivors desperately scanned the horizon for plumes of steamer smoke.

Equally compelling is the story of the man who led the expedition north and whose mysterious death there threw it into chaos—a self-taught, by-your-bootstraps American explorer by the name of Charles Francis Hall. Hall had grown up in a poor farming family in New Hampshire and served an apprenticeship as a blacksmith before heading west to Cincinnati and starting his own penny newspaper. Combining a powerful blacksmith's build and bull-like constitution with a "poetical" turn of mind, Hall caught the Arctic bug through his voracious readings. The quest for the Pole suited his

109

obsessive personality. One biographer of the era noted: "Above all, he had that impression of fatalism, that inspiration of a personal mission, which looked to some of his friends like a mania, but which was a convincing voice to him that success was possible, and that he was the person to succeed."

Leaving behind a wife and two children in Cincinnati, Hall struck out for the Arctic in 1860, convinced that God had chosen him for the job. With virtually no financial backing, he hitched a ride for his little open boat on the deck of a whaling ship heading up to Baffin Island. His grandiose plan was to sail west from there to King William Land, nearly a thousand miles away, to rescue any survivors of the Franklin Expedition, all on the hope—however faint—that some had survived for the last fifteen years.

A storm dislodged his craft from the whaler's deck and smashed it even before he set out, but Hall clung to his vision. He remained on Baffin Island for two years and learned to live and travel and eat like the Inuit, eventually traveling to King William Land. By learning from the people who actually lived in the Arctic, he became one of the first Arctic explorers, as Farley Mowat writes, to understand that rather than in "brute force" or British military-style assaults like Franklin's, "the secret of survival lay in adapting oneself to the conditions of the hard land, in abandoning, in effect, the entire superstructure of 'civilized' attitudes and methods."

By 1871, when an international race for the North Pole was heating up, Hall managed to finance an expedition in the *Polaris*— a sail-steam vessel that had served a former incarnation as a U.S. Navy tugboat. Wedging the *Polaris* in winter's ice off Ellesmere Island, Hall embarked in stages with dog teams to set a new record of "farthest north," if not reach the Pole itself. It was while returning from one of the first dogsled expeditions that Hall came aboard the *Polaris,* drank a cup of coffee, and fell suddenly and fatally ill. As he lay in a delirium on his deathbed, he accused certain members of the ship's company of poisoning him, for there were those who were convinced that Hall's mania for the Pole would kill them all.[1]

With Hall's death, the *Polaris* was now under the command of Captain Buddington, who wanted to abandon all attempts at the Pole and steam south at the first opening of the ice. This was against the wishes of another officer, the experienced whaler Captain Tyson, who, keeping loyal to Hall's dream, urged to push north again. The following summer the ice didn't open until August, however, and, under Buddington, the *Polaris* made little progress southward before she was caught once more by winter. As freeze-up began ice "nipped" the ship, squeezing it as in a vise, and Buddington gave the order to throw their supplies onto the floes for fear she would go down. Suddenly the ice shattered and released the ship, leaving a pile of supplies and a party of crew members and Inuit, as well as Tyson, stranded on an ice floe in the blizzarding night. Buddington, officers, and the rest of the crew sailed off, never returning to rescue them.

Thus began Tyson and company's six-month drift on an ice floe. This excerpt from Tyson's diary begins with the mysterious death of Hall one year earlier.

[Oct. 24th, 1871] "*Afternoon.* Captain Hall and the rest returned to-day about one o'clock; all well, and have lost no dogs. Have been gone just two weeks. Captain Hall looks very well. They expected to go a hundred miles, but they only went fifty. I saw them coming, and went to meet them. Captain Hall seems to have enjoyed his journey amazingly. He said he was going again, and that he wanted me to go with him. He went aboard, and I resumed my 'banking.'"

---

[1]An expedition to Ellesmere Island in 1968 led by Chauncey Loomis opened Hall's grave and took fingernail clippings from his well-preserved body. Chemical analysis proved in fact that Hall had died of arsenic poisoning, although in his book *Weird and Tragic Shores*, Loomis postulates that in addition to the possibility that he was murdered, Hall may have administered the arsenic himself, as it was a common medical treatment at the time.

"*Oct.* 24, *Evening.* I kept at work till it was too dark to see, and then came aboard. Captain Hall is sick ; it seems strange, he looked so well. I have been into the cabin to see him. He is lying in his berth, and says he feels sick at his stomach. This sickness came on immediately after drinking a cup of coffee. I think it must be a bilious attack, but it is very sudden. I asked him if he thought he was bilious, and told him I thought an emetic would do him good. He said if it was biliousness it would. Hope he will be better to-morrow.

"*Oct.* 25. Captain Hall is no better. Mr. Morton and Mr. Chester watched with him last night; they thought part of the time he was delirious.

"*Evening.* Captain Hall is certainly delirious; I don't know what to make of what he says. He sent for me as if he had something particular to say, but— I will not repeat what he said; I don't think it meant any thing. No talk of any thing in the ship but Captain Hall's illness; if it had only been 'the heat of the cabin,' which some of them say over-came him, he could have got out into the air, and he would have felt better. I can not hear that he ate any thing to make him sick; all he had was that cup of coffee.

"*Nov.* 1. Captain Hall is a little better, and has been up, attempting to write; but he don't act like himself—he begins a thing, and don't finish it. He begins to talk about one thing, and then goes off on to something else: his disease has been pronounced paralysis, and also apoplexy. I can't remember of any one dying of apoplexy in the north except Captain M'Clintock's engineer, and he died very suddenly; went to bed well at 9 P.M., and was found dead in his state-room in the morning. I always thought that might have been heart disease. Hope the captain will rally.

"*Nov.* 3. Captain Hall very bad again. He talks wildly—seems to think some one means to poison him; calls for first one and then an-other, as if he did not know who to trust. When I was in, he accused — — and — — of wanting to poison him. When he is more rational he will say, 'If I die, you must still go on to the Pole;' and such like re-marks. It's a sad affair; what will become of this expedition if Captain Hall dies, I dread to think.

"*Nov.* 5. No change for the better—worse, I think. He appears to be partially paralyzed. This is dreadful. Even should he recover his senses, what can he do with a paralyzed body?

"*Nov.* 8. Poor Captain Hall is dead; he died early this morning. Last evening Chester said the captain thought himself that he was better, and would soon be around again. But it seems he took worse in the night. Captain Buddington came and told me he 'thought Captain Hall was dying.' I got up immediately, and went to the cabin and looked at him. He was quite unconscious—knew nothing. He lay on his face, and was breathing very heavily; his face was hid in the pillow. It was about half-past three o'clock in the morning that he died. Assisted in preparing the grave, which is nearly half a mile from the ship, inland; but the ground was so frozen that it was necessarily very shallow; even with picks it was scarcely possible to break it up.

"*Nov.* 11. At half-past eleven this morning we placed all that was mortal of our late commander in the frozen ground. Even at that hour of the day it was almost dark, so that I had to hold a lantern for Mr. Bryan to read the prayers. I believe all the ship's company was present, unless, perhaps, the steward and cook. It was a gloomy day, and well befitting the event. The place also is rugged and desolate in the extreme. Away off, as far as the dim light enables us to see, we are bound in by huge masses of slate rock, which stand like a barricade, guarding the barren land of the interior; between these rugged hills lies the snow-covered plain; behind us the frozen waters of Polaris Bay, the shore strewn with great ice-blocks. The little hut which they call an observatory bears aloft, upon a tall flag-staff, the only cheering object in sight; and that is sad enough to-day, for the Stars and Stripes droop at half-mast.

"As we went to the grave this morning, the coffin hauled on a sledge, over which was spread, instead of a pall, the American flag, we walked in procession. I walked on with my lantern a little in advance; then came the captain and officers, the engineer, Dr. Bessel, and Meyers; and then the crew, hauling the body by a rope attached to the sledge, one of the men on the right holding another lantern. Nearly all are dressed in skins, and, were there other eyes to see us, we should look like any thing but a funeral cortége. The Esquimaux followed the crew. There is a weird sort of light in the air, partly boreal or electric, through which the stars shone brightly at 11 A.M., while on our way to the grave.

"Thus end poor Hall's ambitious projects; thus is stilled the effervescing enthusiasm of as ardent a nature as I ever knew. Wise he might not always have been, but his soul was in this work, and had he lived till spring, I think he would have gone as far as mortal man could go to accomplish his mission. But with his death I fear that all hopes of further progress will have to be abandoned.

"*Adrift, Oct.,* 1872. Blowing a strong gale from the north-west. I think it must have been about 6 P.M., on the night of the 15th, when we were nipped with the ice. The pressure was very great. The vessel did not lift to it much; she was not broad enough—was not built flaring, as the whalers call it; had she been built so she would have risen to the ice, and the pressure would not have affected her so much; but, considering all, she bore it nobly. I was surprised at her great strength.

"In the commencement of the nip, I came out of my room, which was on the starboard side of the ship, and looked over the rail, and saw that the ice was pressing heavily. I then walked over to the port side. Most of the crew were at this time gathered in the waist, looking over at the floe to which we were fastened. I saw that the ship rose somewhat to the pressure, and then immediately came down again on the ice, breaking it, and riding it under her. The ice was very heavy, and the vessel groaned and creaked in every timber.

"At this time the engineer, Schuman, came running from below, among the startled crew, saying that 'the vessel had started a leak aft, and that the water was gaining on the pumps.' The vessel had been leaking before this, and they were already pumping—Peter and Hans, I think, with the small pump in the starboard alley-way.

"I then walked over toward my room on the starboard side. Behind the galley I saw Sailing-master Buddington, and told him what the engineer said. He threw up his arms, and yelled out to 'throw every thing on the ice!' Instantly every thing was confusion, the men seizing every thing indiscriminately, and throwing it overboard. These things had

previously been placed upon the deck in anticipation of such a cata-
strophe; but as the vessel, by its rising and falling motion, was constantly breaking the ice, and as no care was taken how or where the
things were thrown, I got overboard, calling some of the men to help
me, and tried to move what I could away from the ship, so it should not
be crushed and lost; and also called out to the men on board to stop
throwing things till we could get the things already endangered out of
the way; but still much ran under the ship.

"It was a dark night, and I could scarcely see the stuff—whether it
was on the ice or in the water. But we worked away three or four
hours, when the ice on the starboard side let the ship loose again. We
had been tied to the floe of ice by ice-anchors and hawsers, but when
the piece on the starboard drifted off she righted from her beam-ends
and broke away. I had been on board just before she broke loose, and
asked Buddington 'how much water the vessel was making?' and he
told me, 'no more than usual.'

"I found that the engineer's statement was a false alarm. The vessel
was strong, and no additional leak had been made; but as the ice lifted
her up, the little water in the hold was thrown over, and it made a rush,
and he thought that a new leak had been sprung. When I found she was
making no more water, I went on the ice again to try and save the provisions, if possible. While so engaged, the ice commenced cracking; I
told Buddington of it, he meantime calling out to 'get every thing back
as far as possible on the ice.' Very shortly after, the ice exploded under
our feet, and broke in many places, and *the ship broke away in the
darkness, and we lost sight of her in a moment.*

" 'Gone!
But an ice-bound horror
Seemed to cling to air.'

"It was snowing at the time also; it was a terrible night. On the 15th
of October it may be said that the Arctic night commences; but in addition to this the wind was blowing strong from the south-east; it was
snowing and drifting, and was fearfully dark; the wind was exceedingly
heavy, and so bad was the snow and sleet that one could not even look

to the windward. We did not know who was on the ice or who was on the ship; but I knew some of the children were on the ice, because almost the last thing I had pulled away from the crushing heel of the ship were some musk-ox skins; they were lying across a wide crack in the ice, and as I pulled them toward me to save them, I saw that there were *two or three of Hans's children rolled up in one of the skins;* a slight motion of the ice, and in a moment more they would either have been in the water and drowned in the darkness, or crushed between the ice.

"It was nearly ten o'clock when the ship broke away, and we had been at work since six; the time seemed long, for we were working all the time. Hannah was working, but I did not see Joe or Hans. We worked till we could scarcely stand. They were throwing things constantly over to us till the vessel parted.

"Some of the men were on small pieces of ice. I took the 'little donkey'—a small scow—and went for them; but the scow was almost instantly swamped; then I shoved off one of the whale-boats, and took off what men I could see, and some of the men took the other boat and helped their companions, so that we were all on firm ice at last.

"We did not dare to move about much after that, for we could not see the size of the ice we were on, on account of the storm and darkness. All the rest but myself—the men, women, and children—sought what shelter they could from the storm by wrapping themselves in the musk-ox skins, and so laid down to rest. I alone walk the floe all night.

"Morning came at last; I could then see what had caused the immense pressure on the ship, though I knew she must go adrift when I heard the ice cracking. The floe to which the ship was fastened had been crushed and pressed upon by heavy icebergs, which was the immediate cause of its breaking up. This I could not see last night, but I saw all in the morning."

"Fortunately, we had the two boats on our piece of the floe. This was a nearly circular piece, about four miles in circumference. It was not level, but was full of hillocks, and also ponds, or small lakes, which had been formed by the melting of the ice during the short summer. The ice was of various thicknesses. Some of the mounds, or hills, were probably thirty feet thick, and the flat parts not more than ten or fifteen. It was very rough; the hillocks were covered with snow; indeed, the surface was all snow from the last storm. Some of the men whom I now found on the ice were those whom I had picked off of the smaller pieces last night in the darkness. I could now see who they were. These men were thirty or forty yards from the main floe, and I pushed off the boat and went for them. Some of the men, too, had taken their shipmates off of small pieces. I do not think any body was lost last night. I think all that are not here are on the ship. I should think they would soon be coming to look for us.

"Those who laid down on the ice were all snowed under—but that helped to keep them warm. Perhaps I should have lain down too, if I had had any thing to lie on; but the others had taken all the skins, and I would not disturb them to ask for one.

"*Oct.* 16. Why does not the *Polaris* come to our rescue? This is the thought that now fills every heart, and has mine ever since the first dawn of light this morning. I scanned the horizon, but could see nothing of the vessel; but I saw a lead of water which led to the land. The gale had abated; it was almost calm. I looked around upon the company with me upon the ice, and then upon the provisions which we had with us. Besides myself there were eighteen persons, namely:

" 'Frederick Meyers, meteorologist; John Herron, steward; William Jackson, cook.—*Seamen:* J. W. C. Kruger (called Robert); Fred. Jamka; William Lindermann; Fred. Anthing; Gus. Lindquist; Peter Johnson.—*Esquimaux:* Joe; Hannah, Joe's wife; Puney, child; Hans; Merkut or Christiana, Hans's wife; Augustina, Tobias, Succi—children; Charlie Polaris, baby of Hans's.'

"Now, to feed all these, I saw that we had but fourteen cans of pemmican, eleven and a half bags of bread, one can of dried apples, and fourteen hams; and if the ship did not come for us, we might have to support ourselves all winter, or die of starvation. Fortunately, we had the boats. They were across the crack where I had hauled away the musk-ox skins and found the children; we had hauled both the boats on the ice to save them. I had shortly before asked Captain Buddington if he would haul the boats on board; but he had only answered by ordering every thing to be pulled as far back on the ice as possible.

"As soon as I could see to do so, I walked across the floe to see where was the best lead, so that we could get to shore; and in the mean time I ordered the men to get the boats ready, for I was determined to make a start, and try and get to the land, from which I thought we might find the ship, or at least, if we did not find her, that we might meet with Esquimaux to assist us. I thought that perhaps the *Polaris* had been lost in the night, as I could see nothing of her.

"I had called to the crew to rouse up and see to the boats, and at last succeeded in getting them out of the snow, and fairly awake. I told them we must reach the shore; they thought so too, but they seemed very inert, and in no hurry; they were 'tired' and 'hungry' and 'wet' (though I think they could not have been more tired than I, who had been walking the floe all night while they slept); they had had nothing to eat since three o'clock the day before; and so they concluded they must get something to eat first. Nothing could induce them to hurry; while I, all impatience to try and get the boats off, had to wait their leisure. I might have got off myself, but I knew in that case, if the *Polaris* did not come and pick them up, they would all perish in a few days; so I waited and waited. Not satisfied to eat what was at hand, they must even set about cooking. They made a fire out of some wood which they found upon the ice. They had nothing to cook in but some flat tin pans, in which they tried to cook some of the canned meat, and also tried to make some coffee or chocolate. Then some of them insisted on changing their clothing; for several of them had secured their bags of clothing. But every thing has an end, and at last I got started about 9 A.M.; but, as I feared, it was now too late; the leads were closing, and I feared a change of wind which would make it impossible to reach the shore.

"The piece of ice we were on was fast, between heavy icebergs which had grounded, and was therefore stationary. The wind had now hauled to the north-east. I had no means of taking the true bearings, but it was down quartering across the land, and it was bringing the loose ice down fast. But though I feared it was too late, I determined to try. And at last we got the boats off, carrying every thing we could, and intending to come back for what was left; but when we got half-way to the shore, the loose ice which I had seen coming, crowded on our bows so that we could not get through, and we had to haul up on the ice; and soon after I saw the *Polaris!* I was rejoiced indeed, for I thought assistance was at hand.

"She came around a point above us, eight or ten miles distant. We could see water over the ice that had drifted down, and we could see water inshore. I wondered why the *Polaris* did not come and look for us. Thinking, perhaps, that she did not know in which direction to look—though the set of the ice must have told which way it would drift—and though the small ice had stopped us, it was not enough to stop a ship, I did not know what to make of it. But, determined to attract her attention, if possible, I set up the colors which I had with me and a piece of India rubber cloth, and then with my spy-glass watched the vessel. She was under both steam and sail, so I went to work securing every thing, hoping that she would come for us and take us aboard. I could not see any body on deck; they, if there, were not in sight. She kept along down by the land, and then, instead of steering toward us, dropped away behind the land—Littleton Island, I suppose it is. Our signal was dark, and would surely be seen that distance on a white ice-floe. I do not know what to make of this.

"I wanted some poles to help build a house or tent, and I sent some of the men to the other side of the floe to get some; I knew there must be some there belonging to a house I had built of poles in which to store provisions. In going to this portion of the floe they saw the vessel behind the island, and so came back and reported; they said she was 'tied up.' I did not know what to think of it; but I took my spy-glass, and running to a point where they said I could see her, sure enough there she was, *tied up*—at least, all her sails were furled, and there was no smoke from her stack, and she was lying head to the wind. I suppose she was tied up to the bay-ice, which I could see with the glass.

"And now our piece of ice, which had been stationary, commenced drifting; and I did not feel right about the vessel not coming for us. I began to think she did not mean to. I could not think she was disabled, because we had so recently seen her steaming; so I told the men we *must* get to the other side of the floe, and try and reach the land, perhaps lower down than the vessel was, but so that we might eventually reach her. I told them to prepare the boats. I threw away every thing to make them light, except a little provision—enough to last perhaps two or three days.

"I told the men, while they were getting the boats ready, I would run across the ice and see if there was an opportunity to take the water, or where was the best place, so that they would not have to haul the boats uselessly. I ran across as quick as I could. I was very tired, for I had had nothing but some biscuit and a drink of the blood-soup to eat; but I saw there was an opportunity to get through, and that seemed to renew my strength. The small ice did not now appear to be getting in fast enough to prevent our getting across. But in these gales it is astonishing how quickly the ice closes together, and I knew we were liable to be frozen up at any moment; so I hurried back to the boats and told them 'we must start immediately.'

"There was a great deal of murmuring—the men did not seem to realize the crisis at all. They seemed to think more of saving their clothes than their lives. But I seemed to see the whole winter before me. Either, I thought, the *Polaris* is disabled and can not come for us, or else, God knows why, Captain Buddington don't mean to help us; and then there flashed through my mind the remembrance of a scene and a fearful experience which had happened to me before, in which his indifference had nearly cost me my life and those of all my crew. But I believed he thought too much of Puney and the cook to leave us to our fate without an effort. Then the thought came to me, what shall I do with all these people, if God means we are to shift for ourselves, without ship, or shelter, or sufficient food, through the long, cold, dark winter? I knew that sometime the ice would break up; that at least it would break up into small pieces—too small to live upon. From the disposition which some of the men had shown, I knew it would be very difficult to make them do what was needful for their own safety. And then there were all those children and the two women!

"It appeared to me then that if we did not manage to get back to the ship, that it was scarcely possible but that many, if not all of us, would perish before the winter was over; and yet, while all these visions were going through my brain, these men, whose lives I was trying to save, stood muttering and grumbling because I did not want the boats overloaded to get through the pack-ice. They insisted on carrying every thing. They were under no discipline—they had been under none since Captain Hall's death. They loaded one boat full with all sorts of things, much of which was really trash, but which they would carry. We were going to drag the boat across the floe to where we could take the water. I went on, and told the Esquimaux to follow me across the floe. I had not gone more than two hundred yards before a hurricane burst upon me. I nevertheless persevered and got across the ice, and when I got to the lead of water saw that the natives had not followed me! Whether they thought too much of their property, or whether they were afraid of the storm, I do not know; but the cook had followed me, and when he saw they had not come he ran back for them.

"The men still murmured about getting into the boat which they had dragged over so overloaded, but I would have shoved off as long as I had the strength to do it; but when I looked for the oars, there were but three, and there was *no rudder!* I had told them to prepare the boat while I was gone to look for a lead, and this was the way they had done it. I had told them to see that all was right, including sails; but they did not wish to go, and that probably accounts for it. I am afraid we shall all have to suffer much from their obstinacy.

"Perhaps if we had started we could not have reached either land or ship, but it was certainly worth trying. Why they prefer to stay on this floe I can not imagine; but to start with only three oars and no rudder, the wind blowing furiously, and no good, earnest help, was useless. I tried it, but the men were unwilling; and in the crippled condition of the boat it was no wonder that we were blown back like a feather. I was, therefore, compelled to haul the boat back on the ice. The men by this time were really exhausted, and I could not blame them so much for not working with more energy.

"Night was now coming on; our day was lost, and our opportunity with it. We must prepare for another night on the ice.

"We had to leave the boat where she was; we were all too tired to attempt to drag her back. We also left in her the clothing and other things the men had been so anxious to save in the morning.

"I went back toward the centre of the floe, and put up a little canvas tent, and then, eating a little frozen meat and a little ship-bread, I was glad enough to creep in, pull a musk-ox skin over me and get a little rest, drifting in the darkness I knew not whither; for I had had no rest since the night of the 14th—the night before we parted with the ship. All of the afternoon of the 15th I was at work, and all of that night I walked the floe. All the next day I was going and coming across the ice, and laboring with the men and boats, trying to work through the pack; and when night came the ice-floe proved a refreshing bed, where I slept soundly till morning, when I was suddenly awakened by hearing a loud cry from the natives, which made me quickly crawl out from between my wet ox-skins.

"It had snowed during the night; but that was nothing. *The ice had broken!* separating us from the boat which we had left, being unable to haul it the night before. The old house, made of poles, in which there was also six bags of bread, remained on the old floe, and we were left on a very small piece of ice. The Esquimaux, Mr. Meyers, and myself had made our extemporized lodgings on the thickest part of the floe, and when the ice parted we were all on this portion. As soon as I saw the position of affairs, I called the men out, desiring them to go for the boat and bread. It could have been done with safety, for there was no sea running between the broken floe, and they had not separated much at that time; but I could not move them—they were afraid. At least they did not go.

"So we drifted, having one boat on our piece of ice, while one of our boats, part of the provisions, and the house of poles, remained on the main part of the original floe. And so we drift, apparently to the southwest, for I have neither compass nor chronometer with me; my compass is in that other boat, and even my watch is on board of the

Polaris. Our piece of ice is perhaps one hundred and fifty yards across each way.

"*Oct.* 17. Quite a heavy sea is running; piece after piece is broken from our floe. God grant we may have enough left to stand upon! The vessel could now come to us in clear water, if she is in condition either to steam or sail. I told the natives who are with me they must try and catch some seal. Hans was engaged as hunter, servant, and dog-driver; and Joe is one of the best hunters to be found, if there is any thing to catch. If we can only get seal enough, we can live; but without seal we can have no warm food, for we shall have to cook with the blubber-oil, as the natives do. The natives have caught three seals, and could have caught more, but for the thoughtlessness of the men who gathered around and frightened them off; then the weather set in so bad they could do no more; it was thick and heavy. Weather continued bad, but the gale moderated toward the morning of the 18th. When it cleared, I could see the land—about six miles away. I thought it might be the east shore; but, having no compass and no chart, could hardly be sure where we were. 'Young ice,' or new ice, had formed between us and the land; but it was not strong enough to walk upon. I was in hopes it would get firmer, and then we might perhaps get to land.

"One morning—the 21st, I think—Joe was spying around, and saw the end of our abandoned boat on the same floe where we had left it. He called to me, and as soon as I saw it I started off with him to try and recover it. It was about twelve o'clock in the day, and we had not yet had our breakfast. But I was afraid we should not have so good a chance again to get it, and would not wait for any thing, for we could now get across to the old floe from our own piece of ice. Joe and I started, and got it back, with all the things, and also loaded in what bread I could carry. I fortunately had five or six dogs with me. We harnessed them to the boat, they dragging and we pushing over the bad places. We at last got it back safely to the piece of ice we were encamped upon. We saved all. We have now both boats, the natives' kyacks, and are together again.

"*Oct.* 23. We have now given up all hopes of the *Polaris* coming to look for us. All we can do is to wait for the ice to get strong enough for us to get on shore. The worst of it is, we have no sledges; and hauling the loaded boats over the rough ice is likely to injure them, so that they would be unfit for use, should we need to take to them; but it is the only way we can do to get them over to the large floe, which now lies halfway between us and the shore. There is, too, but little time to see to work; all the light we have now is about six hours a day, and not very clear then. On cloudy and stormy days it is dark all the time. But this piece of ice will not do to winter on. So to-day, the ice appearing strong enough, I got the boats loaded, harnessed on the dogs, and started to regain the large floe; succeeded with the first, and then went back for the second. It is fortunate, indeed, that we have the boats. Humanly speaking, they are our salvation, for on an emergency we can use them either for the water or as sledges. Got the second one over safe, and am rejoiced at that; and they do not appear to have received any injury except what can be readily repaired. There are still two kyacks on the small floe. A native will stick to his kyack like a white man to his skin, and Joe and Hans got theirs out of the ship when Captain Buddington ordered them off.

"We had now got all our principal things on the large floe, except a little stuff and these kyacks. I wanted the crew to try and help save them, but could not get them to do any thing toward it. At last Joe started alone, and then two of the men ventured over: one was the negro cook, and the other William Lindermann. One of the kyacks was saved, but the other was lost. These little boats are invaluable to the Esquimaux, who are accustomed to manage them; but no one else can do any thing with them. One might almost as well launch out on an ostrich feather and think to keep afloat, as in these unballasted little sealskin shells. But I'm glad enough they have got one of them.

"The weather has come on very bad; but, fortunately, we have got our snow-houses built. We have quite an encampment—one hut, or rather a sort of half-hut, for Mr. Meyers and myself; Joe's hut for himself, Hannah, and their adopted daughter, Puney; a hut for the men, a store-hut for our provisions, and a cook-house, all united by arched alley-ways built of snow; one main entrance, and smaller ones branching off to the several apartments, or huts. Hans has built his hut separately, but near by.

"Joe did most of the work of building these huts—he knew best how to do it; but we all assisted. They are made in the regular Esquimau style, and the natives call them *igloos*. The way they go about it is this: the ground is first leveled off, and then one-half of the floor toward the end farthest from the entrance is slightly raised above the other or front half. The raised part is parlor and bedroom, and the front part is workshop and kitchen. The walls and arched roof are composed of square blocks of hard snow, packed hard by the force of the wind. A square of about eighteen inches of thin, compressed snow or ice, or sometimes a piece of animal membrane, is fixed in for a window. The entrance is very low, and is reached through the alley-way, so that one has to almost crawl in. At night, or whenever it storms or is very cold, the entrance is closed up, after the inmates are all in, by a block of snow.

"There is hardly room to turn round in these huts, and an ordinary-sized white man can only just stand up straight in them; it is as much as an Esquimau can do in some of them; but from their form they stand the weather well. A hut is often snowed under, so that it can not be distinguished from a natural hillock; but it can not be blown over; and when there is a sufficiency of oil to burn in the lamps, these kind of huts can be kept warm enough. But from their arched form, and the material of which they are constructed, it can easily be seen that they can not be made spacious enough to properly accommodate a large party of men. The centre of the dome only admits of the upright position being maintained, as from that point the walls slope gradually, until they meet the ground. In the men's hut, for instance, the dais, or raised platform, on which they sleep, just accommodates them, lying like herrings in a box, with no superfluous room in which to turn; and only two or three of them can stand up at a time.

"These huts are only used by the natives in winter. The summer sun is as fatal to them as rain would be if it fell there; but when they begin to thaw and melt, the Esquimaux take to their seal-skin tents for shelter.

"The ordinary lamp in use among the natives is made out of a soft kind of stone, indigenous to the country; it is hollowed out, like a shallow dish, with an inverted edge, on which they place a little moss for wicking, which, when lighted, sucks up the oil from the blubber; and this is all the fire they have in this cold country, either for heating their huts or for cooking. To dry their clothing, they put them in nets suspended over the lamp.

"We, however, did not have even a proper lamp; but we soon contrived one out of an old pemmican can, and having no moss, we cut up a piece of canvas for wicking, and it answered very well for us; but somehow the men could not seem to understand how to use it; they either got the blubber all in a blaze, or else they got it smoking so badly that they were driven out of their hut; and so I am sorry to say that they have begun to break up one of the boats for fuel. This is bad business, but I can not stop them, situated as I am, without any other authority than such as they choose to concede to me. It will not do to thwart them too much, even for their own benefit.

"These boats are not designed to carry more than six or eight men, and yet I foresee that all this company may have yet to get into the one boat to save our lives, for the ice is very treacherous. But they will do as they like.

"I have been taking account of stock. By our successive expeditions, in which we gathered nearly all together which was on the ice when we were first drifted off, I find that we have our two boats (but one is being destroyed) and one kyack, and, thank God, plenty of ammunition and shot.

"Of provisions we have eleven and a half bags of bread, fourteen cans of pemmican, fourteen hams, ten dozen cans of meats and soups, one can of dried apples, and about twenty pounds of chocolate and sugar mixed. The pemmican cans are large, each weighing forty-five pounds; the meats and soups are only one and two pound cans; and the hams are small ones; the dried-apple can is a twenty-two-pounder. Divide that into portions for nineteen people, with a certainty of not getting any thing more for six months (unless we reach the land, or can catch seals to live on), and it is plain we could not exist. And if we have to keep to the floe, it will be April or May before we shall drift to the whaling-grounds.

"We must try once more to get on shore. To-morrow, if the weather permits, I will try and get the house and the lumber where we can have the use of it.

"Have had a talk with Mr. Meyers about the locality of our separation from the *Polaris;* he thinks we were close to Northumberland Island, but I believe it was Littleton Island; he says 'he ought to know, for that he took observations only a day or two before,' and of course he *ought* to be right; but still my impression is that Northumberland Island is larger than the one the *Polaris* steamed behind. I wish I had a chart, or some means of knowing for certain.

"*Oct.* 24, *Morning.* Blowing strong from the north-east, and the snow is drifting; quite cold. Robert and Bill have started for the old house to get two planks to make a sledge to haul the rest of the house over on, and for general use. If it is a good day to-morrow, I hope to get all the lumber and the remains of the canvas from the old place.

"*Afternoon.* The men came back with the planks; they were very hungry—so hungry I was compelled to break the rules, and give them some bread and pemmican to eat.

"We only allow ourselves two meals a day, and Mr. Meyers has made a pair of scales, with which to weigh out each one's portion, so that there should be no jealousy. We use shot for weights. Our allowance is very small—just enough to keep body and soul together; but we must economize, or our little stock will soon give out altogether.

"One bad symptom has appeared: we have only had chocolate prepared for the party four times, and it is *nearly all gone!* Some one has made free with the store-house. It is too cold to set a watch; but it is plain enough to be seen that things have been meddled with.

"The wind is mostly from the E.N.E. Have succeeded in getting a sledge made, and the men have brought in a load of lumber and poles from the old house; no doubt we shall be able to get it all. But our blubber is almost out, and we see no seals; if we do not get some soon we shall be in darkness, and have to eat our frozen food without thawing it—to say nothing of cooking it. We need it, too, very much to melt the fresh-water ice for drink. Fortunately there is enough of this ice in the ponds on this floe, if we can only get the means of melting it.

"Our present daily allowance is eleven ounces for each adult, and half-rations for the children. I was obliged to establish a regular rate, and insist upon its observance, or we should soon have had nothing. There appears to be a good deal of discontent in some quarters, but I fear they will get less before any of us get more. Before this rule was established, some got a great deal more than others. It was hard for some of them to come down to it in consequence; and in fact it has weakened them down; but it is absolutely necessary to be careful of what we have. I am so weak myself that I stagger from sheer want of strength; and, after all, the men bear it as well as could be expected—considering, too, that they do not realize, as I do, the absolute necessity of it.

"Hans has just taken two of the dogs, killed and skinned them, and will eat them. I give each of the natives the same amount of bread, and whatever else we have, as I deal out to myself. But the Esquimaux are, like all semi-civilized people, naturally improvident; while they have, they will eat, and let tomorrow take care of itself. I do not suppose an Esquimau ever voluntarily left off eating before his hunger was fully satisfied, though he knew that the next day, or for many days, he would have nothing. Sailors have some kind of an idea that a ship's company must, under some circumstances, be put on 'short allowance;' but that is an idea you can never beat into the head of a native, and yet of all people they are the most subject to fluctuations of luck—sometimes having abundance, and then reduced to famine; but there is no thrift in them. They will sometimes store away provisions, and build *caches* on their traveling routes; but this is always done when they have more than they can possibly consume at the time—as when they have been fortunate enough to kill a whale or a walrus, and by no possibility can eat it all.

"*Oct.* 26. We lost sight of the sun's disk three days ago—

> " 'Miserable we,
> Who here entangled in the gathering ice,
> Take our last look of the descending sun;
> While full of death, and fierce with tenfold frost,
> The long, long night, incumbent o'er our heads,
> Falls horrible.'

"May the great and good God have mercy on us, and send us seals, or I fear we must perish. We are all very weak from having to live on such small allowance, and the entire loss of the sun makes all more or less despondent. But still we do not give up; the men have got another sled-load of poles in to-day; but the ice is very rough, and the light so dim that they can fetch but little at a time. There seems now no chance of reaching the land—we have drifted so far to the west. We are about eight or ten miles off shore. Northumberland Island bears about east from us—should think forty or fifty miles off. Should judge the latitude to be about 77° 30'. Have not drifted any the last three days. The sled has come in with two additional dogs—'Bear' and 'Spike:' these dogs were on the large floe, where the most of our provisions were. I suppose, since we brought the food away, they thought best to follow it. A portion of the sun just showed for a little while to-day—his upper limb about 7' above the horizon.

"*Jan.* 28. Fair; light wind from the south-west. Joe and Hans off again this morning hunting for meat to feed the hungry. Very cold still; −40°.

"I do not see my way clear yet. Can see no land either to the east or west, so we must be far from both shores, and are probably near the middle of the strait, with a slight set to the west. We can not be near the east coast, that is certain, for they have not so low a temperature there in this latitude. They catch whales off the coast there in February, ordinarily at Holsteinborg, and sometimes even at Disco. Yet the 'German Count,' as the men begin to call Mr. Meyers in jest, makes his countrymen believe that we are near to the east shore.

"What convinces me that we are a long way from Disco, which I know so well, is, that Disco is a very high rocky island, which, if we were near it, could certainly be seen. I have been there many times, and know all the coast south of it well. Disco can easily be seen on a clear day eighty miles distant, and I have seen it when one hundred miles off, raised by refraction—not an uncommon phenomenon on the Greenland coast.

"If Meyers had been left on board the *Polaris,* these foreigners would probably have behaved better, for then they would not have had any one to mislead them about our position. His influence is naturally considerable over them, because they think he is educated, and ought to know; and being also their countryman, they probably fancy he takes more interest in their welfare; just as if it was not as much my interest to get to dry land as theirs! But I have sailed these seas too often to be much deceived about our course.

"I know not whether I can keep these men quiet until the temperature rises. Perhaps it may moderate in March, and then they may yet be saved; but, should they start for the shore in February, they are lost. The sun has not yet much influence. They will find no water to drink, have but little to eat, must sleep unprotected except by their wet ox-skins, if they have the strength even to drag them along; in fact, they must perish. But if they can be induced to hold on until the season is further advanced, many cracks will be found in the ice, and some of them may lead us near the coast, or at least to open water; and in these cracks we shall find plenty of seals, and on them we can live till it is a suitable time to attempt reaching the land. At our present rate of drift, we may even be picked up by some whaler.

"I have relieved parties on the ice. They had not drifted so long, to be sure, nor come so far, nor so many of them; they were all men, too—not a boat-load of women and children—but they were far away from their ships, hungry and destitute. There were some runaways from the *Ansel Gibbs,* and also another party—I forget the circumstances now—from the brig *Alert.* I have also relieved Captain Hall two or three times on his former voyages; so I hope Providence may send *us* a rescue before it is too late.

"It is now, past 3 P.M., quite light. The mercury is frozen again. It is extremely cold. Joe and Hans have not returned yet. The men are cooking, or, rather, trying to warm, some seal-*skin,* which serves us all to-day for lunch. We eat it *hair on,* as there is not sufficient heat to scald it off. Boiling water will take it off, but we can't get that. It is very tough. My jaws and head too ache with the exertion made to masticate it. The dogs have the advantage of us there; they will bolt down long strips of it, if they are so well off as to get it, without apparently any chewing at all. They will eat any thing but stone or metal, and make very short work of their harness, or any thing of that kind, which is left in their way.

"6 P.M. The natives have returned; have had no success, and we have now lost our only dog. Joe had him with him to-day. On returning, the poor animal was taken sick and died. I fed him last night on what I was eating myself, seal-skin and pretty well-picked bones; it may be that the bones caused his death, as they swallow such large pieces, or it may be something has happened to him that I do not know of. Well, it is the first and only natural death that has occurred, and that, surely is wonderful; but it is astonishing what men can endure. It must be that the *hope* keeps us alive, and the poor beasts have not that to sustain them. They feel all their present misery, and can not anticipate relief. It will be a very difficult matter to capture a bear now, without a single dog.

"*Jan.* 29. Foggy, with light east wind. The Esquimaux off, as usual, on the hunt. They do not stop for fog, cold, or wind. They understand the situation they are in, and consequently they are the only ones here I can in any measure rely on. Were it not for 'little Joe,' Esquimau though he be, many, if not all, of this party must have perished before now. He has built our snow-huts, and hunted constantly for us; and the seals he has captured have furnished us not only with the fresh meat so essential to our position, but without the oil from the blubber we could neither have warmed our food nor had any means of melting ice for drink. We survive through God's mercy and Joe's ability as a hunter.

"We are all well but one—Hans's child, Tobias. I can doctor a sailor, but I don't understand what is the matter with this poor little fellow. His stomach is disordered and very much swollen; he has been sick now for some time. He can not eat the pemmican; so he has to live on dry bread, as we have nothing else to give him. The wonder is not that one is sick, but that any are well.

"The mercury is still frozen. The men are seldom outside of their hut now. From the nature of the food we live on, and the small quantity of it, there is no imperative necessity which calls them outside—perhaps not more than once in fourteen days. Oh, it is depressing in the extreme to sit crouched up all day, with nothing to do but try and keep from freezing! Sitting long at a time in a chair is irksome enough, but it is far more wearisome when there is no proper place to sit. No books either, no Bible, no Prayer-book, no magazines or newspapers—not even a *Harper's Weekly*—was saved by any one, though there are almost always more or less of these to be found in a ship's company where there are any reading men. Newspapers I have learned to do without to a great extent, having been at sea so much of my life, where it is impossible to get them; but some sort of reading I always had before. *It is now one hundred and seven days since I have seen printed words!* What a treat a bundle of old papers would be! All the world over, I suppose some people are wasting and destroying what would make others feel rich indeed.

"As it is, the thought of something good to eat is apt to occupy the mind to an extent one would be ashamed of on shipboard or ashore. We even dream of it in our sleep; and no matter what I begin to think about, before long I find, quite involuntarily, as it were, my mind has reverted to the old subject. Some of the ancients, I believe, located the soul in the stomach. I think they must have had some such experience as ours to give them the idea. I miss my coffee and soft bread-and-butter most. Give me domestic bread-and-butter and coffee, and I should feel content until we could better our condition.

"Joe has returned (at 1 P.M.); the weather too thick and cold for him to accomplish any thing. He was, of course, very hungry; so was I. We had two or three yards of frozen seal's entrails left from the last seal, and on that we lunched, eating a little blubber with it. Poor Captain Hall used to say he really liked blubber. I like it a good deal better than *nothing!* To men as hungry as we, almost any thing is sweet; this that we ate was frozen as hard as the ice we are on.

"*Jan.* 30. The change of the moon has not benefited us. There is no opening in the ice; the weather is too calm and cold, $-34°$. Could we get a heavy southerly gale, it would rapidly break up the ice; but we have not had a strong gale from the south all winter.

"It is as well to look the future fairly in the face, and none of us can tell who will survive to see this business out. Death is liable to come to all men; and especially may one in my situation prepare himself for it at any moment; and therefore, considering the possibility, I wish here to set down a few facts, as well as my own opinion, which, whether I live or die, I sincerely hope will come to light.

*   *   *   *   *   *   *   *

"I make the above statement not knowing whether I shall get through this affair with life. I have told Joe and Hannah, should any thing happen to me, to save these books" [this, with other notes, was written on small pocket blank-books.—*Ed.*] "and carry them home. It is very badly written with pencil, in a dark hut, and with very cold fingers; but, so help me God, it is all true.

"My present life is perilous enough; but I can truly say that I have felt more secure sleeping on this floe, notwithstanding the disaffection of some of the men, than I did the last eleven months on board the *Polaris.*

"*Jan.* 31. Fair; light east wind; the natives off hunting very early. They found water yesterday, but got no seals. The weather is much warmer—only 22° below zero this morning. We are evidently drifting westward. I hope to see the land soon; but both east and west there is a heavy mist, which the sun has not power enough to disperse.

"*Afternoon.* It has now come on thick; wind north-east. I have just lunched on seal-skin. This time we have been enabled to cook it, and I discover that it is all the better—quite tender. We not only ate the skin, but drank the greasy water it was boiled in. The time occupied in heating five quarts of water over the lamp is from two to three hours.

"Hannah is now pounding the bread, preparing our pemmican tea. We pound the bread fine, then take brackish ice, or saltwater ice, and melt it in a tin pemmican can over the lamp; then put in the pounded bread and pemmican, and, when all is warm, call it 'tea,' and drink it. It reminds me very much of greasy dish-water; but in this climate a man can eat many things which in a warmer latitude the stomach would revolt at. The offal of better days is not despised by us now. As to dirt, we are permeated with it; and the less I think about it the better I feel, for I know not how it is to be remedied. We can scarcely get water enough melted to serve for drink.

"The temperature this evening is 34° below zero—6 P.M. The Esquimaux have returned again without game. They have been a long distance to the eastward in the direction where they discovered water yesterday, but to-day it was all frozen over. They started at seven this morning, and have but just returned; and they do all this traveling on a few ounces of food daily. It is indeed a hard struggle for life, and the result doubtful.

"We have just had our pemmican tea, and have each taken a few scraps of refuse from the dirty lamp. It all helps to fill up, and keep the blood circulating. Poor little Tobias is very low—nothing but a skeleton; he can eat seal-meat, but steadily rejects pemmican. I wish I knew what to do for him.

"*Feb.* 1. It is blowing very heavy from the north-west; too much wind for any hunting to-day. We keep closely housed in our dens. Should an accident happen to our floe serious enough to turn us out of our burrows, leaving us shelterless in such a storm of wind, with our blood so thin, we should none of us live long.

"We are poorly off indeed to-day; not even a bit of skin or entrails to appease the biting hunger. For the last six or eight days we have had *something* to lunch on—either skin or frozen entrails; to-day we have neither; and now we realize the value of those unsavory morsels, and feel the want of them more and more every hour. So do the most unappreciated 'blessings brighten as they take their flight.'

"*March* 28. We have got a bear at last! Shortly after dark last evening, we heard a noise outside of our hut. I had just taken off my boots, preparing for rest. Joe, too, was about retiring, but on hearing the noise thought it was the ice breaking up, and that he would go out and see what the situation was. He was not gone more than ten seconds before he came back, pale and frightened, exclaiming, 'There is a bear close to my kyack!' The kyack was within ten feet of the entrance to the hut. Joe's rifle, and also mine, were outside—mine lying close to the kyack—Joe's was inside of it; but Joe had his pistol in the hut. Putting on my boots, we crept cautiously out, and, getting to the outer entrance, could hear the bear distinctly eating. There were several seal-skins and a good deal of blubber lying around in all directions. Some of the skins we were drying for clothing, and some were yet green. Getting outside, we could plainly see his bearship. He had now hauled some of the skins and blubber about thirty feet from the kyack, and was eating away, having a good feast. Joe crept into the sailors' hut to alarm them. While he was gone, I crept stealthily to my rifle, but in taking it I knocked down a shot-gun standing by. The bear heard it, but my rifle was already on him; he growled, I pulled the trigger, but the gun did not go; pulled the second and third time—it did not go; but I did, for the bear now came for me. Getting in the hut, I put another cartridge in, and put two reserves in my vest-pocket, and crept out again, getting a position where I could see the animal, although it was what might be called quite dark. He saw me, too, and again faced me; but this time, to my joy and his sorrow, the rifle-ball went straight to its mark—the heart I aimed for. Joe now came out of the men's hut, and cracked both a rifle and pistol at him. The bear ran about two rods, and fell dead. On skinning him in the morning, I found that the ball had entered the left-shoulder, passed through the heart, and out at the other side—a lucky shot in the dark!

"This bear will at least give us a change of diet, if it is still meat. He is a fine large animal, and every part good but the liver. The meat tastes more like pork than any thing we have had to eat for a long time.

"It may be thought strange by those who have never lived in this climate in an igloo, that we should leave our guns outside of the hut, instead of keeping them by us; but if brought in they would soon be spoiled, because the exhalations from the lungs condense in this atmosphere, and form moisture, which settles on every thing, and would spoil fire-arms, unless carefully cased, and we have no casings.

"This bear was what is called by the whalers the 'sea bear' (*Ursus maritimus*), and it is almost amphibious, as it swims quite as well as it walks, only I suppose it could not live entirely in the water; and it might live exclusively on land if it could get sufficient food. It is a modification of the common Arctic bear, and necessity makes it seek its food, which is principally seals, either upon the ice or in the water, as opportunity offers.

"*March* 30. Night before last the wind sprung up strong from the north-west. Yesterday it increased to a gale. Huge bergs—and I do not in the least exaggerate when I say hundreds in number—were plowing their way through the ice: there was quite a heavy swell under the ice, and the broad bases of these bergs are sunk many fathoms deep in the water. The floe-ice had refrozen mostly together again, after the break-up in the middle of March, and was now once more in fragments. The gale continued heavy through the night of the 29th, keeping us on the lookout for the safety of our piece. It is still blowing heavy, with considerable swell. In the night I felt a great thump, as if a hammer a mile wide had hit us, and getting out to see what was the cause, found we had drifted foul of a large berg, and the collision had produced the sensation I have described. Well, we thumped a while on the berg, and I did not know but we should go to pieces and founder; but after finally we cleared it, and sailed on, apparently without serious injury to our brittle craft.

"This morning it is snowing again, with heavy drift. We can see but a short distance before us. We are somewhere off the mouth of Hudson Strait, but how far from shore I have no means of ascertaining. Our little ice-craft is plowing its way through the sea without other guide than the Great Being above.

"6 P.M. Still blowing strongly, but little snow drifting. This afternoon saw two "bladder-noses" floating on the ice; got the boat launched, and went for them. The male escaped to the water; but we got the female and her little young one. Hans, later in the day, shot another young one. When the young of the seal can be secured without shooting, it is customary to press them to death by putting the foot down heavily upon them, as by this means not only all the blood is saved, but the milk in the stomach; and among the Esquimaux this milk is highly relished. The men put some of the milk in their blood-soup. These bladder-noses, when attacked, often show considerable fight, if approached with spears or clubs. But they can do nothing against bullets but get out of the way.

"Our piece of ice is gradually wearing away; last night there was a heavy sea, water all round us, and scarcely any ice to be seen; but it may close again. Latitude at noon reported 59° 41' N.

"*April* 1. We have been the 'fools of fortune' now for five months and a half. Our piece of ice is now entirely detached from the main pack, which is to the west of us, and which would be safer than this little bit we are on, and so we have determined to take to the boat and try and regain it. To do this we must abandon all our store of meat, and we have sufficient now to last us for a month, and many other things. Among the most valuable, much of the ammunition will have to be left, on account of its weight—all the powder being put up in metallic cartridges, for preservation against damp and other accidents.

"We got launched, and made some twenty miles west, but were very nearly swamped, for, notwithstanding all we had abandoned, we were still excessively overloaded, what with nineteen persons and the heavy sleeping-gear. When it is considered that the boat was only intended for six or eight men, and that we had to carry twelve men, two women, and five children, with our tent, and with absolutely necessary wrapping of skins for protection from the weather, it is not surprising that we did not make much headway. We were so crowded that I could scarcely move my arms sufficiently to handle the yoke-ropes without knocking over some child—and these children frightened and crying about all the time. Having got about twenty miles, we were compelled to hold up on the first piece of good ice we could find. It was with much difficulty that through these changes I preserved Captain Hall's writing-desk from destruction; some of the men were bound to have Joe throw it overboard, but I positively forbade it, as it was all we had belonging to our late commander.

"On this ice we spread what few skins we had, set up our tent, and ate our little ration of dry bread and pemmican. Hans and his family had the boat for sleeping-quarters.

"On the morning of the 2d we started again, still pushing to the west; but the wind, with snow-squalls, was against us, being from the quarter to which we were steering, and we made but little progress; what we made was S.S.W. Hauled up on another piece of ice, and encamped.

"*April* 3. Spent part of the day repairing the boat, and fitting her up with wash-boards of canvas, to keep the water from dashing over the sides. Seals are so plenty around us now that I do not hear any more croaking about the want of meat. We can get all we want as long as our ammunition holds out. After rigging our boat up, started again, heading to the west.

"*April* 4. After a desperate struggle, we have at last regained the 'pack,' and are now encamped. The sun showed itself at noon, but we are again blessed with a heavy wind from the north and snow-squalls. Our tent is not as good a protection from the wind as the snow-huts. Joe, with a little help, can build a hut in an hour, if the right kind of snow-blocks can be procured. If we were on land we could find stones to help make them of. Mr. Meyers has saved his instruments, and gives us the latitude of our new home as 56° 47′ N.

"We are now on a heavy piece of ice, and I hope out of immediate danger: it looks compact to the westward, but there is no ice to be trusted at this time of the year. We have had a hard battle to reach it, however, and we are all pretty well tired out.

"I did not make any conversation with either Meyers or the men about abandoning the small floe; for the time had come when it was absolutely necessary to do so. I told them in the evening that if the wind abated through the night we must leave in the morning. Some objected to go back into the pack-ice, but wanted to take to the water in the boat.

Had I consented to that, most would probably have been lost in the first gale; for we should have had to throw overboard every thing, sleeping-gear, even guns and ammunition; and some of the men, by their expressions, seemed to intimate that they would not have hesitated to throw over the women and children to save their own lives. Then, also, we should have had no water to drink, nor any opportunity to catch game, and, getting once thoroughly wet, our clothes would have frozen on us in the night, and we probably have frozen too, as it is still very cold.

"When we finally got into the boat to try and reach the pack-ice, some again insisted, instead of sailing west, on getting out to seaward, by trying to work south in the boat, which was laden very heavy, and was, of course, low in the water, with nineteen souls aboard, ammunition, guns, skins, and several hundred pounds of seal-meat; and, consequently, the sea began to break over us, and the men became frightened, and some of them exclaimed that 'the boat was sinking.' Of course, I wished to reach the pack without losing any thing more than was absolutely necessary, for we really had nothing to spare; but the boat took water so badly that I saw we must sacrifice every thing, and so the seal-meat was thrown over (the loss of which nearly caused our ruin), with many other things we sadly needed; but the boat had to be lightened, and so I set the example of throwing away some things I prized most highly, that the men might be induced to rid themselves of 'dead-weights;' and after all was done, the boat was still overloaded fearfully; but, turning to the west, by careful management we reached the pack as I have narrated, through great peril and much loss, but with all our company saved.

"*April* 5. Blowing a gale from the north-east, and a fearful sea running. Two pieces broke from our floe at five o'clock this morning. We had to haul all our things farther back toward the centre. Soon after another piece broke off, carrying Joe's hut with it. Fortunately, the snapping and cracking of the ice gave some warning, so that they had time to escape, and able to throw out and save some few things. No telling where it will split next. It has been a dreadful day—the more so that we can do nothing to help ourselves. If there was any thing to be done, it would relieve the mind of much anxious watching. If the ice breaks up much more, we must break up with it. We shall set a watch to-night. Joe has rebuilt his hut, or rather built another. This sort of real estate is getting to be 'very uncertain property.'

"*April* 6. Blowing a gale, very severe, from the north-west. We are still on the same piece of ice, for the reason that we can not get off—the sea is too rough. We are at the mercy of the elements. Joe lost another hut to-day. The ice, with a great roar, split across the floe, cutting Joe's hut right in two.

"We have such a small foothold left that we can not lie down to-night. We have put our things in the boat, and are standing by for a jump.

"*April* 7. Wind still blowing a gale, with a fearful sea running. At six o'clock this morning, while we were getting a morsel of food, the ice split right under our tent! We were just able to scramble out, but our breakfast went down into the sea. We very nearly lost our boat—and that would be equivalent to losing ourselves.

"Of course, while this storm and commotion has been raging around us we could not shoot any seals, and so are obliged to starve again for a time, hoping and praying that it may not be for long. The worst of our present dearth of seals is that we have no blubber to feed the lamp, so that we can not even melt a piece of ice for water. We have, therefore, no water to drink. Every thing looks very gloomy again. All we can do is to set a watch, and be prepared for any emergency. We have set the tent up again, as we held on to that and saved it. Half of the men have got in under it to get a little rest, while the others walk around it outside. This is a very exciting period. If one attempts to rest the body, there is no rest for the mind. One and another will spring up from their sleep, and make a wild dash forward, as if avoiding some sudden danger. What little sleep I get is disturbed and unrefreshing. I wonder how long we can fight through this sort of thing.

"*April* 8. Worse and worse! Last night at twelve, midnight, the ice worked again right between the tent and the boat, which were close together—so close that a man could not walk between them. Just there the ice split, separating the boat and tent, and with the boat was the kyack and Mr. Meyers, who was on the ice beyond the boat. We stood helpless, looking at each other.

"The weather as usual, blowing, snowing, and very cold, with a heavy sea running, the ice breaking, crushing, and overlapping. A sight grand indeed, but most fearful in our position—the helpless victims of this elemental rage.

"Meyers can manage neither the boat nor the kyack—the boat is too heavy, the kyack of no use to any one unaccustomed to its management. Should he get in it, he would be capsized in an instant. So he cast the kyack adrift, hoping it would come to us, and that Joe or Hans could get it and come for him, and bring him a line, or assist him some way. Unfortunately, the kyack drifted to the leeward. However, Joe and Hans took their paddles and ice-spear and went for it, springing from one piece of ice to another, and so they worked over. It looks like dangerous business. We may never see them again. But all the rest of us will be lost without the boat, so they are as well off as we. They are lost unless God returns them. After an hour's struggle through what little light there is, we can just make out that they have reached the boat, which is now half a mile off. There they appear to be helpless.

"It is getting too dark to see the end; it is colder, and the ice is closing around us. We can do nothing more to-night. It is calmer, and I must venture to lie down somewhere and get a little rest, to prepare for the next battle with ice and storm.

"Daylight at last! Wee see them now with the boat, but they can do nothing with her. The kyack is about the same distance away in another direction. They have not strength to manage the big boat. We must venture off and try to get to them. We may as well be crushed in the ice as remain here without a boat. So I determine to try and get to them. Taking a stick in my hand, to help balance and support myself on the shifting ice-cakes, I make a start, and Kruger follows me. We jump or step, as the case may be, from one slippery wave-washed piece of ice to another—a few steps level, and then a piece higher or lower, so that we have to spring up or down. Sometimes the pieces are almost close together; then we have a good jump to reach the next, and so we go, leaping along like so many goats. On arriving where the boat was, we found our combined strength—Mr. Meyers, well, he was too used up to have any—Joe, Hans, Kruger, and myself—could not stir it. I called over to the other men, and two others got over in the way we had, and still our strength was insufficient. At last all came over but two, who were afraid to venture, and after a long struggle we got her safe back to camp again, bringing Mr. Meyers with us. Both he and Frederick Jamka fell in the water, but were pulled out again. Luckily for them, there were two or three dry suits among the men, so that they could change. We are all more or less wet, and Mr. Meyers badly frozen.

"We have taken our tent down once more, and pitched it nearer to the centre of our little piece of ice, and the boat is alongside, so that we feel comparatively safe once more. Joe has built another hut alongside the tent, and we have breakfasted on a few morsels of pemmican and bread. We have also set a watch to observe the movements of the ice, and the remainder of the men are lying down to get some sleep, of which we are all much in need. Where we are the wind is west-north-west, but outside of the 'pack' there is no wind.

"*April* 9. Things have remained quiet the last twelve hours. During the night the wind was north-west; now blowing a north-east gale outside of the 'pack.' The sun shone for a few minutes—about long enough to take an observation: lat. 55° 51′, approximates to that. The sea is running very high again, and threatening to wash us off every moment. The ice is much slacker, and the water, like a hungry beast, creeps nearer. Things look very bad. We are in the hands of God; he alone knows how this night will end.

"*Evening*. The sea washed us out of our tent and the natives from their hut, and we got every thing into the boat once more, ready for a start; but I fear she can never live in such a sea. The sun set clear in a golden light, which has cheered us up with the hope of better weather. The women and children now stay in the boat for safety. The ice may split so suddenly that there would not be time to get them in if they were scattered about. The baby is kept in its mother's hood, but the rest have to be picked up and handled every time there is a change of position on the ice; but we have got thus far without losing any of them.

"The sea keeps washing over, so that there is not a dry place to stand upon, nor a piece of fresh-water ice to eat. We have suffered badly with thirst. The sea has swept over all, and filled all the little depressions where we could sometimes find freshwater ice with sea-water.

"10 P.M. The ice closing around us fast. The wind and sea going down.

"12 *o'clock, Midnight.* Things look so quiet, and the ice is so well closed, that we have risked setting up the tent once more, and intend to try and get some sleep, for we are quite worn out.

"*April* 10. Last night it was quite calm. To-day it is cloudy and very warm. The ice is closed around, and we are prisoners still.

"The other morning Mr. Meyers found that his toes were frozen—no doubt from his exposure on the ice without shelter the day he was separated from us. He is not very strong at the best, and his fall in the water has not improved his condition.

"*April* 11. Calm and cloudy. We can not, I think, be far from shore. We have seen a fox, some ravens, and other land birds. The ice is still closed around us—nothing but ice to be seen. We have two large bergs almost on top of us; but, fortunately, there is no movement of the ice, or a portion of these overhanging bergs might fall upon and crush us. It is at present calm and still.

"*April* 12. Light wind from the south-east; nearly calm at times. Have seen some seals, but can not get them. Are very hungry, and are likely to remain so. The sun is shining for the first time in a good many days, and the weather is very pleasant. Got an observation to-day: lat. 55° 35′ N.

April 20th: This morning while resting in our tents we were alarmed by an outcry from the watch and almost at the same moment a heavy sea swept across our floe carrying away everything that was loose. This was but a foretaste of what was to follow. We began shipping sea after sea. Finally a tremendous wave carried away our tent, skins, most of our bed clothing, and left us destitute. Only a few things were saved which we had managed to get into the boat. The women and children were already in the boat, or the little ones would have been swept into a watery grave. All we could do under this flood of disaster was try to save the boat. All hands were called to man it in a new fashion – namely to hold on to it with might and main to prevent it being washed away. Fortunately we had a boat warp and another strong line made out of strips of oogjook skin and with these we secured the boat as well as we were able to projecting points of ice; but having no ice anchors these fastenings were frequently unloosed and broken, and the boat could not for one moment be trusted to their hold. All our strength was needed and we had to brace ourselves and hold on.

As soon as possible I got the boat to the edge of the ice where the seas first struck, for I knew if she remained toward the farther edge the momentum of the waves would more than master us and the boat would go. As it was we were nearly carried off, boat and all, many times during this dreadful night.

We stood from nine at night till seven in the morning enduring what I should say few, if any, have ever gone through and lived. Every little while one of the tremendous seas would lift the boat up bodily and us with it and carry it and us forward almost to the extreme opposite edge of our piece of ice. Several times the boat got partly over the edge and was hauled back by superhuman strength, which the knowledge of our desperate condition gave us. Had the water been clear it would have been hard enough. But it was full of loose ice rolling about in blocks of all shapes and sizes, and with almost every sea would come an avalanche of these, striking us on our legs and bodies and bowling us off our feet like so many pins in a bowling alley. We were all black and blue with bruises for many a day after.

So we stood, hour after hour, the sea as strong as ever, but we weakening from fatigue so that before morning we had to make Hannah and Hans's wife get out and help hold on too. This was the greatest fight for life we had yet had. Had it not been for the strength imparted to us by that last providential gift of seal meat it does not seem possible that we would have lasted the night. For twelve hours there was scarcely a sound uttered save and except the crying of the children and my orders to "hold on," "bear down," "put on all your weight," and the responsive "Aye, aye, sir," which for once came readily enough.

When daylight came I perceived a piece of ice riding quite easy near to us, and made up my mind we must reach it. The sea was fearfully rough and the men hesitated, thinking the boat would not live in such a sea. But I knew that the piece of ice we were on was still more unsafe and told them they must risk it and launch away. And away she went, the women and children being all snugly stowed in first and the rest all succeeding in getting in safely but the cook, who went overboard, but managed to cling to the gunwale of the boat and was dragged in and saved. We succeeded in reaching the other piece of ice without other accident, and having eaten a morsel of food, lay down on our new bit of floe in our wet clothes to rest. And we are all today well and sound except the bruises we received from the blows and falls.

"April 28th 4.30. A JOYFUL sight—*a steamer* right ahead and bearing north of us! We hoisted our colors, and pulled toward her. She is a sealer, going south-west, and apparently working through the ice. For a few moments what joy thrilled our breasts—the sight of relief so near! But we have lost it! She did not see us, and we could not get to her; evening came down on us, and she was lost to sight.

"We boarded, instead of the hoped-for steamer, a small piece of ice, and once more hauled up our boat and made our camp. The night is calm and clear. A new moon, and the stars shining brightly—the first we have seen for a week. The sea is quiet too, and we can rest in peace; for, though one steamer has passed us, we feel now that we may soon see another—that help can not be far off. We take the blubber of the seals, and build fires on the floe, so that if a steamer or any vessel approaches us in the night she will see us.

"We are divided into two watches, of four hours each. We had a good pull this afternoon, and made some westing. The hope of relief keeps us even more wakeful than does the fear of danger. To see the prospect of rescue so near, though it was quickly withdrawn, has set every nerve thrilling with hope.

"*April* 29. Morning fine and calm; the water quiet. All on the lookout for steamers, except those who had 'turned in,' as we still call it. Sighted a steamer about eight miles off. Called the watch, launched the boat, and made for her. After an hour's pull, gained on her a good deal; but they did not see us. Another hour, and we are beset in the ice, and can get no farther.

"Landed on a small piece of ice, and hoisted our colors; then, getting on the highest part of the ice, we mustered our rifles and pistols, and all fired together, hoping by this means to attract their attention. The combined effort made a considerable report. We fired three rounds, and heard a response of three shots; at the same time the steamer headed toward us. Now we feel sure that the time of our deliverance has come.

"We shout, involuntarily almost, but they are too far off yet to hear voices. Presently the steamer changes her course, and heads south, then north again, then west; we do not know what to make of it. We watch, but she does not get materially nearer. So she keeps on all day, as though she was trying to work through the ice, and could not force her way.

"Strange! I should think any sailing ship, much more a steamer, could get through with ease. We repeated our experiment of firing— fired several rounds, but she came no nearer, being then four or five miles off. All day we watched, making every effort within our means to attract attention. Whether they saw us or not we do not know, but late in the afternoon she steamed away, going to the south-west; and reluctantly we abandoned the hope which had upheld us through the day. For a while she was lost to sight, but in the evening we saw her again, but farther off.

"While looking at her, though no longer with the hope that she had seen us or would reach us, another steamer hove in sight; so we have two sealers near—one on each side of us. And though as yet neither have made any sign (except the firing in the morning, the cause of which now appears doubtful), yet we are beginning to count the hours which we can not help hoping will bring us help. Some of these sealers will surely come by us, or we may be able to work down to them. What if we had abandoned our boat, as the men proposed in February!

"*Sunset.* Sighted land this evening in the south-west, about thirty-five miles distant. Mr. Meyers thinks we are in lat. 49°. We are not so far south as that.

"Hans caught a baby seal to-day, the smallest I have seen this season. Our latitude, approximate at noon to-day, 53° 0' 5"N.

"*April* 30. The last day of April, and the last, I hope, of our long trial.

"*Evening.* At 5 A.M., as I was lying in the boat, it being my watch below, but which had just expired, the watch on the lookout espied a steamer coming through the fog, and the first I heard was a loud cry, 'There's a steamer! there's a steamer!' On hearing the outcry, I sprang up as if endued with new life, ordered all the guns to be fired, and set up a loud, simultaneous shout; also ordered the colors set on the boat's mast, and held them erect, fearing that, like the others, she might not see or hear us, though much nearer than the others had been.

"I also started Hans off with his kyack, which he had himself proposed to do, to intercept her, if possible, as it was very foggy, and I feared every moment that we should lose sight of her; but, to my great joy and relief, the steamer's head was soon turned toward us. But Hans kept on, and paddled up to the vessel, singing out, in his broken English, the unmeaning words, 'American steamer;' meaning to tell them that an American steamer had been lost, and he tried to tell them where we came from; but they did not understand him. We were not more than a quarter of a mile off when we first sighted her. In a few minutes she was alongside of our piece of ice.

"On her approach, and as they slowed down, I took off my old Russian cap, which I had worn all winter, and, waving it over my head, gave them three cheers, in which all the men most heartily joined. It was instantly returned by a hundred men, who covered her top-gallant-mast, forecastle, and fore-rigging. We then gave three more and a 'tiger,' which was appropriate, surely, as she proved to be the sealer *Tigress*—a barkentine of Conception Bay, Newfoundland.

"Two or three of their small seal-boats were instantly lowered. We, however, now that relief was certain, threw every thing from our own boat, and in a minute's time she was in the water, while the boats of the *Tigress* came on, and the crews got on our bit of ice and peeped curiously into the dirty pans we had used over the oil-fires. We had been making soup out of the blood and entrails of the last little seal which Hans had shot. They soon saw enough to convince them that we were in sore need. No words were required to make *that* plain.

"Taking the women and children in their boats, we tumbled into our own, and were soon alongside of the *Tigress*. We left all we had behind, and our all was simply a few battered smoky tin pans and the *débris* of our last seal. It had already become offal in our eyes, though we had often been glad enough to get such fare.

"On stepping on board, I was at once surrounded by a curious lot of people—I mean men filled with curiosity to know our story, and all asking questions of me and the men. I told them who I was, and where we were from. But when they asked me, 'How long have you been on the ice?' and I answered, 'Since the 15th of last October,' they were so astonished that they fairly looked blank with wonder.

"One of the party, looking at me with open-eyed surprise, exclaimed,

" *'And was you on it night and day?'*

"The peculiar expression and tone, with the absurdity of the question, was too much for my politeness. I laughed in spite of myself, and my long unexercised risibles thrilled with an unwonted sensation.

"At this time the captain came along and invited me down into the cabin. I then told him that there was another officer in the party—Mr. Meyers, of the Scientific Department—and he then invited him also to the cabin.

"We had been sitting talking of our 'wonderful,' or, as he called it, 'miraculous' escape, some half an hour. I was very hungry, having eaten nothing since the night before, and I wanted a smoke *so* much;

but I saw no signs of either food or tobacco. So I finally asked him if he would give me a pipe and some tobacco.

"He said he 'did not smoke.'

"However, I soon procured both from one of his officers, and had a good long smoke—the first I had had since Joe gave me the two pipefuls, one of those dreary days in our snow-hut. In course of time breakfast came along—codfish, potatoes, hard bread, and coffee!

"Never in my life did I enjoy a meal like that; plain as it was, I shall never forget that codfish and potatoes. No subsequent meal can ever eclipse this to my taste, so long habituated to raw meat, with all its uncleanly accessories.

The great sea
Has sent me adrift,
It moves me as the weed in a great river,
Earth and the great weather
Move me,
Have carried me away
And move my inward parts with joy.

—Uvavanuk (Iglulik Eskimo woman)

The Entrail Thief

ONCE THREE MEN journeyed to the edge of the Inland Ice to hunt reindeer. As the reindeer were plentiful, they decided to stay there for a while. So they made a comfortable little ice-hut. They were fast asleep one night when an old hag came to visit them. She was Aukjuk, stealer of entrails. And she passed directly through the ice of their hut. Dish in hand, she walked up to the first man and sucked out his entrails as he lay in his sleeping skins. She did the same thing with the second man. And the same thing with the third man as well. She put all their entrails in her dish and headed back out through the ice again.

Now the men became so light that they proceeded to rise into the sky, right up to the moon. Once they landed, they went straight to the House of the Man in the Moon and complained about their ill-treatment. "Intestines and such-like are very important to us human beings," they said. "I know nothing about this," the Man told them. "You must see Aukjuk." And so they went outside and saw Aukjuk, who was preparing supper. "Oh, please don't eat our entrails," they told her. But she had already begun to cook the Man in the Moon's supper. Their entrails were the main course.

The men had to return home to their wives all hollow inside. Such is the punishment for those who visit the ice-edge.

—West Greenland legend

BOOK II

THE PUSH TO
THE POLE

With the fate of Franklin solved by Rae and McClintock and the Northwest Passage traversed on foot (but shown impracticable for navigation) by McClure and company, Arctic adventurers in the last half of the nineteenth century swung their energies due north—to the Pole itself. Like the great space race between the Soviet Union and the United States in the 1960s, national pride and great sums of money were staked on the respective polar teams. Simply to set a new record for "farthest north"—even by a few miles—was considered a great achievement.

Part of the lure was the notion of a "ring of ice" and "open polar sea." Few if any of the whaling captains, with their long Arctic experience, believed that one would find anything farther north but more ice; nor did the Inuit. Still, many Arctic explorers, as well as the public, believed that something besides ice and cold lay in the Polar regions—something extraordinary and magical. A number of expeditions placed all their hopes on these theories, not the least of them the DeLong Expedition, which planned to follow an alleged spit of land that extended from the Siberian regions to the Pole itself.

By 1909, and many tragedies later, both Frederick Cook and Robert Peary had claimed the North Pole as theirs. They'd each done it by dogsled, not by ship, struggling over the hummocks of ice. The prize is usually accorded to Peary, though neither Cook's claim nor Peary's has stood the test of history well. The bitter feuding between the two explorers that was initiated by Peary and his backers threw a money-and-fame-grubbing taint over all forms of Polar exploration, which hasn't entirely vanished to this day. Nor did the Peary-Cook feud put an end to future attempts to be "first" to the Pole. Following them, other adventurers sought to be *first* by airship, *first* by airplane, *first* by snowmobile, *first* to traverse the polar regions, *first* by skis. There was even one adventurer who, for reasons one can only guess, wished to be *first* by motorcycle to the North Pole.

And still the Pole remains aloof, reachable but not really graspable, this odd pinpoint that the rest of the earth spins around. It's a concept as much as a place. Perhaps better still, the Pole is a state of mind. For all the struggle to reach it, each person who attempts to do so brings his own particular symbolism to the try. Almost inevitably, any victory is tinged with disappointment, the earth's northern axis unable to provide whatever it is that the explorer truly seeks.

Hunger

Fear hung over me.
I dared not try
to hold out in my hut.

Hungry and chilled,
I stumbled inland,
tripping, falling constantly.

At Little Musk Ox Lake
the trout made fun of me;
they wouldn't bite.

On I crawled,
and reached the Young Man's River
where I caught salmon once.

I prayed
for fish or reindeer
swimming in the lake.

My thought
reeled into nothingness,
like run-out fishing-line.

Would I ever find firm ground?
I staggered on,
muttering spells as I went.

—Kingmerut (Copper Eskimo man)

DeLong's
Last Words

BY LIEUTENANT GEORGE W. DELONG (AMERICAN, 1881)

After a British Arctic expedition led by George Nares and Albert Markham managed to drag sledges over the ice to 83 degrees north, James Gordon Bennett, owner of the *New York Herald*, outfitted a yacht named *Jeannette* that was put in the command of Lieutenant George W. DeLong of the U.S. Navy to reclaim the glory of the "farthest north" for the Americans.

Departing early in the summer of 1879, DeLong figured he'd reach the North Pole by sailing from San Francisco to Wrangel Island, off the northern coast of Siberia. He mistakenly believed that the island's landmass extended nearly to the Pole itself and all he had to do was follow it. Ice trapped the *Jeannette* that September near Wrangel and the ship drifted with the pack northwest for nearly two years. In early summer of 1881, ice closed in on the ship and pinched her in a death grip as she listed over on her side and groaned and shook, cracking and humming from end to end with an unearthly sound. "I can never forget the manner in which the gang ladders leading to the bridge jumped from their chucks, and danced on the deck like drumsticks on the head of a drum," wrote the expedition's naturalist, Raymond Newcomb. "In the midst of this wild scene a crash was heard. A man came up from below and said:—'The ice is coming through the coal bunkers.' ... After the smash, no sound save the silent rush of water."

The *Jeannette* went down, and DeLong and crew headed for the Siberian coast, six hundred miles south, dragging over the ice three small boats laden with gear until they reached open water. Storms caught them while crossing the open sea toward Siberia, one boat was lost, and the other two became separated. DeLong's boat landed on the western part of the broad Lena River Delta, and the other boat, commanded by his engineer, Melville, landed on the eastern side.

By now it was early autumn and the survivors of both parties, far separated, were acutely aware that they must reach help before the onset of winter. The crew of Melville's boat soon encountered native Siberian hunters along the Delta who took them in and fed them. In the Delta region where DeLong's party landed, however, the hunters already had moved south to their winter settlement; the party encountered only their abandoned encampments. With the river icing over and snow beginning to fall, DeLong and his starving crew stumbled up the Lena, desperately hoping to find a settlement before their strength gave out entirely. As the party weakened, DeLong sent ahead two men, Nindermann and Noros, to reach a settlement and bring back relief.

Relief never arrived. DeLong's journal was discovered the following spring beside his body, inside the tattered remains of a tent buried by snow. Near him were the bodies of expedition members Dr. Ambler and the cook, Ah Sam. What follows are DeLong's last journal entries; one can feel the hope go out of them and sense between the lines the will not to cannibalize the dead. Contrast these spare, haunting notes of DeLong's with the doomed hero's farewell letters that Scott would scrawl and that would be found beside *his* body thirty years later in a collapsed tent in Antarctica. "I do not regret this journey," wrote Scott in a message to the public, "which has shown that Englishmen can endure hardships, help one another and meet death with as great a fortitude as ever in the past."

SATURDAY, October 1st,—111th day, and a new month.—Called all hands as soon as the cook announced boiling water, and at 6.45 had our breakfast, half a pound of deer-meat and tea. Sent Nindermann and Alexai to examine the main river, other men to collect wood. The doctor resumed the cutting away of poor Erickson's toes this morning. No doubt it will have to continue until his feet are gone, unless death ensues or we get to some settlement. Only one toe left now. Weather clear, light northeast airs, barometer 30.15 at 6.05. Temperature eighteen degrees at 7.30. Nindermann and Alexai were seen to have crossed, and I immediately sent men to carry our load over.

At 8.30 made the final trip and got our sick man over in safety. From there we proceeded until 11.20, dragging our man on the sled. Halted for dinner—half pound of meat and tea. At 1 went ahead again until 5.05. Actually under way 8.30 to 9.15, 9.30 to 10.20, 10.30 to 11.20, 1 to 1.40, 1.50 to 2.10, 2.20 to 2.40, 3 to 3.25, 3.35 to 4, 4.15 to 4.35, 4.45 to 5.05. At 8 P.M. crawled into our blankets.

SUNDAY, October 2d.—I think we all slept fairly well until midnight, but from that time forward it was so cold and uncomfortable that sleep was out of the question. At 4.30 we were all out and in front of the fire, daylight just appearing. Erickson kept talking in his sleep all night, and effectually kept those awake who were not already awakened by the cold. Breakfast at 5 A.M.—half pound of meat and tea. Bright, cloudless morning, light northern airs; barometer 30.30 at 5.32; temperature at 6, thirty-five degrees. At 7 went ahead, following the frozen water whenever we could find it, and at 9.20 I felt quite sure we had gone some distance on the main river. I think our gait was at least two miles an hour and our time under way 2h. 40m. I calculate our forenoon work at least six miles, 7 to 7.35, 7.45 to 8.05, 8.15 to 8.30, 8.40 to 8.50, 9.20 to 9.40, 9.50 to 10.12, 10.22 to 10.40, 10.55 to 11.15. Dinner, 1 to 1.30, 1.40 to 2, 2.15 to 2.35, 2.45 to 3, 3.20 to 3.40, 3.50 to 4.05, 4.15 to 4.20. Camp. Total, 5 h. 15 m.

Two miles an hour distance make good ten to twelve miles, and where are we? I think it the beginning of the Lena River at last. Sagaster has been to us a myth. We saw two old huts at a distance, and this was all; but they were out of our road and the day not half gone. Kept on the ice all the way, and, therefore, think we were over water; but the stream was so narrow and so crooked that it never could have been a navigable stream. My chart is simply useless. I must go on plodding to the southward, trusting in God to guide me to some settlement, for I have long since realized that we are powerless to help ourselves. A bright, calm, beautiful day brought sunshine to cheer us up. An icy road, and one day's rations yet. Boats frozen, of course, and hauled up. No hut in sight, and we halt on a bluff to spend a cold and comfortless night. Supper—half pound meat and tea. Built a rousing fire. Built a log bed. Set a watch, two hours each, to keep fire going and get supper. Then we stood by for a second cold and wretched night. There was so much wind we had to put up our tent halves for a screen and sit shivering in our half blankets.

MONDAY, October 3d, 1881,—113th day.—It was so fearfully cold and wretched that I served out tea to all hands, and on this we managed to struggle along until 5 A.M., when we ate our last deer-meat and had more tea. Our morning food now consists of four-fourteenths of a pound of pemmican each, and a half-starved dog. May God again incline unto our aid! How much farther we have to go before making a shelter or settlement, He only knows. Brisk winds, barometer 30.23 at 1.50 temperature. Erickson seems failing. He is weak and powerless, and the moment he closes his eyes talks, mostly in Danish, German and English. No one can sleep, even though our other surroundings permitted. For some cause my watch stopped at 10.45 last night while one of the men on watch had it. I set it as near as I could by guessing, and we must run by that until I can do better. Sun rose yesterday morning at 6.40 by the watch when running all right. 7.05 to 7.40, 7.50 to 8.20, 8.30 to 9, 9.15 to 9.35, 9.50 to 10.10, 10.25 to 10.40, 11. Back. 11.20, 11.30, 11.40, 11.50. Dinner. 35, 30, 30, 20, 20, 20-total, 155—2 hours 35 minutes, say five miles.

Our force means work. I put as above five miles. Some time and distance were lost by crossing the river upon seeing numerous fox-traps. A man's track was also seen in the snow, bound south, and we followed it until it crossed the river to the west bank again. Here we were obliged to go back again in our tracks, for the river was open in places and we could not follow the man's track direct. Another of the dozen shoals that infest the river swung us off to the eastward, too, and I hastened to get on the west bank again, reaching there at ten minutes to twelve for dinner—our last four-fourteenths of a pound of pemmican.

At forty minutes past one got under way again and made a long spurt until twenty minutes past two. While at the other side of the river Alexai said he saw a hut, and during our dinner camp he said he again saw a hut. Under our circumstances my desire was to get to it as speedily as possible. As Alexai points out, it was on the left bank of the river of which we were now on the right side, looking south, but a sand bank gave us excellent walking for a mile or two until we took to the river and got across it diagonally. Here, at twenty minutes past two, I called a halt, and Alexai mounted the bluff to take a look again. He now announced he saw a second hut, about one and a quarter miles back from the coast, the other hut being about the same distance south and on the edge of the bluff. The heavy dragging across the country of a sick man on a sled made me incline to the hut on the shore, since, as the distance was about the same, we could get over the ice in one-third of the time. Nindermann, who climbed the bluff, saw that the object inland was a hut; was not so confident of the one on the shore. Alexai, however, was quite positive, and not seeing very well myself, I unfortunately took his eyes as best and ordered an advance along the river to the southward.

Away we went, Nindermann and Alexai leading and had progressed about a mile when, plash, in I went through the ice up to my shoulders before my knapsack brought me up. While I was crawling out, in went Gortz to his neck about fifty yards behind me; and behind him, in went Mr. Collins to his waist. Here was a time. The moment we came out of the water we were one sheet of ice, and danger of frost-bite was imminent. Along we hobbled, however, until we reached, at 3.45, about the point on which the hut was seen. Here Nindermann climbed the bluff, followed by the doctor. At first the cry was, "All right; come ahead"; but no sooner were we well up, than Nindermann shouted, "There is no hut here."

To my dismay and alarm nothing but a large mound of earth was to be seen, which, from its regular shape and singular position, would seem to have been built artificially for a beacon. So sure was Nindermann that it was a hut that he went all round it looking for a door, and then climbed on top to look for a hole in the roof. But of no avail. It was nothing but a mound of earth. Sick at heart, I ordered a camp to be made in a hole in the bluff face, and soon before a roaring fire we were drying and burning our clothes, while the cold wind ate into our backs.

And now for supper nothing remained but the dog. I therefore ordered him killed and dressed by Iverson, and soon after a stew was made of such parts as could not be carried, of which everybody except the doctor and myself eagerly partook. To us two it was a nauseating mess, and—but why go on with such a disagreeable subject. I had the remainder weighed, and I am quite sure we had twenty-seven pounds. The animal was fat, and as he had been fed on pemmican, presumably clean; but, immediately upon halting, I sent Alexai off with his gun inland toward the hut, to determine whether that was a myth like our present one. He returned about dark, certain that it was a large hut, for he had been inside of it, and had found some deer-meat scraps and bones.

For a moment I was tempted to start everybody for it, but Alexai was by no means sure he could find it in the dark, and if we lost our way we would be worse off than before. We accordingly prepared to make the best of it where we were. We three wet people were burning and steaming before the fire. Collins and Gortz had taken some alcohol, but I could not get it down. Cold weather, with a raw northwest wind impossible to avoid or screen, our future was a wretched, dreary night. Erickson soon became delirious, and his talking was a horrible accompaniment to the wretchedness of our surroundings. Warm we could not get, and getting dry seemed out of the question. Every one seemed dazed and stupefied, and I feared some of us would perish during the night.

How cold it was I don't know, as my last thermometer was broken by my many falls upon the ice; but I think it must have been below zero. A watch was set to keep the fire going, and we huddled around it, and thus our third night without sleep was passed. If Alexai had not wrapped his sealskin around me, and sat alongside of me to keep me warm by the heat of his body, I think I should have frozen to death. As it was, I steamed and shivered and shook. Erickson's groans and rambling talk rang out on the night air, and such a dreary, wretched night I hope I shall never again see.

TUESDAY, October 4th,—114th day.—At the first approach of daylight we all began to move around and the cook was set to work making tea. The doctor now made the unpleasant discovery that Erickson had got his gloves off during the night, and that now his hands were frozen. Men were at once set at work rubbing them, and by 6 A.M. had so far restored circulation as to risk moving the man. Each one had hastily swallowed a cup of tea and got his load in readiness. Erickson was quite unconscious, and we lashed him on the sled. A southwest gale was blowing and the sensation of cold was intense. But at 6 A.M. we started, made a forced march of it, and at 8 A.M. had got the sick man and ourselves, thank God, under cover of a hut large enough to hold us. Here we at once made a fire and for the first time since Saturday morning last got warm.

The doctor at once examined Erickson and found him very low and feeble. He was quite unconscious, and under the shock of last night's exposure was sinking very fast. Fears were entertained that he might not last many hours, and I therefore called upon every one to join me in reading the prayers for a sick person before we sought any rest for ourselves. This was done in a quiet and reverent manner, though I fear my broken utterances made but little of the service audible. Then, setting a watch, we all, except Alexai, lay down to sleep. At 10 A.M. Alexai went off to hunt, but returned at noon wet, having broken through the ice and fallen in the river. At 6 P.M. we roused up, and I considered it necessary to think of some food for my party. Half a pound of dog meat was fried for each person, and a cup of tea given, and that constituted our day's food; but we were so grateful that we were not exposed to the merciless southwest gale that tore around us, that we did not mind short rations.

WEDNESDAY, October 5th,—115th day.—The cook commences at 7.30 to get tea made from yesterday's tea-leaves. Nothing to serve out until evening. Half a pound of dog meat per day is our food until some relief is afforded us. Alexai went off hunting again at nine, and I set the men gathering light sticks enough to make a flooring for the house; for the frozen ground thawing under everybody, kept them damp and wet and robbed them of much sleep. Southwest gale continues. Barometer, 30.12 at 2.40. Mortification has set in in Erickson's leg, and he is sinking. Amputation would be of no use, as he would probably die under the operation. He is partially conscious. At twelve Alexai came back, having seen nothing. He crossed the river this time, but unable longer to face the cold gale was obliged to return. I am of opinion we are on Titary Island, on its eastern side, and about twenty-five miles from Kumak Surka, which I take to be a settlement. This is the last hope for us. Sagaster has long since faded away. The hut in which we are is quite new, and clearly not the astronomical station made on my chart. In fact, the hut is not finished, having no door and no porch. It may be intended for a summer hut, though the numerous fox-traps would lead me to suppose that it would occasionally be visited at other times. Upon this last chance, and another sun, rest all our hopes of escape, for I can see nothing more to be done. As soon as the gale abates I shall send Nindermann and another man to make a forced march to Kumak Surka for relief. At six P.M. served out half pound of dog meat and second-hand tea and then went to sleep.

THURSDAY, Oct. 6th—116th day.—Called all hands at 7:30. Had a cup of third-hand tea, with half an ounce of alcohol in it. Everybody very weak. Gale moderating somewhat. Sent Alexai out to hunt. Shall start Nindermann and Noros at noon to make the forced march to Kumak Surka. At 8:45 our messmate, Erickson, departed this life. Addressed a few words of cheer and comfort to the men. Alexai came back empty-handed—too much drifting snow. What in God's name is going to become of us? Fourteen pounds of dog meat left and twenty-five miles to a possible settlement. As to burying Erickson, I cannot dig a grave, for the ground is frozen and we have nothing to dig with. There is nothing to do but bury him in the river. Sewed him up in the flaps of the tent and covered him with my flag. Got ten men ready, and with half an ounce of alcohol we will try to make out to bury him, but we are all so weak I do not see how we are going to travel. At 12:40 read the burial service and carried our departed shipmate to the river, where a hole having been cut in the ice he was buried, three volleys from our Remingtons being fired over him as a funeral honor. A board was prepared with this cut on it:—

"In memory of H. H. Erickson, October 6, 1881. U.S.S. Jeannette." And this will be stuck in the river bank almost over his grave.

His clothing was divided up among his messmates. Iverson has his Bible and a lock of his hair. Supper at five P.M., half a pound of dog meat and tea.

FRIDAY, Oct. 7th—117th day.—Breakfast, consisting of our last half pound of dog meat and tea. Our last grain of tea was put in the kettle this morning, and we are now about to undertake our journey of twenty-five miles with some old tea leaves and two quarts of alcohol. However, I trust in God, and I believe that He who has fed us thus far will not suffer us to die of want now. Commenced preparation for departure at ten minutes past seven. One Winchester rifle being out of order, is, with 161 rounds of ammunition, left behind. We have with us two Remingtons and 243 rounds of ammunition. Left the following record in the hut:—

"FRIDAY, Oct. 7th, 1881.—The undermentioned officers and men of the late United States steamer Jeannette are leaving here this morning to make a forced march to Kumak Surka or some other settlement on the Lena River. We reached here Tuesday, October 4th, with a disabled comrade, H. H. Erickson, seaman, who died yesterday morning and was buried in the river at noon.

"His death resulted from frost bite and exhaustion due to consequent exposure.

"The rest of us are well, but have no provisions left, having eaten our last this morning."

Under way by 8:30 and proceeded until 11:20, by which time we had made about three miles. Here we were all pretty well done up, and seemed to be wandering in a labyrinth. A large lump of wood swept in by an eddy seemed to be a likely place to get hot water, and I halted the party for dinner—one ounce of alcohol in a pot of tea. Then went ahead and soon struck what seemed like the main river again. Here four of us broke through the ice in trying to cross, and, fearing frost-bite, I had a fire built on the west bank to dry us up. Sent Alexai off, meanwhile, to look for food, directing him not to go far or stay long; but at 1:30 he had not returned, nor was he in sight. Light southwest breeze, foggy. Mountains in sight to southward. At 5:30 Alexai returned with one ptarmigan, of which we made soup, and with half an ounce of alcohol had our supper. Then crawled under our blankets for a sleep. Light west breeze, full moon, starlight, not very cold. Alexai saw the river a mile wide, with no ice in it.

SATURDAY, Oct. 8th—118th day.—Called all hands at half-past five. Breakfast, one ounce of alcohol in a pint of hot water.

Doctor's Note.—Alcohol proves of great advantage. Keeps off craving for food, preventing gnawing at stomach and has kept up the strength of the men, as given—three ounces per day, as estimated, and in accordance with Dr. Ambler's experiments.

Went ahead until half-past ten. One ounce alcohol. Half-past six to half-past ten, five miles struck Big River at 11:30. Ahead again. Snow banks. Met small river, have to turn back. Halt at five; only made advance one mile more. Hard luck. Snow. South-southwest wind, cold. Camp. But little wood. Half an ounce of alcohol.

SUNDAY, Oct. 9th—119th day.—All hands at 4:30. One ounce of alcohol. Read divine service. Send Nindermann and Noros ahead for relief. They carry their blankets, one rifle, forty rounds of ammunition and two ounces of alcohol. Orders to keep the west bank of river until they reach a settlement. They started at seven. Cheered them. Under way at eight. Crossed the creek. Broke through the ice. All wet up to knees. Stopped and built fires. Dried clothes. Under way again at 10:30. Lee breaking down. At one struck river bank. Halt for dinner; one ounce alcohol. Alexai shot three ptarmigan. Made soup. We are following Nindermann's track, although he is long since out of sight. Underway at 3:30. High bluff. Ice moving rapidly to northward in the river. Halt at 4:40 on coming to wood. Find canal boat. Lay our heads in it and go to sleep. Half ounce alcohol. Supper.

MONDAY, Oct. 10th—120th day.—Last half of ounce of alcohol at 5:30. At 6:30 sent Alexai off to look for ptarmigan. Eat deer skin scraps. Yesterday morning ate my deer skin foot nips. Light southeast wind. Air not very cold. Under way at eight. In crossing creek three of us got wet. Built fire and dried out. Ahead again until eleven; used up. Built fire; made a drink out of the tea leaves from alcohol bottle. On again at noon. Fresh south-southwest wind. Drifting snow. Very hard going. Lee begging to be left. Some little beach and then long stretches of high bank. Ptarmigan tracks plentiful. Following Nindermann's track. At three halted, used up. Crawled into a hole in the bank. Collected wood and built a fire. Alexai away in quest of game. Nothing for supper except a spoonful of glycerine. All hands weak and feeble, but cheerful. God help us.

TUESDAY, Oct. 11th—121st day—Southwest gale, with snow. Unable to move. No game. Teaspoonful of glycerine and hot water for food. No more wood in our vicinity.

WEDNESDAY, Oct 12th—122d day.—Breakfast, last spoonful of glycerine and hot water. For dinner we had a couple of handsful of Arctic willow in a pot of water, and drank the infusion. Everybody getting weaker and weaker. Hardly strength to get firewood. Southwest gale, with snow.

THURSDAY, Oct. 13th—123d day.—Willow tea. Strong southwest winds. No news from Nindermann. We are in the hands of God, and unless He relents are lost. We cannot move against the wind, and staying here means starvation. After noon went ahead for a mile, crossing either another river or a wind in the big one. After crossing missed Lee. Went down in a hole in the bank and camped. Sent back for Lee. He had laid down, and was waiting to die. All united in saying the Lord's Prayer and Creed. After supper strong gale of wind. Horrible night.

FRIDAY, Oct. 14th—124th day.—Breakfast, willow tea. Dinner, half tea, spoonful sweet oil and willow tea. Alexai shot one ptarmigan. Had soup. Southwest wind moderating.

SATURDAY, Oct. 15th—125th day.—Breakfast, willow tea and two old boots. Conclude to move at sunrise. Alexai broken down; also Lee. Came to an empty grain raft. Halt and camp. Signs of smoke at twilight to southward.

SUNDAY, Oct. 16th—126th day.—Alexai broken down. Divine service.

MONDAY, Oct. 17th—127th day.—Alexai dying. Doctor baptised him. Read prayers for sick. Mr. Collins' birthday, forty years old. About sunset Alexai died. Exhaustion from starvation. Covered him with ensign and laid him in the crib.

TUESDAY, Oct. 18th—128th day.—Calm and mild. Snow falling. Buried Alexai in the afternoon. Laid him on the ice of the river and covered him over with slabs of ice.

WEDNESDAY, Oct. 19th—129th day.—Cutting up tent to make foot gear. Doctor went ahead to find new camp. Shifted by dark.

THURSDAY, Oct. 20th—130th day.—Bright and sunny, but very cold. Lee and Kaack done up.

FRIDAY, Oct. 21st—131st day.—Kaack was found dead about midnight between the doctor and myself. Lee died about noon. Read prayers for sick when we found he was going.

SATURDAY, Oct. 22d—132d day.—Too weak to carry the bodies of Lee and Kaack out on the ice. The doctor, Collins and myself carried them around the corner out of sight. Then my eye closed up.

SUNDAY, Oct. 23d,—133d day.—Everybody pretty weak. Slept or rested to-day, and then managed to get enough wood in before dark. Read part of divine service. Suffering in our feet. No foot gear.

MONDAY, Oct. 24th—134th day.—A hard night.

TUESDAY, Oct. 25th—135th day.

WEDNESDAY, Oct. 26th—136th day.

THURSDAY, Oct. 27th—137th day.—Iverson broken down.

FRIDAY, Oct. 28th—138th day.—Iverson died during early morning.

SATURDAY, Oct. 29th—139th day.—Dressler died during the night.

SUNDAY, Oct. 30th—140th day.—Boyd and Gortz died during the night. Mr. Collins dying.

My Breath

This is what I call my song, because it is as important for me to sing it, as it is to draw breath.

This is my song: a powerful song.
Unaija-unaija.
Since autumn I have lain here,
helpless and ill,
as if I were my own child.

Sorrowfully, I wish my woman
to another hut,
another man for refuge,
firm and safe as the winter-ice
Unaija-unaija.

And I wish my woman
a more fortunate protector,
now I lack the strength
to raise myself from bed.
Unaija-unaija.

Do you know yourself?
How little of yourself you under-
    stand!
Stretched out feebly on my bench,
my only strength is in my memo-
    ries.
Unaija-unaija.

Game! Big game,
chasing ahead of me!
Allow me to re-live that!
Let me forget my frailty,
by calling up the past!
Unaija-unaija.

I bring to mind that great white
    one,
the polar bear,
approaching with raised hind-
    quarters,
his nose in the snow—
convinced, as he rushed at me,
that of the two of us,
he was the only male! . . .

This is how it was.
Now I lie on my bench,
too sick to even fetch
a little seal oil for my woman's
    lamp. . . .

—Orpingalik (Netsilik Eskimo man)

The Rescue of Greely

BY ADOLPHUS GREELY (AMERICAN, 1884) AND
COMMANDER W. S. SCHLEY (AMERICAN, 1884)

There is a rule of thumb that applies today for climbers of great mountains like Everest and was true even more rigorously for polar explorers of a century ago: the difficulty is not so much in getting up there. The real difficulty is getting back.

Such was the case with the Greely expedition. It is a favorite example held up by Arctic historians to illustrate bad choices, mismanagement, ill preparation, and rigidity of command in a land that tolerates none of these failings. In the spring of 1881, a U.S. Army expedition under Lieutenant Adolphus Greely, whose closest Arctic experience amounted to a three-day blizzard while serving in the Sioux country of the American West, set out for Greenland in the ship *Proteus*. Ostensibly, Greely's was a scientific expedition undertaken as part of the International Polar Year, 1882–83, which had been declared in an effort to turn attention away from the race for the Pole and focus on contributions to humanity. But Greely was also driven by the hope to beat the British record set by Markham for the farthest north, or to reach the Pole itself. While the U.S. Navy's DeLong expedition was still missing in the *Jeannette* somewhere north of Siberia, the rival U.S. Army with its Greely expedition would show its stuff.

As he departed, Greely understood that a supply ship would sail north the following summer and a relief expedition would arrive the summer after that, in 1883. *Proteus* dropped the party of twenty-five, including two Inuit hunters, on northern Ellesmere Island and the expedition wintered in a quarters it had built named Fort Conger. There were personality conflicts from the first day, especially between the expedition's civilian physician, Dr. Pavy, who was something of a bohemian, and the straight-arrow Greely. Despite this, and the death of a number of their dogs, the following spring three of the men surpassed Markham's record by four miles; and other forays added valuable geographic knowledge to the coast and interior of Ellesmere Island. But that summer the much-awaited supply vessel did not show up. The party had brought plenty of food, however, and game was plentiful in the area; so they stayed on through the following winter. Then the summer of 1883 also passed without the arrival of a relief ship.

Unknown to them, the first supply party had turned back due to ice without unloading its rations at the designated caches. During the next year's attempt, the relief ship, the *Proteus* (again), was under the command of an officer who had no experience in ice. It was crushed and sunk, although the party did manage to unload a very small cache for Greely at Cape Sabine on Ellesmere Island. Setting out in whaleboats, the survivors from the sunken *Proteus* chased far south along the Greenland coast in open boats trying to catch up to their helper ship, the *Yantic*. When they finally reached the *Yantic*, in Godhavn, nearly a thousand miles south, it was too late in the season to head back north to help Greely's party.

Greely, rigidly adhering to military decorum and orders and realizing no relief party was coming north to Fort Conger, finally determined to head south late that same summer, in 1883, in a steam launch that towed three whaleboats. But the party had left too late in the season and was blown about by storms in the moving ice, making little progress. Losing all their boats but one, they finally struggled back to the shore of Ellesmere Island, near Cape Sabine. They tried to hold out for their third winter in the Arctic in a makeshift stone-and-snow hut covered by their whaleboat, under which they could barely sit up.

This excerpt from Greely's *Three Years of Arctic Service* begins in April as rations run low and tempers run short and health breaks down. The second excerpt is from the account of Commander Schley, who rescued the survivors in their last hours before death. In the weeks and months after the rescue, the press revealed that some of the recovered corpses had been cannibalized but Greely denied any knowledge of it and none of the survivors ever admitted to it.

The Beginning of the End.

April opened favorably, for Long killed eleven dovekies and two ptarmigans, and saw a seal and walrus. On the 3d we had yet remaining five pounds of meat, three of bread, and nearly two of stearine to each man. Rice, too, was bringing in from twenty to thirty pounds of shrimps daily, and reported that sea-weed, or kelp, was visible, and might be reached, he thought, at the spring tides. Our first really depressing day came with April 5th. The night before Christiansen, one of the Eskimos, had been somewhat delirious; but in early morning he grew worse, and at nine o'clock died. During the previous week considerable extra food had been issued him in the hope of saving him. His body was carefully examined by Dr. Pavy and Steward Bierderbick. The doctor reported that a few illy-defined signs of scurvy were visible, but that death resulted from the action of water on the heart induced by insufficient nutrition. We dreaded to use or hear the word starvation, but that was the plain meaning of it. His death could not fail to have a very injurious effect on the weak and despondent.

On Sunday, April 6th, Lynn became unconscious at 1 P.M., and died at 7. He asked for water just before dying; we had none to give. It was noticeable, in after cases, that almost invariably from six to twelve hours before consciousness ceased thirst began, and a request for water was repeatedly made. Lynn's death affected us all deeply.

Near midnight of April 6th Sergeant Rice and Private Frederick started southward to Baird Inlet. They went to attempt the recovery of the hundred pounds of English beef which had been abandoned in November, 1883. Such abandonment, it will be remembered, was necessary to save the life of Sergeant Elison, then dangerously frost-bitten.

April 15th "Bierderbick made oath to-day about the truthfulness of his statements charging Dr. Pavy with taking Elison's bread, last autumn, and appropriating to his own use four cans of extract of beef."

"April 19th.—Long detected Dr. Pavy this morning drinking part of Schneider's allowance of rum. The doctor to-day complained very bitterly to me of Elison's ingratitude to him for the kindness and attention he has shown him. I cannot blame Elison for giving vent occasionally to his feelings, as he has long realized the part the doctor has played toward him. Bierderbick and Ellis were much worse to-day, being unable to eat the shrimps. It worries me a great deal, for if one cannot eat them he must certainly die soon.

This evening Schneider broke down morally, if I may use the word, and refused to obey my orders to prepare supper. The doctor reported him well, yet Schneider said he could not do it; in consequence of his refusal, I left my bag and took his place as cook for the other mess, despite the entreaties and remonstrances of the enlisted men of the party."

"April 23d.—Schneider cooking again. I told him yesterday that if he did not cook the breakfast he could have none; that if he could not work here he could not eat here. I pity the man's condition, but deem it necessary that he should cook. I plead with him as a man, as a soldier, and as a German, but for a long time in vain. Bender and Henry to-day tore out the inside of the boat, and Ralston carried out six tubs of ice which had formed on the inside of the boat during the winter. Ralston's toe is in a very bad condition, but yet he is willing to do what he can. We used the last of the stearine for cooking this evening, and begin on the boat in the morning. We have yet seven gallons of alcohol, but I think it better to use it as food to eke out our remaining rations, of which we have about three hundred and thirty pounds. Our chances are still fair of getting through, but more good men may yet fall before plenty and safety come to us."

"April 24th.—I called Dr. Pavy at 4 A.M., and he went down to set the shrimp-nets. Sergeant Brainard went at 8 A.M. to draw the nets, and found only about four ounces; the doctor had arranged everything in such an ingenious way that the shrimps could not get into the bags. He admitted afterward that he was thinking of something else at the time. I had a terrible attack of illness this morning, losing much blood and experiencing great pain, with resulting physical weakness."

"April 26th.—A bad day for hunting; Long saw but one seal. The party generally are in poor spirits. Brainard was too much run down by previous work to enable him to go for shrimps again this afternoon, and his trip was taken by Frederick, who got about seven pounds. Brainard is working far too hard, and if he should break down we certainly would be in a very bad way. Am taking a grain of mild chloride of mercury a day. Suffered much pain, and in consequence am depressed in spirits and physically very weak. My bowels seem to have completely lost their power. Private Henry took advantage of my illness and of others being down in their bags this morning to mix the "moonshine," and drank extra alcohol to such an extent as to become helplessly drunk. His condition was discovered by Lieutenant Kislingbury, who was next to him. The disgust of every one at such baseness is excessive. Yesterday Long saw about a dozen white whales, which were travelling from the north; they unfortunately did not come within shooting distance."

"April 29th.—A fatal day for us. Breakfast at 5 A.M., instead of 6, for accommodation of the hunters. Jens and Long got away at 6:45 A.M. in excellent spirits. Jens appeared to be in particularly good humor; and for the first time in many weeks came and shook hands with me before he left, laughing pleasantly during the while. At 2:30 P.M. Long returned, and reported that Jens was drowned at 11:30 A.M., losing the kayak and our only reliable rifle, the army Springfield. Every one grieves very much over the 'Little Man's' death, not alone on account of the critical condition in which we are left as regards food, but on account of the strong affection we all had for his great heart, unvarying truthfulness and integrity.

Jens Edward, though an Eskimo, was a man and a Christian of whom no evil word was ever spoken, and on whom no shadow of fault rested in his three years' life with us."

The Last of our Rations.

May opened dismally, with a snow-storm. Brainard continued indefatigably his work of catching shrimps, of which he brought in no less than four hundred and fifty pounds from April 8th to 30th. On May 3d, however, our last bread was gone, and but nine days' meat remained, even at the small ration then issued. Every one favored, for once, a reduction to the minimum. Our hunters kept the field daily but saw little game. On the 3d Long visited Rice Strait and killed a seal, which, drifting toward him, sank within ten feet of him.

In the early days of May I was very ill, and expected hourly to pass away. When I was in the worst condition Whisler was detected by Bender and Henry with bacon from the storehouse. The three men were outside, and Whisler claimed that the door was forced by the others, and he, passing by, saw the food, and was too ravenous to resist. Bender and Henry said that Whisler forced the door, and they detected him. I was too sick to do much in the matter. The entire party expressed themselves in the harshest manner, and Whisler, pleading guilty to having been unable to resist the temptation to take the food, announced himself ready to pay any penalty. Henry, who was on parole, joined in the cry.

"May 6th.—A violent storm commenced at three o'clock this morning, and gradually abated, dying away at noon. Dr. Pavy made trouble to-day by false statements on three different points, as regards his reports made daily to me in French, and an acrid discussion followed. I ordered him four times to drop the matter, and finally told him were he not the doctor I would kill him. As a consequence Private Bender attempted to defend the doctor, and, despite repeated orders, would not be quiet. A mutiny seemed imminent and I would have killed him could I have got Long's gun. Things have come to such a point that my orders, by these two men, are considered as binding or not at their pleasure. I fear for the future."

"May 11th.—The temperature at 2 A.M., when Frederick returned from hunting, was −4° (−20°C.), an extremely low one for this time of the year. Frederick succeeded in killing an oosuk seal in a water-pool, but unfortunately he sank instead of floating into the fast ice. The temperature at noon in the sun was 37° (2.8°C.). The party are in much better spirits than for some time. It seems strange that it should be so, as we have, after to-morrow, but two or perhaps two and half days' rations."

"May 18th.—Very stormy last night and this morning. I heard a raven croaking this morning and called Long, who succeeded in killing him. Gave Long the liver, and concluded to use the bird for shrimp-bait, thinking we could obtain more from him that way than in eating. A violent storm kept everybody in the hut to-day except Brainard, who went for shrimps. Ellis very weak to-day. Bender treated him brutally, so that even Henry rebuked him. I reprimanded Bender sharply for his lack of feeling, although he is probably somewhat insane and not entirely responsible."

"May 19th.—Frederick going out to get ice to cook breakfast this morning returned immediately, reporting that as he emerged from the passageway he saw a bear within a few yards of the house. Long and Frederick dressed for the hunt, and started after the bear, but returned about 10:30 A.M., having been unable even to get a shot at him. Their weakened condition was such that the bear easily outstripped them. Our agony of hope and fear while the hunters were absent cannot be adequately expressed by language. The last alcohol issued to-day, except a few ounces for medical purposes which the doctor will prescribe. Israel and Whisler have quite broken down, and the whole party is in lower spirits than ever before. Private Ellis died at 10:15 A.M."

"May 21st.—A saxifrage seen in blossom. We are now mixing saxifrage in our stews; fully nineteen-twentieths of it is the dead plant, with but the faintest tinge of green at the ends. My appetite and health continue good. It is evident that I shall die, as have the others, of lack of food, which induces dropsy of the heart. Lieutenant Kislingbury and Ralston are very weak."

"May 22d.—It is now eight days since the last regular food was issued. It is astonishing to me how the party holds out. I have been obliged to feed Ralston for a couple of days past. About 2 P.M. he succeeded in eating a part of his dinner, but the rest he could not force down. When tea came, about 3:30 P.M., I asked him if he wanted it, and he said yes. I raised him up, but he became unconscious in my arms, and was unable to drink it. The strength of the party has been devoted to-day to pitching the wall-tent some three hundred yards southeast of the present hut, on a level, gravelly spot in the sun's rays. The doctor says that the party will all die in a few days without we succeed in moving from this wretched hut. The melting snow rains down such a quantity of water upon us that we are saturated to the skin and are in a wretched condition."

"May 23d.—Ralston died about 1 A.M. Israel left the bag before his death, but I remained until driven out about 5 A.M., chilled through by contact with the dead. I read the burial service over him, and ordered him to be buried in the ice-foot northwest of the camp, if the party were unable to haul him to the hill. The weakest of the party moved to the tent upon the hill this afternoon.

"May 24th.—The tent is much more comfortable. The temperature reached 39° (3.9° C.) inside it this morning. Whisler unconscious this morning, and died about noon."

"May 26th.—The storm was so bad this morning that Brainard could not go shrimping, but this afternoon he got eight pounds. Owing to his failure to obtain shrimps, we had a stew last night and this morning of the seal-skin thongs which have been used in lashing together the sledge and for similar purposes. How we live I do not know, unless it is because we are determined to. We all passed an exceedingly wretched night. The stronger of the party succeeded in burying Whisler very early this morning. Israel is now in an exceedingly weak condition, and unable even to sit up in his bag. I am compelled to raise him and feed him, which is a tremendous drain on my physical strength. He talks much of his home and younger days, and seems thoroughly reconciled to go. I gave him a spoonful of rum this morning; he begged for it so exceedingly hard. It was perhaps not fair to the rest to have given it to him, as it was evident it could not benefit him, as he was so near his end. However it was a great comfort and relief to him, and I did by him as I should like to have been done by in such a time."

"May 27th.—Long killed a dovekie, which he could not get. Israel died very easily about three o'clock this morning. I gave him yesterday evening the last food he ate. A very unpleasant scene occurred to-day. Dr. Pavy in the afternoon took all the remaining iron from the medicine-chest. I ordered him to return it there, he having been accused to me by Steward Bierderbick, Sergeant Elison, and others of taking large quantities of Dover's powders, and he has lately failed to issue iron to the party as he promised. There was a violent scene, and Lieutenant Kislingbury, as usual, thought Dr. Pavy right. Lieutenant Kislingbury interfered more than I thought proper, and I ordered him to cease criticizing."

The End—By Death and By Rescue.

Summer opened wretchedly, with a howling gale and driving snow, and a temperature near the freezing-point. For a day and a half an unbroken fast depleted our little strength. We were yet fourteen in number, but it was evident that all must soon pass away, unless our hunters were more fortunate or relief came speedily. My journal continues:

"Long saw to-day a flock of long-tailed ducks. Had breakfast this morning of shrimps and sea-weed, after a fast of thirty-four hours without either food or drink. Everybody very wretched, not only from the lack of food, but from the cold, to which we are very sensitive. Lieutenant Kislingbury, who was exceedingly weak in the morning at breakfast, became unconscious at 9 A.M., and died at 3 P.M. The last thing he did was to sing the Doxology and ask for water."

"June 6th.—Fine, warm, clear day. Frederick detected Henry stealing shrimps out of the general mess-pot when his back was turned. Later Henry made two trips to our old winter-quarters, and when returning from the second trip, while passing me, I stopped him and questioned him as to what he had been doing, and what he had with him. After a while he admitted he had taken from there, contrary to positive orders, seal-skin thongs; and, further, that he had in a bundle, concealed somewhere, seal-skin. He was bold in his admissions, and showed neither fear nor contrition. I ordered him shot, giving the order in writing:

" 'NEAR CAPE SABINE, June 6, 1884.
" 'SERGEANTS BRAINARD, LONG, AND FREDERICK:
" 'Notwithstanding promises given by Private C. B. Henry yesterday, he has since, as acknowledged to me, tampered with seal-thongs, if not other food at the old camp. This pertinacity and audacity is the destruction of this party, if not at once ended. Private Henry will be shot to-day, all care being taken to prevent his injuring any one, as his physical strength is greater than that of any two men. Decide the manner of death by two ball and one blank cartridge. This order is *imperative,* and *absolutely necessary* for *any chance* of life.
" 'A. W. GREELY,
" '*First Lieutenant Fifth Cavalry, U.S.A., and Assistant,*
" '*Commanding L.F.B. Expedition.*'

"About two o'clock shots were heard, and later the order was read to the general party. Every one, without exception, acknowledged that Henry's fate was merited. On searching his bundles very considerable quantities of seal-skin were found, as well as a pair of my seal-skin boots which I had loaned to Long a short time since, and which had been stolen from him two nights before. There was found in his pocket a valuable silver chronograph left by me with other scientific instruments at Conger, and stolen by him on our departure. Fully twelve pounds of seal-skin were found cached among his effects."

"I learned this afternoon from Steward Bierderbick that Dr. Pavy, while at the medicine-chest yesterday, took away the extract of ergot, and has since drank all in the bottle, about three ounces. Bierderbick says that, after Dr. Pavy left the medicine-chest, he examined it to see what had been taken, but did not notice the absence of the ergot bottle, as it was a medicine for which we had no use. Dr. Pavy is now (5 p.m.) at the point of death, which has doubtless been hastened a day or two by this action on his part. Bender is also dying."

"Later.—Bender died at 5:45 P.M. very easily. I think his death was hastened by Henry's execution. Dr. Pavy died at 6 P.M. His death has evidently been hastened by the narcotics. Bierderbick thought that he believed the ergot to be iron. By all accounts he has dosed himself continually, and to this I ascribe his sudden break-down, as, until the 2d of this month, he was one of the strongest of the party. There are now but nine left. Long killed a dovekie, which I ordered to be divided between the hunters and Frederick. Long saw many ducks to-day. Brainard was out nearly seven hours, and got less than three pounds of shrimps. We must begin on our seal-skin clothing. I got to-day a large quantity of tripe de Roche lichen, and found them very nutritious; they certainly are very palatable."

"June 9th.—A calm, fair day; temperature ranging from 36° to 42°(2.2° to 5.6° C.). The party succeeded in getting Dr. Pavy and Bender into the ice-crack. All are very weak. Connell shows signs of scurvy in bleeding gums, and Schneider in his swollen, stiff knees, while Gardiner and Bierderbick are weaker. I was out on rocks fifty yards distant for six hours, and got a quart of tripe de Roche; and Bierderbick the same. Had nothing but tripe de Roche, tea, and seal-skin gloves for dinner. Without fresh bait we can do little in shrimping, and so live on lichens and moss alone."

"June 10th.—A calm, cloudy day, with temperature from 35° to 40° (1.7° to 4.4° C.). Gardiner is suffering very much. Long killed last night a Brent goose, which he lost, and a dovekie. The dovekie went to the hunters to-day, although there were some unpleasant remarks made about it. Very few shrimps were obtained. In the evening had only a stew of the tripe de Roche which was gathered by Bierderbick, Schneider, and myself. I was out nearly five hours, until driven from the rocks thoroughly chilled. The stewed tripe de Roche to-day was delicious, having boiled it for the first time. It leaves a sweetish taste in the mouth. Bierderbick told me this evening that inflammation of the bowels had set in in Gardiner's case, which must soon prove fatal."

"June 12th.—A clear, calm day, the temperature ranging from 34° to 38° (1° o 3° C.). Long came in with no game; and Brainard brought back the unfortunate news that the floes at his shrimping-grounds had broken up and been driven out by the late gale, so that he lost not only the shrimps, but the nets and rope. In consequence we have for breakfast only tea and such roasted seal-skin as each one has left from the part issued a few days since. The misfortunes of the day are very discouraging, and affected the spirits and temper of some of the party. Gardiner died to-day of inflammation of the bowels and starvation. He was apparently dead at 11 A.M., and was removed from the tent; but, showing signs of life, later was deposited on an old buffalo-robe, where he died about 5 P.M.

"June 13th.—Strong southerly gale, with the temperature at the freezing-point (0° C.) at 7 A.M., but with a clear sky. Formally discharged Bierderbick to-day, his term of service having expired. Having no regular blanks, I gave him a written certificate of discharge, to be replaced by a regular one. Was unable to give him 'final statements.' The cold gale which sprang up early this morning rendered it impossible, owing to the low temperature, for us to collect lichens. It reduced us to extremities for dinner, as Brainard got but a few shrimps. Issued to the party my seal-skin jumper, which had been reserved for shrimp-bait. Connell, Bierderbick, and Schneider succeeded in eating all their allowance; I was able to eat but very little of mine, but ate instead about an ounce or two boiled lashings which I had saved; also cut off the dirty, oil-tanned covering of my sleeping-bag, and divided it between the party, so that each man could have his part as desired."

"June 14th.—Re-enlisted Bierderbick as a hospital steward of the first class, subject to approval.

"June 16th.—A strong northwest gale commenced in the straits last night, but abated this morning. The temperature 37° (2.8° C.), at 7 A.M. It was too cold and cloudy in the forenoon to pick lichens. The party are now eating oil-tanned skin, which is very repugnant to us. All are weaker and much discouraged. I do not know how we live, except on our hopes and expectations of a ship. Schneider last evening begged for opium pills, with which he could end his life, but found no one to help him to them. He was in better spirits this morning, but had to be handled like a child this afternoon, being as helpless physically as Elison. Connell's mouth seems much worse. Whether his scurvy is increasing or not I cannot say, but his gums are certainly in very bad condition, swollen and bleeding. Brainard found the minimum thermometer (No. 590) which was blown away by the gale of December last."

"June 18th.—The temperature was down to 30° (−1.1° C.) last night, and but 30.5° (−0.8° C.), with a fresh wind and clouded sky, at 7 A.M. Schneider was very weak and out of his head in the morning, and later became unconscious. He wandered a great deal, but not unpleasantly, and died at 6 P.M. Brainard got no shrimps; I am afraid we will have to give it up until we get birds or other bait. He is now collecting tripe de Roche with all the rest of us."

My diary says: "20th, 7 A.M., clear, calm, 29°, minimum 26.8° (−1.7° and −2.9° C.). Six years ago to-day I was married and three years ago I left my wife for this Expedition, what contrast! When will this life in death end?"

The morning of the 21st broke with the gale still raging, and it was with the greatest difficulty that Frederick was able to cook our wretched stew of lichens and heat up some stewed seal-skin, the remnant of the oil-tanned and filthy covering of my sleeping-bag. During the day the gale continued with unabated violence, with a mean temperature of 31° (−0.6° C.), and a minimum of 28° (−2.2° C.), an unprecedented degree of cold for a midsummer day. Our tent gradually gave way inch by inch before the gale, and all efforts to straighten it or to improve our condition proved futile, owing to our enfeebled condition. By evening the front portion of the tent rested on the ground, pinning Brainard, Long, and myself in our sleeping-bags so we could hardly stir.

My diary says: "21st, 11 A.M., south gale, 34° (1.1° C.). At 8:30 A.M., it commenced snowing. Connell's legs paralyzed from knee down. Bierderbick suffering terribly from rheumatism. Buchanan Strait open this noon a long way up the coast."

With these words my journal ends.

It was half past eight o'clock in the evening as the cutter steamed around the rocky bluff of Cape Sabine, and made her way to the cove, four miles further on, which Colwell remembered so well from his hurried landing with the stores on the terrible night following the wreck of the *Proteus.* The storm, which had been raging with only slight intervals since early the day before, still kept up, and the wind was driving in bitter gusts through the openings in the ridge that followed the coast to the westward. Although the sky was overcast, it was broad daylight—the daylight of a dull winter afternoon—and as the cutter passed along, Colwell could recognize the familiar landmarks of the year before; the long sweep of the rocky coast, with its ice-foot spanning every cove, the snow gathered in the crevices, the projecting headlands, and the line of the ice-pack which had ground up the *Proteus,* dimly seen in the mists to the north, across the tossing waters of Kane Sea. At last the boat arrived at the site of the wreck cache, and the shore was eagerly scanned, but nothing could be seen. Rounding the next point, the cutter opened out the cove beyond. There, on the top of a little ridge, fifty or sixty yards above the ice-foot, was plainly outlined the figure of a man. Instantly the coxswain caught up the boathook and waved his flag. The man on the ridge had seen them, for he stooped, picked up a signal flag from the rock, and waved it in reply. Then he was seen coming slowly and cautiously down the steep rocky slope. Twice he fell down before he reached the foot. As he approached, still walking feebly and with difficulty, Colwell hailed him from the bow of the boat:

"Who all are there left?"

"Seven left."

As the cutter struck the ice, Colwell jumped off and went up to him. He was a ghastly sight. His cheeks were hollow, his eyes wild, his hair and beard long and matted. His army blouse, covering several thicknesses of shirts and jackets, was ragged and dirty. He wore a little fur cap and rough moccasins of untanned leather tied around the leg. As he spoke, his utterance was thick and mumbling, and in his agitation his jaws worked in convulsive twitches. As the two met, the man, with a sudden impulse, took off his glove and shook Colwell's hand.

"Where are they?" asked Colwell, briefly.

"In the tent," said the man, pointing over his shoulder, "over the hill—the tent is down."

"Is Mr. Greely alive?"

"Yes, Greely's alive."

"Any other officers?"

"No." Then he repeated absently, "The tent is down."

"Who are you?"

"Long."

Before this colloquy was over, Lowe and Norman had started up the hill. Hastily filling his pockets with bread, and taking the two cans of pemmican, Colwell told the coxswain to take Long into the cutter, and started after the others with Ash. Reaching the crest of the ridge, and looking southward, they saw spread out before them a desolate expanse of rocky ground, sloping gradually from a ridge on the east to the ice-covered shore, which at the west made in and formed a cove. Back of the level space was a range of hills rising up eight hundred feet, with a precipitous face, broken in two by a gorge, through which the wind was blowing furiously. On a little elevation directly in front was the tent. Hurrying on across the intervening hollow, Colwell came up with Lowe and Norman, just as they were greeting a soldierly-looking man who had come out from the tent.

As Colwell approached, Norman was saying to the man:

"There is the Lieutenant."

And he added to Colwell:

"This is Sergeant Brainard."

Brainard immediately drew himself up to the "position of the soldier," and was about to salute, when Colwell took his hand.

At this moment there was a confused murmur within the tent, and a voice said:

"Who's there?"

Norman answered, "It's Norman—Norman who was in the *Proteus*."

This was followed by cries of "Oh, it's Norman!" and a sound like a feeble cheer.

Meanwhile one of the relief party, who in his agitation and excitement was crying like a child, was down on his hands and knees trying to roll away the stones that held down the flapping tent cloth. The tent was a "tepik" or wigwam tent, with a fly attached. The fly with its posts and ridge-pole had been wrecked by the gale which had been blowing for thirty-six hours, and the pole of the tepik was toppling over, and only kept in place by the guy ropes. There was no entrance except under the flap opening, which was held down by stones. Colwell called for a knife, cut a slit in the tent cover, and looked in.

It was a sight of horror. On one side, close to the opening, with his head towards the outside, lay what was apparently a dead man. His jaw had dropped, his eyes were open, but fixed and glassy, his limbs were motionless. On the opposite side was a poor fellow, alive to be sure, but without hands or feet, and with a spoon tied to the stump of his right arm. Two others, seated on the ground, in the middle, had just got down a rubber bottle that hung on the tent pole, and were pouring from it into a tin can. Directly opposite, on his hands and knees, was a dark man with a long matted beard, in a dirty and tattered dressing-gown with a little red skull cap on his head, and brilliant, staring eyes. As Colwell appeared, he raised himself a little, and put on a pair of eyeglasses.

"Who are you?" asked Colwell.

The man made no answer, staring at him vacantly.

"Who are you?" again.

One of the men spoke up: "That's the Major—Major Greely."

Colwell crawled in and in and took him by the hand, saying to him, "Greely, is this you?"

"Yes," said Greely in a faint, broken voice, hesitating and shuffling with his words, "Yes—seven of us left—here we are—dying—like men. Did what I came to do—beat the best record."

Then he fell back exhausted.

The Sun and the Moon and the Fear of Loneliness

It's a fearful thing
to turn one's mind away,
and long for solitude
among a happy crowd of people.
   Ijaija-ja-ja.

It's a happy thing
to feel warmth
come to the great world,
and see the sun
follow its old footsteps
in the summer night.
   Ijaija-ja-ja.

It's a fearful thing
to feel the cold
return to the great world,
and see the moon—
now new, now full—
follow its old footsteps
in the winter night.
   Ijaija-ja-ja.

Where does all this go, I wonder?
For myself, I long to travel east!
But I'll never see
my father's brother,
whom my mind so longs
to open itself to.

—Tatilgak (Copper Eskimo man)

$\mathcal{N}$ansen $\mathcal{S}$trolls
"$\mathcal{F}$arthest $\mathcal{N}$orth"

BY FRIDTJOF NANSEN (NORWEGIAN, 1895)

I n the early part of the nineteenth century the British flung their naval might vainly against the masses of ice, while in the latter part of the century the Americans tried their luck with smaller ships, but without better results. It was then that the Norwegians entered the arena of polar exploration with great skill and energy. One of the most innovative of this new breed was Fridtjof Nansen, who understood profoundly that to succeed in the Arctic one had to put oneself in a position, as he expressed it, to be "assisted by the forces of nature, rather than fighting against her."

Nansen attended the University of Christiana and studied animal life on the Greenland coast before being named a museum curator. In 1888, at the age of twenty-seven, Nansen proposed a crossing of the Greenland Ice Cap, which had defeated both Adolph Erik Nordenskiöld, who first sailed the Northeast Passage, and Robert Peary, later of polar fame. But Nansen proposed to do it differently: He and his men would glide along on skis when possible, their sledges would be equipped with sails to harness the wind, and, most controversially, they would begin on Greenland's east coast, where there were no settlements, and travel to the west coast, where Europeans lived and where their only hope of rescue awaited.

There would be no turning back, because there was nothing to turn back to.

Despite the storm of criticism that greeted Nansen's plan from veteran Arctic explorers, such as the recently-back-from-the-dead Greely, he and his small party of Norwegians and Lapps caught a ride on a whaler to Greenland and, despite many difficulties, completed the crossing. His next plan, which had been churning about in his head since the age of twenty-two, was more audacious still. Acutely observant, he had noted that rocks and larch wood washed up on the Greenland shore originated in Siberia, and bits of wreckage from DeLong's doomed *Jeannette,* sunken off the Siberian islands, had been found in southern Greenland. Nansen postulated that the great mass of polar ice drifted in a general direction from Siberia to Greenland, across the North Pole. His plan, then, was to freeze a ship into the ice off Siberia and simply *drift* across the Pole.

He managed to weather another barrage from naysayers, and won an appropriation to fund the building of the remarkable *Fram.* One hundred twenty-five feet long, her hull was built of oak nearly three feet thick, her decks carried six covered boats, each capable of holding the *Fram*'s entire crew, and her holds stocked no less than *five years* worth of provisions. She was designed with an innovative U-shaped bottom so that when "nipped" she'd simply slip up out of the ice "like an eel," as Nansen put it, instead of being crushed like a walnut. He also had the foresight to equip her with a windmill-driven electrical generator to save coal and, to be used when the polar winds weren't blowing, a man-powered treadmill that would generate electricity and give the crew exercise at the same time. Her crew of thirteen were all Norwegian; only Norwegians, as Nansen joked, could sit facing each other for three years on an ice floe and not hate each other.

Nansen said his mission was not so much to reach that mathematical point that constituted the North Pole as to explore the polar region. He sailed from Norway in June 1893 with the plan to "ram the ship as far as she will go into the ice and let her stick there." He succeeded in doing just that off the Siberian islands on September 22 of that year, and for the next nine months drifted about with the ice in a small circle. The polar drift that he'd postulated then caught the *Fram* and began to take her north.

A year passed with the ship locked in the polar pack, heading north and west toward Greenland, with the crew fighting boredom rather than the elements and Nansen wondering if he'd have anything to write about when he got back home. It gradually became apparent that the *Fram* was not going to drift across the Pole, but somewhat to the south of it. On March 14, 1895, a year and a half after freezing her in, Nansen and Lieutenant Johansen left the *Fram* with three sledges, two kayaks, and twenty-eight dogs to make a try at the North Pole. One gets the sense that Nansen was looking for some excitement after the long idleness aboard the *Fram*.

Three weeks into the journey Nansen gave up his hope to reach the Pole and prudently decided to turn back. The ice had become too much for him to battle. Despite their retreat, he and Johansen had reached 86 degrees, 14 minutes—a good deal farther north than anyone had traveled before.

It would be over a year before they saw another human again. They worked their way south toward Franz Joseph Land, over the polar ice that began to deteriorate in the summer sun, and finally made landfall late that summer on an uninhabited island just north of Franz Joseph Land. Demonstrating the prudence that allowed him to survive such epic journeys, Nansen decided to winter on the island while they still had time to build a shelter and kill a large supply of game. They excavated a hole three feet deep, built a stone wall three feet above it, roofed it over with walrus hides and snow, and spent the winter inside, feasting on bear steaks and blubber. Unlike most explorers who have overwintered inadvertently in the Arctic, Nansen and Johansen were actually *fatter* by many pounds at the end of their winter than when they'd left the comforts of the *Fram*.

As for sleeping, writes Nansen in *Farthest North,* "we carried
this art to a high pitch of perfection, and could sometimes put in
as much as 20 hours' sleep in the 24." Their biggest enemies were
boredom and the fathomless sense of isolation. Nansen writes
sensitively about the closeness to the infinite he experienced during the course of that long winter alone with the eternal polar
wind, and about the insignificance of human beings—of all living
things—and their puny endeavors.

Nansen, it bears noting, went on to a distinguished career in sci-
entifc and humanitarian work and won the Nobel Peace Prize in
1922 for his efforts on behalf of refugees.

"Wednesday, November 27th. −23° C. (9.4° below zero, Fahr.). It is
windy weather, the snow whirling about your ears, directly you put
your head out of the passage. Everything is gray; the black stones
can be made out in the snow a little way up the beach, and above you
can just divine the presence of the dark cliff; but wherever else the
gaze is turned, out to sea or up the fjord, there is the same leaden
darkness; one is shut out from the wide world, shut into one's self.
The wind comes in sharp gusts, driving the snow before it; but up under the crest of the mountain it whistles and roars in the crevices and
holes of the basaltic walls—the same never-ending song that it has
sung through the thousands of years that are past, and will go on
singing through thousands of years to come. And the snow whirls
along in its age-old dance; it spreads itself in all the crevices and hol-
lows, but it does not succeed in covering up the stones on the beach;
black as ever, they project into the night. On the open space in front
of the hut two figures are running up and down like shadows in the
winter darkness to keep themselves warm, and so they will run up
and down on the path they have trampled out, day after day, till the
spring comes.

"Sunday, December 1st. Wonderfully beautiful weather for the last
few days; one can never weary of going up and down outside, while
the moon transforms the whole of this ice-world into a fairy-land. The

hut is still in shadow under the mountain which hangs above it, dark and lowering; but the moonlight floats over ice and fjord, and is cast back glittering from every snowy ridge and hill. A weird beauty, without feeling, as though of a dead planet, built of shining white marble. Just so must the mountains stand there, frozen and icy cold; just so must the lakes lie congealed beneath their snowy covering; and now as ever the moon sails silently and slowly on her endless course through the lifeless space. And everything so still, so awfully still, with the silence that shall one day reign when the earth again becomes desolate and empty, when the fox will no more haunt these moraines, when the bear will no longer wander about on the ice out there, when even the wind will not rage—infinite silence! In the flaming aurora borealis the spirit of space hovers over the frozen waters. The soul bows down before the majesty of night and death.

"Monday, December 2d. Morning. To-day I can hear it blowing again outside, and we shall have an unpleasant walk. It is bitterly cold now in our worn, greasy clothes. It is not so bad when there is no wind; but even if there is only a little it goes right through one. But what does it matter? Will not the spring one day come here too? Yes; and over us arches the same heaven now as always, high and calm as ever; and as we walk up and down here shivering we gaze into the boundless starry space, and all our privations and sorrows shrink into nothingness. Starlit night, thou art sublimely beautiful! But dost thou not lend our spirit too mighty wings, greater than we can control? Couldst thou but solve the riddle of existence! We feel ourselves the centre of the universe, and struggle for life, for immortality—one seeking it here, another hereafter—while thy silent splendor proclaims: At the command of the Eternal, you came into existence on a paltry planet, as diminutive links in the endless chain of transformations; at another command, you will be wiped out again. Who then, through an eternity of eternities, will remember that there once was an ephemeral being who could bind sound and light in chains, and who was purblind enough to spend years of his brief existence in drifting through frozen seas? Is, then, the whole thing but the meteor of a moment? Will the whole history of the world evaporate like a dark, gold-edged cloud in the glow of evening—achieving nothing, leaving no trace, passing like a caprice?

"Evening. That fox is playing us a great many tricks; whatever he can move he goes off with. He has once gnawed off the band with which the door-skin is fastened, and every now and then we hear him at it again, and have to go out and knock on the roof of the passage. To-day he went off with one of our sails, in which our salt-water ice was lying. We were not a little alarmed when we went to fetch ice and found sail and all gone. We had no doubt as to who had been there, but we could not under any circumstances afford to lose our precious sail, on which we depended for our voyage to Spitzbergen in the spring, and we tramped about in the dark, up the beach, over the level, and down towards the sea. We looked everywhere, but nothing was to be seen of it. At last we had almost given it up when Johansen, in going on to the ice to get more salt-water ice, found it at the edge of the shore. Our joy was great; but it was wonderful that the fox had been able to drag that great sail, full of ice too, so far. Down there, however, it had come unfolded, and then he could do nothing with it. But what does he want with things like this? Is it to lie upon in his winter den? One would almost think so. I only wish I could come upon that den, and find the thermometer again, and the ball of twine, and the harpoon-line, and all the other precious things he has taken, the brute!

"Thursday, December 5th. It seems as if it would never end. But patience a little longer, and spring will come, the fairest spring that earth can give us. There is furious weather outside, and snow, and it is pleasant to lie here in our warm hut, eating steak, and listening to the wind raging over us.

"Tuesday, December 10th. It has been a bad wind. Johansen discovered to-day that his kayak had disappeared. After some search he found it again several hundred feet off, up the beach; it was a good deal knocked about, too. The wind must first have lifted it right over my kayak, and then over one big stone after another. It begins to be too much of a good thing when even the kayaks take to flying about in the air. The atmosphere is dark out over the sea, so the wind has probably broken up the ice, and driven it out, and there is open water once more.*

"Last night it all at once grew wonderfully calm, and the air was surprisingly mild. It was delightful to be out, and it is long since we have had such a long walk on our beat. It does one good to stretch one's legs now and then, otherwise I suppose we should become quite stiff here in our winter lair. Fancy, only 12° (21 1/2° Fahr.) of frost in the middle of December! We might almost imagine ourselves at home—forget that we were in a land of snow to the north of the eighty-first parallel.

"Thursday, December 12th. Between six and nine this morning there were a number of shooting-stars, most of them in Serpentarius. Some came right from the Great Bear; afterwards they chiefly came from the Bull, or Aldebaran, or the Pleiades. Several of them were very bright, and some drew a streak of shining dust after them. Lovely weather. But night and day are now equally dark. We walk up and down, up and down, on the level, in the darkness. Heaven only knows how many steps we shall take on that level before the winter ends. Through the gloom we could see faintly only the black cliffs, and the rocky ridges, and the great stones on the beach, which the wind always sweeps clean. Above us the sky, clear and brilliant with stars, sheds its peace over the earth; far in the west falls shower after shower of stars, some faint, scarcely visible, others bright like Roman candles, all with a message from distant worlds. Low in the south lies a bank of clouds, now and again outlined by the gleam of the northern lights; but out over the sea the sky is dark; there is open water there. It is quite pleasant to look at it; one does not feel so shut in; it is like a connecting link with life, that dark sea, the mighty artery of the world, which carries tidings from land to land, from people to people, on which civilization is borne victorious through the earth; next summer it will carry us home.

---

*It often blew very fresh there under the mountain. Another time, one of my snow-shoes, which was stuck into the snowdrift beside the hut, was broken short off by the wind. It was a strong piece of maple.

The Abduction
Kilime sings:

Let me cleave words,
sharp little words,
like the fire-wood
that I split with my axe!
A song of old times,
a gust of soul from ancestors,
a song of oblivion for my wife,
a song to soothe the longing
overwhelming me!
This loud-mouth's
ravished her, belittled her:
a wretched cannibal
who loves to eat men's flesh,
in times of scarcity!

Eqerqo replies:

Shameless impudence!
Half-hearted coward!
You want to put the blame on me
and scare me, with your mockery?
But I'm indifferent
to the risk of being killed.
Look: it's my wife that you sing about.
She was yours once,
but you weren't quite so loving
at the time.

When she was all alone,
you never praised her
in your fighting challenge-songs.
Now she's mine,
and won't go visiting
false lovers, womanisers,
singing beautifully
in strange tents.

—Kilime and Eqerqo (East Greenland Eskimo men)

$\mathcal{M}inik\ \mathcal{D}emands\ \mathcal{H}is$ $\mathcal{F}ather's\ \mathcal{B}ody$

MINIK INTERVIEWED BY *SAN FRANCISCO EXAMINER* (GREENLANDIC, 1909)

T he American explorer Robert Peary made it his life's ambition
to be the first man to stand at the North Pole, and he spent
twenty-three years trying to get there. To fund his burning ambition, Peary employed many methods, including, as was a
common practice among the British explorers, naming prominent
landmarks after his expeditions' benefactors. (Thus a prominent
peninsula in the Canadian Arctic is named the Boothia Peninsula, in
honor of the London gin manufacturer who backed the Ross expedition of 1829, and the northernmost cape of Greenland bears the
name Morris Jesup, after the banking and railroad magnate who was
one of Peary's leading backers.) Peary also brought back goods from
the Arctic and converted them to cash, according to Kenn Harper's
Give Me My Father's Body. Among these were packets of furs and
narwhal tusks ostensibly destined for the American Museum of Natural History in New York City, Harper writes, thus avoiding U.S.
Customs duties, and big meteorites that he plucked off of Greenland
and that had served as the Polar Inuits' main source of iron to make
harpoon heads. Peary, through his wife, sold the meteorites to the
museum, one of which weighed nearly forty tons, for $50,000.

Worse, he brought six Polar Inuit to New York in 1897. Housed
in the museum's basement, four of the six quickly died of pneumo-

193

nia, one returned to Greenland, and the eight-year-old boy Minik survived. After Minik's father died in the boy's arms, museum officials arranged a fake burial for young Minik to witness and then kept the father's body for the museum's collections. Minik was adopted by the museum's building superintendent and learned to speak English fluently. Still, it was years before he realized his wish to return to Greenland and not until many years later was Minik's father's body returned to his homeland. On his return to Greenland, Minik stayed seven years but felt he no longer fit in his own culture. He returned once more to the United States and died soon after during the influenza epidemic of 1918 while working at a logging camp in northern New Hampshire. Minik today has a kind of legendary status among the Inuit of northern Greenland, and many stories are told about him.

The following excerpt appeared in the *San Francisco Examiner* on May 9, 1909, a month after Peary supposedly reached the Pole but before he's broken his ship out of the ice and informed the world of his alleged accomplishment. It is difficult to know whether the dramatic language is that of Minik, nineteen years old at the time, or of the newspaper writer. The newspaper titled the interview "Why Arctic Explorer Peary's Neglected Eskimo Boy Wants to Shoot Him."

Minik Wallace's Dilemma

When Mr. Peary came to us, twelve years ago, we had never seen a white man. Our tribe welcomed him and helped him with guides, hunters, dogs and every hospitality.

At the start, Peary was kind enough to my people. He made them presents of ornaments, a few knives and guns for hunting, and wood to build sledges. But as soon as he was ready to start home his other work began.

Before our eyes he packed up the bones of our dead friends and ancestors. To the women's crying and the men's questioning he answered that he was taking our dead friends to a warm and pleasant land to bury them. Our sole supply of flint for lighting and iron for hunting and cooking implements was furnished by a huge meteorite. This Peary put aboard his steamer and took from my poor people, who needed it so much. After this he coaxed my father and that brave man Natooka, who were the staunchest hunters and the wisest heads for our tribe, to go with him to America.

Our people were afraid to let them go, but Peary promised them that they should have Natooka and my father back within a year, and that with them would come a great stock of guns and ammunition, and wood and metal and presents for the women and children. So that my father believed that for so much good and comfort to his people they should let him and Natooka risk the trip. Natooka could not part from Artoona, his wife, and his little girl, Ahweah, so he took them with him. My mother was dead, and my father would not go without me, so the five of us said a last farewell to home and went on Peary's ship.

We were crowded into the hold of the vessel and treated like dogs. Peary seldom came near us. When we reached the end of the sea voyage we were given the most miserable and unhealthy quarters on the steamship Kite, and lay off Brooklyn for several days on exhibition.

After this we were sent to the Museum of Natural History in New York. There we were quartered in a damp cellar most unfavourable to people from the dry air of the North. One after another we became ill and began to die off; during the fourth month my poor father died; at last I alone remained.

After my father died they took me out into the garden of the museum to see him buried. They lowered a big box into the ground and told me to say goodby to him. That box was filled with stones, and father—my father—his body even then was in the museum being prepared for exhibition. My father on exhibition!

Unexpectedly one day I came face to face with it. I felt as though I must die then and there. I threw myself at the bottom of the glass case and prayed and wept. I went straight to the director and implored him to let me bury my father. He would not. I swore I never would rest until I had given my father burial.

I have lived on and on and have made appeal after appeal, but none has been granted. Mr. Wallace has been good to me, but he can do nothing. Mr. Beecroft has been a true friend, but he has not the power to give me what I want. I prayed to Peary to take me with him upon this last voyage and leave me in my home in Greenland, but he refused me. I had tried to study at Manhattan College so that I could be wise and go North in good time and help my unhappy people, but I am not fitted for your ways or your life.

I have felt that I must go North, back to Greenland somehow, some way. I am a burden on my friends and I see clearly that as long as I live they will have me a weight upon their hands helping me always. I would die for Mr. Wallace and Mr. Beecroft, but I won't be a burden on them. I can never forgive Peary and I hope to see him to show him the wreck he has caused.

I have lost hope. I lost it when Peary refused to take me with him this last trip. And I have given up believing your Christian creed that you taught me was meant for one and all—Christian and savage alike. I gave that up finally when Professor Bumpus at the museum told me for the last time I could not have my father's bones to bury them. Where is your Christianity? My own people are kinder and better, more human, and I am going back to them. My land is frozen and desolate, but we can bury our dead there. What has your civilization done to my people and me but harm us? We are tens now where we were thousands, and what is left is dying fast through your work.

I shall go back to die with my people as soon as I am well enough again to start. My father knows that if I cannot give his bones burial it is not because I have not tried with all that is in me. I even went to Albany because I believed the Assembly would help me, but now I know they won't.

Let me tell you more about my father and me. They brought me down from my home, where I would naturally have fallen into the way of making a living, and where, no doubt, I would have been at least happy and healthy, and they set me adrift where everything is strange and nearly everything hostile. I am in no way fitted to follow a business life such as you people have been trained in for generations. I cannot bear the confinement of a public school class room—it makes me deathly sick in a few days—and I have no funds nor will I burden my few friends for them to secure tutoring or private instruction; so I can only grow into a nonentity, useless to myself and more or less a freak to those about me. It was so at Manhattan College and I saw it could never be different. So much for me.

My father was taken from me, a martyr to the cold-blooded, scientific study of your people. His body was refused a burial, even after he gave his life to your science, and is now degraded to a mere exhibition relic for no greater purpose than to amuse the visitors of a museum. He was dearer to me than anything else in the world—especially when we were brought to New York, strangers in a strange land.

You can imagine how closely that brought us together, how our disease and suffering and lack of understanding of all the strange things around us, and the ominous death of the three other Eskimo of our party, who one by one bade us a sad farewell, made us sit tremblingly waiting our turn to go—more and more lonesome and alone, hopelessly far from home, we grew to depend on one another, and to love each other as no father and son under ordinary conditions could possibly love. Every morning he would come and sit beside me until I wakened, almost crazy to know how I felt, and yet too tender to arouse me from my rest. How he would smile if I was a little better, and how he would sob, with big tears in his eyes when I was suffering.

Aside from hopeless loneliness do you know what it is to be sad— to feel a terrible longing to go home, and to know that you are absolutely without hope? Ah, you cannot know! And then add to this the horror of knowing that death was waiting near for us, and that one must go first and leave the other all alone—awfully alone, no one who even understands your language—no one except grief. Aside from these tortures my poor father was suffering frightfully from disease. His neck was terribly swollen from tuberculosis, and his chest ached so badly that he could not rest. And yet, in spite of all this, his whole thought was constantly of me. He watched over me night and day, denying himself sleep and even food, and when anything was brought for me to eat he insisted on giving it to me himself—coaxing me and praising the food—and if I seemed to like it big tears would come in his eyes and he would laugh—half laugh and half cry—and pat me on the cheeks.

He wanted to do everything for me with his own hands and watched every one who came near me. His greatest suffering was when he grew so weak that he was obliged to remain still in bed and could not come to me. And I cried all the time, and could no longer eat for fear my father would die. Then I grew better, probably because I was so anxious to be with him, and soon I was allowed to go to him and lie near him. He did not notice any of the doctors' torture after that.

One day a doctor accidentally or carelessly burnt my arm with an iron. My father saw the sore, and when I told him that it was a burn, he got out of bed, enraged, as weak and sick as he was, and I am sure he would have killed the doctor. I was terribly frightened, and for the first time I lied to my father. I told him that I had burned my arm on a gaslight. Then he took me in his arms and kissed me and said in Eskimo, 'Mene must be careful for his father's sake.' The next morning my father was dead. The strain had been too great for him, and he nearly suffocated during the night, and cried out for his home, his family, his friends and me. I put my head under a pillow crying hard. They tried to take me from the room, and my father saw them and realized what it was. He called to me and I ran into his arms. He knew that he must leave me, and his grief was terrible. 'Father's spirit will stay with Mene always,' he said in Eskimo, choking hard. Father was dying then I know, but I think his poor heart broke and that is what killed him.

I thought my heart was broken, too! That sad, long lonesome day! . . . Oh, they have given me a thousand deaths! When I could be of no further use to them and my illness frightened them, they turned me adrift—and yet I am not dead. I wish I was, I wish I was!

How can I get justice from those who took me from my home, robbed me of all that was dear to me and have made me a prisoner here.

Think of the injustice of it all. Think of that burial of stones or a piece of wood instead of what I thought was my father's body. When I found out can any one imagine what I felt? You see, we Greenlanders have some curious beliefs about burial. We think a spirit cannot rest unless it is safely in the earth. My father, who held to the beliefs of the tribe had begged me again and again to see that he was buried according to the rites of the tribe. But how could a child see to this? Since I have found out about the way they did, I have tried everything. What I wanted to do was to get the remains of my father, take them with his spear and sled and carry them with me up to Greenland. That would be the way I could have justice. Surely this country owes me justice; the State owes it.

Song of Derision about Wife-Swapping

Kangitsukaq (The Little Headless One) once challenged Kuitse (The Spilt Water) before the latter was quite grown up. Kuitse did not forget the challenge, and reported himself ready for song-contest the moment he was a grown man.

A gust of air hangs over me!
I'm like this,
I can't help it,
Sing I must,
and open up my mouth
to words and notes.
Perhaps it may turn out a useful song,
a song that finds its mark
in somebody who needs it:
useful to some easily-disgusted man,
a man who breaks a friendship suddenly,
a man who's soon disgusted with the friend
he swaps his wife with!

You are such a man, my enemy!
Isn't it true
you quickly broke with
Angutange,
with whom you'd shared
the pleasant game
of putting out the lamps with women?

Isn't it true
you soon got bored and sick of him—
and since then, been a lonely man,
with no one to swap wives with you?

But look at me!
Good men flock around me

and present their women
in exchange for mine.
They come in trust
because they know
I'm not a reckless man,
rejecting women,
separating man from wife.

This is how I am:
I won't get hurt,
I won't risk witchcraft
and revenge.
I love women.
I'm a woman-lover.
I don't let them pass me by.

Evil news was often
brought us from Cape Dan,
when men in kayaks came and visited.
It was pleasant things one heard!
It has been said
(Yes, a little rumour reached my ear)
that my opponent
nearly killed his wife-swap friend!

The reason?
They say it was a dog
he had presented to his friend,
a token from the days
they'd happily swapped wives.
But later, he forgot those joys,
and tried to kill his gift,
to kill the dog.

Yes, this is what he's like,
my contest-enemy.
And as I sing
amusing little details
come to mind:

I was out at sea, on winter ice,
travelling by sleigh outside the vil-
    lage,
hunting bear.
I saw a mother with her cub,
come wandering,
the young one in the mother's
    tracks.
I caught up with them,
and while my barking dogs
forced them to stop,
I quietly
sought the adult out.

His dogs never would approach
that sort of game:
that wretched team
is hardly trained to hunt.
They'll never even see
a living bear:
pitiful bags of skin and bones they
    are,
with coats which could at most
be used for covering a kayak.
Yes, this how my song of mockery's
    turned out.
I hope it reaches folk
who want a bit of entertainment!

Kuitse answers:
Look at him!
Just look at what he's like, my
    song-adversary!

Listen to his rant,
and how he uses that great mouth,
like everybody in his village!

He finds nothing difficult,
nothing's difficult to call to mind.
But I'm more careful in my choice
    of words,
and wouldn't dare to sing of every-
    thing that passed.

Now, there were my male cousins,
and all my dearest female cousins,
who sailed off on a long journey,
and never returned.
All my loved ones
this man mocked in song,
this thin-shitter, this fat-belly!

So what remains for me to sing
    about,
now you've roared your head off
about things I'd rather not recall?
You always were so amiable,
always had such gentle ways:
you haven't got an evil reputation
    to expose.
And yet . . . what was it I heard
    . . .

What was the rumour
that did reach my ears?

IT WAS YOU WHO TRIED TO
    KILL MIGSSUARNIANGA,
    THE MAN WITH CRIPPLED
    LEGS!

When I heard the talk,
I had to stop and ask myself:
could such a carcase-eater,

201

fat of belly, round of loins,
have strength in him to kill?
Well, it was cunning of you
to pick a paralytic,
being such a lazy-bones,

whom no one equals dozing
on the hot fur-covers of the bench!

—Kangitsukaq and Kuitse
(East Greenland Eskimo men)

Cook Makes a Claim on the Pole and Asks: "Was It Worth It?"

BY DR. FREDERICK A. COOK (AMERICAN, 1908)

O n April 21, 1908, Frederick Cook stood with his Inuit companions Ahwelah and Etukishook and their dog teams on the North Pole. Or so he said. Whether he did in fact has been hotly disputed since Robert Peary and his supporters undertook a massive campaign of slander against Cook and his alleged achievement in order to claim the prize for the ruthlessly ambitious Peary. Peary claimed *he* reached the North Pole the following April, while Cook was still on his epic return journey. The laurels were summarily ripped from Cook by the press and public and bestowed on Peary. Here with Peary they remained for the next several decades, while Cook languished in prison on an alleged stock-fraud scheme (he was later pardoned by President Franklin D. Roosevelt). In recent years, however, Peary's claim has come under scrutiny and deep doubt, as the calculations have shown that he would have to have made an incredibly fast return journey to achieve what he claimed.

Whether Cook or Peary reached the Pole is immaterial these many decades later. The lessons of the final race to the Pole, and the inflamed and tawdry controversies that followed, shed less light on geography than they do on the human character and the nature of ambition. The Inuit, whose home was the top of the world, had not the slightest interest in being the first to stand at the Pole. There was no game that far north, so why go? Peary's and Cook's brand of ambition was another of the many imports from the South, and within ambition's narrow confines, as Robert Peary made abundantly clear, there was not room enough to share.

In this respect, whether he "attained" the Pole or not, Frederick Cook, and not Peary, was the explorer who returned from the empty expanses of ice with some worthwhile knowledge. In this excerpt from Cook's *My Attainment of the Pole*, he describes his party's arrival at the Pole and then, upon departing it, wonders whether the human endeavor and suffering expended over the centuries to reach the North Pole had been worth the goal.

With the Pole only twenty-nine miles distant, more sleep was quite impossible. We brewed an extra pot of tea, prepared a favorite broth of pemmican, dug up a surprise of fancy biscuits and filled up on good things to the limit of the allowance for our final feast days. The dogs, which had joined the chorus of gladness, were given an extra lump of pemmican. A few hours more were agreeably spent in the tent. Then we started out with new spirit for the uttermost goal of our world.

Bounding joyously forward, with a stimulated mind, I reviewed the journey. Obstacle after obstacle had been overcome. Each battle won gave a spiritual thrill, and courage to scale the next barrier. Thus had been ever, and was still, in the unequal struggles between human and inanimate nature, an incentive to go onward, ever onward, up the stepping-stones to ultimate success. And now, after a life-denying struggle in a world where every element of Nature is against the life and progress of man, triumph came with steadily measured reaches of fifteen miles a day!

We were excited to fever heat. Our feet were light on the run. Even the dogs caught the infectious enthusiasm. They rushed along at a pace which made it difficult for me to keep a sufficient advance to set a good course. The horizon was still eagerly searched for something to mark the approaching boreal center. But nothing unusual was seen. The same expanse of moving seas of ice, on which we had gazed for five hundred miles, swarm about us as we drove onward.

Looking through gladdened eyes, the scene assumed a new glory. Dull blue and purple expanses were transfigured into plains of gold, in which were lakes of sapphire and rivulets of ruby fire. Engirdling this world were purple mountains with gilded crests. It was one of the few days on the stormy pack when all Nature smiled with cheering lights.

As the day advanced beyond midnight and the splendor of the summer night ran into a clearer continued day, the beams of gold on the surface snows assumed a more burning intensity. Shadows of hummocks and ice ridges became dyed with a deeper purple, and in the burning orange world loomed before us Titan shapes, regal and regally robed.

From my position, a few hundred yards ahead of the sleds, with compass and axe in hand, as usual, I could not resist the temptation to turn frequently to see the movement of the dog train with its new fire. In this backward direction the color scheme was reversed. About the horizon the icy walls gleamed like beaten gold set with gem-spots of burning colors; the plains represented every shade of purple and blue, and over them, like vast angel wings outspread, shifted golden pinions. Through the sea of palpitating color, the dogs came, with spirited tread, noses down, tails erect and shoulders braced to the straps, like chariot horses. In the magnifying light they seemed many times their normal size. The young Eskimos, chanting songs of love, followed with easy, swinging steps. The long whip was swung with a brisk crack. Over all arose a cloud of frosted breath, which, like incense smoke, became silvered in the light, a certain signal of efficient motive power.

We all were lifted to the paradise of winners as we stepped over the snows of a destiny for which we had risked life and willingly suffered the tortures of an icy hell. The ice under us, the goal for centuries of brave, heroic men, to reach which many had suffered terribly and terribly died, seemed almost sacred. Constantly and carefully I watched my instruments in recording this final reach. Nearer and nearer they recorded our approach. Step by step, my heart filled with a strange rapture of conquest.

At last we step over colored fields of sparkle, climbing walls of purple and gold—finally, under skies of crystal blue, with flaming clouds of glory, we touch the mark! The soul awakens to a definite triumph; there is sunrise within us, and all the world of night-darkened trouble fades. We are at the top of the world! The flag is flung to the frigid breezes of the North Pole!

In building our igloo the boys frequently looked about expectantly. Often they ceased cutting snowblocks and rose to a hummock to search the horizon for something which, to their idea, must mark this important spot, for which we had struggled against hope and all the dictates of personal comforts. At each breathing spell their eager eyes picked some sky sign which to them meant land or water, or the play of some god of land or sea. The naive and sincere interest which the Eskimos on occasions feel in the mystery of the spirit-world gives them an imaginative appreciation of nature often in excess of that of the more material and skeptical Caucasian.

Arriving at the mysterious place where, they felt, something should happen, their imagination now forced an expression of disappointment. In a high-keyed condition, all their superstitions recurred to them with startling reality.

In one place the rising vapor proved to be the breath of the great submarine god—the *"Ko-Koyah."* In another place, a motionless little cloud marked the land in which dwelt the *"Turnah-huch-suak,"* the great Land God, and the air spirits were represented by the different winds, with sex relations.

Ah-weh-lah and E-tuk-i-shook, with the astuteness of the aborigine, who reads Nature as a book, were sharp enough to note that the high air currents did not correspond to surface currents; for, although the wind was blowing homeward, and changed its force and direction, a few high clouds moved persistently in a different direction.

This, to them, indicated a warfare among the air spirits. The ice and snow were also animated. To them the whole world presented a rivalry of conflicting spirits which offered never-ending topics of conversation.

As the foot pressed the snow, its softness, its rebound, or its metallic ring indicated sentiments of friendliness or hostility. The ice, by its color, movement or noise, spoke the humor of its animation, or that of the supposed life of the restless sea beneath it. In interpreting these spirit signs, the two expressed considerable difference of opinion. Ah-we-lah saw dramatic situations and became almost hysterical with excitement; E-tuk-i-shook saw only a monotone of the normal play of life. Such was the trend of interest and conversation as the building of the igloos was completed.

Contrary to our usual custom, the dogs had been allowed to rest in their traces attached to the sleds. Their usual malicious inquisitiveness exhausted, they were too tired to examine the sleds to steal food. But now, as the house was completed, holes were chipped with a knife in ice-shoulders, through which part of a trace was passed, and each team was thus securely fastened to a ring cut in ice-blocks. Then each dog was given a double ration of pemmican. Their pleasure was expressed by an extra twist of the friendly tails and an extra note of gladness from long-contracted stomachs. Finishing their meal, they curled up and warmed the snow, from which they took an occasional bite to furnish liquid for their gastric economy. Almost two days of rest followed, and this was the canine celebration of the Polar attainment.

We withdrew to the inside of the dome of snowblocks, pulled in a block to close the doors, spread out our bags as beds on the platform of leveled snow, pulled off boots and trousers, and slipped half-length into the bristling reindeer furs. We then discussed, with chummy congratulations, the success of our long drive to the world's end.

While thus engaged, the little Juel stove piped the cheer of the pleasure of ice-water, soon to quench our chronic thirst. In the meantime, Ah-we-lah and E-tuk-i-shook pressed farther and farther into their bags, pulled over the hoods, and closed their eyes to an overpowering fatigue. But my lids did not easily close. I watched the fire. More ice went into the kettle. With the satisfaction of an ambition fulfilled, I peeped out occasionally through the pole-punched port, and noted the horizon glittering with gold and purple.

Quivers of self-satisfying joy ran up my spine and relieved the frosty mental bleach of the long-delayed Polar anticipation.

In due time we drank, with grateful satisfaction, large quantities of ice-water, which was more delicious than any wine. A pemmican soup, flavored with musk ox tenderloins, steaming with heat—a luxury seldom enjoyed in our camps—next went down with warming, satisfying gulps. This was followed by a few strips of frozen fresh meat, then by a block of pemmican. Later, a few squares of musk ox suet gave the taste of sweets to round up our meal. Last of all, three cups of tea spread the chronic stomach-folds, after which we reveled in the sense of fulness of the best meal of many weeks.

With full stomachs and the satisfaction of a worthy task well performed, we rested.

We had reached the zenith of man's Ultima Thule, which had been sought for more than three centuries. In comfortable berths of snow we tried to sleep, turning with the earth on its northern axis.

But sleep for me was impossible. At six o'clock, or six hours after our arrival at local noon, I arose, went out of the igloo, and took a double set of observations. Returning, I did some figuring, lay down on my bag, and at ten o'clock, or four hours later, leaving Ah-we-lah to guard the camp and dogs, E-tuk-i-shook joined me to make a tent camp about four miles to the magnetic south. My object was to have a slightly different position for subsequent observations.

Placing our tent, bags and camp equipment on a sled, we pushed it over the ice field, crossed a narrow lead sheeted with young ice, and moved on to another field which seemed to have much greater dimensions. We erected the tent not quite two hours later, in time for a midnight observation. These sextant readings of the sun's altitude were continued for the next twenty-four hours.

In the idle times between observations, I went over to a new break between the field on which we were camped and that on which Ah-weh-lah guarded the dogs. Here the newly-formed sheets of ice slid over each other as the great, ponderous fields stirred to and fro. A peculiar noise, like that of a crying child, arose. It came seemingly from everywhere, intermittently, in successive crying spells. Lying down, and putting my fur-cushioned ear to the edge of the old ice, I heard a distant thundering noise, the reverberations of the moving, grinding pack, which, by its wind-driven sweep, was drifting over the unseen seas of mystery. In an effort to locate the cry, I searched diligently along the lead. I came to a spot where two tiny pieces of ice served as a mouthpiece. About every fifteen seconds there were two or three sharp, successive cries. With the ice-axe I detached one. The cries stopped; but other cries were heard further along the line.

The time for observations was at hand, and I returned to take up the sextant. Returning later to the lead, to watch the seas breathe, the cry seemed stilled. The thin ice-sheets were cemented together, and in an open space nearby I had an opportunity to study the making and breaking of the polar ice.

That tiny film of ice which voiced the baby cries spreads the world's most irresistible power. In its making we have the nucleus for the origin of the polar pack, that great moving crust of the earth which crunches ships, grinds rocks, and sweeps mountains into the sea. Beginning as a mere microscopic crystal, successive crystals, by their affinity for each other, unite to make a disc. These discs, by the same law of cohesion, assemble and unite. Now the thin sheet, the first sea ice, is complete, and either rests to make the great field of ice, or spreads from floe to floe and from field to field, thus spreading, bridging and mending the great moving masses which cover the mid-polar basin.

There was about us no land. No fixed point. Absolutely nothing upon which to rest the eye to give the sense of location or to judge distance.

Here everything moves. The sea breathes, and lifts the crust of ice which the wind stirs. The pack ever drifts in response to the pull of the air and the drive of the water. Even the sun, the only fixed dot in this stirring, restless world, where all you see is, without your seeing it, moving like a ship at sea, seems to have a rapid movement in a gold-flushed circle not far above endless fields of purple crystal; but that movement is never higher, never lower—always in the same fixed path. The instruments detect a slight spiral ascent, day after day, but the eye detects no change.

After a midnight observation—of April 22—we returned to camp. When the dogs saw us approaching in the distance they rose, and a chorus of howls rang over the regions of the Pole—regions where dogs had never howled before. All the scientific work being finished, we began hastily to make final preparations for departure.

We had spent two days about the North Pole. After the first thrills of victory, the glamor wore away as we rested and worked. Although I tried to do so, I could get no sensation of novelty as we pitched our last belongings on the sleds. The intoxication of success had gone. I suppose intense emotions are invariably followed by reactions. Hungry, mentally and physically exhausted, a sense of the utter uselessness of this thing, of the empty reward of my endurance, followed my exhilaration. I had grasped my *ignus fatuus*. It is a misfortune for any man when his *ignus fatuus* fails to elude him.

During those last hours I asked myself why this place had so aroused an enthusiasm long-lasting through self-sacrificing years; why, for so many centuries, men had sought this elusive spot? What a futile thing, I thought, to die for! How tragically useless all those heroic efforts—efforts, in themselves, a travesty, an ironic satire, on much vainglorious human aspiration and endeavor! I thought of the enthusiasm of the people who read of the spectacular efforts of men to reach this vacant silver-shining goal of death. I thought, too, in that hour, of the many men of science who were devoting their lives to the study of germs, the making of toxins; to the saving of men from the grip of disease—men who often lost their own lives in their experiments; whose world and work existed in unpicturesque laboratories, and for whom the laudations of people never rise. It occurred to me—and I felt the bitterness of tears in my soul—that it is often the showy and futile deeds of men which men praise; and that, after all, the only work worth while, the only value of a human being's efforts, lie in deeds whereby humanity benefits. Such work as noble bands of women accomplish who go into the slums of great cities, who nurse the sick, who teach the ignorant, who engage in social service humbly, patiently, unexpectant of any reward! Such work as does the scientist who studies the depredations of malignant germs, who straightens the body of the crippled child, who precipitates a toxin which cleanses the blood of a frightful and loathsome disease!

As my eye sought the silver and purple desert about me for some stable object upon which to fasten itself, I experienced an abject abandon, an intolerable loneliness. With my two companions I could not converse; in my thoughts and emotions they could not share. I was alone. I was victorious. But how desolate, how dreadful was this victory! About us was no life, no spot to relieve the monotony of frost. We were the only pulsating creatures in a dead world of ice.

Dispute between Women

Songs of derision from a contest between Paninguaq (Little Daughter)
and her cousin Sapangajagadleq (The Pearl)

Little Daughter dances and sings:

It seems high time
I challenged you to song-contest!
Yes, my anger wakes!

I was out fetching fire
(domesticated as ever)
when you, in foolish vanity
began to flaunt yourself
before my step-father.
Do I lie or speak the truth?
Come forward: test me,
while my anger grows!

The Pearl jumps forward,
dances and sings:

Come over to this side,
those who will defend me!
Take the wick of the lamp,
dip it in oil, light it,
allow the light
to fall on Little Daughter's
*   face!*
Do you hear me, cousin?
Do I lie or speak the truth?
I took you by surprise one day
in bed with Asarpana!

Mock her with me,
those who take my side!
Take her, friends,
and throw her to the ground!
Cousin, you don't still think
that you're a match for me?
Let's close our fists and punch!

Come, we'll have a race:
the winner takes the loser's man!

At this point, The Pearl jumps
forward again, with a song intended
to make the audience laugh:

Ija-ja-hrra
ajai-jai-hrra,
aj-ja-a-ha!
Oh let me be
a little naughty!
Ai-ja-a-ha!
Just a little bad!
If only there were
someone who would stroke,
or only touch my cunt:
I shouldn't then
be angry or resent
another woman
smiling at my man!
Ai-ja-a-ha!

Little Daughter:

Umaya—ima,
Ha-ja-ja!
I'm easy to make jealous,
quick to rage!
Here I stand,
forgetting my poor songs.

But listen, cousin:
you're too eager
to deride me in your song;
let's pay a visit
to the people by the sand.

There I'll make an answer
to your clumsy mockery!

The company rises, and goes down to
the village by the sand. On the way,
The Pearl sings:

I'll have no mercy
for the people by the sand:
they won't be friends of yours for long.
I'll show them
what you girls are really like:
all smiles outside,
but unchaste underneath,
willing to fuck casually with men,
and then give birth
in secret in the hills.
Do I lie or speak the truth?
I often envy
folk who slept at night
in ignorance of what went on.
Chaste people don't see anything.
But there are those who say
that you, too, secretly gave birth.
Do I lie or speak the truth?

At this, Little Daughter bursts into tears. And
now The Pearl has an idea:

Let's sing,
let's go and see the people by the
*   sand!*
We'll open Little Daughter's
*   sewing-box,*
mess it up, reveal
her secrets!
Catch hold of Little Daughter,
friends!

They grab her, and hold on to her, while The
Pearl continues singing:

The festival unites us,
draws us close!
Twist her loins,
rock her hips!

And they force Little Daughter to dance, while
The Pearl goes on singing:

We'll ruthlessly reveal,
her hidden thoughts!
Together we'll expose her:
she who always coveted my man.
My anger, cousin, has arrived!

They reach the village. But here The Pearl's
husband unexpectedly leaps
forward into the circle and sings:

Now my anger wakes!
Do you hear! Do you hear!
I'm feeling like a fight!
Do you hear! Do you hear!
Let's break into the house,
upset the piss-pot,
tear the membrane window out,
chuck the lamp on the shit-heap,
let the boiled meat follow suit!
Destroy, destroy the racks
of meat and skins!
I'm ready for a fight:
I'm hot with rage,
I'm hot for song, for song!

Look, here's this wretched girl
I had my fun with.
Like animals in heat we were,
when we went walking in the
*   hills.*

Oh, I remember how we hid
up on the Great Lichen mountain,

213

that sweet playground
for male animals!
Wagging our tails,
we looked out on
the sunny country of the south,
while we threw ourselves
down into the heather . . .

But what is happening?
Will no-one answer me?

Then shut your mouths!
We're going home,
and you can rest.
Daylight envelops the mountain.
Dawn has taken over from the
      night.

—Paninguaq and Sapangajagadleq
(West Greenland Eskimo women)

214

Amundsen Answers, "Yes."

BY ROALD AMUNDSEN (NORWEGIAN, 1927)

oald Amundsen of Norway was one of the most methodi-
cal, exacting, and by most measures successful of all Arctic
explorers. Amundsen as a boy idolized the great Nansen,
his countryman, and began training to become an Arctic
explorer when he was fifteen, though his mother was pushing him
toward medical school. He nearly lost his life at age twenty-two
when he attempted a winter traverse of one of Norway's mountain
plateaus, but from that experience he learned invaluable lessons
about planning. Studying other Arctic expeditions that had failed,
he realized that he needed to know how to navigate a boat as well as
command an expedition. He signed on as a sailor and eventually
joined the Belgian Antarctic Expedition to research the South
Magnetic Pole. The ship was trapped in the Antarctic ice for thirteen months, though unprepared for even a single Antarctic winter.
The ship's doctor happened to be the young Frederick Cook, of
later notoriety, and for whom Amundsen developed a lifelong affection and admiration. It was the good-natured Cook whose ingenuity and energy on several occasions saved the expedition, such as

when he fashioned mats of penguin skins to cushion the ship's hull against the battering ice.

On his return to Europe after two years, Amundsen, then in his late twenties, decided to make an attempt at sailing the Northwest Passage, which had eluded and destroyed would-be European discoverers for the last four hundred years though McClure and company had completed it on foot. He sought and received the blessing of Nansen and eminent scientists who wished for data on the magnetic pole. He then bought a small fishing smack and began to stock it for three years, but had trouble lining up enough financial backers for the expedition. When one of his suppliers threatened to have Amundsen arrested for fraud unless he received payment within twenty-four hours, Amundsen hastily gathered his six-man crew and in pouring rain at midnight on June 16, 1903, cast off the lines on the *Gjoa* and sneaked from the harbor.

Three years later the world was informed by telegraph that Amundsen and his crew had successfully completed the Northwest Passage. It is a measure of the explorer's skill and ambition that to send the telegraph, he left his ship where it was locked in the ice the final winter among a whaling fleet north of Alaska, traveled by dogsled five hundred miles south over a range of 9,000-foot mountains to the closest telegraph station, sent the telegram, and dogsledded back to the ship, sailing it down to San Francisco when the ice broke.

It was with dogsleds, of course, that Amundsen and his team reached the South Pole in December 1911, just a few weeks ahead of the doomed British expedition led by Scott that attempted to drag sleds by Shetland ponies and by human power. Amundsen prepared so carefully that he and his men shaved down their sleds for weight, paid attention to such detail as redesigning the handles of their dog whips, and, to save weight in packing along food, ate their dogs one by one on the return from the Pole.

This brief excerpt is from the chapter "The Serious Business of Exploration" in Amundsen's *My Life as an Explorer*. It demonstrates some of his practical temperament compared to romantics like Cook. "Victory awaits him who has everything in order—luck, people call it," writes Amundsen. "Defeat is certain for him who has failed to take the necessary precautions—this is called bad luck." And where Cook wonders if the race to the Pole is worth the loss of life and the diversion of energy from more humane endeavors, Amundsen answers that it is.

I find that most people think of "adventure" when the word "exploration" is used. It may, therefore, be well to explain in detail the difference between the two words from the explorer's point of view. I do not mean to belittle the thirst for adventure. It is a perfectly natural longing for excitement that affects any man in normal health. Doubtless, it is an inheritance of our race from those remote ancestors whose struggle for existence involved the uncertainties of the chase, the hazards of combat with wild beasts, and the perils of the unknown. To them, life was a constant adventure, and the thrill that suffuses us in reproducing their experience is the normal thrill of healthy nerves reacting to the natural struggle for self-preservation. Our ancestors had to take the chances of death to get their daily livelihood. When we "flirt with death," we are going back to the compensating nervous pleasure of primitive man, which protected and elevated him in his daily struggle.

To the explorer, however, adventure is merely an unwelcome interruption of his serious labours. He is looking, not for thrills, but for facts about the unknown. Often his search is a race with time against starvation. To him, an adventure is merely a bit of bad planning, brought to light by the test of trial. Or it is unfortunate exemplification of the fact that no man can grasp all the possibilities of the future. Every explorer has adventures. He gets a thrill out of them, and he takes pleasure in thinking back upon them. But he never goes about looking for them. Exploration is too serious a business.

Not all would-be explorers realize this truth. The result is many a grave needlessly occupied before its time, and many a blasted hope.

"What is the good of Arctic exploration?"

How many times that question has been put to me! Doubtless, every serious explorer has had it put to him numberless times.

The most practical value of Polar exploration is the new knowledge it provides to science regarding the phenomena of terrestrial magnetism and regarding the nature of the climate and winds in those regions (which are the weather makers of the world). Elsewhere in this book I have elaborated somewhat on both these points, but here I would add that the greatest advance likely soon to be made in the accurate prediction of day-to-day weather in the North Temperate Zone will come from the erection and maintenance of permanent weather observatories on the north coasts of America, Europe, and Asia. These observatories, completely encircling the Polar Sea, and reporting several times daily by wireless to some central station, will provide far more reliable and valuable information upon which to base weather predictions than has heretofore ever been made available to man. I got some conception of how important such a chain of observatories could be by the excited gratitude of scientists that was aroused when twice daily wireless reports of the weather encountered by the *Maud* off the north coast of Asia were sent.

The other "good" of Polar exploration cannot be so definitely translated into terms of human comfort or of money saved to the world. Personally, however, I have no doubt that it is of equal value. Whatever remains to man unknown, in this world of ours, is by so much a burden on the spirits of all men. It remains a something that man has not yet conquered—a continuing evidence of his weakness, an unmet challenge to his mastery over nature. By the same token, every mystery made plain, every unknown land explored, exalts the spirit of the whole human race—strengthens its courage and exalts its spirit permanently. The trail breaker is an indispensable ally of the spiritual values which advance and sustain civilization.

The Wide Road of Song

The hunter Qaqortingneq had been out of his mind with fury because his uncle, Piuvkaq, had eaten up one of his largest caches of musk ox meat, during a spell of unsuccessful winter hunting. He was so enraged, that he threatened his uncle's life. As a result of this, Piuvkaq sang this song of derision:

Eager to breathe out,
I have prepared
this little bit of song,
along the wide road of the song:
mocking in expression,
well composed,
pointed in words,
out west, out west!

Here I am,
yes, fresh awake,
and ready for defence!

It was a winter night in the dark season.
While others lay asleep,
a sound approached:
it hit my ear,
it hit my ear,
out west, out west!

It said my kinsman,
nick-named Tight Belt,
started raving,
made a frenzied scene,
on the firm winter ice.

Petty and ill-tempered,
he gabbled about stolen food,
when everybody else was starving.

Here I am,
yes, fresh awake,
and ready for defence!

In a bitter spell
of hopeless winter hunting,

we tried to save our lives
with a little meat from your store.
That was all!

Should hunters
be so miserly?
Out west, out west!
But out you came,
with a knife in your hand,
meat-mad, raging!

In my innocence,
I didn't understand
what you were shouting.
Murder never crossed my mind!
Foolishly, I quite forgot
that—aj—a miser's mind
could be obscured like that!

But here I am
to douse you with my mockery,
to deluge you with laughter:
a cheap correction,
easy punishment!

I weave together
bits of song to answer you.
The voice must ring out clear
to drown that voice of yours!
I'm strong enough:
just feeble at inventing wickedness.
Fist-fighting's more my style
than shouted tongue-disputes.
Words all too often disappear:
words disappear like hills in mist.

—Piuvkaq (Utkuhikjalik Eskimo man)

The Short, Unhappy Flight of the Italia

BY UMBERTO NOBILE (ITALIAN, 1928)

Once humans had reached it by dogsled, a new race for the North Pole took to the air. Salomon Andrée made the first air attempt, by balloon, launching the *Eagle* in July 1897 from Spitsbergen, accompanied by two teammates. Nansen, just off the ice after three years, warned him what he was up against, but Andrée persisted. A Swedish scientist, he had prepared meticulously for the flight but couldn't contend with the Arctic fog that weighted down his craft. It bumped along, its gondola "stamping" the ice, as he put it in his diary, until the party finally abandoned the *Eagle* sixty-four hours into the flight. The threesome started walking for land that lay some two hundred miles to the south. Fighting against the breakup of the ice and contrary currents but finding plenty of game, they made landfall two months later on uninhabited White Island. They prepared to winter there, but apparently their cookstove malfunctioned and they suffocated in their shelter a few days after they arrived. In 1930 a scientific expedition discovered their preserved bodies and journals and undeveloped film, thus solving the mysterious fate of the *Eagle*, which had simply disappeared into the Arctic after lifting off from Spitsbergen thirty-three years before.

In the 1920s, with the development of longer air travel, several reconnaissance flights winged over sections of the Arctic. In 1925, the great explorer Roald Amundsen, who'd become convinced of the value of air travel as the future of Arctic exploration, and the American adventurer Lincoln Ellsworth mounted an expedition in two Dornier flying boats and attempted to land at the North Pole. Due to headwinds, they touched down on open leads 120 miles short of their destination, but the leads closed up before they could take to the air, destroying one plane and trapping the other. It took the crews a month of desperate, heavy labor to build ramps and runways on the ice before they were able to lift off from the polar pack.

A year later, in May 1926, the American Richard Byrd flew to the Pole and back, though he didn't risk a landing. A few days later, Ellsworth and Amundsen set out in the airship *Norge* to traverse the entire polar region from Spitsbergen to Alaska, directly over the Pole itself. They made the journey to Teller, Alaska, relatively smoothly in seventy-two hours.

Among the *Norge*'s crew of sixteen was the dirigible's designer and pilot, the Italian colonel Umberto Nobile. In 1928, supported in the effort by Mussolini's government, Nobile embarked on his own flight to the Pole in the sister ship to the *Norge*, the *Italia*. The expedition planned to land a research party at the Pole and return south with prevailing wind patterns to reconnoiter unexplored territory. After a preliminary flight into the islands of the Siberian Arctic, the *Italia* left her moorings at King's Bay, Spitsbergen, for the Pole at 4:28 A.M. on May 23. The wind quickly propelled the party of sixteen, which besides the Italian crewmen included a Czech scientist, Behounek, and Swedish meteorologist, Malmgren, to the Pole at speeds over sixty miles per hour and arrived there after a twenty-hour flight. The problem was getting back. Winds and fog cancelled plans for the landing party. Nobile, according to his account, wished to ride the wind toward the Siberian or Canadian coast, but meteorologist Malmgren advocated turning into the wind and pushing back to King's Bay, predicting that the wind would soon reverse direction.

It didn't. For a day and a half the *Italia* fought its way into a headwind that averaged around thirty miles per hour. She had to fly low in the fog in order to measure speed and drift against the pack ice. An ice coating began to collect on the gas bag and the ship grew heavy. Bits of ice flying from the propellers cut small rents in the bag. What happened next Nobile tells in this excerpt from his memoir, *My Polar Flights*.

The international search for Nobile became the twentieth century equivalent of the nineteenth century's search for Franklin, with nearly as many miscalculations and lost chances. Those who survived owed their lives to a Russian peasant near Archangel who operated an amateur radio set and picked up the Nobile party's faint distress signal emanating from out on the sea ice. A final tragedy befell the searchers: The great Amundsen, who had quarreled bitterly with Nobile after the *Norge* flight but who now flew to his rescue, disappeared in a French search plane along with his crewmates. The only indication of its fate was its wing pontoon later found bobbing in the waters off the Norwegian coast.

The excerpt picks up as Nobile and crew battle their way into headwinds on the return toward Spitsbergen from the Pole.

On the morning of May 25th the bitter struggle against the wind went on without respite.

For nearly 30 hours a stiff head-wind of 24 or 30 m.p.h. had been blowing. We advanced with difficulty, swerving now to one side, now to the other. It had become extremely difficult to keep on our course. Often the squalls got the upper hand of our helmsman, producing deviations of 20 or even 30 degrees.

Wind and fog. Fog and wind. Incessantly. And from time to time flurries of snow.

Everyone on board went about his business in silence. Some looked tired. The damp, grey, chilly atmosphere surrounding us weighed on our spirits. For a whole day and more we travelled thus. Not a glimmer of light through the fog above us; fog and cloud all the time. And below us, the colourless, monotonous pack.

Zappi and Mariano had charge of the route, dividing their attention between the steering-wheel, the speed-measuring apparatus, and the table on which the charts were spread. Trojani and Cecioni took turns at the elevator. Malmgren helped the Naval officers, taking long spells at the steering-wheel. Behounek, calm and impassive as ever, was beside his instruments. Pontremoli and Lago had gone to sleep some hours before in the fur bags laid down towards the stern. I was supervising everything, more or less, but for some time my attention had been given to checking the speed and to the radio-goniometrical reports, which served to determine our position.

There was great uncertainty as to this. We were making far less headway than our speed measurements indicated. Obviously, the zigzag course into which we were driven diminished our actual progress along the route. Only so could it be explained that we had not yet seen the land that ought to have been sighted some hours previously.

It was a really difficult situation. But—as always in similar circumstances—the difficulties had excited my energy: I did not feel tired, but even more alert than usual.

I divided my time between the navigation table, the wireless cabin, and speed measurements. When I got Biagi's reports I myself marked them on the map. Now and again I went into the front of the pilot-cabin to see that everything was all right. Then passing by my child's photograph—an old photograph which had already accompanied me on the *Norge* and had been fixed up again on the wall this time—I gave it a rapid glance. Maria's lovely eyes looked back at me. I was struck by the sadness of their expression—they seemed to be misted with tears.

Given the uncertainty as to our position, the radio-goniometrical data had assumed a vital importance. The trouble was that the radio did not tell us the exact spot where we were, but only the direction in which the *Città di Milano* heard our signals most strongly. So one could trace a bearing on the chart, somewhere along which the airship was at that moment; but where on this line, we did not know.

Towards seven in the morning my anxiety at not yet seeing land grew still keener. By this time, if we could rely on our calculations—

according to which at 1.30 a.m. we had been 100 miles NE. of Moffen Island—we should have already sighted the coast. But there was nothing to be seen. In front of us, to the extreme limit of the horizon, nothing but frozen sea.

I felt more than ever the need of checking our position: we must reckon with the drain on our petrol caused by the forced speed at which we were travelling; that was still my chief worry.

I was anxious to put an end to this uncertainty, somehow or other. So it occurred to me to order that for half an hour at least, we should travel westwards, at right angles to the line given by these reports, instead of straight along it, as we had done until then. The angle between the two observations made at the beginning and end of this course, would give us an approximate idea of our position on the line, and so of our distance from King's Bay.

At 7.40 a.m. we were on a radius from King's Bay passing about 10 miles NE. of Moffen Island. I gave orders to steer westwards. At 8.10 the new observation showed that the radius had approached the island by 3 or 4 miles. This experiment had not lasted long enough to give a reliable result, but I dared not go on with it because the wind, blowing hard on the bow, reduced our speed too much.

So we resumed our course towards North-East Land, steering southwards. The wind seemed even stronger.

At 9.25 I was standing by the door of the wireless cabin waiting for news when suddenly I heard someone cry: "The elevator wheel has jammed!" I ran up at once and saw Trojani—who had been for some time at this helm—trying to turn the wheel, to raise the nose. But he could not manage it. The controls of the helm were blocked.

I realized the gravity of the danger. We were at a height of 750 ft. The ship, being down by the nose, was dropping. In a few minutes we should strike the pack.

There was nothing to be done but to stop the engines—which I did at once. When I looked out and saw the three propellers at a standstill I breathed once more. There was nothing now to fear, for the ship was so light that soon it would stop sinking and go up again.

As I had foreseen, the moment the engines were stopped the descent slowed down abruptly, and about 250 ft. from the pack it ceased altogether. We began to rise gently.

In the meantime Cecioni—who had been asleep in the keel—came down into the cabin, and by my orders paid out the ballast chain, which was lying on the floor. As the chain was heavy this little operation took some time, and I thought it would be much better to let the chain hang out, ready in case of need. At that moment I had not the faintest idea how soon the event would justify this small precaution.

While we were slowly rising, Viglieri had released the elevator by a sharp blow. I ordered Cecioni to take it to pieces and examine the mechanism. As he worked, the airship went on rising. Some time before I had opened all the air-valves, so that the gas-pressure had been reduced below zero. Now it showed signs of going up again. I kept an eye on the pressure-gauges.

Soon we were swallowed up in fog. At this moment Mariano came to me and said: "Don't you think, sir, we might take the opportunity of getting above the fog and taking the height of the sun?"

I agreed, all the more readily because the fog around us was becoming steadily more luminous, showing that it was thinning out. Besides, Cecioni had not yet finished his work.

During the ascent I saw the pressure-gauges register a slight rise. At a certain point I noticed that the pressure in the last compartment of the stern was much higher than in the others. I then let out a little gas, to equalize the pressure in this compartment with that of the others. We were still going up.

At 2,700 ft. we at last emerged from the fog and found blue sky. A glorious sun flooded the cabin with its rays. Mariano and Zappi made their observations.

Cecioni had finished. On dismounting the casing of the elevator he had found nothing wrong with it, so probably the obstruction had been caused by ice forming on the inside. In any case, the helm was now working perfectly well.

We were at 3,300 ft. by this time. The gas began to dilate, making the liquid rise rapidly in the pressure-gauges; but before they reached the height at which they were normally kept when flying, I ordered two engines to be started—the centre and the left.

It was 9.55 a.m.

We set off again, and flew for a few minutes longer above the fog, scanning the horizon in front to see if by any chance the highest peaks of the Svalbard were rising up in the far distance out of the mist. But there was nothing to be seen. Nothing, as far as our field-glasses would reach, except the sea and the fog.

I then decided to come down to the height at which we had until lately been sailing. It was essential to find the pack again, so that we could go on checking our drift and speed.

We plunged back into the fog and slowly descended until the frozen sea appeared clearly in sight. We were about 900 ft. up.

The Crash

My first thought was to measure our speed. We had only two engines working, but it seemed to me all the same that we were making a bit more headway than before.

Our first measurement, in fact, showed a velocity in relation to the pack of about 30 m.p.h. The wind had gone down, then, and there was no need to start the third engine. I was relieved at this, for it deferred our anxiety about the petrol. I was also glad not to have to go on straining the ship by an excessive speed.

Once more I turned my attention to the course, with Mariano and Viglieri. Combining the position given by the recent height measurement with the radio-goniometrical report at 10 o'clock, we had located our position with approximate certainty. We were apparently 45 miles NE. of the Ross Islands and 180 miles NE. of King's Bay.

On the basis of this distance I calculated that we should reach the Bay between three and four in the afternoon, and intended to announce this by wireless a little later on.

Everything on board was now in order and each man had resumed his post. Malmgren was at the helm, with Zappi giving him instructions from time to time. Cecioni had not left the elevator since he had tested its casing. Beside him, between the pressure-gauges and the engine controls, stood Trojani.

In the rear of the cabin with me, sitting round the navigation table, were Mariano and Viglieri. One of them was taking speed measurements with the Goertz apparatus clamped to the side of the table. Behounek stood behind us, making observations with his instruments. Pontremoli and Lago, as I said before, had been asleep for some hours up in the stern.

The mechanics were all awake, in their respective engine-boats, Arduino, helped by Alessandrini, was in the gangway, superintending the inside of the ship.

We were flying between 600 and 900 ft. up. The dirigible was still light, so to keep it at the proper height we had to hold the nose down.

At 10.30 I again ordered a speed measurement. When this had been taken I walked to the front of the cabin and looked out of the right-hand porthole, between the steering-wheel and the elevator. To test the height, I dropped a glass ball full of red liquid, and stood there, timing its fall with a stop-watch.

While I was attending to this, I heard Cecioni say excitedly: "We are heavy!"

I turned with a start to look at the instruments.

The ship was right down by the stern, at an angle of 8 degrees to the horizon; nevertheless, we were rapidly falling.

The peril was grave and imminent. A short distance below us stretched the pack. I at once gave the orders which had to be given, the only ones that could save the ship in this emergency—if that was possible: to accelerate the two engines, start the third, and at the same time lift the nose of the dirigible still higher. I hoped by these means to overcome the unexpected heaviness.

Simultaneously, I shouted to Alessandrini to run out on the top of the ship and inspect the stern valves, as I thought gas might be escaping—the only explanation that occurred to me at the moment of this serious and rapid increase in weight.

Meanwhile, the mechanics had carried out my orders. Pomella and Caratti had speeded their engines up to 1,400 revolutions and Ciocca, with surprising promptness, had started his own. The ship began to move faster, and tilted at an angle of 15 or 20 degrees.

The dynamic lift obtained in this way must certainly have represented several hundredweight.

But unfortunately we went on falling. The variometer—on which my eyes were fixed—confirmed it; in fact, we seemed to be dropping even faster.

I realized that there was nothing more to be done. The attempt to combat the increased weight by propulsion had failed. . . . A crash was now inevitable; the most we could do was to mitigate its consequences.

I gave the necessary orders: to stop the engines at once, so as to avoid fire breaking out as we crashed; and to drop the ballast-chain. Sending Cecioni to do this, I put Zappi in his place.

It was all that could have been ordered; it was ordered promptly and with absolute calm. The perfect discipline on board was unbroken, so that each man carried out my orders as best he could, in the vertiginous rapidity of the event.

In the meantime the pack was approaching at a fearful speed. I saw that Cecioni was finding it difficult to untie the rope which held the chain. "Hurry up! Hurry up!" I shouted to him. Then noticing that the engine on the left, run by Caratti, was still working, I leaned out of a porthole on that side, and at the top of my voice—echoed, I think, by one of the officers—repeated the order: "Stop the engine!" At that moment I saw the stern-boat was only a few tens of yards from the pack. I drew back into the cabin.

The recollection of those last terrible instants is very vivid in my memory. I had scarcely had time to reach the spot near the two rudders, between Malmgren and Zappi, when I saw Malmgren fling up the wheel, turning his startled eyes on me. Instinctively I grasped the helm, wondering if it were possible to guide the ship on a snow-field and so lessen the shock. . . . Too late! . . . There was the pack, a few yards below, terribly uneven. The masses of ice grew larger, came nearer and nearer. . . . A moment later we crashed.

There was a fearful impact. Something hit me on the head, then I was caught and crushed. Clearly, without any pain, I felt some of my limbs snap. Some objects falling from a height knocked me down head foremost. Instinctively I shut my eyes, and with perfect lucidity and coolness formulated the thought: "It's all over!" I almost pronounced the words in my mind.

It was 10.33 on May 25th.

The fearful event had lasted only 2 or 3 minutes!

After the Crash

When I opened my eyes I found myself lying on the ice, in the midst of an appalling pack. I realized at once that others had fallen with me.

I looked up to the sky. Towards my left the dirigible, nose in air, was drifting away before the wind. It was terribly lacerated around the pilot-cabin. Out of it trailed torn strips of fabric, ropes, fragments of metal-work. The left wall of the cabin had remained attached. I noticed a few creases in the envelope.

Upon the side of the crippled, mutilated ship stood out the black letters ITALIA. My eyes remained fixed on them, as if fascinated, until the dirigible merged in the fog and was lost to sight.

It was only then that I felt my injuries. My right leg and arm were broken and throbbing; I had hurt my face and the top of my head, and my chest seemed all upside down with the violence of the shock. I thought my end was near.

Suddenly I heard a voice—Mariano's—asking: "Where is the General?" And I looked around me.

I had never seen such a terrible pack: a formless, contorted jumble of pointed ice-crags, stretching to the horizon.

Two yards away on the right, Malmgren was sitting, and a little farther off lay Cecioni, moaning aloud. Next him was Zappi. The others—Mariano, Behounek, Trojani, Viglieri, and Biagi—were standing up. They appeared unhurt, except for Trojani, whose face was stained by a few patches of blood.

Here and there one could see wreckage—a dreary note of grey against the whiteness of the snow. In front of me a strip of bright red, like blood which had flowed from some enormous wound, showed the spot where we had fallen. It was the liquid from the glass balls.

I was calm. My mind was perfectly clear. But now I was feeling the seriousness of my injuries—worst of all, a terrible convulsion in my chest. Breathing was a great effort. I thought I had probably sustained some grave internal injury. It seemed that death was very near—that maybe I had only 2 or 3 hours to live.

I was glad of this. It meant that I should not have to watch the despair and slow death-agony of my comrades. What hope was there for them? With no provisions, no tent, no wireless, no sledges—nothing but useless wreckage—they were lost, irremediably lost, in this terrible wilderness of ice.

I turned towards them, looking at them with an infinite sadness at heart. Then I spoke: "Steady, my lads! Keep your spirits up! Don't be cast down by this misfortune." And I added: "Lift your thoughts to God!"

No other words, no other ideas, came to me in those first unforgettable moments when death seemed imminent. But suddenly I was seized by strong emotion. Something rose up from my soul—from the depths of my being: something stronger than the pain of my tortured limbs, stronger than the thought of approaching death. And from my straining breast broke out, loud and impetuous, the cry: *"Viva l'Italia!"*

My comrades cheered.

Beside me on the right Malmgren was still sitting silent in the same place, stroking his right arm. On his face, frowning and ashen pale, a little swollen from his fall, was a look of blank despair. His blue eyes stared fixedly in front of him, as if into the void. Lost in thought, he seemed not even to notice the other men around him.

I had been very fond of this young scientist, ever since we had shared in the *Norge* expedition. And lately my affection for him had grown. He had become my most valued collaborator—the only one to whom I confided my plans, my ideas, my thoughts. I attached a good deal of weight to his judgment and advice. Some days previously we had decided the general lines of our future flight—the bold scheme which, if carried out, would have utilized to the utmost the possibili-

ties afforded by our ship and crew. . . . But now all our plans had come
to naught.

Wishing to speak to him, I said softly: "Nothing to be done, my dear
Malmgren!"

Nothing to be done! . . . A painful confession for men of action!

He looked at me and answered: "Nothing, but die. My arm is broken."

Suddenly he got up. He could not stand erect, for his injured shoulder made him stoop. Once more he turned to me and said in English:
"General, I thank you for the trip. . . . I go under the water!"

So saying, he turned away.

I stopped him: "No, Malmgren! You have no right to do this. We will
die when God has decided. We must wait. Please stop here."

I shall never forget the look he turned on me at that moment. He
seemed surprised. Perhaps he was struck by the gentle and affectionate
seriousness of my tone. For a moment he stood still, as if undecided. Then
he sat down again.

But suddenly a ray of light pierced the darkness. I heard Biagi cry:
"The field-station is intact!"

By this he meant the little emergency wireless set which had been
placed on board precisely in a case of a descent on the ice.

I began to hope again. If we could send wireless messages—if we
could ask the *Città di Milano* for help, perhaps all was not lost. My
comrades might yet be rescued.

Then I called Mariano.

"I feel myself dying," I told him. "I think I have only a few hours to
live. I cannot do anything for you. Do all you can, yourself, to save our
men. . . . God help you! God grant you may return to Italy. . . . What a
pity if our country were to lose men like you!"

He answered gently: "Yes, General! Set your mind at rest. . . . There
is still hope. We have found the wireless, and very soon we shall be in
communication with the *Città di Milano.* And we have picked up a
case of provisions too. We can hope."

Then all at once the memory of home came back to me: "When you
are in Italy, do what you can for my child and my sisters' children!"

"Yes, General—don't worry. . . . I'll see to it," he replied, and then added: "I've always been fond of you. . . . In my own fashion—but always."

I was delighted with the optimism and energy that this young man was showing in such terrible circumstances.

Suddenly my glance fell upon a large dark heap in front of me, between two hummocks of ice, and about 10 or 15 yds. away. I recognized one of the two waterproof bags in which Pontremoli and I had put everything that might be useful in case two or three of us made a descent at the Pole, as I had thought of doing. One of the bags was inside the ship; the other, strapped to the ceiling of the wireless cabin, had fallen amidst the wreckage.

I pointed it out to Mariano: "Get that sack opened! You will find valuable things inside—a tent and provisions. There's a sleeping-bag too. Please bring it here to me and get me into it, if you can. Then I shall be able to die there in peace."

Shivers of cold were running through my body. Unlike the others, I had not a heavy coat lined with lamb's-wool.

They brought the sleeping-bag to the spot where I was lying, and little by little slid me into it. This was not easy, because my right arm, leg, and foot gave me excruciating pain at the least movement. Besides, I was on top of a hummock, where there was not even enough flat surface for me to lie comfortably.

Once inside the sack I thought of Titina and called to her. The dear little thing was scampering gaily to and fro on the ice, happy to be free at last and no longer in the air . . . so happy that she was not even surprised at this novel method of landing, and still less disconcerted at the terrible aspect of the pack. I called her to me, but she refused to understand and continued to frisk about, wagging her tail and sniffing the air.

I recommended her to the care of one of the men.

Having done this I put my head inside the bag and lay motionless, waiting for death to steal over me.

Half an hour passed thus—perhaps even longer. But death did not come. In its stead I felt life gradually creeping back. It did me good to lie still. The effects of the violent shock on my lungs were beginning to wear off.

All of a sudden I began to wonder what my comrades were doing. I put my head out of the bag to have a look.

Mariano, Viglieri, Trojani, and Behounek were wandering about on the ice picking up materials. Biagi, having improvised a wireless mast, had begun to transmit. Cecioni, sitting up, was still cursing his luck. As soon as he caught sight of me he called: "I've broken my leg, sir!" I noticed he had bandaged it as best he could.

Malmgren, gloomy and ashen pale, was still motionless in the same position. He sat there, nursing his right arm, and staring fixedly in front of him. On the other side, on my left, Zappi was lying stretched out. He had been slightly hurt about the face, and was complaining of a pain in his chest, just by one of his ribs: "Do you think it's broken, General?"

"If it doesn't hurt you much when you breathe, that means it isn't broken," I hazarded in reply. But to tell the truth I was not at all sure of the accuracy of this remark.

Meanwhile I heard Viglieri, Trojani, and Mariano discussing the best spot to pitch the tent. It must be put up as quickly as possible because the cold was intense, and the wind (although only blowing 12 or 15 ft. to the second) made us feel it still more.

At last the spot was chosen—a sheet of ice about 50 yds. square—some yards away from me and on a lower level. Trojani, helped by some of the others, set to work.

Once the tent was ready they carried me there. The going was painful. More than once I had to set my teeth, not to cry out with the agony of my fractures. But at last they dragged me inside and laid me at the back of the tent, along the wall facing the entrance.

Then they carried in Cecioni and put him beside me. They slit up my fur bag, and thus opened it made a bed for us both.

Meanwhile Mariano, Viglieri, Behounek, and Trojani went on looking for provisions. Some of the tins had fallen through the holes in the framework where the cabin and the stern engine-boat had been. Later on it was suggested that Arduino and the others, on their own initiative, had thrown down stuff to lighten the ship, but this does not seem probable.

By the evening about 150 lb. of provisions—pemmican and chocolate—had been collected. This would suffice for 25 days, allowing a ration of 11 oz. per head.

Biagi had already sent out the first S.O.S., trying in vain to call the *Città di Milano;* then a flaw had developed in the apparatus which he had been unable to set right.

A little later everyone gathered in the tent and Mariano distributed 1/2 lb. of pemmican to each. Some of them began to masticate it, not without signs of distaste. Cecioni and I put ours aside: we had no appetite.

Then they gave me the news of Pomella's death. They had found him seated on the ice near the wreckage of his engine-boat. He had taken off one of his leather shoes. There was no sign of suffering on his face—no apparent injury.

Pomella was very dear to me; yet that tragic night his loss left me indifferent. It was not hardness of heart—but involuntarily I reflected that it was better for him to have died then and there and escaped the lingering death reserved for us. For my part, I envied him his lot.

Then having speculated a little about the fate of the other six we settled down to sleep. Nine men, huddled up together in that cramped space. A tangle of human limbs. Outside, the wind was howling, and one could hear the canvas of the tent flapping with a lugubrious rhythm. Cecioni rambled on until weariness overcame him. It overcame me too, and I fell asleep.

The Woman of the Sea

IN THE TIME of the earliest forefathers, there lived a handsome young woman known far and wide for her long, thick hair. When she bunched this hair in a top-knot, it was almost the size of the rest of her body. Entire weeks she would spend combing it. Also, she had nice fat hands which many men admired.

One day this woman was picking berries when a fulmar flying overhead happened to see her. Immediately he swooped down and said:

"Marry me, my dear . . ."

The woman laughed and said sea-birds weren't much to her taste.

Then the fulmar went away and changed himself into a man. He put on a garment of the richest sealskin, a colorful tunic, and sun-spectacles made from walrus tusks. Now he came back and appeared at the woman's door. Once again he put the question to her.

"Well, you're a fine piece of man," she said, and left with him despite her parents' objections.

Now the woman lived with the fulmar in a little rock hut at the end of the sea. As she was fond of blubber, each day the fulmar would bring her a fresh seal. As she was fond of singing, he would sing to her while they made love. And so they had a happy marriage. But one day the fulmar's spectacles fell off and the woman saw his eyes. She said:

"You're just an ugly fellow, like all the others . . ."

All this time her parents had been paddling around in search of her. At every cove and headland they called out: "Daughter, daughter, where have you gone?" They searched the shore all the way to the Inland Ice. At last they arrived at the little rock hut at the end of the sea and beseeched her to return with them. She agreed to go. Because, she said, "I can't stand my husband's hideous eyes anymore."

Now the fulmar was searching for the woman himself. First he couldn't find her. But then he put on his walrus-tusk spectacles and saw the little boat in the sea below. Whereupon he flapped his wings wildly, more and more, and a terrible storm rushed over the water. Wind swept down the mountains. The boat looked as if it might capsize. The woman's parents said: "*You* brought on this storm. If you don't get out, we'll drown. Out, out with you!"

She protested that the storm was her husband's fault. It did no good. Her parents tossed her overboard. But she caught hold of the gunwale and clung to it. Her father took out his knife and cut off a few of her fingers. Still she clung there. He cut off a few more. Still she clung. And then he chopped off both her hands. She tried to hold on with her stumps, but she had no grip and as a result she slipped away. Immediately the waters subsided and her parents were able to paddle home, happy that they've survived even if it meant the sacrifice of their daughter.

The woman sank to the bottom of the sea. There she acquired her name Nerrivik, Food Dish. Her chopped-off fingers came back to her as fish, whales, seals, and walruses, all making their homes in her hair. But she couldn't comb this hair as she'd been able to before. Try as she might, she couldn't. For she didn't have any hands. All she could do was sit there at the sea-bottom, legs drawn up to her chest, and watch her hair get more and more filthy with each passing day.

Thus it is that *angakoks* must swim down to the depths and comb Nerrivik's hair for her. And, in her gratitude, she offers mankind all the creatures of the sea. The bounty in her long, spreading hair is endless. Friend, respect this woman.

BOOK III

THE SEARCH TO UNDERSTAND

With the *Italia* disaster and end of the air race for the North Pole, the great "firsts" of Arctic exploration had been completed—at least for the moment. Ships and airplanes, radios and telegraphs knit together the scattered outposts of the Far North, and the Arctic opened up to visitors from the South as never before. They each came with their own reasons: some to learn which of the Arctic's resources—furs or gold, oil or fish—could be shipped south at a profit; some to extend territorial claims across the tundra islands; some to build a great necklace of early warning systems that could detect Russian attacks launched over the top of the world; and some for no other reason than curiosity itself. While only males participated in the early European expeditions to the Arctic, some of these new visitors were women, and we start to hear more women's voices in the literature of the Arctic. These Southerners began to listen to the legends and songs and life stories of the Inuit instead of regarding the natives as a threat, or a source of food, or a flock of heathens to be converted. They studied the animals and plants of the Arctic, the landforms and geology, the ice and the weather. Perhaps most important of all, instead of trying to score another "first" or to name newly discovered lands after themselves and their friends, these new visitors sought to *understand* the Arctic for its own sake.

Walrus

The sea lay shining brightly
near my hut.
I couldn't sleep.

I paddled out.
A walrus came up
by the boat.

He was too close
for a harpoon-throw.
So I drove it
down and into him,
and the float went hopping
across the water.

But up he came,
and laid his flippers
just like elbows
on the surface,
as he tried to tear
the float to bits.

He tired himself in vain:
an unborn lemming's skin
(protective amulet)
was sewn to it.
Blowing angrily,
he gathered all his strength,
but I closed in
and put him out of pain.

So listen, boastful men
from distant fjords,
so eager always to draw breath
in praise of your own skill:
fill your lungs
with songs
about the daring exploits of a stranger!

—Aua (Iglulik Eskimo man)

The Story of Comock the Eskimo

BY COMOCK (CANADIAN INUIT, 1912)

Robert Flaherty came north as a mining engineer and lived for many years among the Inuit, gaining a deep appreciation of their culture, which eventually led to his making of the film *Nanook of the North*. As he relates in the preface to *The Story of Comock the Eskimo*, he was out hunting one day in 1912 on Cape Wolstenholme at the northeastern end of Hudson Bay when he saw a very strange *umiak*—Inuit skin-hulled passenger boat—approach the shore. In it was Comock and his family, oddly dressed, who told this story of their ten years on an uninhabited island.

The story shows the resourcefulness and forbearance and patience of the Inuit, as well as the emotional struggles they suffer in a land where human life vanishes so suddenly and so swiftly. On the one hand, this story is a microcosm of Inuit life; on the other, as Edmund Carpenter writes in his introduction, Comock's story tells of the rebirth of mankind—"human life reduced to a man, a woman, fire-making stones, and the will to perpetuate life."

In the year 1912 I was in a little Hudson's Bay Company post at Cape Wolstenholme, the northeast extreme of Hudson Bay. Over breakfast

241

one morning the manager of the post said, "How about some hunting? We'll take the sloop and sail around the nose of Cape Wolstenholme. We might see something in the way of game. A walrus, perhaps, or possibly a bear among the cliffs."

We started. We came to a ledge jutting off from the cliff face, landed upon it and, climbing up some fifty feet, sat down. I was looking through my glass at thousands of little specks, sea pigeons flying among the rocks of a nearby island. Suddenly on the water before the island I saw a small boat rowing toward us. It sprawled clumsily over the lumpy sea. It drew nearer. Its occupants were Eskimos. A man was steering at the stern, two others were at the oars. It drew nearer, close in. It was almost a third as broad as it was long, which was not more than fifteen feet, but within it we counted thirteen people, grown-ups and children, huddled together, and among them two dogs as well. Over the children and the dogs a woman held a stick to hit them if by moving suddenly they should threaten the balance of the cockleshell. Why the amazing craft did not capsize we could not understand, until I saw its waterline, a series of in-flated seal bladders tied at intervals around it. They alone kept the craft afloat. The Eskimos, their dogs—as wild as wolves—cowering between their legs, stared at us out of their twinkling slant-eyes. They looked like something half bird and half man, for their costumes were not made of the usual deerskin or bearskin or hairy seal, but of the skins of the ivory duck, feathers and all, sewn together. They were not afraid. The mother's babe that she carried naked in the hood of her *koolitah* [parka] suddenly crawled halfway out along her bare shoulder, looked up at us for a few moments with big brown eyes, then stuck out its tiny arm and smiled. That broke the ice. I took its hand, it smiled again, the mother smiled and then the father, one of the finest looking Eskimos I have ever seen. He had a long, finely chiseled nose, a chin as solid as a rock and penetrating, far-seeing eyes. His hair hung to his shoulders. "*Chimo* [hi!]," he said.

"Chimo," echoed his wife.

"Chimo," piped the children. The mother twitched her shoulder on which the baby lay; it understood and smiled again.

"Who are you?" I asked.

"My name is Comock," he answered, smiling expectantly.

"Where in the world have you come from?"

"From far away, from big island, from far over there," he answered, pointing out to the west. "You see, our *umiak* [boat] is not very good," and he laughed and his family laughed with him. We took them all aboard and, with this incredible contraption in tow, sailed on back toward the post. He told me this story.

—Robert Flaherty

Comock's Story

For ten winters and ten summers we had been living on an island, far out on the sea (said Comock). See, my wife has kept count. She has written it here on the handle of my harpoon. (And he showed me the harpoon, the wooden handle of which was notched from end to end, a notch for each moon.)

The land where we used to live was poor; no walrus, few seals, no deer. I had two wives and many children. I did not know anymore how to keep them alive, but I had an idea. I'd had it for a long time. Far out at sea from my land there is an island. None of my people had ever seen it, it was so far away. I heard about it from the White Chief of a whaler. He told me there were days when the sky over it was almost black with the flight of birds, the big birds that honk, and there were many lakes and ponds, the Chief of the big whaler said, and around them the big birds brought up their young. There were many foxes, there were many deer and there were many bear and schools of walrus on the little islands along the coast, and seals—many, many seals.

And they'd be so easy to hunt, the Chief of the whaler said, because no Eskimo lived on all that land. Never had he seen such game as was on this island. He told me if I could get out to it I would never be hungry. I could not keep from thinking of that land; I talked about it over and over with my wives. There was only one way to go, we all agreed—by sled over the ice fields in winter, in the moon of the most cold when there is the least chance of the ice field parting and drifting off.

"Two days sledding," I told my family. "Two long days it will take us if our dogs are strong and we are strong, and there is not too much rough ice."

"*Ae* [yes,]" my wife said, "the rough ice will be the worst." You see, we could be caught and travel no farther in one sun than a seal might swim from one breathing hole to another. Winter came on; we had little food. More than most winters it was poor; no deer upon the land, no walrus at the ice edge and the seals—not many.

"We will go," said my wife.

"Yes, we will go," said my sons.

And there was another, Annunglung, who sailed with me. He was not a good hunter; he had only one wife, but he was not afraid. "Yes," he said, "I will go too." And so said his wife.

The sun got lower every day. We watched the ice from the high cliffs that lean out over the sea. Day by day we watched that ice. On the days when we had to go hunting one of the women watched it for us. The ice grew fast, for it was cold, until at last nowhere was there water, and the big smokes of the freezing were gone—the ice was everywhere. "Now is the time, now we will go. *Twavee* [quick]!" I said.

"Twavee!" said everyone. We could hardly hear the howling of our dogs. We had three sleds of dogs, twelve dogs to each sled. They were good dogs. We had taken care to feed them well, and now they howled to be off.

In the beginning the ice was rough for the first big wind of the winter had jammed the ice hard against the coast and piled it up to many times the height I stand. It was heavy going, but at last we worked out of it without hurting our sleds and we got smooth ice. We traveled fast on this smooth ice for the wind had packed the snow hard, and our feet did not sink and the dogs' feet moved so fast my eyes would swim to look at them. We never had so little use for the long whip—their tails never fell, their traces never touched the snow. We only rested twice— to untangle the traces and to clear the ice from between the toes of the dogs' feet. There was good hunting too—my leader dog was always turning his head, so many were the breathing holes of the seal—but "We must not stop," I said.

"We must not stop," said my wife, "ae," and everyone agreed.

At last the long shadows in the snow grew blue like the sky. The shining left the edges of the ice and the long shadows drew away like the edge of an ice field moving slowly out from the land. Still the traces of the dogs did not touch the ground. There was not much light from the stars, and we stumbled.

When the moon did rise it was only half a moon. It did not give us much light, and we stumbled, and there were wails from the dogs and that was because we were now truly tired and it took much shaking to keep our children awake. "*Tiamak*" [here-now; that's it], I said. "We will stop."

"Ae," said everyone. And the dogs sank into the snow, too tired to fight, and they buried their noses between their paws and let the snow-smoke drift over them, and while our women sat in the shelter of our sleds and nursed the small children, Annunglung and I went off with our snow knives and harpoons, and by good luck we found along a crack in the ice a deep drift of snow. We cut out a block of snow. The edges cut sharp and did not crumble and then we cut out block after block and built our igloo.

The dogs between sleep kept watching us and when we had built our igloo and from the inside cut out the door and crawled out, they were all around us howling for their seal. I had to use my long whip to keep them away, and then our wives crept inside and they were all smiling for they were away from the burn of the cold, and they lit our seal-oil lamps and put our willow mats and deerskins down while the children chewed their pieces of raw seal. Outside we gave our dogs their meat, and then they bedded themselves in the snow in the shelter of the sleds and the igloo, and let the snow cover them again. Annunglung and I went inside, and our wives cut seal meat and filled our mouths, and we said the night was full of good signs, though there were growls now and then running through the ice, growing louder and louder as they came toward us, and sounding in our ears like Nanook the bear rushing toward the spear, but I said, "Never mind, there is always growling from the sea." So we fell asleep, cold though our igloo was, as a new igloo always is when there is no wind.

When I awakened I was happy, for our ice window was blue, and by that I knew that there was no snow-smoke in the air. My head wife made fire in her willow down, and she blew it into a flame and lit the lamp. "Look at our children, Comock," she said, "they are warm." There were little smokes rising from the deerskin robes under which they slept.

We were out early. There was still fire in the stars. It was so cold that the spit from our mouths froze before it struck the ground. We were out on the ice so far now that looking backward I could not see land, and besides there was rough ice—much rough ice. I climbed up on one high piece, and looking ahead all I could see was rough ice. We moved very slowly, up and down, up and down—the smallest child who walks could keep up with us. Many times this rough ice would tangle the long traces of the dogs and it was hard to keep them from laming or wounding one another, for all this tangling gave them the madness to kill.

Not until the sun was high could we get out of this rough ice, and though it was cold our bodies were wet with sweat, and the muzzles of the dogs were white, and they were quick with their breathing and wanted to lie down. "But we must keep on," I said. "Look—I do not like the sky."

"No, we do not like the sky," said everyone. There were clouds in it, and they began to cross the sun and there was more and more wind, and everywhere over the ice the smoke of the snow was rising.

We kept on and we went fast for a while, and then we struck young ice. And then we had to go faster still, for it would bend with our weight—if we stopped we would have broken through. From this young ice we struck old ice once more, and it was smooth and again we traveled fast, though the wind was still stronger and the smoke of the snow was thick in the air.

The wind was growing stronger and there was no blue left in the sky, and all three sleds had to keep close together or we might lose one another.

I did not like this wind. It might part the ice, for it blew off the land, but we all laughed and said it was a little matter, there was no harm in that wind. Darkness came early, so filled was the sky with the flying snow, and we were tired, and we stumbled. "It is enough," I said.

"Ae," said my wife.

"Ae," said everyone, and the dogs sank in the snow.

Though our igloo walls were thick, and we could hear the wind, after we finished eating the red meat and lay down to sleep, we could hear it more. We wondered how far we were still from the big island.

"It is strange that with all this wind we can hear no growling in the sea—the ice now must be very strong," I said.

But someone else said, "Even if the ice is strong there still could be growling of the sea." We did not talk another word for sleep was heavy in our eyes.

I slept near the door so that I could be the first out in the morning. I was deep in sleep. Then I awoke—why I do not know. I could hear the fierce roaring of the wind. But even now though I listened hard I could hear no growling from the sea. Then I wondered why I had wakened—fool, I called myself. I looked at Annunglung and his wife and his children asleep. I was trimming the moss wicks of our seal-oil lamp before lying down again, and then I heard it. Far out at first, then quick like the wind it began coming toward me—one long, louder and louder roar! And now under me I could feel trembling. I knew what it was. It was the ice, it was parting, and it cut our igloo in two. The lamp fell; there was no light. "Hold on to each other!" I yelled to everyone in the darkness. "Hold on to each other or we are lost!" The dogs were howling, the children crying, and there were screams from our wives. I could not see it, but open water was at our feet. "Hold together!" I yelled. I could not hear. "Are we all together?" I cried.

"No, we are not together, we are not together!" It was my head wife. "Don't you hear, don't you hear?" she was shrieking.

"Stop," I cried, "then I shall hear." Even so they were already far—I could barely hear them—my young wife, Annunglung's wife, one of his and two of my young children and my second oldest son. Then their calling died away. We called—we listened—we called again, but we could only hear the roaring of the storm and the growling of the sea.

It was black with darkness, and I had to walk from one to another feeling their hands. We stumbled in our walking and fell down, but we held our hands and we got into the hollow of some big blocks of ice. We stood there until the light came into the sky and then we tried to see across the open water which was not far, but we could not see well, for it was covered with its own thick smoking from the cold. I was glad we could not see, for we could do nothing even if we did see our people and my wife still had her fits of screaming.

I went off to see the place where our igloo had been standing but there was only the smoke and water of the sea. Everything—all but one sled—was gone. All that we owned was gone—the willow mats, the deerskins, the stone pots, the stone lamp for our snow melting, all my knives, spears, harpoons—everything gone. Then a thought struck me and I was truly frightened and I walked fast and I called out to my wife as I walked, "The stones, the stones—have you got them?"

"The stones, did you say?" asked my wife, and she stood still and she looked frightened.

"Yes," I said, "the stones, have you got them?" Then quickly her hands went to the pouch in her koolitah. And for a long time she was feeling. And then at last, "Yes, Comock," she said, "I've got them." They were the stones we must have to make the sparks for our fires.

Then I said to my wife, "There surely will not be time for grieving now. Everything is gone. We have only one sled, my ivory knife with which to cut the snow blocks for our igloo building and your stones for fire-making."

My wife said, "It is well, Comock, we have something."

"Yes," I said, "but no spears, no harpoons—we cannot kill bear—we cannot kill seal."

"There are the dogs," my wife said, "and there are the harnesses of the dogs that are gone. We can eat them," my wife said.

"No," said my eldest son, "we cannot eat the harnesses. The harnesses they are gone. They were tied to the lost sleds."

"Well, anyway, there are the dogs," my wife said.

"Ae," I said, "there are the dogs."

"Ae," said everyone.

For one moon we were on the broken ice, drifting—we drifted one way many days—we drifted another way many days. It made us feel small to drift in this foolish way upon the sea.

We shared with our dogs the dog meat upon which we lived. "The meat of the dogs does not keep one warm like the meat of the seal," someone said.

"Yes, and our dogs are no longer warm," someone said.

And then someone else said, "They will bear watching, what with all the children and we with no spears to kill."

"I will make clubs," I said. "There are a few crosspieces of the sled that can be spared, and they will make clubs."

And we took the crosspieces off our sleds and they made clubs. Besides these crosspieces, I had my long whip—I could kill ptarmigan with it, and if I had to, I could split a dog's ear in two.

"But the crosspieces and whip are not enough," said my wife. "There are some dogs we will have to tie up. The dogs upon which we live are the weaker dogs—the dangerous ones are those that are strong."

"We must have patience with the dogs," I said, "even if they try to kill, for we will need our dogs even more than fire if we ever come upon land again."

"Yes," said my wife, "but what of the children, Comock? If they should stumble—I get sick from watching."

There was much hunting to find good stones. We searched far though we were all weak. Not in one day did we find the good stones, but we found them just the same. My young sons found a piece of driftwood buried in the snow. I made a knife and a spearhead of the stones, and we cut the driftwood, and at least we made a harpoon. Everyone laughed and said they had seen better harpoons. That night when we all lay down to sleep, someone said, "It will be good when we get seal."

And then someone said, "Yes, it will be good when we get oil."

"Yes," said someone, "it is the oil we need most. Hunger is one thing, but these nights of darkness are the worst." We went to sleep.

There was another storm and for a long time we could not see. But when the smoke of the snow cleared from the sky we saw the edge of our ice breaking high upon something. It was land. This land was low like the sea, but we knew it was land because we could see black specks in the whiteness and those black specks in the whiteness were rocks sticking up through the snow. "This must be the big island," said my wife.

"Yes," I said.

When we got to this land we built an igloo, and in the darkness, for we had no lamp, we lay down to sleep. "It is funny," said someone, "the land is so still." For a long time we could not sleep because the land was so still.

With the daylight coming I took my leader dog to find me a breathing hole of the seal, and not far out on the ice he stopped and he smelled a hole. And there I waited all day until the seal had made his rounds of his breathing holes, and at last the bubbles of his breathing began to rise in my hole, and I took up my harpoon and killed the seal.

There was darkness in the igloo when I clubbed my way against the dogs through the long tunnel dragging my seal. Everyone made noise, and the dogs in the tunnel made much noise. And there was talking and laughing, and my wife soon got oil and from her stones struck fire, and there was light in our igloo, and everyone smiling could see one another. The seal which lay before us was a big seal, and we fed our dogs, and we kept on eating and sleeping and eating. It was all mixed up together.

We made more knives and better knives, and we made more harpoons. And on all these days there were seals. "The dogs do not show their ribs now," said my wife. "And did you ever see such strong children? But we soon must get skins for new clothing. Are there deer on this island?"

"We will find out," I said, "if there are deer on this island."

"It will be good to have soft deerskins for clothing," said my wife.

"Which way shall we go? To the north or to the south?" For a long time we did not know, and then my wife said, "I have a feeling—let us go north."

"Ae," said everyone, "let us go north."

We were many days traveling for there was much hunting. All the way there were bear and there were seal and there were walrus, and at last we saw deer. And we made our kill, and my wife got the skins for our clothing.

The days now were all light. The ice was scattering on the sea, and the warm sun bared the ground, and the big birds that honk came up from the south and they nested round the edges of the lakes and ponds. Everywhere were these big birds and their crying and their flying filled the sky, but in time they lost the feathers of their wings. Then we ran after them and ran them down.

From driftwood and sealskins we made a kayak and I hunted the little islands off the shore, and on some there were walrus. From the tusks of the walrus we got the ivory for our sled runners, ivory for our snow knives, ivory for our harpoons, and ivory for needles for my wife.

There were bear. We made trips over the land far in from the sea, and in one camp, where we fished salmon from the stream, the bear were so many that I had to tie bones together on a string so that in the wind they would knock and make noise and so keep the bear away while we had our sleep.

During the warmest days of the summer we were camped along a shore where there was a river in which many salmon were swimming. We had just finished with our day's fishing when our children came running to us over the sand. Their eyes were big and they were saying, "We have seen something strange, a monster which has come up from the sea and it is now lying on the shore." We all went to where they said the monster was. Soon we came to a point. It lay behind that point, they said. We walked carefully to the point and we looked over the point, and then we saw it. Its black holes looked like eyes. It had been shoved far up from the water by the ice. It was very old, I could see by the moss and the whiteness of its wood. My wife did not like to go near.

"Something might come out of the holes," she said.

"Don't be foolish," I said, but she hung behind. With Annunglung and my sons I climbed up on it, and the first thing we found was iron, good iron, not only gray iron, but yellow iron and the red iron which is softer than the yellow iron. And these two, when we rubbed them, gleamed in the sun. And all of that ship was good wood. Some of this wood was hard like stone, and there was enough of it to make the runners for sleds and handles for spears and harpoons for ten times more people than there are fingers on my hands. "Come," I yelled to my wife. "Come," I said, "you will not believe your eyes."

But she said, "No, something might come out of the holes."

We found pots for my wife, pots of gray iron, pots of red iron, pots of yellow iron, and, the best of all, we found axes and knives, knives for my wife for the cutting of meat, knives for the cutting of skins, knives that were big and knives that were small and knives for the cutting of wood, big knives as long as my arm, and we ground them and ground them with stones until blood came to our fingers we ground them so sharp.

But for all this treasure my foolish wife was too frightened to go near the ship, and my children would only peep at it from behind big rocks. They could see them, they said, the ghosts of white men going in and coming out of the holes. But I used to go and my sons used to go and we found many things, and a glass that could see was one of the things. "Ae," said my wife when I gave it to her, "there are truly good things that come out of the black holes of the ghosts."

"Yes," I said, "but even ghosts will do you no harm, no more than the ghost of your face in the glass."

"Maybe you're right, Comock," she said, and she looked and she smiled at the ghost of her face in the glass.

"We are rich," I said. We were all sitting on the sand around a big driftwood fire.

"Yes," said my wife, "we are rich, but if only the rest of the people were with us, they would have everything too. We could all be happy together."

"We can't have everything," I said. "No one has everything."

"It is true," said Annunglung. "No matter how much we have, there is always more that we are wanting."

"But if only I could have those that went off in the ice," said my wife. "When the storms come across from our land I cannot keep their calling out of my ears, and dead they may be, but they are still on the ice. I am sure that I can hear them."

Our second winter on the island was a good winter. We were happy, even my wife. But as the winter drew on she talked more of our old land, much hunger she had for our old land and for our people who had been lost on the ice of the sea. "Maybe they landed on our old land," she said, "maybe their ice came back again and they landed there, after all, who can tell?" she said.

"It is foolish your talk," I said. "You have forgotten all that hunger we had in our old land, and if you have not forgotten that hunger, have you forgotten the ice that lies between? That ice," I said—"for myself I would rather trust a hungry dog."

"Maybe you are right, Comock," she said.

The oldest of my sons was growing big. He was almost a man and he was learning fast in his kayak and learning fast with his sled and he was good at his hunting—he had already killed his first deer.

One night—it was winter again—he had been away two days with Annunglung on the ice out at sea. He came into our igloo with the children laughing and screaming and helping him drag in his first seal— not a small seal, but a big square-flipper seal. We could not believe he could kill such a big seal.

"Yes," said Annunglung, "there was much fighting, but he killed him—I sat over one breathing hole and he sat over another, and when the seal came to his hole he stood up and struck down with his harpoon. The seal sounded and dived, so fast with his line he was pulled to the ice, so hard I thought surely some of his bones were broken. But he had the end of his line wrapped around him where he lay over the hole. I got him to his feet, but he was pulled down again and again. At last he was mostly on his feet, and he pulled in some of his line, and he pulled in more of his line and then more of his line and then it came easy, and at last the seal was dead."

My son said that anyone could have killed such a seal—a child could have killed almost such a seal. But my wife said, "Lie down beside it; it's longer than you."

But my son said, "My dogs, they are hungry," and he crawled out of the tunnel with all the children behind him.

My wife turned to me and said, "Comock, our son is now a hunter."

"No," I said, "but maybe he will be before the end of this winter—there is still his first walrus and there is still his first bear."

During the moon of the shortest days a big storm blowing again from our old land drove in big fields of ice and piled it high along the shores. At sea there was no open water for a long time, and that was the end of our good hunting. For many days I was hunting with my sons on the ice for seals, but all that we got was hardly enough to keep us alive. In these days Annunglung began to stay at home—something had come over him. Annunglung was always a silent man, never speaking much, not even of his lost wife and his lost children; but now, said my wife, he would sit in the igloo all day, just looking. This went on for days. We would come home perhaps with a seal, and Annunglung would say, "It's a poor man, Comock, who shares your igloo and eats your seal and does not do his share of hunting."

And then I would say, "Why do you not come out with us hunting?" And for a long time we would be silent though all our eyes would be upon him and waiting to hear what he would say. But it would be as if his mouth had been frozen—he would not move it again.

This would happen many times, and when we came home there would be Annunglung sitting in the igloo and my wife would say, "He has not moved all day long."

One night we came home with two big seals—we had been away two days—and there was Annunglung sitting and saying nothing, and I saw by my wife's face that she was frightened. My wife took me into the tunnel to be away from his hearing, and my wife made her voice very small and she said, "Comock, you must not leave me and my young children here alone again—I am frightened. Have you seen his eyes?"

"No," I said.

"You must see his eyes," she said.

As soon as the dogs were fed, my eldest son fastened the snow-block door for the night. And then we gathered around our seal and sat down to our eating, and we could not help looking at Annunglung who did not sit with us but sat near the lamp, not even eating the seal meat we had put into his hand. My wife, who sat near me, kept touching my arm. "Annunglung, are you not hungry?" I asked, hoping he would look up in the way that there would be light in his eyes. He looked and the light of the lamp was in his eyes, and then the meat in my mouth stood still, and truly I was frightened—the little black balls of his eyes—they had grown so small.

Then I told my sons to go alone to the hunt. I found and hid Annunglung's spears and harpoons. His knives, my wife said, he always kept under his sleeping mat. I found them and hid them too. There were many days of storms. My sons brought home no seals. We grew hungry. "Let our sons stay at home," my wife said. "You go for a seal this time, for we must soon have seals." I went out on the ice and stayed away two days, but the storms were too heavy. I could do no hunting. I had to come home. The night was half done when I did come home, and late though it was there was still a bright light shining through the ice window. Then I knew something was wrong. When I crawled into my igloo my wife was sitting up and not moving and there was fright on her face, and my sons were sitting up, and they were frightened too. Annunglung was sitting like a stone, not moving and not talking, but there was something in his eyes that told me that three men would not be so strong.

We took turns sitting and watching all that night and all the next day, and I tried to think what I would have to do. "Maybe he will get well," said my wife. And sometimes it looked as if this would be so, for in these times he would sleep a little, and he would eat a little, but I knew in the end that he would never be well. And truly this was so, for there were now deep lines on his face, and his teeth were set hard and sometimes they ground. And there was blood from his tongue, and in his eyes there was that shine and the black balls of them were truly very small.

We were hungry and my dogs were hungry—they were all ribs and there was whiteness on their mouths. We had one family of young dogs—those the dogs had already killed and eaten. And there was Annunglung, more and more still, and there was more and more hunger and my wife said, "Soon, Comock, you must kill some seals."

Then there was a night, and on this night everyone was asleep. And I who was watching was almost asleep, and then I heard a noise. It was Annunglung. I looked. He could not see my half-open eyes. He got up and he looked—he looked toward me a long time, then he looked at my sons a long time, and then he looked at my wife and my children, and then he looked all over the igloo and then he looked under his mat and there was no knife, and then he looked around again, and at last with no noise he began to crawl out through the tunnel of the igloo. This tunnel was narrow—he could not quickly turn. I followed him. I came upon him as he reached the end of the tunnel and stood up to get a knife and spear. Then he heard me, but I struck. Then he struck. Then I was glad, and if it had not been so I would not be alive. It was his blood the dogs smelled first.

When I came into the igloo again, no one had heard the fight or the fighting of the dogs. They were still asleep.

There was no more want that winter, or the next winter or the next winter. Our children were growing. One daughter was almost a woman. "It is well," my wife said, for it was more than she could do to take care of my kills and our son's kills and sew the skins for our boots and clothing.

Then the day came when my son all alone speared his first bear. My wife said, "Our son now is a man, Comock."

"Ae," I said, "he is now a man." But my wife still kept on with her talking as a woman will.

"Does it mean nothing to you, Comock, now that he is a man?"

"What do you mean?" I asked her.

But she said, "How can we go on living on this big island, and no wife for our son who is now a man? Besides," she said, "our other sons, too. They will all soon kill their first bear. We are only one family on all this big island, Comock," she said. "We will have to go sometime—if we don't we will die out on this big island, for all of its deer and all of its bear and all of its walrus and the bones of the white man's ship from which we get the good wood and the good iron for our knives and our harpoons. Besides, there's the ghost of Annunglung, Comock. We must leave this big island."

"The ghost of Annunglung," I said, "will come to us wherever we are. We must stay, we are fools to trust the sea—if we do, maybe we will die," I said.

"Maybe," said my wife, "but here it is sure—longer maybe, but sure."

"But I am afraid of the ice that lies between this big island and our old land," I would say, "and it will break on our crossing."

"The break of the ice on our crossing will not be so bad as if we stay here," was always my wife's answer. To this no words would come to my mouth.

Now came days that were still—there were no more big smokes rising from the sea, and these days were the days of the most cold. The nights of these days were the nights of the Big Lights, and these Big Lights were the red of pale meat and like the warm coat of the bear and like the weed of the sea. And my wife said these Big Lights were truly the spirits of unborn children playing in the sky, and she said for many days they may be playing in the sky, and now, she said, it was the time we should be crossing the big ice on the sea.

She said this many times and at last I said, "Maybe you are right—if ever we go, now is the time. In all our ten winters on this big island never have there been such good signs, such stillness on the sea or so much of the Big Light playing in the sky. We will go," I said. "Tiamak, to this big island."

"Ae," she said.

"Ae," said everyone.

There were yet some stars when we started. The air was still. "Twavee," I said.

"Twavee," said everyone. We had strong dogs, two sleds, twelve dogs to each sled. All day we traveled over the sea. We did not stop for seal and we did not stop for bear. There was much smooth ice and there was bad ice, but mostly the ice was smooth. We never traveled so fast over the ice of the sea.

On the next day it was the same, it was wonderful how fast we were going. On the third day we saw the land. We got close in, and the land we saw was our own land—the land which leans over the sea.

But now the ice was rough and piled higher than any I'd ever seen; from one high place one sled fell, and it fell so hard it broke in two. We had to leave this sled where it was and its load of good deerskins and good pots and the whole of one seal. We kept on, it was a long time, but at last we got close to the land which leans over the sea, and we could see, high up, its caves and dark places, but we had to lift our heads to look up at its edge, it rose so high in the sky.

We were deep in one place in this big ice, and the dogs, their traces all tangled, were all thrown together like fish in a net, and they were fighting to kill. We were trying to stop them and then with my feet I felt something. It was the ice—it was moving. My wife and my children were on a high ledge behind us, and though I could not hear them above the great noise of the dogs, I could see them waving their arms. At first it looked as if it was the big land that moved, passing us by. "Twavee," I yelled, "twavee." We must go back—we must go back out of this rough ice. We threw away half the load of the sled, and we turned and we began to work back. And it took all day to get onto the smooth ice, and all the time the ice field we were on was drifting. By nightfall it looked small, the land which leans over the sea.

For a long time, two moons, we drifted. And then one morning again we saw land, the big land on one side, but nearer to us still an island which rose high, almost straight up from the sea.

Our ice closed on this island like a big hand on a throat, and after the ice had done with its piling and breaking and rafting we climbed and we crawled through it, and got on to the shore, and climbed its big cliffs and on the top made our camp. Here we lived for the rest of the winter and through the spring and through the summer. And there were the eggs of eider ducks to eat and the skin of eider ducks for clothes, and there were sea pigeons which we caught in the cliffs and there were seals sometimes as well.

In these days we were much troubled for we did not know how we could get off this island, for between us and the big land, though it was not far, there was always the tide that runs swift like a river. And always, if there is ice in it, it is not ice we could cross, for it is the ice that is loose and the ice that is wild, always turning and tumbling and going up and down.

"If there were no ice and we had an umiak," I said, "then we might cross."

"Yes," said someone, and there was much laughing. "If our legs were long enough we could walk through the sea."

"Yes, but just the same if we had an umiak, we could cross," said my wife.

"We have no wood," said someone.

"We have no skins," said someone else, "and there are steep shores on this island, and the tide washes so high. Where shall we find driftwood?"

"But we have some skins of seal," I said, "and maybe we can get more. And the handles of our harpoons will be some wood, and maybe we can get more."

We began to search hard everywhere upon the shores, and the search took many days and we did not find much. But we found some driftwood buried in the sand. It was old and not too strong, but it was driftwood just the same. And we killed more seals, and my wife was careful when she skinned the seals. We found also some bones and we saved the bones, even those which were very small, and the time came and though we had only half enough I started to build the umiak. "There will never be enough wood to build this umiak," someone said. And then one would find more driftwood. And then I kept on to build more of the umiak until there was no more wood, and at last everyone said, "There will be no umiak." And for many days there was only half an umiak and no one knew what to do.

We had used all the bones of our kills, all the wood we could find and even the ivory snow knife for a part of a rib. And then one day I heard sounds from my wife and our children, and when I looked down they were on the shore and they were digging up sand. "The bones of a whale," they were yelling, "the bones of a whale."

The bones of a whale. I could not believe what I was hearing. The bones of a whale. And they were good bones, these bones of a whale, and they were big bones, and I finished the umiak. Then everyone came and we sat down around it, and we laughed. "It is a funny umiak," everyone said.

We lowered it down by the traces of the dogs (all tied in one) over the edge of the steep cliffs and we put it in the water, and someone said, "Now it looks more funny still." Some of us climbed in, but, even so, with few of us in it, it was shaking all over.

"It will never carry us," said my wife.

"No, never," said everyone.

"Yes," I said, "it will carry us." And I said to my wife, "Get me a roll of your good sealskin line, and the bladders of the seals I told you to save." All around the umiak I fastened the line. And then I blew up the bladders of the seals and I tied them. And I fastened them to the sides, and then I said, "Now you who always doubt, get in."

And they got in, and my wife got in, and she said, "It will do, Co-mock, it will do."

And everyone said, "Ae, it will do."

Now we waited some days for no wind. But in these days, though the ice was all gone, with even a small wind there was always some sea. We waited more days, and now there were no more seals, and the eiders were gone, though there were still in the cliffs some sea pigeons. Upon these we lived. We waited more days, and on this day of today my wife said, "This is the smoothest of all our days on this island."

"Ae," I said, "we will wait, there is still enough sea."

But she said, "We should lower the umiak over the cliffs and all of us climb down and be ready to go." But I said, "No, we will wait until there is more smoothness come over the sea." But she said, "No, we will go"; and then I said, "No, we will wait until there is more smooth-ness come over the sea." But she said, "No we will go"; and then I said, "No"; then she said, "Yes"; then I said, "No." Then she went off and sat by herself, still like a stone.

Suddenly there were yells: "Umiak! Umiak!" And when I stood up there it was, your white sail going around the nose of the cape. And though there was not too much smoothness on the sea, we lowered our umiak over the cliff and put it in the water and we all got in.

And my wife said, "I have here in my hands a stick, and if anyone moves they will feel this stick, for there is not too much smoothness on the sea." And all the way she kept good watch with her stick.

"And now," concluded Comock, "we have come over to you on the sea, and you have taken us on your boat, and here we are."

"Ae," said his wife.

"Ae," said Comock, his wonderful face alight. "Ae, and now there are no more words in my mouth. Tiamak," he said.

Reindeer

I wriggled silently through the swamp,
carrying bow and arrow in my mouth.
The marsh was broad, the water icy cold,
and there was no cover in sight.

Slowly, soaked, invisible,
I crawled within range.
The reindeer were eating;
they grazed the juicy moss
without concern,
till my arrow sank
tremblingly deep
into the bull's side.

Terrified, the unsuspecting herd
hastily scattered,
and vanished at the sharpest trot
to shielding hills.

—Aua (Iglulik Eskimo man)

Stefansson's Crucial Caribou Hunt

BY VILHJALMUR STEFANSSON (CANADIAN, 1917)

Vilhjalmur Stefansson was one of the new breed of Arctic explorer, but in some ways he was also the last of the old. Stefansson spent a year early in his career living with the Inuit to learn their language, travel techniques, and how to live off the land for years on end. During his five-year Canadian Arctic Expedition (1913–18), he explored the western islands of the Canadian archipelago and became the last explorer to discover significant new lands in the North American Arctic—Borden, Brock, Meighen, and Longheed islands. Stefansson was the consummate expert, and for this reason his writings make less gripping reading than those of explorers beset by incompetence and disaster. Instead, they are full of instructive discourses about how to survive in the Arctic. "In general my polar experience has been nearly free from the hardships that most impressed me in the books I read before going north," he wrote in his memoir, *The Friendly Arctic*. "For nine winters I have never frozen a finger or a toe nor has any member of my immediate party."

Still, Stefansson had his share of close calls. One occurred in the spring of 1917 when he and his party were far north in the Canadian archipelago and two of his men succumbed to scurvy because they had ignored his instructions to eat plenty of fresh meat in the weeks and months before rendezvousing with him. Stefansson was out of fresh meat at the time, and now found himself out on the sea ice 125 miles from the nearest land, six hundred miles from his base camp, with two men quickly weakening. Storms prevented good seal hunting on the ice. He decided to head for the nearest land and hoped to find caribou enough to bring the men back to health. What follows is Stefansson's description of this crucial hunt. It reveals the precision and intelligence with which one must act to survive living off the land in the Arctic.

Apart from the islands actually discovered by my expedition, there is no known country in the northern hemisphere that has been so little visited as Isachsen Land, in north latitude 79°, west longitude 103°. We feel sure that no Eskimos ever saw that island. From the beginning of the world to our own time it had been visited only once—by Captain Isachsen in 1901. Isachsen made a hurried sledge trip round the island. The journey took him about a week. In one place he saw some caribou tracks, and I think he may have seen some caribou at a distance, but he did not try to hunt them. The next visitors were my sledge party in 1916, and on that occasion we saw no caribou and had to feed ourselves and our dogs entirely on seals.

My second visit, and the third visit of human beings to the island, was in 1917. We were then on the most dangerous adventure that has ever fallen to our lot. By the road we had to travel we were some five hundred miles away from the nearest Eskimos and six hundred miles away from our own base camp. Four of us had been on a long journey out on the moving sea-ice to the north-west. When we were more than a hundred miles north-west from Isachsen Land two of my three companions were taken seriously ill. We turned towards shore immediately, and it was a hard fight to make land. When we got there after a struggle of two weeks we found ourselves with one man so sick that he could not walk, another who could barely walk, but was of no use otherwise, and with two teams of dogs that were exhausted with hard work and so thin from short rations during the forced march towards shore that they were little more than skeletons. It had been my pride through many years never to lose a dog. Furthermore, I was exceedingly fond of every one of these dogs, for they had worked for me faithfully for years. I was concerned for their safety, and still more concerned for the safety of the sick men. By that time, however, my confidence in our ability to make a living in the Arctic had become so strong through eight years of experience that I felt more worry for the lives of the men on the score of illness than for fear they might actually die of hunger.

But the first day on Isachsen Land was a depressing contradiction of my hopes and expectations. The one man in good health and the two men who were sick had to make their way as best they could along the coast while I hunted inland parallel to their course. I walked that day twenty miles across one of the very few stretches of entirely barren land that I have seen in the Arctic. Under foot was gravel without a blade of grass. Much of the land was lightly covered with snow, as in other typical Arctic lands in winter, and I looked in vain in the snow for track or other sign of any living thing.

That evening my men were depressed, partly because of their illness and also because it looked as if we had at last come into a region as barren as many people think the polar countries generally are. It was clear that if we saw game the next day we should simply have to have it. Where game is plentiful you may lose one chance and soon get another; but where it is scarce you must not allow any opportunity to slip through your fingers.

I am telling this particular hunting story rather than any other to illustrate the principle of how you must hunt caribou in the polar regions if it is essential that you should get every animal you see. It certainly was essential in this case, for I wanted not only to stave off immediate hunger, but to secure meat enough to enable us to camp in one place for several weeks and give the sick men a chance to become well.

On our second day at Isachsen Land the men again followed the coastline with the sledges, cutting across the shortest distance from point to point, while I walked a much longer course inland. I had gone but a few miles when I came upon the tracks of a band of caribou. You can seldom be sure from the tracks of the minimum number in a band if there are more than ten animals, for caribou have a way of stepping in each other's footprints. There are always likely to be more animals in a band than you have been able to make out from the tracks.

The trail showed that these caribou were travelling into the wind, as they usually do. There were only light airs, and the snow had on it a crust that broke underfoot with a crunching noise. Under such conditions the band were likely to hear me four or five hundred yards away. The country now was a rolling prairie—not barren gravel as yesterday. It was impossible to tell which ridge might hide the caribou from me, so instead of following the trail ahead I went back along it for about half a mile, studying the tracks to see just how fast they had been moving. They had been travelling in a leisurely way and feeding here and there. I estimated that their average rate of progress would not be more than three or four miles per day. I could not rely on this, however, for a wolf may turn up any time and begin a pursuit which takes a band twenty-five or fifty miles away. Should a wolf pass to windward of them, so that they got his smell without his knowing about them, they would be likely to run from five to ten miles.

When I had made up my mind that these caribou were moving slowly I went to the top of a neighbouring hill and through my glasses studied the landscape carefully. With good luck I might have seen some of them on top of some hill, and the problem would have become definite. But I watched for half an hour and saw nothing. Clearly they were either feeding in some low place or else they were lying down, for caribou are like cattle in their habit of lying down for long periods. I now commenced a cautious advance, not along the actual trail, but criss-crossing it from high hill-top to high hill-top, hoping to get a view of the animals while they were at least half a mile from me and while I was beyond the range of their eyesight, for they cannot see a man even under the most favourable conditions farther off than half a mile. Under ordinary conditions they would not see you much beyond a quarter of a mile.

Finally I saw the band lying quietly on some flat land. There was no cover to enable me to approach safely within five hundred yards, and that is too far for good shooting. I thought these might be the only caribou in the whole country. We had thirteen hungry dogs and two sick men, and now that I had a large band before me it was my business to get enough food at one time to enable us to spend at that place two or three weeks, while the men had a chance to regain their health and the dogs to regain their flesh and strength.

On a calm day, when caribou can hear you farther than you can shoot, there is only one method of hunting. You must study their movements from afar until you make up your mind in which direction they are going. Then you must walk in a wide curve round them until you are in the locality toward which they are moving and well beyond earshot. This takes judgment, for they usually travel nearly or quite into the wind, and you must not allow them to scent you. You therefore have to choose a place which you think is near enough to their course for them to pass within shooting distance, and still not directly enough in front to enable them to smell you.

On this occasion the glaring light on the snow had been so hard on my eyes that I did not feel they were in perfect condition, and no one can shoot well if his eyes are not right. Unless there is a change of wind caribou are not likely to turn their course back along the trail by which they have come. I accordingly selected a hill across which they had walked that morning and half a mile away from where they now were. On the top of this hill, where I could see them, although they could not see me (because my eyes were better than theirs) I lay down, covered my head with a canvas hunting-bag to keep the sun away, and went to sleep. Sleeping is the best possible way of passing time, but my object now was not only to pass the time until the caribou began moving, but also to get my eyes into perfect condition.

When you go to sleep at twenty below zero you have in the temper-ature an automatic alarm clock. My clothes were amply warm enough to keep me comfortable while I was awake, but I knew that when I went to sleep my circulation would slow down. This reduces the body temperature, and the same weather that will not chill you when you are awake will chill you enough to wake you from a sleep.

In this case the chill woke me in about half an hour to an unpleasant situation. A fog had set in, and I could not see the caribou, nor had I any means of knowing whether they were still lying down or whether they had started to move. If this had been a good game-country I might have taken chances on advancing through the fog a little, but I was so impressed with the possibility that these were the only animals within a hundred miles that carelessness was not to be considered. At this time of year we had twenty-four hours of daylight. The fog was bound to lift sooner or later, and whenever it did I would commence the hunt over again.

The fog did lift in about two hours, and I did have to commence the hunt all over again, for the caribou were gone. I was to the north of them, and I felt sure that they had not gone by near me; so they must have gone east, west, or south. I was probably so near them that I could not with safety go on top of any of the adjoining hills, so I went back north half a mile and climbed a high hill there. From that hill I saw nothing, and went half a mile to one side to another hill. Then I saw the caribou. They were now feeding half a mile south of where they had been when the fog covered them up. In the meantime the breeze had stiffened, so that now there was no longer danger of my be-ing heard. I did not, therefore, have to circle them and lie in wait in front, but could follow up directly behind.

Eventually I got within about three hundred yards. But I wanted to get within two hundred, so I lay still and waited for them to move into a more favourable locality. During my wait an exceedingly thick fog-bank rolled up, but with it the wind did not slacken. Under cover of this fog I felt safe in crawling ahead a hundred yards, for I knew that I could see through the fog quite as well as the animals, and that they could not hear me because of the wind. The reason I had not approached them in the previous fog was that the weather then had been nearly calm and they would have heard me.

At two hundred yards I was just able to make out the outline of the nearest caribou. I did not dare to go closer, and, of course, I could not begin shooting with only one or two animals in sight when I wanted to get them all. I had before now counted them carefully. There were twenty-one, which I estimated would be enough to feed our men and dogs between two and three weeks, giving them a chance to recuperate.

After about half an hour the fog began gradually to clear, and in another half-hour I could see all the animals. I was near the top of a hill and they were in a hollow, the nearest of them about a hundred and fifty yards away and the farthest about three hundred.

In winter the ground in any cold country will split in what we call frost-cracks. These are cracks in the frozen surface of what in summer is mud. They are ordinarily only half an inch or so wide, but I have seen cracks four or five inches wide. These cracks form when the mercury is dropping and with a noise that resembles a rifle-shot. Under the same conditions the ice on the small lakes cracks similarly. These loud noises are so familiar to the caribou, and the report of a rifle is so similar, that the mere sound of a rifle does not scare them. Of course, we have smokeless powder, so they cannot see where the shots come from. What does scare them is the whistle of the bullet and the thud as it strikes the ground. It is instinctive with all animals to run directly away from the source of any noise that frightens them. It is another instinct of caribou when they are alarmed to run towards the centre of the herd. A band that has been scattered while feeding will bunch up when they take fright. When you know these two principles it is obvious that the first caribou to kill is the one farthest away from you. On some occasions when I have been unable to get within good shooting distance of a band, I have commenced by firing a few shots into a hill on the other side of them, hoping that the noise of the striking bullets would scare them towards me. Frequently it works.

On this occasion, however, I merely took careful aim at an animal about three hundred yards away. It dropped so instantaneously that although the sound of the bullet striking it induced the other caribou to look up, they recognized no sign of real danger. They were, however, alert, and when they saw the second caribou fall they ran together into a group and moved somewhat towards me. I now shot animals on the outer margin of the group, and as each fell the others would run a little away from that one. Their retreat in any direction was stopped by my killing the foremost animal in the retreat, whereupon the band would turn in the opposite direction.

It would not have been difficult for me to kill the whole band alone, but I was not shooting alone. From a point somewhere above and behind me I could hear other shots, and some animals I was not aiming at were dropping. Without looking round I knew what this meant. My companions travelling along shore on the ice had seen the caribou, and had waited for some time until they began to fear that I might have missed the band. The two sick men had been left behind in camp, while their Eskimo companion had come inland to try to get the caribou. When he got near he saw that I was approaching them, and very wisely did not interfere. There is nothing so likely to spoil a caribou-hunt as two hunters whose plans conflict. Even when they have a chance to consult at the beginning of the hunt, two men are less likely to be successful than one. For one thing, caribou may see a black dot on the landscape and take no warning from it, but if they see two black dots and later notice that they are either close together or farther apart than they were a moment before, this makes a danger signal which they understand. That is the main reason why I always hunt alone. If there are two hunters to go out from the same camp on any given day, they should go in opposite directions. In this way they double the chance of finding game, and each has a fair chance of getting the animals he does find.

On our journeys we never kill more animals than we need, but in this case we needed the whole twenty-one. The Eskimo and I went down to the ice with my hunting-bag filled with the tongues of the caribou. This gave the sick men a more appetizing meat than they had had for a long time. The dogs had to wait for their food until we were able to move camp right to where the caribou had been shot. Although they were thin and tired, they became so excited at the smell of the fresh-killed caribou which they got from our clothes that they pulled towards shore as if they had been well fed and of full strength.

On the hill from which I had shot the caribou we pitched camp. During the next two weeks the invalids rapidly gained in health. We called the place Camp Hospital. Few hospitals have ever been more successful. When we left it three weeks later the dogs were fat and the men well.

Spirit Song

Do you hear
The voice from the deep!
  ajai-jija.
The voice from the deep!
  Ajai-jija.

I will visit
unclean women,
probe behind man,
break taboo.
Aj, let the lace of the boot hang loose.
  Ajai-jija.

Do you hear
the voice from the deep?
  Ajai-jija.
The voice from the deep!
  Ajai-jija.

I will visit
unclean women,
probe behind man,
break taboo.
Aj, smooth the wrinkles
from the rounded cheeks!
  Ajai-jija.
I walked out on the sea.
Marvelling, I heard
the voice from the deep,
the song of the sea.
I went out slowly,
pondering myself.
The vast young ice-floes sighed,
  ajai-jija
  ajai-jija.
Helping spirit seeks the feasting-house.

—Netsit (Copper Eskimo man)

Rasmussen Meets the Iglulik Eskimos

BY KNUD RASMUSSEN (GREENLANDIC, 1922)

During his epic Fifth Thule Expedition (1921– 24), the Greenlander and ethnologist Knud Rasmussen spent three years traveling by dogsled across the whole of the Canadian and American Arctic, from east to west, staying with various Inuit groups and recording their customs. The first winter, 1921–22, the expedition was quartered at Danish Island at the northern end of Hudson Bay. It was from here that Rasmussen made contact with Inuit who had undergone relatively little exposure to white culture.

The following excerpt, from the opening pages of Volume VII of his massive report of the Fifth Thule Expedition, contains the abbreviated life story of the woman Takornaq. She gives a startling picture of the keen joys and unimaginable hardships of the traditional way of life, and the way in which the Eskimos' world was circumscribed by taboo. The song that Takornaq makes up on the spur of the moment to give thanks for her guest has in the seventy-odd years since that moment of recitation become one of the best-known of Inuit poems. Without Rasmussen there to write it down, it undoubtedly would have vanished like thousands of other improvised Inuit poems.

273

The excerpt opens with some of Rasmussen's thoughts on Eskimo religion and Christian missionaries, and then describes the first encounter with Takornaq.

Takornâq and her husband Padloq.

My visit to Repulse Bay proved of the greatest importance in the subsequent arrangement of my work. The natives here were frank and genial folk, with whom it was easy to enter into conversation on ordinary matters of everyday life. Nor had they any reluctance to tell a story, or sing a song accompanied by the whole household as chorus. But as soon as I ventured to touch on more serious themes, they showed more reserve. There were great and difficult questions here which were best left alone. Only when actual happenings called for some decision, some course of action in face of threatening circumstances, would the subject be discussed with the wise men of the tribe. The earth grew angry if men out hunting worked too much with stones and turf in the building of their meat stores and hunting depots; so also the spirits that guided men's fate might be offended if men concerned themselves over much with such things. Men knew so little of things apart from their food and sleep and rest; it might easily seem presumptuous if they endeavoured to form any opinion about hidden things. Happy folk should not worry themselves by thinking.

And old Ivaluardjuk held to his view at first, maintaining a profound reserve when I endeavoured to draw him out. Moreover, apart from this innate reluctance to speak of such things as life itself and the purpose of life, and its guiding powers, the Eskimos of these regions were extremely cautious in expressing their views at all when dealing with white men. True, no missionaries ever came here—save for a few brief visits—to condemn their religion, but the little they knew of "that sort of white men", who were so unlike the traders and whalers, was not calculated to render them more communicative. As far as they could understand, it seemed that the strangers regarded them pityingly on account of their belief in such unreasonable things as their wise men maintained to be the foundations of all wisdom. A kind of spiritual shyness, not unmixed perhaps with a certain sense of dignity, made them reticent on the subject; they merely acknowledged that the missionaries otherwise appeared to be good men in their daily life.

"The other sort" of white men comprised the traders and whalers. These were bright, smart fellows, caring only for their hunting and trading. But when any of them occasionally happened to be present at the solemn seances of the angákut, they would merely shrug their shoulders, or make some scornful remark, as to the relations of these shamans with the supernatural. Furthermore, all white men looked with supreme disdain on the system of taboo by which the balance of the Eskimo community was maintained.

I understood then, that if I were to succeed in gaining the full confidence of these people, it was absolutely necessary to place myself in their position. I was not concerned to guide or correct them in any way, but had come to their country expressly for the purpose of learning what they could teach. The thing to do, then, was to make friends with some of the elders, those most familiar with the traditions of the tribe. Once I had won their friendship, the rest would come of itself.

It was not long before I made just the sort of acquaintance I had in mind; it happened indeed on the way back from Repulse Bay to Danish Island. Peter Freuchen had gone on further south to continue his investigations, and Nasaitsordluarssuk and I were driving home alone to inform our companions of all that we had learned. In order to save time, we decided to make a short cut from Haviland Bay down to Gore Bay. We had not got far inland when we came upon an old woman fishing for trout in a lake. The ice was thick already, and she lay half hidden among broken hummocks, with her head bent over the hole where her line was down. We thus took her entirely by surprise. She started up as the dogs gave tongue, and stumbled backward in confusion at the sight of us. We had already been told that the natives here were not usually pleased to encounter strangers unawares; there was no knowing whether it was friend or enemy. We were not surprised then, that the old woman endeavoured to run away; in this, however, she was unsuccessful; in fact, a moment after she was sitting on my sledge—albeit much against her will—and driving down towards the place where she lived, our dogs having already scented human dwellings near. She had with her a little puppy, that she had not wished to leave behind, and held it in her lap with a convulsive clasp, looking up at me at the same time with such an expression of terror in her eyes that I could not help laughing. She had heard nothing of our arrival in the district and saw now only two men and two sledges, every detail revealing the stranger. The fashion of our clothes, the build of our sledges, the dogs' harness, and even our manner of speech. She was sitting behind me, and as I bent down to explain who we were and what we wanted, I suddenly noticed a sound I had not perceived before, and now discovered, tucked away down at the back of her behind the fur hood, a little naked infant with its arms round her neck, squealing in concert with the puppy. I now hastened to mention the names of all the new friends I had made during my stay at Repulse Bay, and this, as showing that I was well known to people she knew as neighbours, changed her attitude entirely. So delighted was she to find herself among friends that her eyes filled with tears. As soon as she had calmed down a little, I explained where we had come from. It was easier now to do so than in the case of our first meeting with natives at Haviland Bay, for I could now give the Eskimo names of the places. I knew that Ponds Inlet was called Tununeq, and explained therefore that we came from a country beyond the great sea that washed the shores of Baffin Land. Hardly had I finished speaking when she told me that she herself was called Takornâq ("the recluse" or "the one that is shy of strangers") and came from Iglulik. She had moved down to Repulse Bay with her husband, Padloq, expressly in order to be near white men and all the wealth which one could obtain by bartering with them .She had often been to Ponds Inlet, and had met Scottish whalers there. They had told her of the people from whose land we came, who spoke the same language as she did, and lived over on the other side. So pleased was she at finding that we belonged, as it were, to her own world after all, that she became frankly communicative, not to say garrulous herself. It was not long before we had the village in sight and soon came up to the three snow huts which were all it amounted to. They were built close to a lake where trout were to be caught. The inhabitants came running towards us but without knowing quite how to receive us, for they also had recognised at once that we were strangers. But on catching sight of Takornâq, who was laughing delightedly, they came up and gathered round us. Takornâq certainly did not bear out the character implied in her name. She chattered away, recounting all the information she had just acquired, and pointing to us, explained that we were real live human beings, from a country far, far away beyond the sea from Tununeq.

Takornâq was conscious of her position at the moment, as the principal actor in the scene, and when I asked her the names of those about us, she took me by the shoulder and led me, laughing herself all the time, from one to another, mentioning their names. This one was Inernerunashuaq ("the one that was made in a hurry") an old shaman, and I noticed that he wore, as a mark of his dignity, the belt of office round his waist, consisting of a broad strip of skin hung about with many odd items, bones of animals, little implements, knives and whips cut out of walrus ivory. His wife, who was conspicuously tattooed on the face, was called Tûglik ("northern diver"), a big, fat woman with a whole crowd of little children hanging to her skirts. Then there was Talerortalik ("the one with the forepaws"); his wife was the shaman's daughter, Utsukitsoq ("the narrow vulva"). The young couple stood modestly in the background, but Takornâq, who was not afraid of saying what she thought, declared openly that it was they who kept the shaman and his family alive. Inernerunashuaq might be a great shaman—that was none of her business to say, she put in laughing— but he was certainly a very poor hunter. This lack of respect for a shaman interested me very much, albeit the remark was only made in jest, for I had always understood that the natives were very careful about what they said to the shaman. I learned afterwards that this was indeed the rule, and Takornâq the exception, being not only remarkably free with her tongue, but equally sincere in what she said. She was herself skilled in shamanism, though practising more in secret, and would thus know something of the limitations of the craft. Finally, there was Talerortalik's brother Peqingajoq ("the crooked one"), who was actually a cripple, with a pronounced hunchback figure. Takornâq informed me that he was a most hardworking fellow, and so keen on his fishing that there was always ice on the front of his dress—from lying face downward on the ice at his fishing hole. There were other natives in the party, but it would take up too much space to mention every one.

Takornâq, maintaining that she had a sort of right to us, as having been the first to meet us, now invited us in to her house. It was a well-kept snow hut, but rather cold until we got the blubber lamp going. Nasaitsordluarssuk and I clambered up on to the bench, which was completely covered with warm skins of caribou, a pot of meat was set to boil, and these domestic preparations finished, our hostess sat down between us and declared that now she was married to both of us, for her husband was away on a journey. She burst out laughing herself at this observation, and seemed to enjoy her own joke immensely. It was indeed, not to be understood in any ill sense, for she added directly after that she knew no better man than her husband. It was only her fun, she said, and there was no harm in talking nonsense when one felt a little jolly.

As soon as the place was warmed up a little, she pulled out the infant from her amaut, and laid it with motherly pride in a sleeping bag of hare's skin. The child's name was Qahîtsoq, it had been called after a mountain spirit. It was not her own child but one of twins, belonging to a certain Nagjuk ("deer's horn") of the Netsilingmiut, and Takornâq had bought it of him as it would otherwise have been killed. "Twins", she added, "are hardly ever allowed to live in our country, for we are always travelling about, and a mother cannot carry more than one in her amaut". The price paid for Qahîtsoq was a dog and a frying pan; really too much for such a skinny little bit of a thing. Takornâq was evidently sore at the recollection that Nagjuk had cheated her, and kept the fatter of the twins for himself.

Takornâq talked incessantly, and it was not long before we were quite like old acquaintances. There was no need for me to say much, a grunt here and there, an encouraging remark, sufficed to keep her going. She was proud of her descent, for the Iglulingmiut, which of all the tribes has had least to do with white men, is reckoned as having the cleverest hunters and the best women. She was therefore anxious that we should not mistake her birthplace for that of the others in the village, these being all Netsilingmiut. They were dirty with their clothes, she said, and not at all clean in their houses. She and her husband, now, had special vessels for urinals indoors, which showed how cleanly they were even when living in snow huts, whereas the Netsilingmiut did not hesitate to make water on the floor, or even on the bench under their pillows, simply lifting up the skins that covered it.

When the talk began to quieten down a little, I told her about my own childhood in Greenland, that she might understand how I came to speak her language, and having ended my story, I declared that I would rather listen to others than talk myself. At this she burst out laughing, and observed that it was just the other way with her: she would much rather talk herself than listen to other people. I therefore took her at her word and begged her to tell me about her own life, as far as she could remember, from her earliest childhood. And now for the first time since we had entered the hut, Takornâq seemed inclined to talk seriously. She closed her eyes and sat for a long time without speaking; then when at last she began, she gave us the whole story of her life, all her experiences recounted without hesitation, in clear and fluent language.

"My father and mother often had children that died. My father was a great shaman, and as he was very anxious to have children, he went up inland to an ice loon and asked it to help him. My father and mother say that it was with the aid of this creature that I was born; a strange creature it was, half bird, half human. So it was that I came into the world. And I lived.

"Some time after I was born, there came a season of scarcity, and we were in want of food. My father had gone out to a hole in the ice, and here, it is said, he spoke as follows:

" 'If my daughter is to live, you will remain as you are. If my daughter is to die, you will close over, and keep away all the seal. Now give me this sign.'

"The hole in the ice did not change, there was no movement in the water, and my father began to catch seals, and he knew that I was not to die.

"When he came home in the evening, he said to my mother:

" 'Today a sign has been given to tell me that our daughter is not to die like the others. Therefore you need no longer trouble about all those rules for women who have had a child.'

"And though it is the custom among our people for women with young children to refrain from many kinds of food which are considered harmful to the child, my mother now ate whatever she liked, and nothing was forbidden to her. But then it came about that I fell ill after all, and they thought I should die. Then my father said to my mother:

" 'Take the meat fork and stand it up in the pot! If it falls down she will die; if it stays upright she will live.'

"The fork was laid across the pot, and slipped down of its own accord and stood upright. Thus once more they learned that I was to live, and my mother again took to eating whatever she liked.

"Thus I began to live my life, and I reached the age when one is sometimes as it were awake, and sometimes as if asleep. I could begin to remember and forget.

"One day I remember I saw a party of children out at play, and wanted to run out at once and play with them. But my father, who understood hidden things, perceived that I was playing with the souls of my dead brothers and sisters. He was afraid this might be dangerous, and therefore called up his helping spirits and asked them about it. Through his helping spirits my father learned that despite the manner in which I was born, with the aid of a magic bird, and the way my life had been saved by powerful spirits, there was yet something in my soul of that which had brought about the death of all my brothers and sisters. For this reason the dead were often about me, and I could not distinguish between the spirits of the dead and real live people. Thus it was that I had gone out to play with the souls of my dead brothers and sisters, but it was a dangerous thing to do, for in the end the dead ones might keep me among themselves. My father's helping spirits would therefore now endeavour to protect me more effectively than hitherto, and my father was not to be afraid of my dying now. And after that, whenever I wanted to go out and play with the spirit children, which I always took for real ones, a sort of rocky wall rose up out of the ground, so that I could not get near them.

"The next thing I remember is hearing people talk of evil spirits, which were said to be about us; evil spirits that would bring misfortune and spoil the hunting. When I heard this I was very much afraid, for I was now old enough to understand that our life was set about with many perils, and I fell to crying. Then I remember we all went away, to escape from that dangerous place, and travelled long and far until we came to Qiqertaq (Ship Harbour Island, near Haviland Bay). It was here that I first saw the white men, and I learned later on that they were whalers. I remember some curious things from those days. There was an old woman who wanted to sell a puppy to the white men, but they would not buy it, and I thought how hard it was on the old woman, for she was very poor. I remember she tried to work magic and do the white men harm because they would not help her.

"Another thing I remember about the white men is that they were very eager to get hold of women. A man with a handsome wife could get anything he wanted out of them; they never troubled much about what a thing cost as long as they could borrow the wife now and again. And they gave the women valuable gifts. I was only a little girl myself at that time, and had but little knowledge of what took place between man and woman when they were together, but I remember there were some of our men who would have no dealings with the white men, because they did not wish to share their wives with them. But most of the men did not mind; for it is quite a common thing among us to change wives. A man does not love his wife any the less because she lies with someone else now and again. And it is the same with the woman. They like to know about it, that is all; there must be no secrets in such matters. And when a man lends his wife to another, he himself always lies with the other man's wife. But with white men it was different; none of them had their wives with them to lend in exchange. So they gave presents instead, and thus it was that many men of our tribe looked on it as only another kind of exchange, like changing wives. And there were so many things in our way of life that did not agree with the white man's ways, and they did not feel obliged themselves to keep our rules about what was taboo, so we could not be so particular in other matters. Only the white men had less modesty than our own when wishing to lie with a woman. Our men always desired to be alone with the woman, and if there was no other way, they would build a snow hut. But the white men in the big ship lived many together in one place, lying on shelves along the steep sides of the ship, like birds in the face of a cliff. And I remember a thing that caused great amusement to many, though the ones to whom it happened were not pleased. One evening when a number of women had gone to the white men's ship to spend the night there, we in our house had settled down early to rest. But suddenly we were awakened by the sound of someone weeping outside. And this was what had happened. A woman named Atanarjuat had suddenly fallen through the shelf where she was lying with one of the men on the ship, and rolled stark naked on the floor. She burst out crying for shame, put on her clothes in a great hurry and went home weeping, saying that she would never again lie with a white man. It was she whom we had heard outside our house, and as I said before, these things took place at a time when I did not rightly know what went on between man and woman. But all the same, when I heard about this, a thing most of the others laughed at, I could not help feeling that the white men must have less sense of decency than we had.

"Then I forgot all that happened at that place, and did not remember again until we came to Malukshitaq (Lyon Inlet), where we had taken land. One thing I remember from that time is that my mother always had a urine bucket for a pillow when she lay down to sleep. This she did in order that my father might be successful in his hunting. Thus she helped the hunters, and they killed a walrus. There was a great feast, and I was there, and I remember there was a fight between father and son. I was afraid, and ran away.

"All this that I have told you I remember only as in a mist. My first clear remembrance is of the time when we lived at Utkuhigjalik (Wager Bay); my father died there. Soon after his death, my mother married Mánâpik ("the very much present") but they could not live together, and it was not long before they separated, and my mother was married to a man named Higjik ("the marmot"). Shortly after, we went away from there, and lived at Oqshoriaq (the word means quartzite; it is the Eskimo name for Marble Island). There were many people there at that time, and life was very amusing. The men often had boxing matches, and there were great song feasts at which all were assembled. It was there I saw for the first time an old woman from Qaernermiut (Baker Lake). I was told that this old woman was the first who ever saw Oqshoriaq. Before that time, it was nothing but a heap of pressure ridges in the ice. It was not until later that the ice turned to the white stone we call Oqshoriaq. I remember the first time we came to that island, we had to crawl up on to the land, and were not allowed to stand upright until we reached the top. That was done then, and it is done to this day, for the Island is a sacred place: magic words made it, and if we do not show respect for it by crawling it will change to ice again, and all the people on it will fall through and drown."

—At this point in Takornâq's story the meat in the pot began to boil, and she interrupted her narration to serve up a meal. Tea was made from our own supply, and the old woman was so pleased at this little trivial courtesy, that she at once improvised a song, the words of which were as follows:

> Ajaja—aja—jaja,
> The lands around my dwelling
> Are more beautiful
> From the day
> When it is given me to see
> Faces I have never seen before.
> All is more beautiful,
> All is more beautiful.
> And life is thankfulness.
> These guests of mine
> Make my house grand,
> Ajaja—aja—jaja.

We then settled down to eat, but Takornâq herself would not join us, for in order to preserve the life of the delicate infant she had bought, she was obliged to refrain from eating any food cooked in a pot with meat intended for others; she must have her own special cooking pot, and eat from no other.

As soon as we had finished, she went to a store chamber at one side of the hut, and dragged out the carcase of a caribou, which she gave us with the following words:

"Go out and give this to your dogs. I am only doing as my husband would have done had he been at home."

We then went out and fed our dogs, and when we re-entered the hut, the talk naturally turned upon her husband, Padloq (properly, "he who lies face downwards"). She had already told us that she had been married several times before. She now resumed her story where she had left off, as follows:

"When I was old enough to begin taking part in games with the young men, I was married. My first husband was called Angutiashuk ("one who is not a real man"). We were only married a very short time. I did not care for him, he was no good, and so we separated. He died of hunger shortly after.

"It was not long before I was married again, this time to one named Quivâpik, but everyone was afraid of him, because he was always threatening to kill people if he did not get exactly what he wanted. He went up inland hunting caribou, and I went with him to help carry the meat. We lived quite alone, far from any people, and I often wept with misery at our loneliness. I felt the need of being among others, and having someone to talk to, for Quivâpik was a man who hardly ever spoke. We stayed up inland all that summer. The only means we had of getting fire was by using firestone (pyrites) but once we could not find any, and could make no fire. Then Quivâpik called up his helping spirits, and while doing this he cried to me suddenly:

" 'Close your eyes and clutch at the air!' And I did so, and a piece of fire-stone came flying through the air and I caught it, and we were able to make a fire once more.

"Summer came to an end, and autumn set in, and when the darkness came, we could sometimes see beings in human form, but we did not know what they were. We were afraid of them, and returned home to our own place, where at that time there was scarcity of game and great want of food. Before long a walrus was captured, and then there was meat for all once more.

"Real knives of iron and seel, such as we use now, were very rare in those days, and the men often lost them. Then my husband would hold a spirit calling, and in that way recover the lost knives.

"Once while we were at Southampton Island, Quivâpik was attacked by some of his enemies, and wounded by a harpoon in one eye and one thigh, but so great a shaman was he that he did not die.

"Quivâpik once tried to catch a dead man who was trying to return to his village. A corpse thus trying to come to life again is called an anerlartukxiaq. They are persons at whose birth magic words have been uttered, so that if they die, they can come to life again and return to their place among men. But it was a hard matter for Quivâpik to catch this one, so he got another shaman to help him, and even then they did not succeed. Quivâpik said it would have been easy to bring the dead man to life again if only the moon had given leave. But the dead man's mother had sewn garments of new caribou skin on the island of Oqshoriaq, and that is not allowed there, so the moon would not let her son come to life again.

"Another time we were out after salmon, and I could not catch any. But my husband came and took the fish hook and line from me and held the hook between his legs, and after holding it there a while, he swallowed it, and drew it out from his navel, and the line the same way. After that I caught plenty of salmon.

"I was married to him for seven years, but then he was killed by some people who were afraid of him. A man named Ikumaq ('the flame') stabbed him with a snow knife, and took me to wife himself. He was not my husband for long, and when I married again, it was Padloq. It is not our custom to call our husbands by their names. I call Padloq o'maga ("the one that keeps me alive"). From the day I married him, my life became restful.

"In the course of my life, from childhood to old age, I have seen many lands, and lived in many different ways. There were times of abundance, and times of dearth and want. The worst thing I remember was when I found a woman who had eaten her husband and her children to save herself from starvation.

"Ûmaga and I were travelling from Iglulik to Tununeq when he dreamed one night that a friend of his had been eaten by his nearest kin. Ûmaga has the gift of second sight, and always knows when anything remarkable is going to happen. Next day we started off, and there was something remarkable about our journey from the start. Again and again the sledge stuck fast, but when we came to look, there was nothing to show what had stopped it. This went on all day, and in the evening we halted at Aunerit ('the melted place', in the interior of Cockburn Land). Next morning a ptarmigan flew over our tent. I threw a walrus tusk at it, but missed. Then I threw an axe, and again missed. And it seemed as if this also was to show that other strange things were to happen that day. We started off, and the snow was so deep that we had to help pull the sledge ourselves. Then we heard a noise. We could not make out what it was; sometimes it sounded like a dying animal in pain, and then again like human voices in the distance. As we came nearer, we could hear human words, but could not at first make out the meaning, for the voice seemed to come from a great way off. Words that did not sound like real words, and a voice that was powerless and cracked. We listened, and kept on listening, trying to make out one word from another, and at last we understood what it was that was being said. The voice broke down between the words, but what it was trying to say was this:

" 'I am not one who can live any longer among my fellows; for I have eaten my nearest of kin'.

"Now we knew that there should properly be no one else in this part of the country but ourselves, but all the same we could distinctly hear that this was a woman speaking, and we looked at each other, and it was as if we hardly dared speak out loud, and we whispered:

" 'An eater of men! What is this we have come upon here!'

"We looked about us, and at last caught sight of a little shelter, built of snow with a piece of a skin rug. It lay half hidden in a drift, and was hardly to be noticed in the snow all round, which was why we had not made it out before. And now that we could see where it was the voice came from, it sounded more distinctly, but still went on in the same broken fashion. We went slowly up to the spot, and when we looked in, there lay a human skull with the flesh gnawed from the bones. Yes, we came to that shelter, and looking in, we saw a human being squatting down inside, a poor woman, her face turned piteously towards us. Her eyes were all bloodshot, from weeping, so greatly had she suffered.

" 'Kivkaq,' she said (literally, 'you my gnawed bone,' which was her pet name for Padloq, whom she knew well) 'Kivkaq, I have eaten my elder brother and my children.' 'My elder brother' was her pet name for her husband. Padloq and I looked at each other, and could not understand that she was still alive and breathing. There was nothing of her but bones and dry skin, there seemed indeed hardly to be a drop of blood in all her body, and she had not even much clothing left, having eaten a great deal of that, both the sleeves and all the lower part of her outer furs. Padloq bent down quite close, to hear better, and Ataguvtâluk—for we knew her now, and could see who it was—said once more:

" 'Kivkaq, I have eaten your fellow-singer from the feasting, him with whom you used to sing when we were gathered in the great house at a feast.'

"My husband was so moved at the sight of this living skeleton, which had once been a young woman, that it was long before he knew what to answer. At last he said:

" 'You had the will to live, therefore you live.'

"We now put up our tent close by, and cut away a piece of the fore curtain to make a little tent for her. She could not come into the tent with us, for she was unclean, having touched dead bodies. When we went to move her, she tried to get up, but fell back in the snow. Then we tried to feed her with a little meat, but after she had swallowed a couple of mouthfuls, she fell to trembling all over, and could eat no more. Then we gave her a little hot soup, and when she was a little quieter, we looked round the shelter and found the skull of her husband and those of her children; but the brains were gone. We found the gnawed bones, too. The only part she had not been able to eat was the entrails. We gave up our journey then, and decided to drive back with her to Iglulik as soon as she felt a little stronger. And when she was once more able to speak, she told us how it had all come about. They had gone up country hunting caribou, but had not been able to find any; they then tried fishing in the lakes but there were no fish. Her husband wandered all about in search of food, but always without success, and they grew weaker and weaker. Then they decided to turn back towards Iglulik, but were overtaken by heavy snowfalls. The snow kept on, it grew deeper and deeper, and they themselves were growing weaker and weaker every day; they lay in their snow hut and could get nothing to eat. Then, after the snow had fallen steadily for some time there came fierce blizzards, and at last her husband was so exhausted that he could not stand. They kept themselves alive for some time by eating the dogs, but these also were wasted away and there was little strength in them as food; it simply kept them alive, so that they could not even die. At last the husband and all the children were frozen to death; having no food, they could not endure the cold. Ataguvtâluk had been the strongest of them all, though she had no more to eat than the others; as long as the children were alive, they had most. She had tried at first to start off by herself and get through to Iglulik, for she knew the way, but the snow came up to her waist, and she had no strength, she could not go on. She was too weak even to build a snow hut for herself, and the end of it was she turned back in her tracks and lay down beside her dead husband and the dead children; here at least there was shelter from the wind in the snow hut and there were still a few skins she could use for covering. She ate these skins to begin with. But at last there was no more left, and she was only waiting for the death to come and release her. She seemed to grow more and more dull and careless of what happened; but one morning, waking up to sunshine and a fine clear sky, she realised that the worst of the winter was over now, and it could not be long till the spring. Her snow hut was right on the road to Tununeq, the very road that all would take when going from Iglulik to trade there. The sun was so warm that for the first time she felt thawed a little, but the snow all about her was as deep and impassable as ever. Then suddenly it seemed as if the warm spring air about her had given her a great desire to go on living, and thus it was that she fell to eating of the dead bodies that lay beside her. It was painful, it was much worse than dying, and at first she threw up all she ate, but she kept on, once she had begun. It could not hurt the dead, she knew, for their souls were long since in the land of the dead. Thus she thought, and thus it came about that she became an inukto·majɔq, an eater of human kind.

"All this she told us, weeping; and Padloq and I realising that after all these sufferings she deserved to live and drove her in to Iglulik, where she had a brother living. Here she soon recovered her strength, but it was long before she could bear to be among her fellows. It is many years now since all this happened, and she is married now, to one of the most skilful walrus hunters at Iglulik, named Iktukshârjua, who had one wife already; she is his favourite wife and has had several more children.

"That is the most dreadful thing in all my life, and whenever I tell the story, I feel I can tell no more."

—With these words she set about arranging a sleeping place for Nasaitsordluarssuk and myself on the bench, and for a long time did not speak. Quietly she prepared a little meal for herself, after having entertained us so lavishly, and always taking great care that none of her food came in contact with any we had left; for that might have been dangerous to the adopted child that she was vainly endeavouring to keep alive. She then crawled up on to the bench behind her lamp and soon fell asleep.

Takornâq was the first of all the Hudson Bay Eskimos whose confidence I gained. In her narrative that first evening we were together she gave me, as it were, in a single sum, the life I had now to investigate in detail. Early next morning we set off again, but not before extracting a promise from Takornâq to come and stay with us for a while as soon as her husband returned.

Song of a Diffident Man

I am one who always
has the stream against him.
Slowly, slowly I press on.
If I went to visit
people who live south of us,
it was always difficult.
But eventually I reached
the lonely people
living at the far end of the fjord.

I am one who always
has the stream against him.
Slowly, slowly I press on.
If I wanted to hunt reindeer
near the "Little Spring"
it was always difficult.
At length I did surprise
the black musk oxen
that bellowed on the river-bank.

It was always hard
to join the men up front
who caught the seals:
yet I always kept
my harpoon ready.
    Jaijaija.

It was always hard
to join the men up front
who killed the reindeer:

yet I always carried
arrows on my back
    Jaijaija.

It was always hard
to join the happy company
that sang in the feasting-house:
for I never could remember
the words of my little song
in the drum-dance.
I was always holding back.
I was such a humble creature.
Everything was difficult.

—Qerraq (Copper Eskimo man)

$\mathcal{K}abloona$: $\mathcal{A}\,\mathcal{V}isit\ to$ $\mathcal{F}ather\ \mathcal{H}enry's$ $\mathcal{I}ce\ \mathcal{C}ave$

BY GONTRAN DE PONCINS (FRENCH, 1941)

f I were to recommend a single book about the Arctic, *Kabloona* would be it. Gontran de Poncins was a French aristocrat who gave up a career as an artist to become a freelance journalist who roamed the world. During a fifteen-month, 20,000-mile journey in 1938 and 1939, he traveled to the Central Canadian Arctic—some of the Arctic's most remote reaches. There, he lived for a time with the Inuit, who were relatively untouched by the white man's ways. Written with the collaboration of Lewis Galantiere, *Kabloona*, the book that resulted from this trip, is a stunning piece of literature. Though his distinction between the "primitive" and "civilized" mind will strike modern readers as archaic and even racist, de Poncins for the most part writes with acute sensitivity—not to mention artistry—about the Inuit he encounters, about the significance of the Arctic itself, and about his own struggles to cast off his attachments to the life in Paris he left behind.

It's tempting to excerpt any number of passages, but here is the chapter where he reaches the apogee of his journey—the remote territory around Pelly Bay—and his stay in an icy hole in the earth that serves as the home of a missionary ascetic, Father Henry. The father demonstrates an extraordinary understanding and admiration for the mind and ways of the Inuit, but also, paradoxically, an utter blindness to their own system of belief. Like some sort of oracle at the end of the trail, Father Henry kneels before his altar in the tiny cave with two blubber-oil lamps burning. Here is the being stripped to his essential spirit that de Poncins wishes he could become but knows he cannot.

"Here among these shadows, in these mysterious recesses," writes de Poncins, "the almost incomprehensible Eskimos eat and laugh, live a material existence of inconceivable brutality and at the same time a spiritual life of infinite subtlety, full of shades and gradations, of things sensed and unexpressed."

I am going to say to you that a human being can live without complaint in an ice-house built for seals at a temperature of fifty-five degrees below zero, and you are going to doubt my word. Yet what I say is true, for this was how Father Henry lived; and when I say "ice-house for seals" I am not using metaphorical language. Father Henry lived in a hole dug out by the Eskimos in the side of a hill as a place in which to store seal-meat in summer. The earth of this hill is frozen a hundred feet down, and it is so cold that you can hardly hold your bare hand to its surface.

An Eskimo would not have lived in this hole. An igloo is a thousand times warmer, especially one built out on the sea over the water warm beneath the coat of ice. I asked Father Henry why he lived thus. He said merely that it was more convenient, and pushed me ahead of him into his cavern.

If I were to describe the interior, draw it for you inch by inch, I should still be unable to convey the reality to you. There was a wooden door framed in the side of the slope. You stooped to enter he doorway and found yourself in a passage. On the right, standing as usual on end, were a half dozen frozen seal powdered with snow. On the left lay a bitch, suckled by a puppy. Ahead was a second door and behind it a second passage about ten feet deep and so narrow that you went through it sidewise, so low that your hood scraped the snow that had drifted in and sent it down into your neck. At the end of this passage was the hermit's cave.

Two seal-oil lamps were burning as I went in. These lamps light up an igloo, because an igloo is circular and more or less white: here they gave off only a faint gleam and the corners of the cave were hidden in darkness. The lamps stood on an empty barrel at the left of the door. Above them hung the drying rack, a sort of net suspended from three nails in which, if you looked hard enough, you could see a glove, a boot, but surely not a pair. At the right a shelf had been nailed up, and on it stood a queerly shaped kerosene lamp, the lid of a pot, a circular Eskimo knife, a rag, an empty tobacco tin, and a box of salt. Straight ahead, facing the door, was a couch.

Compared with this hole, an igloo was a palace. From the door to the couch opposite measured four and one half feet. Two people could not stand comfortably here, and when Father Henry said Mass I used to kneel on the couch. "If you didn't, you would be in my way," was how he put it. It was so small that when I came in from outdoors I never contrived to shake the snow off my coat without shaking it all over the couch.

The couch was a rickety wooden surface supported in the middle by a strut, over which two caribou hide had been spread. On these three planks forming a slightly tilted surface, Father Henry slept. To the right was a hole in the ground, which we blocked in part by the packing case containing my effects.

"The box will be your couch," said Father Henry; "and if you remember to keep out of that hole, you'll be perfectly comfortable."

Father Henry has no table knife, and I doubt that he has ever had a fork. His spoon disappeared a few days before my arrival, and he thought it might have fallen into the hole. I pushed the box aside and began to hunt for the spoon. After I had pulled up a dozen frozen fish-heads, an old parka, a sack with a bit of flour still in it, and five Arctic-hare hides, I found the spoon.

No white man has anything to boast of in the Arctic, but Father Henry no longer had the little with which he had started. Whatever he had possessed on first coming out here was to him part of a forgotten past, and he referred to it as "all those things." It had helped in the beginning, but now "all that" was superfluous. What, for example, did he want with a plate when his only meal of the day was a lump of frozen fish, eaten on waking in the morning? What good was that lamp to him, since he had no kerosene? How could he have used a pen here where ink froze? A napkin, which would have stiffened like a board in this cold? The only thing to do was to lick one's fingers, and indeed the gesture had become automatic with him. But since he knew that I was what Frenchy Chartrand at Coppermine had called a "cream puff," he gave me a ptarmigan skin to wipe my fingers on. This is the classic towel of the Arctic. It lasts the whole winter through without washing, and if you really mean to honor your guest, it is with this ptarmigan skin that you wipe his plate.

Father Henry lacked every object known to the civilization of the white man. "Those things make no sense here,"—and with that phrase he disposed of the subject. When I unpacked my gifts for him, rejoicing in advance over the delight they would give him, he stood by shaking his head. No, he can longer eat white man's food: not even rice. He cannot digest the stuff. "That sort of food doesn't keep a man warm. Frozen fish, now . . ." He loves frozen fish. There is nothing like it, he says, to warm you inside. Doctors tell you that you ought to vary your diet. Well . . . For six years he had been living on nothing but frozen fish, and he was none the worse off for it. When he awoke he groped on the ground, picked up a great chunk of fish frozen so hard that he had to thaw it out a little with his lips and breath before he could bite into it, and with this he regaled himself. It was succulent, it warmed you up, it sated your hunger, and you felt fine. As for eating in the evening, no: it would have kept him awake all night.

Despite this discouragement I continued to unpack. The cheese: I should finish it myself. The cigars (Gibson's gift): there was a Belgian priest at Repulse Bay who loved cigars, and they were put aside for him. The pipe: poor Father Henry! He had had a pipe. Smoking it from time to time had been his only luxury. But my Lord Bishop had asked all his missionaries to make one supplementary sacrifice, and Father Henry had sacrificed his pipe. I protested; but I do not believe I quite got him to promise to smoke again. As for the rest of the gifts, he took them and put them to one side, saying absentmindedly, "Very kind, very kind." His thanks were an acknowledgment of the intention: the gifts themselves had no meaning for him, no value.

His possessions were limited to lamps, dogs, sealing nets, and clothes. He spent a great deal of time looking to his lamps, and the Eskimos teased him about it. "You do it better than we do," they would say with their smile; and it is a fact that nothing wants so much attention as a seal-oil lamp. You can spend hours trimming the improvised wick, shortening or lengthening it, adding more seal-oil—or rather blubber which, melting, becomes oil—when you hear it splutter. It used to make me smile to see Father Henry, in the midst of his Mass, between the syllables of an *Introibo ad altare,* turn from the plank on the right that was his altar and trim the wick while he continued his service.

It was six o'clock next morning when I awoke. I had slept badly on my box, unable to stretch my legs and half fallen into the hole. Father Henry had long been up and tended to his lamps, and now he was sitting on the couch. He had slept in his clothes: one could not do otherwise in this terrible cold that rose from the earth, and he was sitting motionless, fearing to wake me, murmuring his prayers to himself. Now that I was awake he prepared his altar by shoving to one side the kerosene lamp and empty tobacco tin, and the Mass began. I "served," squatting on the couch.

"Dominus," said Father Henry; and then ducking beneath a beam overhead he appeared round the other side:

"Vobiscum."

And I, from the couch: *"Et cum spiritu tuo."* . . .

When he heard confession from one of the natives, his box was the outer passage and the scene took place under the vitreous eyes of the frozen seal. In this virtual darkness, at fifty degrees below, the two men would kneel and murmur together.

All day long I was weary, unable to get warm. I lay in my sleeping-bag and drank tea, and as Father Henry drank with me we chatted. I tore the paper off a packet of biscuits and said as I threw the wrapper away:

"An Eskimo would pick up a bit of paper like that as soon as you threw it down."

"So would I," Father Henry said calmly, and he picked up what I had thrown away and put it on a shelf. He told me how he had been informed of my coming. Nothing could better display the mentality of these natives.

An Eskimo had come running into the cavern and had stood breathless before him. He was the bearer of astounding news and proud to be bringing it. But he did not speak. It is ill-bred to be in haste, and it is ill-bred also to attack any subject directly. So, shaking the snow from his clothes, he had taken a mug of tea from the unsuspecting priest and had drunk it in silence. Then, having cut himself a slice of fish, he had eaten, and smoked a cigarette. Time passed, and Father Henry went about his household tasks.

Eventually Father Henry asked him a question.

"Kis-si-wi?" (Are you alone?)

"Nak-ka." (No.)

"Kina-lo?" (Who is it?)

"Oo-shu-tik-sak," said the Eskimo, giving Shongili's true name and refraining from mentioning me.

"Sug-mat?" (How does that happen?)

The Eskimo looked at Father Henry and smiled. Now he was heavy with his news, electrically charged, bursting to speak, proud of his mission of annunciation. And yet he was silent again for a time. Finally he exploded:

"Kabloona-ralu!"

Father Henry stopped short and turned round with a start.

"What is his name?"

"Ma-i-ke."

All this meant nothing to Father Henry, for he knew nothing about me, not even this nickname by which I was known among the Eskimos. (Of themselves, the Eskimos might have called me "He of the Long Ears" or something equally flattering.) He hunted round in his mind. Who could it be?

"What does he do?"

"Nu-nang-juar-le-rie." (He draws the image of the earth.) The Eskimos had seen me sketching.

"Is it Learmonth?"

"That is not his name."

"Is it a policeman?"

"I believe not. He went into the igloos. He saw the Cross. He 'follows' as we do."

"Does he speak Eskimo?"

At this point Father Henry said to me: "Observe the delicacy of these men. He might have said, 'Badly.' Instead, in order not to hurt any one, he said, 'All that he has said to us, we have clearly understood.'

"Then," Father Henry went on, "they brought you gradually into Pelly Bay. I was at work shovelling the snow away from my door while one of them on the watch called out to me: 'He is in sight. He is turning the point. He will be here in a moment.' And I, hunting feverishly for my gloves! 'He is very near.' And then, just as I started out of the door: *'A-ood-lar-mat,'*—He has arrived!"

We talked of many things and among others of dogs, for Father Henry had a superb team of which in his selfless way he was proud.

"The more I see of the dogs," he said, "the better I understand the men. The same defects; the same qualities. And how different they are from our dogs at home! What hypocrisy there is in them at times, and with what pleasure they play tricks on you, turning round each time to give you the same jeering look. On the other hand I have known them to go a week without food, trotting along at a steady pace with no single whimper of complaint. To go three or four days hungry is their frequent lot, and when night falls and the sled is stopped, they will lie down and go to sleep unfed, as if they expected nothing better."

I expressed my regret that I should never know the Eskimo language well enough to grasp its inner essence, and should therefore never know the men who spoke it, seeing that language is the faithful mirror of a people's spirit.

"If you knew what condensation there is in their language!" Father Henry exclaimed. "Their phrases are as sober as their faces. A gleam in an Eskimo's eye tells you more than a half dozen of our sentences concerning desire, repugnance, or another emotion. Each Eskimo word is like that gleam: it suggests at once what has happened and what is to come, and it contains that touch of the unexpressed which makes this people so mysterious and attractive.

"Their shades of expression are infinite," he went on. "They are Asiatic, and perhaps for that reason imperceptible to us. We are so habituated to our simple yes and no that we ignore the existence of a scale of gradations between affirmation and negation. It took me a long time to understand what was going on in their minds, and many things had to be revealed to me before I knew where I stood with these men. They would explain: 'He did not refuse to do as you asked; he merely told you that there were obstacles in the way.' Or: 'He did not deceive you, he did not lie to you; he merely omitted to affirm the thing to you.' It was hard for me to grasp the care they took not to commit themselves. Each time that they speak they leave themselves a back door through which to retreat. For example:

"An Eskimo comes in from trapping. There are several visitors in his igloo. He picks up the snow-beater, and when his clothes are free of snow he takes them off. All this without a word. Then, as he knows that the others are waiting for him to speak, he says: 'Those foxes! There is no way to get them.' Silence. 'And besides, I'm not good for much any more. An old man.' Again silence. Finally, still as if he were speaking to himself: 'But I got three today.' "

I told Father Henry of my trouble getting to Pelly Bay. He was astonished.

"How could it possibly have taken so long?"

"I can't say. And yet, Heaven knows I told those men often enough that I was in a hurry to get here."

Father Henry laughed. "That's it then," he said. "That explains it. You are lucky to have got here at all. You deserved to be led round and round in a circle to teach you a lesson."

And he told me how he went about getting a sled up to Repulse Bay in double time.

He would send for an Eskimo and say to him: "I want you to go to Repulse Bay. It will take you a good bit of time. You are young; probably you do not know the way very well; your dogs are not worth much. Still, nobody else is available, so go along."

Time passes, and the Eskimo is back from the trip.

"Well?" says Father Henry to him.

The man looks crestfallen. Things went badly. The weather was worse than he had expected. Then one of the dogs fell sick. And there were other difficulties, each of which he lists with scrupulous care. But he had gone and come in twelve days, just the same, and he knew that Father Henry knew that was fast travelling.

When we spoke of Eskimo murder, Father Henry told me about a man now at Committee Bay who had come to him one day, and, after the usual tea and silence, had said to him suddenly:

"I took the old woman out on the ice to-day."

It was his own mother that he had driven out and set down at sea to freeze to death. He was fond of her, he explained. He had always been kind to her. But she was too old, she was no longer good for anything; so blind, she couldn't even find the porch to crawl into the igloo. So, on a day of blizzard, the whole family agreeing, he had taken her out, and they had struck camp and gone off, leaving her to die.

"With God's help I hope in time to change these things, to soften some of their ways," said Father Henry; "but it is difficult. They live a hard life, and it is in all respects a material life. They would say, if they knew our words, that they had to 'face facts.' That man had indeed been a good son. You must have seen yourself how they look after the aged on the trail, running back so often to the sled to see if the old people are warm enough, if they are comfortable, if they are not perhaps hungry and want a bit of fish. And the old people are a burden on the trail, a cause of delay and of complication. But the day comes when, after years with no word of complaint, the young people deem the thing no longer possible, and they leave the old man or the old woman on the ice. The old people are told in advance what their end is to be, and they submit peacefully without a word of recrimination. Sometimes, indeed, they are the first to suggest this end for themselves."

There are violent murders, however, that are harder to explain. The murder, for example, that results purely from the instinct of the hunter. One of Father Henry's stories I had already been told at King.

Three men were on the trail together. Evening came and they built an igloo. They sat talking and smoking. The igloo had been hastily put up and a wide hole appeared overhead which one of the men went out to patch up. As the two others continued to sit and smoke, one of them chanced to raise his eyes. Overhead the third was patching the hole. His loose clothing had parted, and his great brown belly was bare and visible as he worked.

"A fine belly," said the first Eskimo.

The other raised his head. *"Eh-eh-eh!"* he affirmed with appreciation, "a very fine belly."

They continued to stare at it. The first man spoke again:

"I could stick my knife into a belly like that."

The second man said nothing. He stood up and planted his snow-knife into that belly. It was irresistible: the belly was too fine.

Father Henry having asked why I had come into these regions, the simplest thing for me to tell him was that I was studying Eskimo manners and trading for primitive utensils. The fact that Eskimo life and objects might be of interest to me must have seemed to this priest pure futility.

"You bother with those things, do you?" he said. It was clear that they had no value in his eyes. Nevertheless, to give me pleasure, he sent for a native called Nibtayok, who arrived with a few articles in a sack. One of these pieces fascinated me and was highly valued by Nibtayok, too, for it was the product of a great deal of labor. It was a *kayok-tak,* a bowl made of the hollowed out skull of the musk-ox. Out of it the natives drank seal blood. These bowls were now so scarce that I had never before seen one either on King William Land or at Perry River. I was about to offer a tin of tobacco for it, and for the rest a packet of cigarette paper; but, uncertain that this would be enough, I asked Father Henry to find out for me. Nibtayok's face brightened the moment the question was put to him.

"A-lie-na-i!" he answered. (I think should so.)

Nibtayok was the only man left in camp, the others having gone off sealing, and I took advantage of his presence to ask him about Eskimo superstitions and legends. This astonished Father Henry.

"I should never have thought of asking about such things," he said; and I teased him a little.

"How," I said, "can you expect to uproot their superstitions if you do not know what they are? You told me yourself that the surest way to be rid of these things is to show bit by bit how ineffectual and absurd they are."

"True, true!" he said, but his mind was on other things and I sensed that for him all this was nonsense.

When I had questioned Nibtayok for about twenty minutes he became exhausted and his eyes began to blink.

"I am sleepy," he said.

Twenty minutes was as long as an Eskimo could go on thinking. And besides, the white man's way of putting his questions made the operation difficult. I would ask a question directly, to begin with. Then I would have to attenuate it, explain in roundabout fashion what I was getting at; and the explanation itself took so much time, that listening to it wearied my man. He had to be reassured about each subject of inquiry, convinced that he need not be afraid to answer, so great is the fear among them of committing themselves.

Nibtayok took me with him on a tour of the camps. This was the season when the whole clan were scattered over the ice throughout the length of Pelly Bay, and to see them one had to go visiting.

As we were about to leave, Father Henry gave me a bit of advice. "Be sure not to run alongside the sled," he admonished me. "Nibtayok would be horribly vexed, for my Eskimos do not do this. Besides, his dogs are very fast, and you might soon find yourself left behind."

I had scarcely time to fling myself on the sled before we were off at a gallop, and for three hours we went on without slackening speed. How different from King William Land! Nibtayok had only to call out to the dogs, and they responded magnificently. Snow on King was often a hindrance; here it was a kind of airy carpet on which we seemed literally to be flying, not dragging ourselves along on a sled that creaked like an old farm cart.

As we moved from camp to camp I was surprised everywhere by the spaciousness, I might almost have said the magnificence, of these igloos. Their porches were invariably built to contain two good-sized niches, one for the dogs, the other for harness and equipment. In some camps I found again the communal architecture of which I had seen a deserted specimen on the trail—three igloos so built as to open into a central lobby. Each igloo housed two families, one at either side the porch, and was lighted by two seal-oil lamps. I measured them and found they were twelve feet in diameter,—so wide at the axis that the *iglerk,* which in the King William Land igloo fills three quarters of the interior, took up less than half the floor space. The seal-oil lamps, or more properly, vessels, were nearly three feet long. All this luxury was explained by the presence of seal in quantity, whereas round King, seal is, to say the least, not plentiful.

Back of each lamp, on a sort of platform of snow, lay the usual larder of the Eskimo rich in provisions, into which every visitor was free to put his knife and draw forth the chunk of seal or caribou or musk-ox that he preferred.

What was admirable about the architecture of these igloos was that it permitted at one and the same time a private life and a communal life. Each woman was free to trim her lamp and sit quietly over her sewing or scraping of hides, attending in silence to her own concerns; but it was also possible for her to converse with the others across the lobby while she worked, to drop her work and, with the child in its hood at her back, come across to sit with her neighbor; or all of them might, if they wished, collect for a chat in the central lobby.

Thanks to the abundance of seal, these people exhibited to me a powerful and dignified community, a life that might have gone on in an ancient civilization with its matrons, its patriarchs, its forum in which the will of a people expressed itself in common discussion and decision. Each detail of life was here an episode: the waking in the morning and first trimming of the lamps; the feeding of children and men and dogs; the hubbub of departure for the sealing; the chatter of the matrons, and their housekeeping; the return when evening fell amid the barking of the dogs, the swearing of the men, the hauling in of the seals; and finally tea, the women sewing or serving while the men stood waiting for their steaming mugs to cool, snorting, joking, cutting off large chunks of meat, and feeling themselves indeed that which their name implied, *Inuit,* "Men, preeminently." What I was seeing here, few men had seen, and it was now to be seen almost nowhere else—a social existence as in olden days, a degree of prosperity and well-being contrasting markedly with the pseudo-civilized life of the western Eskimo and the pitiful, stunted, whining life of the King William clan with its wretched poverty, its tents made of coal-sacks, its snuffling, lacklustre, and characterless men clad in rags; that life like a dulled and smutted painting with only here and there a gleam to speak of what it had once been.

The generosity and courtesy of their hospitality struck me as forcibly as the grace of their life. Hardly had I come into the igloo before my clothes were taken from me, my boots and socks drawn off my feet and hung to dry on the rack. It was as if my presence honored the igloo, and when my clothes were later handed back to me by a little girl in a gesture whose shyness was charming, I saw that they had not been dried only, but scraped clean and soft as well.

I had not been five minutes on the *iglerk* before I heard gay giggles in the next igloo. Bending forward, I looked in and saw—my own image. They were mimicking me, and it was the wife of Ikshivalitak who, seated on her *iglerk,* was taking me off. There was "Ma-i-ke" himself, me to the life, jerky and nervous in gesture, peremptory in speech, practically giving orders: "I want to trade utensils." "I want," not—as it should have been—"I should like"; and my confusion between the two modes of expression sent them into gales of laughter. The notion that I, a white man, alone in this immense country, their country, should take it upon myself to give them orders ("I want . . .") was to them highly comic. And then, the woman continued in my own pidgin-Eskimo, *"Na-mang-nik-to tap-ko-a"* (This thing is worthless): and off into laughter they went again. The idea that objects which they knew to be precious might be said by me to have no value, was very funny to them.

And the mimicry was done with so much art, with such perfection in reproduction of the intonation of my voice, that I was stupefied. These people had never seen me in their lives until ten minutes before, and then in the hubbub of our arrival; yet they had picked up instantly the characteristic traits—the nervousness, the impatience, the stupid arrogance of the white man who thinks himself master wherever he goes. I had never been parodied like this, with an insight at once so penetrating and so little aggressive. Small wonder that I burst out laughing myself.

I made a humiliating discovery among these people, which was that I did not know their language. On King William Land I thought I knew it, but that was because those Eskimos, in their contact with the white man, spoke pigdin-Eskimo in order that he might understand them. Here pure Eskimo was spoken, and I understood scarcely a word. It was embarrassing. I found myself in an igloo with an old man named Krepingayuk and his wife. He was a gentle old fellow, bearded, and speaking in the high-pitched voice usually affected only by a shaman. This respectable old man, with his pious old face, was said to be twice a murderer—his second killing having been done in order to keep to himself the wife of the man he killed, who had been a shaman. He had simply tipped the late husband into open water and had come back saying that his companion had drowned. Everybody was quite sure what had happened, but as so often in Eskimo occurrences, it had been impossible to get at the truth. His wife—probably as the result of having lived with a shaman—spent hours bowed over the lamp, murmuring to herself in true shaman fashion. They would speak to me, would see that I did not understand, and then a long colloquy would be held between them. Was it possible that a man might not know their language? The old chap would try again, repeating carefully several times his words, and when, again, I let him know that I did not understand, he would smile incredulously.

The igloo was constantly filled with visitors come to see the Kabloona. They would come in one after the other, stay only long enough to examine me closely, and then slip out through the porch in order to take home their impression of me. When the parents hadn't time to spare for this scrutiny, they would send a child, and the child would report my appearance and gestures, from which they would draw their conclusions. I, meanwhile, sat not daring to speak or move, conscious that all the words and gestures of the white man were in their eyes violent, direct, and ludicrous. If only Father Henry had been there!

In the way of nourishment, I had brought with me only tea and biscuits, and these I distributed with the feeling that they hardly constituted the acknowledgment of an honored guest. But my hosts appeared to be delighted, as if the intention were the important thing, not the gift. Constantly, I was asked my name—the question was phrased thus: "Who are you?"—and the name, "Ma-i-ke," was repeated again and again. Women would shake their children half out of the hood and say to them:

"Look! Who is this?"

"Ma-i-ke!" the children would answer promptly; and as they gazed at me with sober faces and unblinking eyes everybody present would laugh with pleasure.

Except for Father Henry, these women and children, and even some of the men, had never seen a Kabloona, and they dealt with me as with a friend. True primitive hospitality consists not merely in welcoming the stranger but in seeking to incorporate him into the community. Their intent is to keep him among them as long as possible, and his slightest indication of appreciation increases their hope that he will stay on with them. They discuss at length precisely where and how he is to be lodged, and what can be done to make his visit pleasant. Once he has distributed his little gifts and brewed them a mug of tea, he has done his part. It now becomes their part to look after him solicitously, to see that he is well fed and comfortably bestowed. And if the stranger speaks of leaving them, he will find that he has offended them.

It wants very little time to return to the primitive. Already I had ceased to feel the need of the appurtenances of our civilization; and yet I had been reared in a fair degree of comfort, I was rather more than less sensitive than the average, and I was even, in a manner of speaking, an "intellectual." After a brief few weeks, all this had dropped away from me. I do not mean that I had stopped yearning for telephones and motor cars, things I should always be able to live without. I mean that the thought of a daily change of linen was gone from my mind; that a joint of beef would not have made my mouth water, and I loved the taste of frozen fish, particularly if it had frozen instantaneously and retained its pristine savour all through the winter. As a matter of fact, I do not remember being served anything in France as much to my taste.

Besides, Father Henry was perfectly right: the white man's diet would never have lent me the power of resistance needed for this life. Boiled rice warmed you while you ate it, but its warmth died out of you almost as soon as it was eaten. Frozen fish worked the other way: you did not feel its radiation immediately; but twenty minutes later it began to warm you and it kept you warm for hours. As for raw meat, with its higher vitamin content, the advantage of eating it frozen was that you could absorb enormous quantities of it; and after a hard day on the trail there was no end to what you ate. Even the taste for rotted food came in time, though I never reached the point of considering it a delicacy. "In the beginning," Father Henry admitted, "I was like you; I always chose the freshest piece. But one day I happened upon a bit of *ti-pi,* the high meat, and I said to myself, 'Mm! not bad!' Since then fresh meat has seemed to me almost tasteless."

Father Henry and I took to each other from the beginning. A seal icehouse brings people together more quickly than a hotel room, and a good deal more intimately. Conversation in such a place is frank and honest, untrammelled by the reticences of society.

I said to him one day: "Don't you find this life too hard for you, living alone like this?"

"Oh, no," he said; "I am really very happy here. My life is simple, I have no worries, I have everything I need." (He had nothing at all!) "Only one thing preys on my mind now and then: it is—what will become of me when I am old?"

He said this with such an air of confessing a secret weakness that my heart swelled with sudden emotion, and I tried clumsily to comfort him.

"When you are old," I said, "you will go back among the white men. You will be given a mission at Chesterfield, or at Churchill."

"No, no, no!" he protested, "not that."

What could I say? I had no right to press the point. But at that moment I wished with all my heart that every man who had a warm house and assurance of a comfortable old age might see this lone priest in the Arctic.

Another time I expostulated with him. "You cannot live like this," I said, "devoid of everything. You are not responsible to yourself alone. You have a mission to fulfill, and you must equip yourself for it, must have those things that will ensure your health and well-being so that you may fulfill it properly. Let me take back those foxes of yours"—offerings brought by the natives—"and trade them for you at the Post. I'll send you back the things you need."

He refused categorically. "No, no. I have not the right to dispose of the foxes. They belong to my bishop."

"Never mind your bishop!" I said. "Let me have those five foxes."

But he was unshakable. "No," he said, wagging his head; "impossible!"

"Very well," said I crossly. "You need harness, nets, rope—not for yourself, but for your mission, and I am going to send them to you. You will force me to pay for them out of my own pocket."

Ah, the poor man! I had faced him with a case of conscience, and he was upset. "All right, all right," he agreed. "But it is very bad of you to put me in this position. I'll let you have the foxes."

He didn't, though. When time came for me to leave, his scruples had returned. "I've thought it over," he said, "and I find you are wrong. There is nothing I need."

I had been with him several days when I began to see that something was gnawing at him. Something was on his mind, and he was going round and round in a circle.

"Come," I said, "What is it? You have something on your mind."

It must really have been preying on him for he made no attempt to evade me.

"Ah, well," he said. "You see for yourself how it is. Here you are, a layman, enduring these privations, travelling 'tough' "—another locution of the North—"depriving yourself of your only cheese for me. Well, if you do these things, what should I, a religious, be doing?"

I stared at him. His eyes were hollow, brilliant, strangely brilliant. A religious, indeed! What a distance that one word suddenly placed between him and me! This man was animated and kept alive by something other than the power of nature. Life had in a sense withdrawn from him, and a thing more subtle, more mysterious, had taken its place. He was doubly superior to me, by his humility and by his mystical essence as priest. "I am of the most humble extraction," he had said to me. He was a Norman peasant, and it came to me suddenly that if he had chosen to live in this seal-hole instead of an igloo, his choice had been motivated in part by the peasant instinct to build his own sort of farmstead, even here in the Arctic. He took no particular pride from his origin, nor is it because he referred to it that I speak of his humility, which was Christian, not worldly. He was a direct, simple, naked soul dressed only in the seamless garment of his Christianity.

By grace of that garment, his flesh was as if it were not. When I said, for example, "It is not warm this morning," he would answer mechanically, "No, it is not warm"; but he did not feel the cold. "Cold" was to him merely a word; and if he stopped up the door, or livened up the lamp, it was for my sake he did it. He had nothing to do with "those things," and this struggle was not his struggle: he was somewhere else, living another life, fighting with other weapons. He was right and I was wrong in those moments when I rebelled against his existence and insisted rashly that he "could not live like this." I was stupid not to see, then, that he truly had no need of anything. He lived, he sustained himself, by prayer. Had he been dependent only upon human strength he would have lived in despair, been driven mad. But he called upon other forces, and they preserved him. Incredible as it will seem to the incredulous, when the blizzard was too intense to be borne, he prayed,

and the wind dropped. When, one day, he was about to die of hunger—
he and the single Eskimo who accompanied him—he prayed; and that
night there were two seal in their net. It was childish of me to attempt
to win him back to reality: he could not live with reality.

I, the "scientist," was non-existent beside this peasant mystic. He
towered over me. My resources were as nothing compared to his,
which were inexhaustible. His mystical vestment was shelter enough
against hunger, against cold, against every assault of the physical
world from which he lived apart. Once again I had been taught that the
spirit was immune and irresistible, and matter corruptible and weak.
There is something more than cannon in war, and something more than
grub and shelter in the existence of this conqueror of the Arctic. If,
seeing what I have seen, a man still refused to believe this, he would
do better to stay at home, for he had proved himself no traveller.

Men's Impotence

Maybe—yes
it doesn't matter.
Maybe—yes.
I'll just sing about a man,
"The One at Boiling-Point",
who sat tight-lipped and frightened
among women.
Maybe—yes
it doesn't matter.
Maybe—yes.
I'll just sing about a man,
"The Reindeer-Belly",
who sat tight-lipped and frightened
among women.
His eyes augured ill,
curved like a horn
to carve into an eeling-fork.
Maybe—yes
it doesn't matter.
Maybe—yes.
I'll just sing about a man,
"The Axe",
who sat tight-lipped and frightened,
far, far away from people,
in solitude.
Maybe—yes
it doesn't matter.
Maybe—yes.
My tongue can only put together words
to make a little song.
A mouth, a little mouth,
can that be dangerous?
A little mouth,
that curves down at the corners
like a stick,
bent to form a kayak's rib.

—Netsit (Copper Eskimo man)

Fur Trade Bachelor

BY DUNCAN PRYDE (BRITISH, 1971)

T he Inuit practice of wife exchange has long fascinated Southerners. Many of the early visitors to the Arctic took advantage
of it; the missionaries who came later did their best to eradicate
it. While undoubtedly there was much abuse of the system by
explorers and whalers—Rasmussen records the shame felt by an
Inuit woman when she fell naked from a whaler's bunk onto the ship
cabin's floor—there were also examples of close and enduring relationships. In this chapter from his memoir, *Nunaga*, Duncan Pryde, a
Hudson's Bay Company employee who spent ten years among the
Inuit in the late 1950s and early 1960s, tells of his awkward first
sexual encounter with his exchange wife. He describes how the system
of "spouse exchange," as he calls it, traditionally has served an important societal role: to strengthen kinship bonds among these roaming,
nomadic people and to provide a sort of insurance policy for food
and clothing—and to help in the event one's spouse falls ill or dies.

There is a widespread belief that a man has only to go to the Arctic,
and the first Eskimo he meets will happily turn his wife over to him for

the night. There was indeed at one time, and there remains still in some of the more isolated settlements, a system of wife exchange among the Eskimos, but it was rarely established on a casual basis, and there were always certain social niceties and boundaries to be observed. The custom might better be termed spouse exchange because in many cases the wife, not the husband, initiated the exchange.

This custom used to be accepted, even preferred community behaviour among the Eskimos, and was practised throughout the Arctic. When I was at Perry Island every adult man had an exchange wife, and every woman an exchange husband. There was no question of adultery, or any feeling of 'shame'. In fact, Eskimos thought it shameful, or at least strange, if a man or woman did not have an exchange partner. In white society today, if a teenage girl isn't dating, her mother wonders what is wrong with her and pushes her to get into the swim, to be like everyone else. Similarly, in Eskimo society there was family pressure on young people to obtain exchange mates. The mother of a young bride, perhaps uncertain of her new son-in-law's ability to keep the larder full, might impress upon her daughter the advantage of a liaison with an older, more experienced hunter.

Such relationships did not exclude single people. A man or woman who had lost a mate, by death or desertion, might become involved in a triangle exchange with a married couple. Occasionally young unmarried men and women entered such a relationship.

Sound sociological reasons contributed to the growth and perpetuation of the system, and not the least important was self-preservation. Up to twenty or thirty years ago Eskimos were as bad as the MacDonalds and the Campbells when it came to blood feuds. If Anaqqarniq killed Simigiaq, the next of kin to Simigiaq was duty bound to take revenge on Anaqqarniq, and so on as long as there was anyone left in either family. As we have seen, kinship relationships and blood feuds played a major role in Eskimo life. An Eskimo who was without kin to avenge any wrong done him was exposed and vulnerable. If he travelled to strange territory to hunt or trade, he could fall into a dangerous situation, alone among strangers who might, and generally did, covet anything from his dogteam to his harpoon, and were sometimes more than willing to kill him to get what they wanted. With no kin to avenge his death, he could be murdered with impunity.

To prevent this, the Eskimos evolved spouse exchange as a kind of insurance policy. When a man travelled in distant regions he always took his wife with him, and when they reached a strange settlement, the visitor automatically arranged a wife exchange with one of the local residents, thus establishing the all-important kinship relationship. He acquired all his wife's exchange husband's family as his kin, and they became bound to avenge any injury done to the visitor. It was no longer safe to rob or harm the traveller.

According to Eskimo belief, moulded to fit the circumstance, a one-night stand would never result in pregnancy. Accordingly, a single act of intercourse with a non-spouse had little significance to the immediate family.

Whenever wife or spouse exchange took place within the same band or settlement, choice was virtually unrestricted except for the important taboo of incest. As long as a man or woman chose someone outside his or her kinship circle, any arrangement agreeable to the persons concerned was possible.

Within a tribe or settlement, spouse exchange sometimes developed as a purely sexual thing. One man might like another's wife, and his wife in turn might have her eyes on the other husband, and if feelings proved to be mutual, an exchange was easily established. Among the Eskimos I knew at Perry Island and in some other villages the average length of a spouse exchange relationship was about two years, but such extramarital fidelity was unusual.

The Eskimo attitude towards the custom and towards sex generally is well illustrated by Iqaluut and his wife Qungayuna, an older couple I knew at Bathurst Inlet. One year a missionary came down from Cambridge Bay to hold some services, and he was surprised and pleased at the number of Eskimos who attended. He had brought along his record books and said that he hoped to baptize some of the older Eskimos who had never undergone that sacrament. The missionary wanted to visit his potential converts, and asked me to act as interpreter. One of our first stops was the home of Iqaluut and Qungayuna.

'Well, you seemed to enjoy the services,' the missionary began. After some small talk he asked, 'Would you like me to baptize you so that we will know for sure that you are an Anglican?'

To the missionary's surprise Iqaluut promptly declined: 'Oh no, I don't want to get baptized, and I don't want my wife baptized either.'

'Why not? You are Anglicans. You came to the services.'

'If we get baptized, then we can no longer exchange mates,' said Iqaluut. He and his wife believed that if they were baptized they would have to follow the ways of the missionary, and all Eskimos knew that missionaries frowned on wife exchange.

To make the point clear, Qungayuna, giggling and laughing, butted in: 'That's right. It gets awfully boring when you've just got one man all the time.'

To them it was a poor man who could only attract one woman, and a useless woman who failed to have several admirers.

In my own case it was a beautiful and brazen girl, Niksaaktuq, wife of the young hunter Nasarlulik and daughter-in-law of the shaman at Perry, who initiated the exchange. Almost from the time of my arrival at Perry, Niksaaktuq had flirted provocatively with me. For that matter, so had several other women in the settlement. I was flattered, but I realized that I was considered unusual not because of my appealing Scottish face or my splendid physique, but simply because as the only whiteman in the place, and as the trader, I had enormous prestige. I was something new, a whiteman who spoke Eskimo and who made it obvious that the attention of girls was pleasing.

But I moved slowly. I was neither naive nor celibate, but during my first days at Perry my time was fully engaged in getting the post back on its feet. I was unsure of local customs and dared not risk an already precarious position by committing a social gaffe.

But Niksaaktuq was a delightful girl and I was soon sure she was making a real play for me. Once when I was visiting with Nasarlulik and his mother Arnayak, Niksaaktuq made a point of joking in a rather risqué way with me, smiling and teasing in little ways that women everywhere instinctively use. When Nasarlulik and I left, I discovered I had forgotten my mitts and went back to get them, telling Nasarlulik

I would catch up with him in a minute. Niksaaktuq handed the mitts to me, and when our hands touched she held on to mine, looked knowingly into my face, and smiled. Neither of us said a word, but I knew for sure that this girl was interested.

I was interested too. Very much. Niksaaktuq had caught my eye my very first day at Perry Island. She was an extremely good-looking girl with a beautiful body, slim and vibrant. Although she was only twenty or twenty-one, she had already been involved with eight or nine different men in spouse exchanges.

She had a trick of scratching her instep with the toe of her other foot. I thought she must have a very itchy foot, but later discovered she was using an old Eskimo custom to signal to me that she was interested in a sexual liaison. I was willing all right, but I didn't know quite what to do about it.

Fortunately Niksaaktuq was neither as faint-hearted nor as inhibited as I was. During the next couple of months she made the most of every opportunity to see me, even when Nasarlulik was there. Whenever her husband's back was turned Niksaaktuq would smile at me and try to catch my eye, or she might scuff her mukluk suggestively. When they came over to the post to trade she always seemed to find some opportunity to touch me. I didn't object—to be strictly honest, I tried to make it easier for this to happen. The big problem for me was that I really liked Nasarlulik. We got along well, hunting together, joking and laughing to the point where the other Eskimos called us *kipaqatiqiik* (joking partners), which meant we were close friends.

Finally, the situation came to a head. We had been on a trip together, and when we got back I asked Nasarlulik and Niksaaktuq to come over and have a mug-up with me as soon as they had their dogs chained and their gear stowed away. When they arrived I went to the kitchen to get the tea ready. Niksaaktuq came up behind me, put both arms around me and pulled me back against her. Nasarlulik had plopped down on the chesterfield in the living room, just around the corner from us and barely out of sight where we stood by the stove. I turned round and Niksaaktuq put her hands to my face and pulled my head down to her and rubbed noses with me. The Perry Island people didn't engage in kissing, but they certainly knew how to rub noses, and rubbing noses can be very exciting if it is done the right way with the right noses. First this saucy girl just held the side of her nose against mine. That is considered just affectionate; but when she pressed the side of her nose against the side of mine and started rubbing, then that is not only considered passionate—it is!

She was busy leading the nose rubbing, and I was busy trying to see where Nasarlulik was, when she reached into her parka and brought out a little slip of folded paper which she handed me. I stepped away from her and into the tiny adjacent washroom to see what was on the paper. She had written in Eskimo syllabics three words, *Piyumaguvit uiga kanngunaittuq* ('If you want something, my husband won't be embarrassing'). What it really meant was, 'If you want to go to bed with me, ask my husband for his permission, and he won't embarrass you by saying no.' This was a proposal for a wife-exchange relationship.

As soon as I read it I understood the proposal but lacked the confidence. Never before had I asked a man for permission to take his wife to bed. It might have been easier if I hadn't liked Nasarlulik so much. I was worried that we should both end up badly embarrassed. I was fully aware that Niksaaktuq shared none of my doubts, but not only did I hesitate to go behind my friend's back, I also knew such an action might be dangerous. Loss of face when our activities became known might force Nasarlulik to strike out at me. Normally a man would never ask for an exchange relationship unless he were virtually certain the woman's husband would agree. Nor would he risk an illicit arrangement unless he was prepared for a violent reaction. Of course, in this instance, Niksaaktuq had prepared the way with Nasarlulik, but I didn't know that for certain. I just stalled as though nothing had happened.

I went back into the living room with the tea, and Niksaaktuq smiled expectantly at me and Nasarlulik smiled expectantly at me, and I just grinned back at them. I was thinking furiously to myself. I well knew Niksaaktuq's reputation as an impetuous and headstrong girl, and I wondered if this was something she had cooked up on her own, or if, as she implied, her husband knew about it and was in agreement. I didn't want to move too fast in spite of Niksaaktuq's reassuring note. I thought that if

Nasarlulik did turn me down, it would mean he suspected I had been friendly with him only because I wanted his wife, which wasn't true at all.

So we sat there and drank our tea in silence, each trying to think of something to say. Every once in a while Nasarlulik and Niksaaktuq would flash pregnant smiles at me and make little comments that could be taken two ways. At ten o'clock I excused myself while I made my nightly message broadcast. It was then that I received orders, heard any news that was on the air, and relayed my own messages. Nasarlulik went to the bathroom and Niksaaktuq followed me into the radio room where I was twiddling the dials to tune in the Cambridge Bay station. I stood up to reach for something, and that bold girl threw her arms around my neck, then suddenly reached down and grabbed me by the genitals. Being only human, I grabbed her back—and just then the Cambridge Bay station came on. I had to sit down and answer their call. All the time I was talking to Cambridge Bay, Niksaaktuq was caressing my face until Nasarlulik came back. Then she stopped, and we went into the kitchen and all sat around the little table there.

Niksaaktuq had another of her little notes ready. This time it read, 'What are you waiting for? Ask my husband!'

I was still too embarrassed, so I folded the note up and stuck it in my pocket. She laughed and said, *'Kanngusuktutit?'* (Are you shy?)

'Oh, no,' I replied, and cleared my throat.

'Well, go ahead, do what I asked you to do.'

I didn't know what to do. Somehow Nasarlulik seemed to have become nothing more than an onlooker in this little game between his wife and friend. Then Niksaaktuq picked up her pencil and wrote out another little note, and in the next half hour or so she wrote six or seven little notes and passed them over to me while we made small talk. Some of them I looked at and some I just folded over and shoved in my pocket. I began to devote my exclusive attention to Nasarlulik. I was about to fold another note without reading it and stick it in my pocket with the others, but Niksaaktuq could take no more.

'Give it to me,' she ordered. 'Go on and ask my husband. Don't be shy. Go ahead and ask my husband.' She grabbed the note out of my hand and gave it to Nasarlulik.

Her husband opened the note, looked up and smiled. I was sure it was a smile of relief because now the little comedy was over. Obviously he had known all along what was going on. This had all been talked over beforehand between the two of them.

He asked me plainly, 'Do you desire my wife?'

I still played it cautiously, and said, 'Oh, she's very desirable. Any man would desire her, a woman as good-looking as your wife.'

'Do you like her?' he persisted.

'Sure I like her.'

Then looking right at me, and with Niksaaktuq hanging on every word, he said, 'Do you want to make love with her?'

I was still very cautious. 'Well, she's not my wife, you know.'

Nasarlulik grinned and said, 'Well, Niksaaktuq likes you, and I like you too, so if you want to get my wife' (and that was the term he used), 'then go ahead.'

Still uneasy, I tried to be amiable. 'Okay, that's great . . .'

'Fine,' he said, 'Where do you want to get her?'

'Well, in my bed,' I blurted. There wasn't anywhere else to go. Niksaaktuq jumped up—'Come on, let's go, let's go.'

Off we went while Nasarlulik stayed in the kitchen. The bedroom was just off the kitchen, and there wasn't even a door. It was all wide open. I was in there with Niksaaktuq, not feeling the least bit romantically inclined, with her husband sitting a couple of arm's lengths away in the kitchen. But Niksaaktuq had no such inhibitions. She was trying to hurry me up. Down came her pants and bloomers and everything else, and she jumped into bed. So I got undressed and into bed too, but I still had a strange feeling. 'What about your husband? He didn't go home.'

'Oh, he'll be all right in the kitchen,' said Niksaaktuq.

Nature took its course. We were a bit noisy about it, because Niksaaktuq was just as eager as could be. The thing I most remember is her comment: 'You like me, even though I'm an Eskimo.' I have never heard any other Eskimo say that.

We got up, dressed and went back to the kitchen, and I was a little embarrassed thinking of the noise we had made. Nasarlulik was standing there; he had cleaned up all the dishes and was drying them. He turned to me with a smile and asked, 'Are you feeling better now?'

'Much better,' I smiled.

'I'm glad.' Then he explained, 'Niksaaktuq likes you, and I like you. Niksaaktuq kept telling me that we should share, because you are such a nice fellow, but I didn't want to say anything, because I didn't know how you felt about her.'

We sat down and had another mug-up; then they went home.

By the next day the news had spread. Niksaaktuq was proud to be the first woman in the settlement to 'get' me. She was just like a man who makes love to a beautiful woman and feels so good about it that he wants everyone to know. In typical Eskimo fashion she described to anyone who would listen the entire event, from beginning to end. It didn't make any difference whether men or women or both were listening, Niksaaktuq went into minute detail. Before noon every Eskimo in the settlement had heard all about us. Amirairniq, the young husband of Tuiligaaryuk, who liked to hang around the post, came in and said, 'I hear you slept with Niksaaktuq last night.'

I said that was true.

'How was she?' he asked. 'Was she good? Did she bounce up and down or did she just lie there?'

'She was good,' I replied.

Amirairniq nodded. 'You know that she is Tupilliqqut's exchange wife?'

I said I knew that, and he said, 'Well, she told Nasarlulik this morning that she doesn't want to exchange with Tupilliqqut again.'

Amirairniq said that Niksaaktuq had been all around the settlement that morning, casually bringing up the subject in numerous conversations—it just happened that the trader wanted her, and she just happened to be there, and one thing had led to another, an exchange had happened, and sharing taken place.

After a while Niksaaktuq arrived with Kuptana, Tupilliqqut's wife, another very good-looking girl who had been Niksaaktuq's chief rival for me. I hadn't objected to them competing; it made me feel good. I was surprised to see them together, but I soon realized why Niksaaktuq had brought her competitor along. The two of them sat down in my living room and had a mug-up, and Niksaaktuq said to me, *'Kina nuliasut?'* ('Who's your exchange wife?' Modern young Eskimos would translate it as 'Who's your girl friend?')

I looked at her and said, 'I don't know.'

She bristled. 'What do you mean you don't know? Who did you make love with last night?'

'You,' I said.

She turned triumphantly to Kuptana as she said to me, 'Well, then I'm your exchange wife.' Her smile of triumph was all woman.

Tupilliqqut didn't think much of what I had done, taking his girl away from him, but there wasn't anything he could do. He came over to the post the next day and opened with a remark I was beginning to hear over and over again. 'I hear you made love with Niksaaktuq.'

I said that was right.

'You know she is my exchange wife?' He turned away and looked out of the window.

'Yes, I knew that.' I added carefully, 'Nasarlulik agreed to it.'

He just said, 'Oh.' Then, 'You know, I really like her.'

I said, after a pause, 'I do too.'

'Oh, I see,' he said. That was all I ever heard on the matter from Tupilliqqut.

Every time after that when Nasarlulik or I made a trip, we would wind up at a camp together and we would share Niksaaktuq. Up at his trapping camp there would be Arnayak, his old blind mother, the two kids, Nasarlulik, Niksaaktuq and myself. We would all sleep on the sleeping platform together. At one end would be Arnayak, then me, Niksaaktuq, Nasarlulik, and then the two kids. Several times we made love in that situation. If it seems strange making love to a girl with her husband seven inches from your right knee and her mother-in-law seven inches from your left knee, then that is just another inhibition to be overcome. Everyone politely pretends to be asleep, but all ears are wide open. I can't say it really helped my sexual performance; on the other hand, it didn't stop me.

I didn't know how long this arrangement might last. It seemed that Niksaaktuq was a natural man collector. Among her partners was her father-in-law himself, the shaman. Normally such an alliance would have been taboo because of the kinship factor, but a shaman lies outside all taboos.

Niksaaktuq didn't like Alikammiq, but the shaman was a strong-willed man who dominated the family, including his son and his daughter-in-law. Niksaaktuq was frightened of him, and Nasarlulik could hardly object. One night Alikammiq had wanted Niksaaktuq and simply taken her. I knew that Nasarlulik felt repressed by him, but I didn't know why until after his death when Niksaaktuq told me about it. She said she hadn't wanted to make love to her father-in-law, but that he had forced himself on her. It was close to rape; Alikammiq just bullied her mentally until she gave in.

Nasarlulik and I spent more and more of our time together, hunting and trapping and working together as a unit. When two men share a wife, each has definite responsibilities. If, for instance, Nasarlulik had fallen sick, it would have been up to me to look after him and his family, including his old mother and any children there might be. In turn, if anything happened to me it was Nasarlulik's responsibility to see that I was provided for. If I had had a wife and family, he would have taken care of them until I was able to work again.

At Perry Island, two men who share one wife are called *angutauqatigiik,* and they will become as close as brothers. They will share every confidence with each other, all of each other's problems and troubles. When Nasarlulik was worried by anything, he usually came and told me. Once he confided that he was glad he had agreed to share Niksaaktuq with me; before she fooled around with too many men, but now she had settled down. She knew that other girls around the settlement, like Kuptana, would like to have me and that if she flirted elsewhere, I might look for another girl.

As my exchange wife, Niksaaktuq performed many duties. She did a lot of cooking for me, baking bannock and boiling stews when I was busy at the post. She took care of my clothing, which is no small matter for a man in the Arctic. Any Eskimo woman will try to outdo the others in making elaborate boots and *kamiks,* or the handsomest parka with the best stitching. No one outdid Niksaaktuq. She turned out beautiful clothing for me, embroidered *mukluks,* a caribou parka, perfectly tailored.

When she first began sewing for me, like most Eskimo women, she simply measured me with her eyes to get the proportions. Eskimo women have keen eyes for that sort of thing and seldom make a mistake, but Niksaaktuq decided she must measure me more carefully. She said I was a bit lopsided, probably because I was a whiteman, and produced a short piece of string to measure me with. I was puzzled how she expected to get accurate measurements with that, but she tied it around my head, across my forehead. I didn't see how that helped unless she was going to make me a hat. She called me silly and said that everyone knew that a man's height is always three times the circumference of his head. That was all the measuring she did and everything fitted exactly.

Like couples the world over, Eskimos have their share of marital problems. One day Angulaalik came to the post about nine in the morning sporting a terrific shiner. He kept his head turned away from me to one side but several Eskimos had been in already, and they had told me what happened. The previous night Angulaalik, who must have been in his middle or late fifties, had sneaked over to Nasarlulik's house and made love to the blind, hunchbacked Arnayak. Old Arnayak was reputed to be a real sex-pot. Irvana had found out and given her husband his black eye.

Soon Irvana came over to the trading post. She was a very attractive woman, much younger than Angulaalik, and intelligent into the bargain. Arnayak, proud as punch over what had happened, had gone all round the settlement blathering about the events of the night before. Irvana said she was mad at Arnayak too, but there was nothing she could do about that. Eskimos are taught to respect the older generation. Irvana told me about it all, then reached out and squeezed my foot. 'Don't tell my husband I told you.'

I promised I wouldn't and she returned to her house. I thought no more of it.

Early the next morning I heard Angulaalik's team going past my window, the usual rattle-rattle-bang of the sled and dogs excited and yapping. The noise half-awakened me. I noticed that it was only five o'clock. A few minutes later, I heard my front door open and footsteps coming into the house. I opened my eyes a slit to see Irvana standing beside the bed.

Seeing me awake she said, 'You've frequently desired me?'

My eyes widened, and I answered, 'Because you are desirable.'

She hesitated another moment: 'You always tell me you think I am good-looking, so I came over.'

Then she waited no longer. She climbed into bed with me and we made love. At that particular moment I was all for it. But later I began to have serious misgivings, remembering the gentle Angulaalik's past.

By this time several months had gone by since Niksaaktuq and I had become exchange mates, and I had learned a great deal about the dos and don'ts of the spouse-exchange system. I knew the risk involved in going to bed with Irvana behind Angulaalik's back. I had no agreement or arrangement with Angulaalik as I did with Nasarlulik. The only factor in my favour was that Irvana had come to me; I had not pursued her. Eskimos are quite understanding and tolerant of such little human foibles as errant sex, and I was banking on this, but at the same time was fully cognizant of the fact that Angulaalik might feel obliged to kill me to defend his honour. It was ticklish.

Irvana sneaked out, but in a few minutes she was back and worried herself: 'I wonder if people will see me leaving? It might be better if you didn't gossip about this.' I assured Irvana that I had no intention whatever of gossiping, on that or any future occasion.

Soon afterwards, around Christmas, a couple of Eskimos came down from Cambridge Bay. They brought some yeast with them, and made some home brew for a party at Angulaalik's house. This was nothing like the drunken brawls staged there before, just a good party. But the next morning one of Irvana's daughters, Tuiligaaryuk, came over to the post, giggling and laughing.

'Oh-oh, oh-oh, you've been making love with my mother.'

Thunderstruck, I demanded, 'How do you know that?'

'Because last night Angulaalik and Irvana got tight and she told him that you two had been making love.'

The fat was in the fire. I have to admit I was nervous.

Later in the day Irvana came over to explain. 'I had to tell him,' she said, 'I had *satqara isuirmat'* ('something wrong with my breastbone', which is to say a guilty conscience).

I watched out for Angulaalik, but he didn't come to the post that day. The next morning he arrived at the usual time, but he wouldn't look me in the eye. Finally he said, 'Do you like my wife?'

I knew I might as well admit it. 'Yes,' I said, 'I do.'

He said, 'Well, she likes you, you know, and she told me she's been coming over here when I've been away.'

I admitted that too.

'Well, I just wanted to let you know that it's all right,' said Angulaalik.

I gave a sigh of relief. So we sat down and had a mug-up and talked about women.

Angulaalik was in a mood to philosophize. 'Women are strange. They always like to fool around,' he said. 'I know that the first time Irvana came over here she did it to get revenge on me because I made love with Arnayak. She told me that.'

My curiosity got the better of me. 'How was Arnayak, anyhow?'

'Oooh,' he said, rolling his eyes, 'she was good. That's why Irvana was mad. Everyone knows that Arnayak is good in bed.' I had to remind myself that he was talking about a blind woman, at least fifty-five, and hunchbacked.

So we sat there like any couple of cronies, laughing and talking. Angulaalik said, 'If you like my wife, go ahead whenever you feel like it, because I like you, and you've always been good to us.' With a shake of his head he added: 'I'm an old man now, and can't satisfy her as I used to.' He was close to twenty-five years older than she was.

So life was pleasant at Perry Island. Niksaaktuq was my exchange wife, and others were always willing. Eskimos don't think of sex in the romantic way we do. An Eskimo woman doesn't fall head over heels in love, as we would say. Marriage is a practical matter to her, and sex is something else again.

Niksaaktuq and I became very close and affectionate as time went on. Our relationship was very much like a marriage. She was the most help to me in learning and perfecting the language—the Copper Eskimo dialect. It is natural to lie in bed and talk after making love. Niksaaktuq had a good ear for the shades of meaning and pronunciation that make so much difference. I began to feel that I was really learning to think in Eskimo. And then I could say things to her I would never say to a casual friend, even in bed. Sometimes, when I had been working on my accounts, Niksaaktuq would bring me a mug of tea and just stand there with her arm on my shoulder. Sexuality is listening and touching and wanting to make the other person happy, and Niksaaktuq's ways were very sexual.

I should never have become involved in wife exchange if I hadn't practically adopted the Eskimo way of life. The fact that I spoke their language made a world of difference. Some of the early explorers and many of the fur traders in particular took Eskimo wives or mistresses for a period, and there are many half-white Eskimos in the Arctic today. But that situation has changed. There are few isolated settlements today where the old Eskimo way of life continues. Missionaries, the RCMP, government workers and other whites flocking to the Arctic, the swift movement of Eskimos off the land to the larger villages and towns, and the almost universal education of the children in white schools—all have contributed to what amounts to a new culture in the North. I knew that the missionaries frowned on me for having Niksaaktuq as a shared wife. But what I did, the way I lived, was within the context of the Eskimo society in which I lived, not to be sneered at or scorned by outsiders.

When Niksaaktuq became pregnant, Nasarlulik and I didn't know which of us was the father. Niksaaktuq just kept smiling and assuring me, 'I know it is going to be yours. He'll be born with a nose like yours. You wait and see.' Eskimos believe that every child takes after the father, so they think they can always tell who the father is.

There is no word in Eskimo for illegitimate child. The child of any union belongs to the mother, so it becomes relatively meaningless who the father is. The child is raised by the mother and her husband, and when the child is old enough to understand, it is told who the real father is. Everyone knows, and there is no shame. Identifying the real father enables the incest taboos to be kept.

The matter of kinship has always been vital to the Eskimos. When two strange Eskimos meet in the middle of the tundra, the first thing they do is sit down and have a mug-up and try to find out if they are related in any way. Whenever a new family comes to a region, there is a great cross-examination until everyone is satisfied that all kinship ties are established. A relationship will be identified if any exists.

The Eskimos proved quite right about children taking after their fathers as far as Niksaaktuq's baby was concerned. There was no mistaking; I was the father. Before the birth of the baby, Nasarlulik and Niksaaktuq went to Cambridge Bay for a visit, and the child was born there. Before they returned to Perry, I had been transferred by the Company to a new trading post at Bathurst Inlet, so it was a long time before I was able to see my daughter. But Father Menez, one of the most decent missionaries I ever knew, who saw the child in Cambridge Bay, had no hesitation in confirming my fatherhood to me. 'Don't try to deny it,' he said gaily. 'Everyone knows it is your baby.'

The last thing in my mind was to deny it. I was very proud. My daughter was named Utuittuq, which had been the name of Niksaaktuq's father, one of the men killed by Angulaalik. But little Utuittuq was weak as a baby. She caught the flu when she was still tiny and very nearly died. So Niksaaktuq and Nasarlulik renamed her, as the custom decrees when someone has a brush with death. Her new name was Qummiq, which literally means a thing that one grips between one's knees. But Eskimo names are relatively meaningless. They are also all asexual. After our daughter got her new name, her health improved rapidly and she has developed into a lovely little girl.

Niksaaktuq's mother, Aaruattiaq, and her second husband, Tupilak, had no children. By Eskimo custom, when a couple want a child and can't have their own, they often adopt a grandchild. Niksaaktuq and Nasarlulik didn't want to give Qummiq to them, but Aaruattiaq begged them; she was getting old and wanted the company of a child. An Eskimo daughter can't really stand up to her mother; it simply isn't good manners to go against the wishes of an older woman, so finally Qummiq went to live with her grandparents and now lives in Cambridge

Bay. Niksaaktuq and Nasarlulik eventually moved to Gjoa Haven, where they live today.

Qummiq was not my first—or my last—northern child. Young Eskimo women are at least as eager as young white women. A man isolated in an environment where there are only native women, where he never sees a white woman, doesn't take long to adjust to native standards of beauty. He will soon find that he appreciates their striking looks, and he can always find a girl to sleep with. The problem is which one.

We were all very close at Perry Island. The people had come to that little settlement from all over the Arctic—it was a most cosmopolitan place. We all became related or tied in one way or another, through seal partnerships or wife exchange. We were like one big family; and I was fortunate enough to be considered a member.

Work Song

I'm only a little woman,
who's happy to slave,
happy to toil.
Anxious to be useful,
I pluck willow-flowers
that remind me
of the great wolf's beard.

I wear holes in my kamiks
when I walk far out
to pluck the willow-flowers,
that bring to mind
the great wolf's beard,
the great wolf's beard.

—Kibkarjuk (Caribou Eskimo woman)

Baby Kari Goes to the Arctic

BY MARIE HERBERT (BRITISH, 1973)

I n 1972, a British actress, Marie Herbert, accompanied husband Wally to live for a year among the Polar Eskimos in Northern Greenland—the people among whom Dr. Isaac I. Hayes found such hospitality—while Wally Herbert filmed a documentary about them. Wally Herbert had a few years earlier completed a dogsled journey that traversed the Pole, but for Marie and their ten-month-old baby girl Kari, the Arctic experience was utterly new. The Herberts lived in a hut in a tiny Eskimo village on an island fifteen miles off the Greenland coast near Qaanaaq. This tiny community of Inuit eventually opened up to accept Marie, and especially Kari, but with her husband off on filming expeditions for days or weeks at a time, the year among strangers was often a struggle for her. These selections from Marie Herbert's memoir, *The Snow People,* describe her first trip out on the sea ice with an old Inuit couple, the difficulties of dogsledding through the frigid winter night with an infant aboard, and some of the hardships that Inuit women face in the form of their husbands.

Maria and Avatak are an Inuit couple whom the Herberts befriended and who helped with the documentary.

The boats were up. There was now no way out of Herbert Island until the ice formed. Until the dog teams could take to the ice we were cut off from the rest of the world. The only way out, in an emergency, would be by helicopter from Thule Airbase. The air rescue service was part of the agreement made when the Airbase came into being in 1952. The helicopters are alerted from Qanaq, but the only way to contact Qanaq is by radio. But the radio on Herbert Island was now out of order—so we were really cut off.

The dying sun, as if to compensate for its disappearance, put on a kaleidoscopic display of colour. I would wake in the morning to see a pale moon and an orange sun together in the blue sky. The dogs lay in pools of pink between the black rocks. Against the horizon dark and light bergs alternated: those nearest blushed delicately in the sun. As the day wore on, icebergs like green fortresses sailed into view, outlined in petrol blue and covered with snow. At night their colour deepened into mauve.

When the ice was four inches thick it was safe enough to walk on, though not thick enough to take a dog team. My first venture on to the new ice was a thrilling experience. I went with Taitsianguaraitsiak and Suakuanguak to lay a net under the ice. Each carried a harpoon and the old man had an old tattered canvas bag slung over his shoulders. His wife carried the frail rifle which always seemed to point in my direction, whichever way I moved. It was a cold day and we walked for over half an hour along the coast while the old folk looked with practised eyes for the slight bulge in the ice which suggested the breathing hole of the seal. It was 23rd October—the next day would be the last day of sunlight. Already there was a wide band of ice around the island.

We kept close to the shore line, up and down the rocks and around the tiny inlets, while the squat old man peered out of his good eye towards the blue-grey band of ice. (His other eye had been badly injured several years before when the tip of his whip caught it.) They explained that in places the wind had blown away some of the ice, and that was no good for netting. Eventually, however, we climbed down the steep bank on to a drifting floe near the shore. Stopping first to make sure I was safe, the two of them then skipped across several more floes and waited while I followed gingerly. It is a really strange sensation to walk on sea ice for the first time. An old Alaskan Eskimo Wally had filmed said, 'Sea ice flexible like plastic, fresh ice break like glass.' I was ready to test his theory, and I felt all the thrill and excitement of the beginner explorer. From time to time the old man struck the ice with his harpoon. He sucked contentedly at his little pipe and his wife and I waited respectfully for him to lead the way.

As we left the safety of dry land I thought of the icy water just a few inches beneath me—water that could paralyse the body in a few minutes. Before long we reached a hummock in the ice like a huge boil frozen as it was about to burst. Taitsianguaraitsiak picked a spot about four yards from the mound and began to chip a hole in the ice with the pointed end of his harpoon. He made a hole about a foot in diameter. Then Suakuanguak scooped the mush out with an old frying pan. I could not help noticing how straight their backs were whenever they bent over. They seemed to bend from the hips—'chevron-shaped', as Wally called it.

The old man explained that the seals would come up for air into the little hummock: then, on their way back, they might get caught in his net. 'Imaka. Imaka nagga.' 'Maybe. Maybe not,' he laughed as he said it. His wife chuckled too. The Eskimos always used the word 'Imaka', 'Maybe', when they talked about anything.

It was lovely to see how well these two old folk worked together. They seemed so dependent on each other, so much in tune. I liked their ready smile and the concern they showed that I should be safe and not too cold. It was easy to see in them the spirit that had made their ancestors survive in this inhospitable environment, without the assistance of white men and without the accoutrements of civilized living. These old folk had been brought up the tough way, before the village of Kekertassuak had sprung up. These were the last of the pioneers, the true Inuit.

When the old couple had made three holes, five or six feet apart, they began to put the net together. They stretched it across the ice to unravel any tangles, and tied small stones to one side to weight it down in the water.

The skill came in getting the net into position beneath the ice. The old man tied a length of gut to one of the top corners of the net, and the other end of his harpoon. He then threw the harpoon like a spear through one of the holes in the direction of the next. Suakuanguak or I had to catch it as it glided past. I did manage to catch it after a few attempts.

When the gut line was running from each corner of the net down through the centre hole, and out to the holes at either side, all that remained was to lower the net carefully through the centre hole, tighten the lines, and anchor them so that the net hung taut in position beneath the ice. A quick look into the middle hole and the old man was satisfied that the net was hanging right. We kicked the snow back into the holes to cut out the daylight, and the job was done.

We rubbed our hands together to restore the circulation and looked round for a place to walk ashore. 'When do you think a seal might get caught in the net?' I asked, in Eskimo. 'Akago, imaka.' 'Tomorrow, maybe,' replied Suakuanguak with a mischievous look on her face. 'Kisiane imaka nagga.' 'But maybe not.' We all laughed. These two people were so used to hunting and the joys and disappointments that went with it. If there was a seal they were glad, but if there was not they accepted it calmly.

The few weeks before Christmas are busy ones for the Eskimo women. Traditionally, at this time everyone gets a new anorak and a new pair of kamiks. In a family with many children this means a great deal of work for the mother. Skins have to be scraped, stretched and dried. There is a lot of sewing to be done. The women leave their long kamiks out in the frost to bleach them. Because I am taller than Eskimo women, mine were made out of Harp Seal, but they were as white as the Ringed Seal kamiks worn by the Eskimo women.

I had a lot of presents for the villagers, but still needed to buy a few more things, so we decided to make a quick trip to Qanaq. We could not decide whether to go by dog sledge or by Skidoo. The advantage with the Skidoo was that it was quicker and more direct and we could get to Qanaq and back the same day. We could also park it where we liked in Qanaq. The main disadvantage was that it would be colder, as there was greater wind chill.

Wind chill is one of the most important factors to consider when dressing for a journey in the cold. The faster the speed and the stronger the wind the greater chill the body has to contend with. Thus, if there was no wind and the temperature was $-5°$ F., and we travelled at a speed of 25 miles per hour, the equivalent chill would be $-51°$ F. If, however, there was also a wind blowing the chill factor would increase. Weighed against this was the length of time it would take to get to Qanaq by dogs—possibly three hours as against the Skidoo's 30–40 minutes—and the chore of looking for somewhere to picket the dogs at the other end. This was sometimes difficult if there were other teams visiting. The dogs have to be near snow, as they get very thirsty during and after a journey, and there is no water available in winter.

We decided to take a chance and go by Skidoo. But I set to to make a thick sheepskin bag with a hood on it, inside which I put Kari's sleeping bag. The whole lot we put inside a wooden box which we anchored to the sledge. That would save me the trouble of holding on to her all the time.

As we were leaving, Migishoo came down to see us off. She brought a cotton tablecloth which she said I should put over the box. She showed me how I should feel inside from time to time to make sure Kari's face wasn't too cold. Good Lord, she will smother, I thought to myself as I saw the cloth put over the face of the sleeping child. I didn't realize there is enough air trapped for a baby inside the folds of the cloth and that this protects their delicate faces from the cutting wind.

We had no goggles, as these steam up in the cold. But we needed some protection for our faces and I made sheepskin masks, with holes for the eyes, to cover our noses and cheeks. We didn't dare put them on till we got out of the village, for fear of scaring anyone who caught sight of us. Even the adults were obsessed with imaginary spirits, which they said flew underneath the ice and which could appear at any moment and 'get us'. These things were said half in jest, but there was more than a touch of superstition in the ideas.

For some reason I had decided at the last minute to take Kari's little sledge on the larger one, which would be pulled by Skidoo. I thought it might be useful.

There was enough moonlight for us to be able to see clearly. Setting out was a glorious feeling. The sledge swung like a pendulum from side to side, down the rafted ice in the cove, till its nose pulled round towards the open pack. The Skidoo roared into the silent night and we raced after it. Raised prints of paw marks shone like strange flowers on the frozen sea. It was exhilarating to swish over the moonlit ice in whatever direction we pleased without battling with the wills of thirteen dogs, who always wanted to go the wrong way.

I had just begun to relax—when the wooden shaft which joined the sledge to the Skidoo snapped. Wally managed to fix it. But when it came to starting the Skidoo again it just would not work. Nothing could make it go. It would start, and then peter out in a few seconds. Wally did everything in the book, including changing the spark plugs, but it was no good. It was as dead as a doused fire.

We were about five miles from Herbert Island and still thirteen miles from Qanaq. We couldn't tell what was the matter, but repairs would have entailed putting up a tent and getting a primus going. It was too long for Kari to be outdoors in such an uncomfortable situation. Wally tried the Skidoo again.

'Oh, hell, who'd ever bring a wife and baby to the Arctic!' he blurted out. 'If you were a man I could have left you here and gone back to get the dogs. But I can't leave you alone with Kari—anything might happen. You wouldn't know what to do if a polar bear appeared. Besides it is too cold!'

I nodded glumly. Poor Wally. He had so many things go wrong with this expedition already, without the responsibility of Kari and me.

'Let's push Kari back on her sledge,' I suggested, thanking God I had brought it. Wally agreed there was no alternative. By this time Kari was crying hysterically. I felt inside but she seemed quite warm, just frightened. We pacified her and started the walk back. It was sweaty work in all our polar clothes. Wally trudged ahead, pulling, and I pushed from behind—a silent trio. Wally carried the gun and I had the ice axe. I couldn't help looking round every few minutes to make sure that the forms I saw silhouetted against the light sky were not animal.

The return journey seemed endless and by the time we got back we were exhausted. The runners on the small sledge were rough from the scratches of the rocks at the island. Our clothes were soaked in sweat when we returned and we had to strip them off as soon as we got inside the house. Of course the fire had gone out, and it was cold and dark, but we soon had the place cheered up. We discovered later that the trouble with the Skidoo was water in the fuel. Wally had taken tremendous care when he had mixed the petrol and oil but we learnt that some of the fuel drums already had water in them. At Orla's suggestion we added spirit to the mixture and had no further trouble. When Maria heard about our adventure she told me several stories of adventures she herself had had. She spoke of one occasion when she had been underneath an overhanging cliff, and there was a sudden avalanche: it just missed her and the children, but formed a huge wall of snow between them and her husband. Thinking they could not possibly have survived, he was overcome with grief, and sat on his sledge and wept. By great good luck, they managed to worm their way round behind the wall of snow and came out several yards ahead of the unhappy man. He was in some doubt that it was really them. But her teasing assured him that 'no angel would speak that way.' He still gets embarrassed if the incident is mentioned.

Maria explained that there were two reasons why women carried their baby in the Amaut when they went sledging. Firstly, it was warmer and the child could be twisted round to the mother's breast without taking off any clothes. But, as important was the fact that sledges sometimes went through the ice, and if a mother was trying to save herself from going under, she often had not time to save the baby as well, and there had been many cases in their history of children being lost when the ice gave way. My heart froze as she told me this: and

I made sure when we made Kari's travelling cot that she was easy to get at in case I had to snatch her up suddenly. But the thought of travelling with her seemed less agreeable, and I decided that as soon as I could find someone who would look after her, while we went away on short journeys, the better.

Wally and Avatak left for Savigsavik on the 26th January. A grey pall hung over the sea ice and through it the moon shone like gossamer. Wally's sledge shrank till it vanished from sight with a final flash from his torch. Maria accompanied Avatak out on to the sea ice, dressed in her finest clothes. The husband goes off leaving his wife looking her most beautiful: he would always think of her as he saw her last. I had been up most of the night with Wally doing last-minute things and I went straight back to bed after they had gone.

Maria put on a show of bravado in front of any of the other women, and said it was a good thing our husbands had gone away as there would be hunters visiting from the other settlements on their way north and she would enjoy the change of company for a while. The others laughed and pretended to be shocked. But Maria's cheer would sometimes drop for a while as we chatted intimately together.

She was glad the winter was almost over. It had been unbearable to be cooped up for so long in the house. Didn't we feel the same boredom? Both she and Avatak felt restless during the long dark night. But at least the men knew that in the spring they would go on their long journeys—the women had nothing to look forward to. It was worse for those with a lot of children, like herself, because they rarely got a chance to travel, except in the summer to a camp. That was why she loved summer so much. Sometimes the women got so bored that they fought bitterly with their men.

She glanced at the books on the shelves and pointed to one that she would like to look at. She never remained miserable for long—it was if she thought it a sign of weakness to feel unhappy just because her man had gone, and Maria hated to admit weakness. She pored over the pictures in the book. I watched her, fascinated. Her features were not remarkable, except for her sloping forehead and fair complexion. Like all Eskimos she had almond eyes and high cheek bones. Her thin mouth set itself in a smirk whenever she was with other people as if she found them a constant source of amusement, and she could never resist a laugh at their expense. But at moments I thought her beautiful.

The women in the village were so different in their attitudes to me. There were those like Maria, Nauja and Savfak, who seemed genuinely to treat me as a friend. There were a couple who ignored me, as if I never existed. Others kept our relationship strictly an acquaintanceship, except at those times when beer loosed their tongues.

I used to love to hear these women come alive, when they forgot their shyness. They would go over the old stories of who had fought with whom in the village. There were often quarrels when two hunters set out after one animal. This had happened a few years ago when a bear had appeared on the scene. There were only two old men around and they had both harnessed their dogs simultaneously and dashed out after it. The old custom of dividing the fur into two was forgotten. They had skinned the animal between them and began a furious tug of war. The stronger of the two rushed off with the skin to his own home. His wife proudly scraped it and as usual hung it on the drying frame in the open air. The loser, however, sneaked down and slashed the skin in several places so that it could not be sold or used to make breeches. The battle continued over several months, till they drowned their anger in an orgy of drink.

Nauja loved to tell stories of calamities that had befallen people on their travels. The worst victims were always the Kasdlunas, though she admitted occasionally to some losses on the Inuit side. She was delighted to be able to tell me a couple of tales of cannibalism, which she assured me had happened a long time ago. She remembered a story of an expedition when both Eskimos and white men ran out of food. They could not hunt because they were in poor gaming territory. Eventually the Eskimos had eaten the dogs and survived till they could find a walrus. But all the white men except one had been too squeamish to eat dog meat and had perished.

There were times these days when all the men in the village were away. The women spent their time visiting from house to house. If

there were no skins to prepare or no kamiks to make there was very little else to do. Women without children could not bear to be in the
dreary houses by themselves and they spent the whole day visiting
their neighbours. There was no recreation they could turn to other than
sewing. The few books in the 'library' had not been renewed for a couple of years. They had read them all and didn't see the point in reading
them over again. They suffered all the depressions and ills of boredom.

It was when their menfolk were away that I got to know the other
women in the village better. They enjoyed the brightness of our home
and the many books. I made a great effort to entertain them although I
much preferred to listen to their stories. One night Nauja and I had
spent the whole evening together chatting about our relationship with
our husbands. She admitted that she had been *given* in marriage to her
husband.

'My mother was rather frightening when she got angry—she always
told me not to sleep with a man before I got married. The priests said it
was a very bad thing. But one night she found me sleeping with Inugssuak after a dance. She was very angry and told him he would have
to marry me.'

'But surely you like him?' I asked.

'Oh, I liked him, but there was another man I liked better.' She described how she wept behind the smile she forced at the wedding. The
first two years were stormy, while they lived in his parents' house,
with four of his sisters. It was a happy day for her when they got their
own home.

I handed her a cigarette, which she smoked vigorously. At last she
looked up. 'Was it true that white men never beat their wives?'

I told her that on the whole they didn't. They might have bitter arguments, but some married people managed to discuss their difficulties
without being nasty to each other and this was the way Wally and I
preferred.

'That could never happen amongst the Eskimos. The men think the
women are inferior and should be kept down. They have no understanding of women. They are vicious when they are angry, especially
when they are drunk.' She went on rapidly as if a torrent of feeling had

been unleashed. 'I try not to fight back when he hits me and I just say yes to everything he demands, but sometimes I get fighting mad too. I often want to run away—far away, and take my two girls with me. I get so bored cooped up inside while he goes away. "Go outside," he says, "if you don't like the house." As if it is as easy as all that!' She stubbed out her cigarette as if it required all her strength.

I hesitated before I asked, 'Do you love Inugssuak?'

She thought for a moment, frowning. 'I don't know—I don't know what I feel for him. He is sometime so difficult—I don't understand him!'

I felt sorry for her. From all appearances Inugssuak seemed a fine figure of a man—a good hunter and a loving father. But I heard from other people that when he was drunk he was like a man with a devil in him. His liquor ration had recently been stopped after a very violent argument he had had in another settlement. 'He is difficult,' Nauja repeated reflectively '—but sometimes maybe I love him. I don't know."

Song of a Mother

A young man had killed his hunting companion in a fit of rage.
The murderer's mother sang this song to express her grief:

Ejaja-eja.
A bit of song comes back.
I draw it to me like a friend.
   Ejaja-eja.

I ought, I suppose, to be ashamed
of the child I once carried on my
   back,
when I heard he'd left the settlement.
They're right to tell me so:
I ought to be ashamed.
   Ejaja-eja.

I am ashamed:
because he didn't have a mother
who was faultless
as the clear sky,
wise and without folly.
Now that he's the butt
of everybody's tongue,
this evil talk will finish him.
   Ejaja-eja.

He has become the burden
of my age.
But far from being

properly ashamed,
I'm envious of others
when they break up
after feasts, and set off
with crowds of friends
behind them, waving on the ice.
   Ejaja-eja.

I remember one mild spring.
We'd camped near Cross-Eye
   Lake.
Our footsteps sank
with a soft creak
into half-thawed snow.
I stayed near the men,
like a tame animal.
But when the news
about the murder came,
and that he'd fled,
the ground heaved under me
like a mountain,
and I stood on its summit,
and I staggered.

—Uvlunuaq (Netsilik Eskimo woman)

An American City Sprouts on the Hunting Grounds

BY JEAN MALAURIE (FRENCH, 1976)

For nearly half a century the French anthropologist Jean Malaurie has been an advocate on behalf of the Inuit against exploitation from the South. In 1950, when he was in his late twenties, Malaurie spent a year living with the Inuit in Siorapaluk, Greenland, the northernmost native village in the world, learning their language and skills, such as how to handle a dog team. The cultural integrity of the region that Malaurie had chosen for his studies was shattered early the following summer when the United States military, at the height of the Cold War, constructed the world's largest airbase square in the middle of the Polar Inuit's best hunting grounds at Thule. Malaurie witnessed firsthand the arrival of the airbase, a traumatic event which compelled him to become a leading voice for the Arctic peoples.

The excerpt is from *The Last Kings of Thule*, Malaurie's classic account of his year with the Polar Inuit. It describes the surprise that overtook him and his hunting companions when they dogsledded down a glacier and spotted for the first time the U.S. base under construction.

Sakaeunnguaq, Qaalasoq, and I stood discussing which route to follow. We were all three dirty and smelly; I was worn out and leaned on my napariaq. Suddenly one of the Eskimos touched my shoulder.

"Takkuut! Look!"

A thick yellow cloud was rising into the sky.

"Qallunaat!" he added.

I pulled out my field glasses and, squinting, slowly brought them into focus. Beyond the compact ice field, an extraordinary spectacle took shape on the spotted lens; for a moment, I thought I was seeing a mirage.

A city of hangars and tents, of sheet metal and aluminum, glittering in the sun amid smoke and dust, rose up in front of us on a plain that only yesterday had been deserted. The most fantastic of legends was taking shape before my eyes.

"Takkuut! Look at that!"

Like pustules erupting from the depths, rows of storage tanks stood along the mountain. Their being orange made the vision all the more absurd. As we went down the slope of shining snow, surprise changed to stupefaction. As far as the eye could see, there were lines of trucks and cranes, and mountains of crates. Steel skeletons raised thin metallic arms toward the sky. Along the slopes, the enormous jaws of tentacled diggers chewed away amid smoke and steam, lifting tons of mud and stones which, in one uninterrupted movement, they vomited into the sea from buckets. The sound of the breathing, the panting of this "city," reached all the way to where we stood, and from then on it was to stay with us—the muffled grinding of ceaselessly turning motors. Planes by the dozen wheeled about in the gray sky. One, nearer than the rest, flew back and forth like a huge bumblebee, adding its own deep buzz to the hubbub. Seen from the glacier, the spectacle created by this sudden eruption of civilization looked sinister. Our dogs were howling their heads off. Two of the teams attacked each other. We intervened, but not very energetically. This return to the world of men was a letdown.

We continued our descent toward the coast. The glacier was in very bad shape; the season was too far advanced for us to be able to cross without problems. Small holes opened up in the surface at our feet. The rotten snow did not hold. At one point during the last few miles I was almost engulfed when the bridge over an enormous crevasse suddenly collapsed a moment after I stepped off it. I had no sooner escaped this danger than the whole slope seemed to begin to move; the ice was swelling in the heat of the rising sun. Section after section slid down toward the valley. We traveled the last few miles prepared for the worst.

On the shore we found a wet, yellowish rock on which we rested for a while. We left the two Eskimos' sledges and their equipment beside it and crossed a torrent, carrying my material on our heads. We threw my dogs forcibly into the icy water—they were terrified of it—and with a rope hauled them up onto the opposite bank. We did the same with my sledge.

On June 16, after crossing the frozen fjord, we were finally arriving at the Eskimo "capital" of Thule; in the eyes of the qallunaaq I had once more become, this seemed like a very big word to denote a disorderly cluster of twenty or so molehills—igloos whose relative importance could be assessed by the height of the rubbish pile before each door. We were greeted by an unusual silence; even the dogs slept on. The two Eskimos, disappointed, grumbled and thrashed their teams as they passed through the camp. Discarded wrappers from packs of Camel cigarettes and chewing gum littered the snow.

At one window I glimpsed the chocolate-smeared face of a child. A few yards farther on, a door opened slightly and from a cloud of cigarette smoke a young woman in blue jeans and makeup called out to me, "Hello, boy!" Whatever had happened since February, when I was last here?

We set up our tent near Knud Rasmussen's little white house, which was vacant. The south wind smelled of diesel oil. A message of welcome from Krogh, the Danish administrator, was delivered to me. Old Uutaaq paid us a visit; a few minutes later, he was joined by Inukitsupaluk. Little by little, I heard the news.

"Thousands and thousands of Americans," Uutaaq said in his hoarse voice. "Amerlaqaat, you lose track of how many. They come down from the sky every day. There's the atomic bomb, too. . . . We've been here a thousand years, we Inuit. We always thought Thule was an important place on the earth. . . . After all, we were the ones who discovered it. . . . Thule . . . Inukitsupaluk learned from Tatsiannguaq that fifty big ships sank beneath the ice down there. . . . The Inuit also say that they're going to heat the ice field and make it melt; that way there will hardly be any winter anymore. . . . Then they're going to send us to the North Pole. That's why Piulissuaq spent fifteen years trying to go there with the Inuit. . . . Ah! we understand everything now. . . . None of these Amerikamiut have women. That isn't normal. Sofia has heard that they'd like our hundred girls. . . . The poor things! They could never satisfy those thousands and thousands of men. . . ."

He went on for two hours. I was skeptical and listened with only half an ear. A little later, I was to confront the truth.

Qisuk personified it. Wearing a gray-green jacket with the words "United States Navy" in black block letters on the back, he was pushing a sledge piled high with cases of tinned corned beef, ham, marmalade, and bundles of magazines over the rocky ground. The dogs were struggling to pull the load. Qisuk, streaming with sweat, forced them on by belaboring them with cans of vegetables. He was followed by a crowd of kids wearing jockey caps; Lucky Strikes drooped from their mouths. They were coming from the store; the stock had been replenished, the Americans having generously given their surplus to the Eskimos through the Danish administrator. Already the shore was strewn with empty tin cans and scraps of clothing.

"Now we are richer than the danskerne. We don't have to work anymore," the natives announced. "What are we going to do? No more hunting, no more kayaks." Then, immediately contradicting themselves: "That's just a manner of speaking. You can't eat half of what's in these cans; it's too salty." The Eskimos could not tolerate even lightly salted canned food.

In the village, everyone was arguing and haggling and swapping rumors.

Every morning I walked around the city as a tourist, my camera around my neck and a notebook in hand. I had been "cleared," so I went everywhere. Following the arrows at each crossroad, I walked through dirty white dust in step with the heavy tread of power tools and machines. In less than ten weeks, the world's most formidable air base had risen up on this desert.

Imagine a valley three miles wide and nine miles long, at one end terminated by a glacier, and at the other end closed off by the sea, which was frozen nine months out of twelve. Packed into this valley was a group of Americans numbering more than one-quarter of the native population of Greenland. In the space of a few weeks, the Americans had apparently spent as much as, or more than, the Canadian government had invested in its Eskimo colonies in the last hundred years. The monies for the annual work on the base would amount to more than double Denmark's expenditures for the whole of Greenland since 1721. The creation of this base was part of Operation Blue Jay, which was said to be the biggest military enterprise since the Allied landings in Normandy. Apparently Thule would be the Strategic Air Command's most powerful atomic base.

Song of the Lemming

On a cold winter's day, a little lemming came out of his warm hole.
He looked about him, shivered, shook himself, and sang:

The sky,
like a vast belly,
arches itself
around my burrow.
The air is clear,
no clouds in sight:
icy weather! Aiee!
I'm freezing! freezing!

—Atqaralaq (Caribou Eskimo woman)

$\mathcal{I}\,\mathcal{A}m\,in$
$the\,\mathcal{M}iddle$

BY MINNIE AODLA FREEMAN (CANADIAN INUIT, 1978)

innie Aodla Freeman brings the perspective of both an insider and an outsider to the Inuit as well as the white world. Born to an Inuit family on Hudson Bay's Cape Hope Islands, she was schooled among Cree Indians at an Anglican missionary school on the mainland, where she learned English. In 1957, at the age of twenty-one, after she herself had been a patient, Freeman was hired as a translator in Ottawa to work with the hundreds of Inuit who had been brought to the South for treatment of tuberculosis.

Her memoir, *Life Among the Qallunaat*, consists of a series of short, insightful essays about life in both the North and Ottawa. In this excerpt, she looks at the deleterious effects of social change coming to Frobisher Bay in the late 1950s.

$\mathcal{I}\,\mathcal{A}m\,in\,the\,\mathcal{M}iddle$

In 1958 my job as a translator took me to Frobisher Bay, Baffin Island, Northwest Territories. Because I was a working girl, I lived with a *qallunaaq* woman. Our conversations were simple: good morning and good night. Because I was from somewhere else the Inuit were

347

strange to me and I was strange to them. The *qallunaat* with whom I worked accepted me from 9:00 A.M. to 5:00 P.M.; socially, I did not exist. I was friends with the *qallunaat* as long as I made parkas and translated for them. I should have been sad all the time but I was too busy studying the people around me. Inuit were in the middle as well, like I was.

The Inuk man was caught between his desire to go hunting and the demands of the clock. He would be late for his job and get fired. His mark became unreliable so he would go hunting and feed his wife and children on the seal which he had luck with. Eventually the weather would not allow him to go hunting again or the money that was left from his last pay was all spent on ammunition and grub. But there was always an answer for him—he went on relief for a few months and tried hunting again. If he was successful with his hunting, the strong beliefs of his tradition to share with his neighbours would not allow him to eat alone with his family.

He begins to visit his friends and relatives which he has not seen since he started working like the *qallunaat,* and somehow he borrows money. In the meantime problems and worries are swelling up in his mind. His wife no longer looks up to him with happiness, she is too wrapped up herself with the problems that have arisen in her home. She is doing a lot of visiting herself, trying to get food for her children. The husband finds some friends who are making homebrew or friends who have bought from the *qallunaat,* at five to ten dollars, a bottle. He finds this drink very intriguing and it makes him forget his problems. So now he sleeps in the day and gets up at night when his friends are available.

Then one night someone in the group remembers a card game, a game which his ancestors learned from some explorer or Hudson's Bay man. Instead of playing it just as a game to pass time, as it was played by his ancestors, he turns it into a gambling game and now money is involved. He manages to win now and then and when he does he buys all the ingredients to make homebrew. He then becomes very popular with others who are in the same situation. His home begins to be their regular meeting hall. His wife, usually terrified of people who drink, is no longer amused by her regular visitors. The rules that were given to her by the *qallunaat* to have the children in school are no longer an obstacle. She has a greater obstacle to overcome, her drinking husband.

The children no longer listen to her words. They realize that the language they have learned is much stronger and has more impact. They can tell her to be quiet and to shut up. She feels very tired; she does not get enough to eat; she loses a great deal of sleep and can hardly keep awake during the day while her younger children are running around, going in and out without proper clothing. Then one day a mysterious machine of the *qallunaat* comes around, the *ajjiliurrutik* machine for taking pictures, X-ray. Not very long after she is told that she has to go south to the hospital. She does not know for how long or why; she guesses that she has tuberculosis, one of many gifts her ancestors have received from the *qallunaat.* She no longer sees her former problems but worries about them while in the southern hospital. Her children are now under the care of their grandparents. They can no longer answer back and find their grandparents are much stronger willed. Now they are having to grow up in a different way.

Because all kinds of people fascinate me I also studied the *qallunaat* in the North. They are also in the middle, between their jobs in the North and their authorities in the South. In the North they appear knowledgeable in everything. They give out rules that they understand. When asked a question by the Inuit, their favourite replies are "maybe" and "will write to South." In the South, the ones receiving the letter remember the occasion when they had visited that community. To them the Inuit did not seem to have that problem. They remember their smiles and handshakes and recall that the schools, offices and recreation affairs looked very well at that hour of their visit. Their *siallaat,* servants, had followed their orders. Everything was working according to plan.

The letter has quite a trip itself. It has been in the hands of the receiver, receiver's head, head of the head and finally third head's head.

Everybody now has something to do. The letter even went through a machine and was made into several copies. It has been some months since the letter arrived. By this time the Inuk who had asked the question will have sorted it out himself. A reply is sent finally to the original writer, telling the Inuk that those in the South will write to the people who have something to do with the question. Inuk again sits and waits; to him it sounds as if they are doing something about his problem.

Perhaps his question becomes very pressing in his mind and he decides to write himself. His letter goes to one of the heads, the head sends it to the head of the translators. The translator head sends it to the translator. The translator is very upset on reading the letter. The translator then puts the letter into English; somehow, it does not sound as pressing as it does in Inuttitut. Altogether it does not sound very important to the receiver because we translators lack many important words in English, though we know them in the Inuit language. *"Qittungara anniakuvimmut aullalaursimajuk suli tusangilara naningimaat tusarumavunga iqaumainarakku isumaalugillugo ..."* "My child is gone to the hospital, I have not heard where he is. I would like to hear." I am still learning many things, but I have learned that the *qallunaat* language can be just as pressing as the Inuit language. "Some time ago my child was hospitalized, but I have not yet heard of his whereabouts. I would be pleased to hear as I worry about him a great deal. My mind does not rest from worry."

One day the *qallunaaq* in the North decides to go with the hunter and his dog team. On the whole, he enjoys it, enjoys the freedom of not having to watch the clock. He observes igloo building, the use of harpoons, stalking of seals, dogs being harnessed, the whip being handled. He sees how an Inuk can handle dogs with few commands, how an Inuk can get out of the ice when stuck with his sled. He does not really care for the coffee breaks; it takes too long to be made and when he finally gets it, it is full of *piluit,* caribou hairs, which fall off the outfit he is wearing. What can he do? By the time he picks them out of his cup, the coffee will be too cold to enjoy. He has to gulp it down like an Inuk.

For the first time he sees the Inuk as a capable person. In fact, he is amazed by what the Inuk can put up with. He begins to invite him to his home. While talking with him, he begins to find out a lot of things about how the Inuk lives. He begins to understand the full meaning of his language. He asks him to carve for him; the carving has a meaning itself and the Inuk explains it. He realizes for the first time that the carving speaks like the art work in the South. Bit by bit, he begins to collect. He begins to send carvings as gifts to his relatives in the South. At the same time he realizes that his job no longer deals with "just Inuit." To him the Inuit are human after all, with feelings, able to think, capable of a life which he himself would never choose. His way of approaching the Inuk begins to change; he no longer talks fast, but explains in a way that the Inuk will understand. Even his manner is no longer stiff. It has become thawed, warm, and the Inuk sees he too is human after all.

In the South, the *qallunaaq* is very friendly, he no longer walks as if he is carrying a heavy load. Sitting with his colleagues, he listens to their plans for the North. There will be a new runway for aircraft, a new school building, a new administration building, new quarters for the *qallunaat* who are employed there, a new home economist to teach the Inuit how to be clean and to show them how to wash and prepare meals, new ways to bring the Inuit children in to the school, new community affairs, a survival course for the new *qallunaat* who are to go north. There is no mention of a new way to teach Inuit how to cope with their changing lives, how to cope with liquor, how to cope with a working husband, how to plan their spending now that he is no longer a hunter.

So many things the *qallunaat* have introduced to the simple Inuk. The *qallunaaq* man feels withdrawn after listening to his boss's big plans. He wonders if his boss will understand him if he makes any comments on how to cope with the Inuit. He becomes very quiet and cannot bring himself to explain the things he has seen happen when other new ways of the South have been tried in the old North. What he says will affect his job which he cannot afford to lose. He lets his colleagues and boss dream on with their plans, and he agrees to them. He is trained to respect his superiors; what they say is always right, what they say has to be the way. No matter how he feels and how much he understands the Inuk way, he chooses to be quiet and to sit back and listen. He is now Inuit.

Being in the middle I also studied the young women in the North. At one time it was the Inuit tradition that a young woman's parents chose her husband at the earliest age. Early marriages prevented promiscuity. Now she is also in the middle, between the Inuk man and the *qallunaaq* man. In her changing community she has seen *qallunaat* women who are attired in pretty frocks and wear make-up. In her eyes they choose what they want, eat what they want, speak loudly at husbands, ditch and pick up husbands. She finds that the *qallunaaq* man is friendly towards her; in fact, he notices her looks and tells her so. On the other hand, the Inuk man would notice what she can do and not what she looks like. But the *qallunaaq* man speaks loud and makes it all so exciting for her. He arranges some meeting place where there will be more privacy. He then invites her and gives her a drink. He gives her more than he takes. Everything he says is now agreeable to her.

The meetings go on and on, until she is discovered by the police. The *qallunaaq* man knew the rules all the time—that he was not supposed to mingle with Inuit girls at that place. Somehow he gets out of it, in spite of the promise he made when he signed his contract to work there. The girl is now in the hands of the police. She is asked many questions: "How did you get in there? Where did you get the drink? You are not supposed to go there! What is the name of the man you were with? Who does he work for?" She knows that she will suffer a great deal more if she tells on him. She is warned not to go there again, not to drink or she will go to jail. It makes her afraid, but more so of the *qallunaaq* man whom she is afraid to report.

Then one day she has funny pains and an uncontrollable itch; she now carries one of his gifts—venereal disease—so now she has to go back and forth to the dispensary and take many needles to cure it. If she has not received that gift, she may find herself pregnant. Now the community sees her condition; she is suffering in her mind and it affects her family. The Inuk man whom she had rejected, rejects her for carrying a *qallunaaq* child. The *qallunaaq* man has disappeared, or if he sees her, he avoids her and acts as if he had never been intimate with her. She has to carry her problem alone. After the birth her parents become understanding again; they have gained a grandchild and they know the child did not ask to be born on its own. They also know that the new mother has paid enough for her promiscuity. Not all young women suffer this experience; yet I watched it happen, being in the middle, in my one-year stay in this community. And, of course, it does not happen only in that community; it has happened in the four corners of the world.

Dancing Song

Two little girls squat opposite each other, and hop up and down, singing repeatedly.
They sing again and again, hopping faster all the time.

Aj-ja-japa-pé.
Bring out your hair-
ornaments!
We're only girls
rejoicing with each other!
Aj-ja-japapé.

Difficult times,
shortages of meat
have smitten everyone:
stomachs hollow,
meat-trays empty.
Aj-ja-japapé.

Can you see out there?
The men are coming home,
dragging seals
towards our village!
Aj-ja-japapé.

Joy has distorted
everything in sight:

the leather boats lift themselves
away from their ropes,
the straps follow them,
the earth itself
floats freely in the air!
Aj-ja-japapé.

Plenty visits us again:
times when feasts
bind us together.
Aj-ja-japapé.

Do you recognise
the smell of boiling pots,
and blubber squelching
in the corner of the bench?
Aj-ja-japapé, hu-hue!
Joyfully we welcome
those who bring us wealth!

—Tutlik (Iglulik Eskimo woman)

A Seal Hunt in the Moon of the Returning Sun

BY RICHARD K. NELSON (AMERICAN, 1980)

ichard K. Nelson is an anthropologist who has lived for long periods of time among the native peoples of Alaska. In his book *Shadow of the Hunter*, Nelson retells, month-by-month, the annual cycle of activity among the Inupiat, an Inuit group who live along the Arctic Ocean. This excerpt, the first chapter in the book, follows the hunter Sakiak as he leaves his wife and children and warm house and walks far out onto the sea ice on a cold January morning for a day of hunting seal. "The Moon of the Returning Sun" refers to the Inupiat term for the first month of the new year. Nelson wonderfully captures the precise details of the ice—a key element of the Inuit world—and how carefully the hunter must think about ice and its behavior. Para-doxically, the task falls to an outsider or an anthropologist like Nelson to explain the Inuit techniques of survival. In the stories told by the Inuit, these techniques are not explained because, of course, it is assumed that the listener already knows them.

This excerpt picks up as Sakiak leaves the village and steps out onto the sea ice.

For the first half-mile the ice was almost perfectly flat, except for a few low hummocks, or ice piles, where the floes had moved and been crushed the previous fall. The surface was also punctuated by the minor undulations of snowdrifts, packed hard as a wooden floor by the pounding winds. Sakiak's practiced eye could tell which drifts had been shaped by the cold northeasters and which by the warmer south winds. If fog or a blinding snowstorm caught him, he would navigate by watching, or even feeling, the configuration of the drifts.

Shortly, he reached the first high ridges of piled ice. He picked his way up the side of a huge mountain of tumbled slabs and boulders, from which he could look far out over the pack. When he stood at the top, he scanned the vast expanse of snow-covered ice that stretched beyond him. It was still gray twilight, but in the crystal air and brightness of snow the sea ice stood out sharply to the distant horizon. From his lofty perch, Sakiak looked over an environment that appeared totally chaotic and forbidding. Huge ice piles and ridges interlaced the surface everywhere, encircling countless small flat areas and occasionally fringing a broad plain of unbroken ice.

To the unpracticed eye this jumbled seascape would have seemed utterly impenetrable and unattractive. But to the Eskimo it held a different promise. He would find an easy trail by weaving among the hummocks, crossing them at low places. And he would find his prey, the seal, that now swam dark dark waters beneath the pavement of ice. For although this world appeared silent and lifeless, the sea below was rich with living things. The currents carried millions of tiny planktonic organisms, the basis of a long chain of biological interrelationships. Larger invertebrates and fish fed upon the drifting clouds of krill, and they in turn fell prey to warm-blooded animals that rose to the surface for air. Seals fed all winter among the congealing floes, gnawing and scratching holes through the ice to reach the air above or rising in the steaming cracks. And, on the ice surface, polar bears and Eskimos stalked the seals.

Sakiak searched the pack with his binoculars, their cold eyepieces stinging his skin. He was attentive to minute details, hoping to pick out the yellowish color of a polar bear's fur against the whiteness of the snow. He looked also for the fresh black lines of cracks and for rising clouds of steam that would mark open holes and leads. Long minutes passed before he took the binoculars from his eyes, satisfied that there were no bears or open places in the area. The ice was packed firm against the coast and would not move today unless the wind or current changed. It was a perfect time for an old man to wait for a seal at its breathing hole.

In a moment Sakiak was down from the ice pile, walking seaward again along the sled trail. About a mile out from the coast he passed the frozen carcasses of two old dogs, half-covered by blown snow. They had been shot early in the winter by their owner, who was replacing them with strong pups. This fate awaited all dogs that outlived their usefulness, for though Eskimos appreciated their animals they could ill afford the luxury of emotional attachment to them. Sakiak had used dogs all his life, but like all the older hunters he often preferred to walk. Animals frequently saw or heard a dog team long before they could detect a lone man afoot, so it was better to hunt this way. If the kill was heavy, a man could drag part of it home and return with a team for the rest.

The trail wound and twisted across the ice, which made it long but relatively smooth. Still, it crossed many ridges that the Eskimos had laboriously chopped and smoothed to make the passage as easy as possible. About two miles out the trail entered a field of very rough ice, with some ridges forty to sixty feet high. Broad slabs of ice four feet thick had been tossed on end and pushed into the air like huge monuments that towered high above a man's head. The far edge of this rough area was marked by a single ridge that stretched unbroken for miles, its direction generally paralleling the distant coast. The outer face was a sheer wall of pulverized ice, ground flat and smooth by the motion of the pack.

Sakiak sat down to rest and cool off beside this ridge. His long walk had generated too much warmth, and if he did not stop he would begin to perspire. He knew that moisture robbed clothing of its warmth, so he always tempered his labors during these cold months to avoid overheating. The long ridge where Sakiak rested marked the outermost edge of the landfast floe, an immobile apron of ice that extended far out from the land. An early winter gale had driven the ice against the coast and caused it to pile so high and deep that the entire floe had become solidly anchored to the bottom of the ocean. The ice beyond it was the mobile Arctic pack, which moved according to the dictates of current and wind.

Hunters knew that landfast ice rarely moved during the winter unless a tremendous gale arose, with an accompanying high tide that lifted the ice free of the bottom. Landfast ice meant safety because it would not drift away, carrying men out to sea with it. But the pack was different. Hunters who ventured onto it were suspicious and watchful, constantly checking wind and current to be sure the ice would not break away from the landfast floe. If this happened, and sometimes did, they would be stranded beyond a widening lead, an open crack that blocked their return to shore. Men who drifted away often died without seeing land again.

A week earlier, powerful onshore winds had driven the pack against the landfast ice, where it had remained without moving ever since. Sakiak would now decide if it was safe to go beyond the final grounded ridge. He walked along its edge until he found a narrow crack covered with dark, thin ice. With the point of his *unaaq,* he chiseled a fair-sized hole through it. Then he cut a bit of sealskin thong from his boot tie chewed it until it was moist, and dropped it into the black water. The white thong sank slowly downward until it cleared the bottom edge of the ice, then drifted off eastward, toward the land. Finally it was enveloped in the blackness.

Sakiak stood up and looked out onto the pack. The current flowed from the west, from the sea toward the land, gently but with enough force to hold the ice ashore against opposing pressure from the easterly breeze. He had studied the movements of ice throughout his life, and he remembered well the lessons taught him by old hunters during his youth. With this knowledge and experience he could judge to near perfection the mood of the pack. Today it would be safe, so long as the wind and current pushed against each other. He would look for breathing holes somewhere not far from the landfast ice, where he could scurry to safety if conditions changed. Old men knew there was no point in taking chances. "The ice is like a mean dog," they warned. "He waits for you to stop watching, and then he tries to get you."

Sakiak climbed to the top of a nearby ridge and scanned the pack with his binoculars. Jagged lines of hummocks pierced sharply into the brightening sky. The day was now full and blue, brilliant refracted twilight glowing high above the seaward horizon. He smiled as he squinted into the brightness. Indeed, it was *Siqinyasaq tatqiq,* "moon of the returning sun." But the cold needling his cheekbones reminded him that it was still midwinter, and that he must work fast to hunt before darkness closed over the sky again.

He saw no hint of life on the pack, but the configurations of ice told him where best to look for it. Just beyond a low ridge several hundred yards away there was a long plain of flat ice, its color and lack of snow cover indicating that it was not more than three feet thick. This would be an ideal place to search for the breathing holes of seals, because they were easy to see on such ice. The sled trail had ended at the edge of landfast ice, so he picked out an easy route before heading toward the flat. Younger hunters often failed to reconnoiter in this way, considering it a waste of time. But instead of moving faster they were forced to clamber laboriously over the rough ice, and they often came home bruised and exhausted.

It was not long before Sakiak stood at the edge of the big flat. Its surface was completely free of snow but was covered everywhere with large, fluffy crystals of frost, some so thin and feathery that they shivered in the breeze. They were made flexible by salty moisture from the ice, which prevented them from freezing hard, and when Sakiak walked on the frost his tracks were slushy despite the intense cold. This was why ice hunters wore boots soled with waterproof seal hide, which kept their feet dry on the moist surface.

He moved quickly along one side of the flat, searching for the telltale signs of a breathing hole. Presently he stopped, looking at the ice nearby. He saw a little group of thin ice chunks frozen into the surface, scattered in a circle about a handbreadth in diameter. When this ice was newly formed, a seal had broken up through it to breathe, leaving a small opening with bits of ice around it. The hole was never used again, but this frozen scar remained.

If the seal had continued to use such a hole as the ice thickened, it would have looked quite different. Each time the animal returned, water would slosh out over the ice and freeze, eventually building up a small, irregularly shaped dome with a little hole in its top. By scratching and gnawing, the seal kept this dome hollow inside, like a miniature igloo. Beneath this structure the hole widened into a tunnel through the ice, large enough to accommodate the seal's body when it came up to breathe. The Eskimos called such breathing holes *allus.*

Sakiak walked to the far end of the flat without seeing an *allu* or even another scar. So he turned back, following a low ridge that flanked the opposite side. He had not gone far when he spotted an *allu* just a few yards from the base of the ridge. It was very large and nearly cone-shaped, so he knew at a glance that it had been made by the huge *uguruk,* or bearded seal. He bent low, stiff-legged, moving his trunk from side to side and peering into its opening. The interior was very dim, but he could make out its round entryway, covered by a layer of dark gray ice. This was a disappointing find. The ice was almost a day old, indicating that the seal was not using this *allu* often.

If the days were longer he might wait there, for a bearded seal was a fine catch indeed. But with few hours of daylight he needed a hole that was visited more frequently. He would remember this *allu,* and if the ice did not move he might check it again to see if the seal returned. Sakiak memorized the shape of the ridge nearby so he could easily guide himself to this spot another day.

Breathing holes were often somewhat clustered, so he looked carefully around the area. Seeing none, he climbed the ridge to inspect a small flat on its opposite side. He was surprised to find that the flat was cut by a broad crack, perhaps ten yards across, covered with newly frozen ice. The crack, which must have opened during the past week's storm, made a jagged swath across the flat and sliced cleanly through a ridge on its far side. Sakiak marveled at the power of moving ice, which could split a heavy ridge into two sections as a man would cut through blubber with his knife. The crack probably ran for miles, and there would almost certainly be a few breathing holes in its covering of young ice. It also offered Sakiak an easy trail through the hummocky areas.

Sakiak made his way down the ridge and onto the frozen crack. He followed it across the flat, through the chasm of the split ridge, and onto another flat. There he saw what he was looking for. Almost in the middle of the crack was a nearly perfect little dome, the *allu* of a ringed seal, or *natchiq*. He peered closely into its opening and saw deep black inside. "It's good," he murmured softly to himself. The blackness was a circle of open water with a transparent skin of new ice forming at its edges, just a few inches below the quarter-sized opening of the *allu*. Not an hour before, while Sakiak walked out across the landfast ice, a seal had risen here to breathe.

There was no time to waste. For all he knew, the animal might be heading for this hole now, and he was not ready for it. He slipped off his hunting bag and rifle, laying them on the ice together with his *unaaq*. Then he went quickly to the nearest hummock and kicked free two blocks of ice for a stool and footrest. After carrying them back, he again inspected the interior of the *allu*. Its opening was slightly off center, and the tunnel appeared to angle somewhat away from the vertical. From this Sakiak knew which direction the seal would face when it came to breathe, and he would angle his rifle slightly for the deadliest possible shot.

Now he placed the two ice blocks about a foot from the hole, along its southeast side. He calculated automatically, almost without thought, the effects of wind and light. There was enough brightness to create a faint shadow, which must not fall across the hole. And he must not sit upwind lest the seal be frightened by his scent. He also preferred to face away from the biting chill of the breeze. He emptied his hunting bag onto the thick ice alongside the crack and pulled his rifle from its canvas sheath. The bag would insulate and cushion his stool while the sheath insulated the footrest. Eskimos always took pains to minimize loss of heat from their bodies in every way possible, and Sakiak knew the wait would be a cold one even in the best circumstances.

He placed his *unaaq* on the thick ice, where its shadow would not be visible from below, and he adjusted the ice blocks so they could not jiggle or squeak noisily. Then he sat down on one block and put his feet on the other, so that his legs were held straight out before him, Eskimo fashion. He could sit this way for many hours without tiring. When he was seated atop the ice blocks, his menacing presence could not be detected by a seal looking up through the glowing translucence of the gray ice.

The bolt of his rifle clicked loudly in the brittle cold as he thrust a shell into the chamber. Then he placed the weapon crosswise over the tops of his boots, where it was least likely to compress his clothing and cause chilling. Its muzzle faced the *allu* but did not hang over where the seal might see it. He had taken the precaution of standing a flat chip of ice alongside the little opening to screen his intrusive shape from the seal's eyes as it rose to breathe.

Now he would wait.

It was impossible to know when the seal would appear. In fifty winters of hunting at breathing holes, Sakiak had learned not to think too much of time. It might be fifteen minutes, perhaps an hour. Perhaps many hours. Sometimes the animal never returned.

Sakiak knew of old men who, in times of starvation, had waited beside an *allu* for twenty-four hours. Nowadays the young men refused to hunt at breathing holes, preferring to wait until a wide crack or lead formed so they could shoot seals in the open water. When Sakiak was a boy the men had relied upon harpoons, which could not be thrown far enough to strike a seal swimming freely out in a lead. But a harpoon was as good as a rifle for hunting at breathing holes, perhaps better. When a seal was harpooned, a line attached to the point ensured that the animal would not sink or be carried away by the current.

Young men said that breathing-hole hunting was too cold, that it involved too much waiting. The old men said only that people must eat. They had learned the art of enduring patience, as if they could merge their thoughts with the timeless physical world that surrounded them. Life, after all, was a game of waiting. One could not expect that the weather, ice, and animals would do a man's bidding. If a man would live, he must persist, wait, endure.

Sakiak was enveloped in still silence, interrupted only by the occasional buffeting of wind against his parka hood. His breath condensed on the ruff around his face and on his scraggly moustache, coating each hair with thick white frost. He could feel the immensity of the pack surrounding him, its quiet, latent power.

Radiant amber flowed up the wall of the sky before him, hinting of warmth in some distant world, while the pervasive cold drew closer around his body. Time faded away to a dim consciousness at the core of the hunter's mind.

Twilight grew and spread slowly southward, then edged toward the west. The fullest light of midday came, then imperceptibly began to fade. Sakiak drew his arms from the sleeves of his parka and held them against his body for warmth. He was shivering. Frost had collected on his eyelashes and brows. Occasionally he poked a bare hand up through the neck of his parka and held it against his cheek to warm the stiff, numb flesh. His toes felt large and icy cold. Perhaps the temperature was falling, he thought. Indeed, it was now minus forty, but the wind was fading as it grew colder.

Sakiak wished he had brought the boy along. His grandson Patik was old enough to hunt and could make the seal come to the *allu* where he waited. If he walked in a broad circle around Sakiak, he would frighten the seal away from its other holes and force it toward the hunter's station. Had the ice been perfectly smooth, Sakiak could have accomplished this alone by finding every breathing hole in the area and urinating on it. The powerful scent would frighten the seal away, leaving it only the hunted *allu* to use. It was funny to think how a seal must plunge away in frightened surprise when it smelled urine in its *allu*. But in rough ice many breathing holes were concealed in open spaces beneath hummocks and snowdrifts, where a man could never find them.

Almost two hours had passed. A growing ache spread up Sakiak's legs and back, but he dared not move to relieve the discomfort. The seal might be near enough to hear any noise transmitted through the ice to the water below. So he moved only his head and arms, even then very carefully.

It was also important to watch the surrounding ice in case a polar bear happened to approach him. Bears would occasionally stalk a man, if they were so thin and hungry that starvation drove fear out of them. But today it seemed there was no life anywhere, except for the silent lives beneath the pack. Sakiak wondered how deep the water under him might be. And he thought the current could soon shift and flow from the east, as it always did when intensely cold air moved in off the great expanse of land that stretched eastward away from the coast.

He was now shivering hard, and he wondered if his shaking might jiggle the ice stool, making a noise that would scare away the seals. He smiled, thinking what a great joke that would be after such a long, cold wait!

But beneath him at that moment a seal torpedoed through the black-gray water, darting and arcing in pursuit of the fleeting silver of fishes. It dodged between the blue and emerald-green walls of ice protruding downward beneath the hummocks. Huge inverted ice mountains blocked its path, but it sensed them and turned away before striking invisible barriers deep in the blackness.

In the freedom of its dense medium, the seal could ignore the encumbrances of gravity. It swam on its side, then upside down, then coasted to a stop in midwater. There it hung quietly in the dark silence, drifting slowly with the current, like a footloose star in the vastness of space. But this space was far from an empty void. Nervous shoals of fish left glowing trails as they spun and needled through luminescent plankton. Tiny jellyfish pulsed and parachuted, trailing delicate streamers beneath them. And, far below, crabs littered the bottom, waiting for those above to die and become their food.

For more than a minute the seal remained motionless, ignoring the fish that swam too near. It was in need of air and was listening. Then it suddenly whirled and shot upward toward a circle of white that glimmered faintly in the high distance.

When it reached the underside of the ice, the seal turned slowly beneath the circle. It hesitated a moment, then swam slowly upward into the narrow passage. Reaching the surface, it poked its nose out for an instant, sampling the air, then dropped again. The air was fresh and stinging of cold. It rose again, emerging into the bright igloo of ice, globed eyes wide and black, nostrils flaring and closing.

In the silence of the pack, after a long wait, the seal's approach was startling and exciting. Sakiak first heard, almost sensed without hearing, a pulsation of the water inside the *allu.* Then he saw water flow through the opening and over the ice outside, where it instantly froze to a fresh glare. This water was forced up ahead of the seal as it rose from below.

Sakiak heard scratching as the seal cleared away newly formed ice at the tunnel's upper opening. He quickly slipped his arms into the sleeves of his parka, then remained perfectly still. The cold had vanished. Shivering ceased as warmth spread from mind to muscle.

He fixed his eyes on the *allu,* consumed with intense concentration. His lips moved slightly, almost imperceptibly. "Come seal," he whispered, asking the animal to give itself to him. "Come. . . ." It was only a thought this time.

In a moment the seal obeyed Sakiak's will. It took a first short, hissing breath, smelling the air for signs of danger. He did not move. He expected the brief silence that followed, knowing the next breath would be a deep one.

Whoosh!

It was a long, drawn-out hiss that sent a misty spray from the opening. This noise was loud enough to drown out the sound of Sakiak's movement as he reached down and picked up his rifle from his legs. He was careful to spread his arms so his clothing would not scrape noisily, and he was still before the deep breath was finished.

Whoosh!

Again the animal breathed. Sakiak lifted his rifle, and held it vertical, with the thumb of his upper hand against the trigger. Again he waited, as the second breath stopped.

Whoosh!

On the third breath he moved his rifle straight above the *allu,* its muzzle inches from the opening. His face was expressionless. His resolve was complete. Without a second's hesitation, he deliberately squeezed the trigger.

For the seal, breath cut short. A sudden *crack!* only half heard before the world was shot out in closing clouds of black.

For the hunter, a sudden deafening explosion. The *allu* split and shattered. Fragments of ice dyed crimson. The seal bobbing on the pulse of water, grotesque and broken, instantly detached from the reality of life.

Sakiak ran to fetch his *unaaq*. Using its sharp point, he chipped the rest of the *allu* away, then snagged the animal with the metal hook on its other end. The seal was still quivering, so he held it until movement stopped. With the knife he carried on his belt he slit the skin of its upper lip, then he pushed the loop end of his seal-pulling harness through this cut and fastened it around the animal's nose.

This done, Sakiak held the line under one foot while he chiseled the hole until it was large enough so he could pull out the seal. If he had not secured the seal quickly with a line, it might have been carried off by the current. In thicker ice, where the seal would enter through a long, cigar-shaped tunnel, this would be unnecessary; winter-killed seals were buoyant from their thick layer of blubber, so they would float well up into the tunnel where the current could not take them away.

Finally, Sakiak pulled the seal out onto the ice. It was completely limp and flexible, like a sack full of liquid. Blood flowed and coagulated on its skin, freezing in thick layers around the wound. It was large for a ringed seal, about four feet long and weighing perhaps a hundred pounds. And its hide was deep black, patterned with small whitish circlets. The *Inupiat* called a dark seal like this *magamnasik*.

The warmth of excitement that had flared inside Sakiak died quickly, and he found himself shivering again. Before starting back he should eat something and drink the hot tea in his thermos. Eskimos knew that food kindled heat inside a man's body, so it was important to eat well and often during the cold hunts. Heavy steam billowed from the thermos when he opened it. He drank quickly, feeling the hot liquid flow down his throat to the cold pit of his stomach. Refreshed, he took the hard-frozen fish he had brought along and peeled off its skin. Then he cut into small sections and hungrily ate the raw chunks. Its oil fat would bring him quick warmth and energy.

More hot tea and a couple of frozen biscuits finished his meal. When he had drunk his fill of tea he spilled the remainder out onto the snow, staining its white surface yellow brown. It made sharp, crackling noises as it immediately frozen to a brittle crust. He felt deep appreciation for the food and for the seal he had killed. He could remember his grandfather chanting thanks to an abiding spirit that helped him, but Sakiak thanked the Christian God with a short prayer in Eskimo.

He rested for a few minutes, looking at the distant sky. The light was fading, and he had a long walk before him. Perhaps in a few days he would return to this *allu*. Often several animals used one hole, and they might eventually come back in spite of the damage done to it. But now there was little time to waste. Sakiak lighted a cigarette and put his equipment back into the hunting bag. When this was finished he took his knife and made a long slit down the seal's belly. Then he cut a wide slab of blubber from the abdomen and both flanks, laying it aside on the ice. Along each side of the slit he made a series of holes in the hide, and through these he laced a piece of heavy cord, sewing the animal back together. Removing the blubber made it almost ten pounds lighter, and ten pounds would make a noticeable difference to an old man pulling a large seal home over the ice.

I Will Walk with Leg Muscles

I will walk with leg muscles
which are strong
as the sinews of the shins of the little caribou calf.

I will walk with leg muscles
which are strong
as the sinews of the shins of the little hare.

I will take care not to go towards the dark.
I will go towards the day.

—Author unknown

———◆•••◆———

Girl of Stone

A GIRL NAMED Kala stood on a lonely headland and she saw two men in a kayak paddling toward her. One of the men shouted that he had no wife. Would she like to lie with him? But she had no interest in him, or the other one, so she told them to paddle on their way or they would taste her spear-point. And as she turned her back to them, she felt her hands and legs become stone. She called out:

"Kayak men, come back. You may take me to wife if you wish."

The kayak men paddled on. Now Kala felt her shoulders and head grow stiff. She called out again:

"Kayak men, dear kayak men. Please take me to wife."

Again they ignored her. Now all but her navel had turned to stone.

"Dear kayak men, you may *both* take me . . ."

Too late! She was now a pillar of stone. For the Stone Spirit had married her as it marries anyone who turns his back on his fellow human beings.

Forever more Kala remained on that headland. She did not have offspring. Sea-birds came and shat upon her.

—told by Nattiq (Canadian Eskimo)

BOOK IV

THE NEW EXPLORERS

The business of "exploration," in the classic sense of the term, has been made obsolete by satellites whose electronic eyes can map a stretch of unknown Arctic coastline in an instant, whereas it would have taken a party of explorers months to sketch traveling by sledge, boat, or slogging along on foot. Though the Arctic lands and seas are "known" in the old geographical usage, there still remains so very much to learn about the regions. What we learn inevitably reflects back on ourselves and our own place here on this earth.

The excerpts in this final section represent a breed of "new explorers" who bring new approaches and perspectives to the Arctic. Thus Barry Lopez explores the interconnectedness between Arctic wildlife and the rest of the planet, and employs wonderful imagery in doing so. He describes, for example, the annual caribou migration as the Arctic's equivalent of a great intake and then exhalation of breath.

Today's native writers from the Arctic likewise bring new perspectives in their ability to "see" their land from both a European and Inuit point of view. For instance, Finn Lynge, a Greenlander, in a fascinating short essay, looks at a porpoise fetus encountered in a market in Nuuk from the perspective of both a horrified group of Europeans and an admiring Inuit.

It is also a sign of the change that has come to the Arctic that Lynge's work, as well as that of Rachel A. Qitsualik, are found on the Internet. The Arctic is now bound intimately to the rest of the world through the vast, glowing network of cyberspace. For the first time, a resident of Barrow or Iqaluit is, in theory at least, no more isolated than a resident of Los Angeles. In terms of communications, the native peoples of the Arctic are on an equal footing with the rest of the world.

While some of the following pieces point toward the future, in the excerpts from Steger and Schurke and Turk we arrive at a kind of fin de siecle of Arctic exploration and circle back to an earlier era. These writers realize that the old style of exploration is obsolete, yet something draws these new explorers powerfully toward the old methods, and so they set out to recreate by dogsled and sea kayak earlier feats of Arctic exploration. Their journeys finally become less about geographic discovery than discovery of the self.

Still, the question lingers—the one that haunts the accounts of all Arctic explorers. It is the question raised, but never answered, by Frederick Cook upon his realizing the ultimate futility of the quest for the Pole, "Why do they do it?"

Prayer for Strength

I am a man.
A bracelet, strong
as the word Yes,
clasps me.
The Yes-word's bracelet
brings me strength.
Aija-ija!

Little gull, high in the air,
fly down to me,
settle on my shoulder,
rest in the hollow of my palm!

Little gull, high in the air,
splitting the wind,
fly down to me,
fly down to me!

Your wings glow
up there in the red cold!
Give me strength!

—Nakasuk (Netsilik Eskimo man)

Some Primitive People's Reflections . . .

BY FINN LYNGE (GREENLANDIC, 1983)

The debate over native hunting rights versus animal rights is one of the most highly charged issues in the Arctic today. Various animal-rights and conservation groups have sought to limit or ban outright the hunting of the marine mammals—such as whales and seals—on which the Inuit have traditionally depended for food and clothing, and which serves as a central activity of their cultural and spiritual life. While these bans are usually aimed at commercial hunting of these animals and make exceptions for subsistence hunting, they can have unintended consequences for the Inuit. For example, the campaign during the 1980s by Greenpeace and other groups against the commercial hunting by whites of baby harp seals off Newfoundland generally destroyed the market for sealskins. The Polar Inuit who relied on the sale of sealskins to buy supplies with which to hunt, to feed their families and dog teams, suddenly found their way of life threatened.

This short essay by Finn Lynge offers a vivid vignette of two cultures—the European farming tradition and the Inuit hunting tradition—colliding head-on over a porpoise fetus in a fish market in Nuuk, Greenland. The "MEPs" Lynge refers to are members of the European Parliament. Lynge, formerly a Catholic priest as well as having served for five years as Greenland's representative to the European Parliament, was born of a Greenlandic father and Danish mother and has been a vocal advocate for the rights of native peoples. Originally appearing in *11 Essays on Whales and Man* with the title "Some Primitive People's Reflections on People's Attitudes to People's Attitudes", this piece can be found on High North Alliance Web site (www.highnorth.no/so-pr-re.htm). The site also offers recipes such as "Whale Steak with Green Peas."

The scene is Nuuk, Greenland, in the spring of 1983, at the open-air market near the old harbour where the hunters deliver their daily catch of birds and seals, fish and whale meat. A group of MEPs are being shown round. An old hunter calls to me, "Come here, Finn. There's something I want to show your friends!" We gather round his end of the stall, there is a carved up porpoise on it. The ladies discretely hold their noses. The old man holds out his cupped hand to us, his weather-beaten face bright and smiling, his eyes running in the heavy frost. He shows us the tiny, pink fetus of a porpoise, 10 cm long. "Isn't it lovely?" he says. The MEPs stand there, trying to find suitable facial expressions. They are polite people. I nod and smile at him. It is lovely, that little fetus.

Looking back, I know why I have never been able to forget that incident. It was two worlds in a nutshell. A meeting of two cultures. The hunter who has spent all his life out there at sea in all kinds of weather, making his livelihood by seeking out and killing wild animals, seals and whales, he never gets tired of it. The fjords are beautiful with mountains and glaciers. The animals out there are good, they give us life. He encounters life and death every day, the animals' lives and the animals' deaths and sometimes even those of his comrades. He knows death, he has blood on his hands every day. It does not occur to him that there might be anything repulsive about it. He also sees how foxes take fledglings, how seals hunt fish and how killer whales hunt the seals. That is how the Almighty arranged it all, and it does not occur to him that someone might want things done differently. He is himself at the top of the food chain, he puts his teeth into it all, and enjoys it. The fact that something can be both beautiful to look at and good to taste is merely part of the excellent order of things. And young animals are among the most beautiful creatures to be found, even more so in a way, when still inside their mothers.

What went on in the heads of the MEPs when they were presented with that tiny small-type whale fetus? It was such a repulsive affair that they lacked words. And indeed, nothing was said. What words went through their heads? *Abortus provocatus,* the most painful and most taboo of all the life-and-death experiences of city dwellers? I should imagine so. Under the best of circumstances, it was hardly something they would wish to remember as a thing of beauty, that's for sure. There was a wall between the old man and the stylish politicians from Central Europe. Two worlds that could only meet at a fleeting glance.

The distance between these two worlds is now on the verge of conflict, a sad and unnecessary conflict. In our part of the world, the hunter has always led his life in his own parts, and the farmer and the city dweller in theirs. Everyone knew that conditions varied from one place to another, as was the case with lifestyles and the varying interests in natural resources, too. There was room enough for us all. Perhaps that is what is lacking: room for us all. Perhaps the world is becoming too small, even in the Far North with its Atlantic distances. Because we now have so many mutual tangent surfaces that we can no longer turn our eyes away and pretend that we don't notice just how different our neighbours are. We must make up our minds as to whether or not we can stand the thought of our neighbour having different views on the killing of animals than we ourselves have. Perhaps it's true that he can both hunt and respect an animal at the same time? Perhaps the whaling, sealing and hunting peoples are not interested in canvassing for their own attitudes in their neighbouring communities, where the distance from Nature and animal life is greater. Perhaps they are less presumptuous than those industrial people who obviously simply will not accept that there are quite legitimately other people who do not share their ideas, religion, political systems and now, believe it or not, their attitudes to animals!

If we are to have a reasonable future on this earth, we must learn to live together with other peoples without devouring their cultures. We all have the right to live here, in mutual respect.

Hymn to the Spirit of the Air

A religious song to be performed wearing a head-decoration
made from the skin of the sacred Great Northern Diver.

I stand here humbly
with extended arms,
for the spirit of the air
has brought dsown game for me!

I stand here
surrounded by great joy,
for a reindeer with tall antlers
carelessly exposed his flanks to me!

Ah, how I crouched
in my hunter's hide!
But scarcely had I
glimpsed his flanks,
than my arrow pierced them.
haunch to haunch.

And then, beloved reindeer,
as you pissed there,
as you fell,
I was surrounded by great joy!

I stand here humbly
with extended arms,
for the spirit of the air
has brought down game for me!

I stand here humbly
with extended arms,
surrounded by great joy:
an old seal-bull
was blowing through his breath-
    ing-hole,
and I, a little man,
stood upright over him.
The tension
made my body longer,
till I drove my harpoon down,
and tied him
to the harpoon-rope.

—Tpakuhak (Copper Eskimo man)

Arctic Dreams

BY BARRY LOPEZ (AMERICAN, 1986)

Barry Lopez's *Arctic Dreams* has probably done more to shape the perception of the Arctic, at least among a U.S. readership, than any other book of recent decades. He blends scientific research, personal experience, and history, along with insight and lyricism to conjure a vision of the complexity and interrelatedness of the Arctic's life and landscapes. Out of many wonderful passages, two are included below. The first, from the chapter titled "Migration," describes the movement of hundreds of thousands of caribou northward in the summer to the calving grounds and the stillness they leave behind when they retreat south again. "Watching the animals come and go," Lopez writes earlier in the chapter, "and feeling the land swell up to meet them and then feeling it grow still at their departure, I came to think of the migrations as breath, as the land breathing. In the spring a great inhalation of light and animals. The long-bated breath of summer. And an exhalation that propelled them all south in the fall."

The final passage is from the book's epilogue, when, after a blood-soaked walrus hunt with the Yup'ik people of St. Lawrence Island, Alaska, Lopez reflects on the Arctic and humans' relation to it, to the earth as a whole. "The great task of life for the traditional

377

Eskimo is still to achieve congruence with a reality that is already given," Lopez writes. He then goes on to quote Albert Schweitzer: "The given reality, the real landscape, is 'horror within magnificence, absurdity within intelligibility, suffering within joy.'"

AFTER the passage of fish and marine mammals through the Bering Sea region, and the arrival of birds at their accustomed deltas and sea rookeries, there is a third great migratory spectacle to behold in the Arctic: the movement of caribou.

North American caribou are divided into three groups. The woodland caribou, the largest of the three, lives in the taiga forests of the subarctic and migrates over only relatively short distances. Peary caribou, the smallest of the three, occupy parts of the Greenland coast and northern islands in the Canadian Archipelago and also move over relatively short distances each year. Barren-ground caribou are the distant travelers. As many as 2 million of them trek hundreds of miles each year between their winter range near the tree line and well-defined calving grounds on the tundra.*

Caribou biologists recognize more than thirty different arctic herds, each occupying a different region. The ones that migrate the farthest each year are the Western and Central Arctic herds in northern Alaska; the Porcupine herd, which straddles the U.S.-Canada border; and, from west to east in Canada, the Bluenose, Bathurst, Beverly, and Kaminuriak herds.

Scientists are uncertain what starts caribou on their northward journey—knowledge that they have stored enough fat to carry them through, perhaps. They endure spring blizzards on their journeys and cross ice-choked rivers with great determination and a sure sense of bearing, but they also choose paths of least resistance over the land, often following in each other's tracks through deep snow. Pregnant cows are normally in the

---

*None of the three caribou is a reindeer. Reindeer, a separate sub-species of *Rangifer tarandus,* are the deer native to northern Europe and Asia. Of the many that have been brought to Alaska as domestic stock, a significant number have joined herds of caribou.

lead; mature bulls may be as much as a month behind the cows, or never arrive at the calving grounds at all. By the end of their arduous journey the females are thin and tattered-looking. Behind them, in places where they have had to cross rivers in a stage of breakup, there may be the carcasses of hundreds of drowned and fatally injured animals. Their calving grounds, writes biologist George Calef, appear "bleak and inhospitable. Meltwater lies in pools on the frozen ground, the land is often shrouded in fog, and the wind whistles unceasingly among the stunted plants and bare rocks." The advantages of these dismal regions, however, are several. The number of predators is low, wolves having dropped away from the herds at more suitable locations for denning to the south. Food plants are plentiful. And these grounds either offer better protection from spring snowstorms or experience fewer storms overall than adjacent regions.

Most calves are born within a few days of each other, and calving occurs at least a month before swarms of emergent mosquitoes, blackflies, warble flies, and botflies embark on a harassment of the caribou that seems merciless to a human observer. If one were to think of events that typify arctic life—the surge of energy one feels with daily gains of ten or fifteen minutes of sunlight in the spring, or waking up one morning to find the ocean frozen—one would also include that feeling of relief that descends over a caribou herd when a wind comes up and puts hordes of weak-flying mosquitoes to the ground.

After calving, cows and their offspring join immature animals, barren cows, and the bulls in "postcalving" aggregations of 75,000 or more animals, their numbers stretching from horizon to horizon. They trek slowly south, breaking up into smaller herds. The first fall storms catch them in open country, and in the cold, snowy air these "gray shepherds of the tundra," as the Alaskan poet John Haines calls them, "pass like islands of smoke." They take shelter in the short timber of the taiga for the winter.

After the herds have gone, the calving grounds can seem like the most deserted places on earth, even if you can sense strongly that the caribou will be back next year. When they do return, hardly anything will have changed. A pile of caribou droppings may take thirty years to remineralize on the calving grounds. The carcass of a wolf-killed cari-

bou may lie undisturbed for three or four years. Time pools in the stillness here and then dissipates. The country is emptied of movement.

The coming and going of the animals during the short summer gives
the Arctic a unique rhythmic shape, but it is to be felt only in certain
places. Mostly, summer and winter, the whole land is still. The arctic explorer George De Long called it "a glorious country to learn patience in."
Time here, like light, is a passing animal. Time hovers above the tundra
like the rough-legged hawk, or collapses altogether like a bird keeled over
with a heart attack, leaving the stillness we call death. In the thin film of
moisture that coats a bit of moss on a tundra stone, you can find, with a
strong magnifying glass, a world of movement buried within the
larger suspended world: ageless pinpoints of life called water bears migrate over the wet plains and canyons of jade-green vegetation. But even
here time is on the verge of collapse. The moisture freezes in winter. Or a
summer wind may carry the water bear off and drop it among bare stones.
Deprived of moisture, it shrivels slowly into a desiccated granule. It can
endure like this for thirty or forty years. It waits for its time to come again.

Long, unpunctuated hours pass for all creatures in the Arctic. No
wild frenzy of feeding distinguishes the short summer. But for the sudden movement of charging wolves and bolting caribou, the gambols of
muskox calves, the scamper of an arctic fox, the swoop of a jaeger, the
Arctic is a long, unbroken bow of time. Twilight lingers. There are no
summer thunderstorms with bolts of lightning. The ice floes, the caribou, the muskoxen, all drift. To lie on your back somewhere on the
light-drowned tundra of an Ellesmere Island valley is to feel that the ice
ages might have ended but a few days ago. Without the holler of con-
temporary life, that constant disturbance, it is possible to feel the slope
of time, how very far from Mesopotamia we have come. We move at
such a fast clip now. We draw up geological charts at a snap, showing
the possibilities for oil in Tertiary rocks in the Sverdrup Basin beneath
Ellesmere's tundra. We delineate the life history of the ground squirrel.
We list the butterflies: the sulphurs, the arctics, a copper, a blue, the
lesser fritillaries. At a snap. We enumerate the plants. We name everything. Then we fold the charts and the catalogs, as if, except for a stray
fact or two, we were done with a competent description. But the land is
not a painting; the image cannot be completed this way.

Lying flat on your back on Ellesmere Island on rolling tundra without animals, without human trace, you can feel the silence stretching all the way to Asia. The winter face of a muskox, its unperturbed eye glistening in a halo of snow-crusted hair, looks at you over a cataract of time, an image that has endured through all the pulsations of ice.

You can sit for a long time with the history of man like a stone in your hand. The stillness, the pure light, encourage it.

THE MOUNTAIN in the distance is called Sevuokuk. It marks the northwest cape of Saint Lawrence Island in the Bering Sea. From where we are on the ice, this eminence defines the water and the sky to the east as far as we can look. Its western face, a steep wall of snow-streaked basalt, rises above a beach of dark cobbles, riven, ice-polished, ocean-rolled chips of Sevuokuk itself. The village of Gambell is there, the place I have come from with the Yup'ik men, to hunt walrus in the spring ice.

We are, I believe, in Russian waters; and also, by a definition to them even more arbitrary, in "tomorrow," on the other side of the international date line. Whatever political impropriety might be involved is of little importance to the Yup'ik, especially while they are hunting. From where blood soaks the snow, then, and piles of meat and slabs of fat and walrus skin are accumulating, from where ivory tusks have been collected together like exotic kindling, I stare toward the high Russian coast. The mental categories, specific desires, and understanding of history among the people living there are, I reflect, nearly as different from my own as mine are from my Yup'ik companions'.

I am not entirely comfortable on the sea ice butchering walrus like this. The harshness of the landscape, the vulnerability of the boat, and the great size and power of the hunted animal combine to increase my sense of danger. The killing jars me, in spite of my regard for the simple elements of human survival here.

We finish loading the boats. One of the crews has rescued two dogs that have either run off from one of the Russian villages or been abandoned out here on the ice. Several boats gather gunnel to gunnel to look over the dogs. They have surprisingly short hair and seem undersize to draw a sled, smaller than Siberian huskies. But the men assure me these are typical Russian sled dogs.

We take our bearing from the far prominence of Sevuokuk and turn home, laden with walrus meat, with walrus hides and a few seals, with crested auklets and thick-billed murres, with ivory and Russian dogs. When we reach shore, the four of us put our shoulders to the boat to bring it high up on the beach. A young man in the family I am staying with packs a sled with what we have brought back. He pulls it away across the snow behind his Honda three-wheeler, toward the house. Our meals. The guns and gear, the harpoons and floats and lines, the extra clothing and portable radios are all secured and taken away. I am one of the last to leave the beach, still turning over images of the hunt.

No matter what sophistication of mind you bring to such events, no matter what breadth of anthropological understanding, no matter your fondness for the food, your desire to participate, you have still seen an animal killed. You have met the intertwined issues—What is an animal? What is death?—in those large moments of blood, violent exhalation, and thrashing water, with the acrid odor of burned powder in the fetid corral smells of a walrus haul-out. The moments are astounding, cacophonous, also serene. The sight of men letting bits of meat slip away into the dark green water with mumbled benedictions is as stark in my memory as the suddenly widening eyes of the huge, startled animals.

I walk up over the crest of the beach and toward the village, following a set of sled tracks. There is a narrow trail of fresh blood in the snow between the runners. The trial runs out at a latticework of drying racks for meat and skins. The blood in the snow is a sign of life going on, of other life going on. Its presence is too often confused with cruelty.

I rest my gloved fingers on the driftwood meat rack. It is easy to develop an affection for the Yup'ik people, especially when you are invited to participate in events still defined largely by their own traditions. The entire event—leaving to hunt, hunting, coming home, the food shared in a family setting—creates a sense of well-being easy to share. Viewed in this way, the people seem fully capable beings, correct in what they do. When you travel with them, their voluminous and accurate knowledge, their spiritual and technical confidence, expose what is insipid and groundless in your own culture.

I brood often about hunting. It is the most spectacular and succinct expression of the Eskimo's relationship with the land, yet one of the most perplexing and disturbing for the outsider to consider. With the compelling pressures of a cash-based economy to contend with, and the ready availability of modern weapons, hunting practices have changed. Many families still take much of their food from the land, but they do it differently now. "Inauthentic" is the criticism most often made of their methods, as though years ago time had stopped for the Yup'ik.

But I worry over hunting for another reason—the endless reconciliation that must be made of Jacob with his brother Esau. The anguish of Gilgamesh at the death of his companion Enkidu. We do not know how exactly to bridge this gap between civilized man and the society of the hunter. The Afrikaner writer Laurens van der Post, long familiar with Kalahari hunting peoples as archetypal victims of our prejudice, calls the gap between us "an abyss of deceit and murder" we have created. The existence of such a society alarms us. In part this is a trouble we have with writing out our history. We adjust our histories in order to elevate ourselves in the creation that surrounds us; we cut ourselves off from our hunting ancestors, who make us uncomfortable. They seem too closely aligned with insolent, violent predatory animals. The hunting cultures are too barbaric for us. In condemning them, we see it as "inevitable" that their ways are being eclipsed. Yet, from the testimony of sensitive visitors among them, such as van der Post and others I have mentioned in the Arctic, we know that something of value resides with these people.

I think of the Eskimos compassionately as *hibakusha*—the Japanese word for "explosion-affected people," those who continue to suffer the effects of Hiroshima and Nagasaki. Eskimos are trapped in a long, slow detonation. What they know about a good way to live is disintegrating. The sophisticated, ironic voice of civilization insists that their insights are only trivial, but they are not.

I remember looking into a herd of walrus that day and thinking: do human beings make the walrus more human to make it comprehensible or to assuage loneliness? What is it to be estranged in this land?

It is in the land, I once thought, that one searches out and eventually finds what is beautiful. And an edge of this deep and rarefied beauty is the acceptance of complex paradox and the forgiveness of others. It means you will not die alone.

Song to the Sea

All winter, the sea on the East coast of Greenland lies frozen and
inaccessible to sledge-riders. But when spring approaches, and the
ice starts loosening, good days for daring hunters have arrived.

I'm not an empty, stubborn man,
bored and taciturn,
Ava-ajaja, ajaja-aja.
I climbed the hills of Sermilik,
and gazed out at the sea,
the great sea,
ava-ajaja, ajaja-aja.

Vast ice-floes
lay scattered along the coast;
a glacier carved its way
into the deep,
and the Uigordlit rocks
stood like pillars
above the waters,
ava-ajaja-aja.

I grew dizzy,
my breath laboured,
and it seemed to me
my life was destined to be short,
too short,
ava-ajaja, ajaja-aja.

—East Greenland Eskimos

$\mathcal{A}$ $\mathcal{M}$odern-$\mathcal{D}$ay $\mathcal{M}$ush to the $\mathcal{P}$ole

BY WILL STEGER WITH PAUL SCHURKE (AMERICAN, 1987)

I n 1986 Will Steger and Paul Schurke, two Minnesotans with a lifelong love of the outdoors, embarked to recreate the dogsled trips to the Pole attempted by explorers like Peary and Cook. Their ambition was to achieve—in their words—the "first confirmed 'unsupported' or 'unsupplied' trek to the North Pole." One must note carefully the qualifying language. Theirs would be a "first" because Peary and Cook's claims on the Pole were never "confirmed" and, in fact, heavily questioned, while other adventurers like Wally Herbert had traveled to the North Pole by dogsled in the years since Peary and Cook but had been resupplied with food by regular airdrops.

One of the fascinating aspects of Steger and Schurke's journey was their team's difficulty in defining what they meant by "unsupported" or "unsupplied." One common practice of the old explorers was to eat any superfluous dogs or feed them to the remaining dogs as the sled loads lightened. But the Steger-Schurke team was determined to treat their dogs well and bring them home alive and in good health. However, the team decided they'd allow airplanes to land on the ice during the course of their journey and fly out the dogs that weren't needed as the team consumed food and fuel and the sled loads lightened, as well as fly out any injured team member, or, in a last-ditch attempt to reach the Pole, fly out some of the team members in order to jettison some of the supplies and equipment the party carried, thus lightening the loads. But they would refuse to *accept* anything whatsoever—not a morsel of food—from the dog-evacuation flights. Some members argued that flying people out constituted a kind of "reverse resupply," because the expedition would no longer have to haul food for them. Also, would the expedition members permit themselves to receive information by radio, garnered from satellite photos, about the easiest passages across the ice? They decided not.

Of course, unlike Peary and Cook's alleged trips to the Pole, once they reached their goal the Steger and Schurke team would be airlifted back to civilization instead of stumbling south hundreds of miles across the fractured, drifting ice to the nearest coast. Despite the modern tents and sleeping bags, communications, airlifts, and the Visa card on which they piled their last-minute expenses, the team found plenty of adventure, as well as hardship almost more than they could bear: temperatures at their departure from the northern coast of Ellesmere Island registering minus 70°F, sled loads so heavy at the outset that they and the dogs, pushing in tandem, could barely budge them, and mile upon mile of pressure ridges to chop their way through.

The excerpt here from Steger and Schurke's *North to the Pole* begins with their encounter out in the middle of the Polar Sea with a French doctor who is *skiing* to the North Pole (as if it's getting crowded up there) and ends with the growing tension of whether they will make it to the Pole, and who may, or may not, be sent back.

Day 32
"SKI TRACKS!"

"It's a travel day, rise and shine!" Paul was shouting as he shook our tent the next morning. It was clear and breezy but bitterly cold, the usual conditions that follow an Arctic storm. We were soon digging out equipment that had been buried under mounds of snow. The cold invigorated us as it cut through clothing dampened by our long session in moist sleeping bags. Brent was painstakingly untangling his knotted traces. As the cold crept in while he unraveled each knot, his movements became steadily faster. Then he would suddenly drop the rope and bolt off at a sprint, running in wide circles and windmilling his arms. After a minute or two, he abruptly stopped and picked up where he had left off. His behavior was pure reflex, just part of our way of life on the polar sea.

During one of our sprints that morning, Richard and I ran a ways back up our trail, curious to see what the winds had done to the lead we had crossed. The gap was now several hundred yards wide. The huge ridge we had encountered just before crossing it was now just a barely discernible bump on the horizon. How terribly fragile this landscape is, I thought. "We're damn lucky we crossed that before the storm hit," Richard commented. I agreed, but I was glad to see that a two-inch skin of fresh ice pavement covered the gap. That meant that though the temperatures were moderating, the cold was still sufficient to repair the damage of these storms. Nonetheless, the rest of our journey would be a real gamble. We were in for some high adventure. After a month of misery and monotonous slogging, I was looking forward to it.

We traveled fast that morning on the freshly wind-packed surface. Richard was well ahead, scouting, when we suddenly saw him stop and get down on hands and knees. "Ski tracks!" he shouted as we approached. We were all stunned, but knew immediately whose they were: Jean-Louis Etienne, the French explorer Ann and McKerrow had met in Eureka. We knew he had departed Ward Hunt Island on his solo attempt to reach the Pole about the same time we left Drep Camp. It was a monumental undertaking, and most of us had guessed that he had given up by now. Though we were somewhat chagrined that he had overtaken us, we were amazed and impressed that he was still on the move. And more than anything, we were stunned at the bizarre coincidence of having encountered his trail amid the trackless expanse of the polar sea.

We wondered if we might run into him. Richard attempted to follow his route, but soon lost the tracks in snow drifts. Four hours later, plodding along with my team out front, I heard a noise in the ridges to my right. Suddenly my dogs lunged in that direction. Looking up, I gaped in amazement as I watched a man in a bright blue jacket step out from behind a pinnacle of ice. He welcomed us with outstretched arms. Here we were, the only two expeditions on the Arctic Ocean, and we happened to meet. Pondering the odds of that happening, I shook my head in disbelief. Ever since McKerrow and Ann had told me about Jean-Louis, I had looked forward to meeting him. But I had never imagined that we would meet under these circumstances. Surely, I thought, this proves that like energies attract. I felt as if I were greeting an old friend after a long separation. The other team members gathered around, each embracing Jean-Louis and glowing with amazement.

He led us back behind the ridge to a tidy little camp. His home was a tiny, one-person tunnel tent. Neatly organized inside were a sleeping bag, a Primus stove, a cookpot, and a plastic bag containing his evening rations. Trailing out the door was his antenna wire, stretched across the tops of wide, stubby mountaineering skis planted in the snow nearby. Then he showed us his small toboggan—a two-by-seven-foot Kevlar shell—that he towed with a waistband and two slender poles as he traveled along each day. As he pulled back its nylon covering, we saw inside seven color-coded plastic bags, each containing a day's rations. Stuffed along the front were seven bright red fuel bottles. We marveled at the beautiful simplicity of his travel system, compared with our complicated operation. Every other week he was resupplied by air. Thus, his sled never had more than about a hundred pounds in payload.

Jean-Louis was only lightly dressed—he'd been huddled in his bag when he heard the commotion from our teams—so we took a quick group photo and made plans to rendezvous along the trail the next day. We carried on a couple of miles before setting camp. Our spirits were soaring.

Day 33

"IT'S SO GOOD TO HAVE SOMETHING DIFFERENT TO EAT."

The next morning I awoke to the singsong sound of my name being repeated over and over. "Will, Will, Will, Will, where are you?" I realized it was Jean-Louis, milling about our campsite, trying to determine which tent I was in. "Good morning!" I shouted. "Please come in." We all sat up and hurriedly began assembling our stove. What a rare treat it was to have a visitor stop by for tea! In honor of our special guest, we allowed the stoves to burn extra long and warm the tent a bit as he came in. In answer to our queries, he told us he was a doctor from Paris who had given up his practice to become an adventurer. Though he had many mountaineering and backpacking expeditions to his credit, his goal was to be the first person to ski alone to the North Pole. An attempt he had made the year before was thwarted only twenty miles out by badly broken ice conditions. His daily rhythm was to travel seven hours, achieving about as many miles. He carried a small beacon from which a satellite tracked his coordinates. Through nightly radio contact with his base manager, Michel, in Resolute, he was kept abreast of his progress.

Later he paid a visit to the other tent, where Paul's crew asked him about his diet. Their mouths watered as he told them that his menu included freeze-dried entrees such as lobster, as well as fruits, nuts, and chocolate bars. The regular airlifts allowed him the luxury of foods that were not as concentrated in calories as ours. In my tent, minutes later, we heard a burst of laughter. "While Jean-Louis was telling us of his wondrous diet," Paul recorded later in his journal, "we were finishing up our umpteenth pot of saltless, sugarless oatmeal. I scraped the last bits of cold, pasty porridge from the bottom of the pot and was about to flip it out the door for the dogs. Jean-Louis grabbed my hand and said, 'Aren't you going to eat that?' I shook my head. He took the spoon, gulped down the porridge, then leaned back and said in his strong French accent, 'It's so good to have something different to eat.' So much for freeze-dried lobster, we thought."

Our jovial new friend went on his way as we loaded our sleds. We expected to overtake him later in the morning. He was looking forward to following our route so that he wouldn't have to break a trail. I watched him plod along over freshly jumbled ice just north of our campsite. His was a tedious job. Trudging at a snail's pace, wielding skis and poles and with a sled lurching along at his heels, he looked like a big blue insect.

Our route took us over young, windswept ice studded with table-sized blocks that protruded a few feet above the surface and looked like giant snowflakes. As we maneuvered our sleds through this obstacle course, we could on occasion see through the clear, thin surface ice to the black sea water below. This was very fragile country; a wind would quickly churn this into a maelstrom of ice and water. Miles ahead along the northern horizon, Paul and I noticed a dark smudge. We hoped our eyes were deceiving us, but as we traveled on, we knew we were looking at sea smoke—the telltale sign of a large system of open leads. This phenomenon results when moisture rises from cracks in the sea ice and condenses as a thick vapor. This lead system, we knew, was the result of the recent windstorm. The piper was being paid. We wondered if we were about to meet our match. Though we had learned to hack our way through pressure ridges of any size and slog our way through endless mounds of drifted snow, we simply couldn't walk on water.

We decided to veer toward the northeast, where the trail of sea smoke seemed to thin out a bit. Within a few miles we began crossing small cracks. As we pushed on, we entered a shatter zone where the cracks became larger and more frequent and crossed at all angles. We were able to thread a trail through this maze by going around the ends of the widest cracks. These maneuvers required deft coordination as a team; each of us ran back and forth among the sleds, jockeying them around fissures and coaxing timid dogs to leap the cracks. It felt great to be operating as the finely tuned machine that we had set out to be during training. The dogs rose to the challenge as well. Though they were initially frightened by the splintered ice, they seemed to catch on to the sport of weaving a way through it, and their noses keyed in on the new smell of open water.

The cracks grew wider and more numerous. When will this maze trap us? I wondered. At 4:00 P.M. we found ourselves on the brink of a thirty-foot-wide gap covered in wafer-thin ice. Brent and Richard scouted to the east and west and found that the lead stretched on for miles. The ice around us creaked and groaned like a haunted house as we considered our next move. We had only one option: we would have to wait and hope that the lead would refreeze or close. It was sufficiently cold—45 degrees—for the lead to firm up adequately within a day's time. And fortunately, with our second dog-pickup flight slated for the next day, we could make good use of this delay. However, a suspicious two-foot gap of open water in the middle of the partially refrozen lead suggested that it might be opening wider. If so, we could only hope that at some section of the jagged-edged lead, the ice might twist and crunch together, forming a bridge.

Paul's sextant shot placed us at 85°22', 310 miles from the North Pole and one degree of latitude north of our first pickup flight. The pan on which we were camped was far smoother than the bone-jarring mogul field we had offered Karl before. Though it was a bit short, we assumed it would serve as a tolerable airstrip. We set camp on a pan alongside the lead, joking about our beachfront view. Despite the delay, we were in good spirits, looking forward to enjoying the woodstoves and anxious to reorganize our teams and sleds for the next phase of the journey. We would be trimming back to just three sleds pulled by seven dogs each; of the other two, the *Indre* would serve as fuel for the layover day, and the *Gaile* would be sent out as a museum piece. Soon the air was filled with the sound of bow saws and axes as the *Indre* was transformed into piles of splintered wood. The name plate was saved; it would go out on the flight as a gift for our support staff member for whom the sled was named.

The news on the radio that evening was disheartening; a storm had closed the airport in Resolute. No flights tomorrow, Jim informed us but perhaps the next day. "Here we sit," I wrote, "another one of the countless moments of waiting on this trip. Our hourglass is now more than half-full." The rest would do us good, but we worried about the twenty-one dogs that were to be airlifted out. In keeping with our rationing schedule, they had not eaten in two days, and now the feast of meat scraps Jim had collected was to be denied them for yet another day. Most of the dogs going out were Geoff's. These Eskimo dogs are accustomed to a feast-and-famine cycle—life in the Arctic demands this—so we knew they would be fine. But their voracious appetites represented a threat. Waiting for a morsel of food, they eyed every move we made and lunged violently against their stakeout lines when we fed the other dogs. We would have to sleep lightly during this layover. If any of these dogs broke loose from their lines during the night, they would wreak havoc with our sled loads.

Jean-Louis joined us at our camp that evening, setting up his little blue tunnel tent a hundred yards away from us. He stopped by my tent for a cup of tea and another pleasant visit. I told him I wanted to cross Antarctica by dogsled. His eyes lit up. He had considered a similar expedition, but had no access to dogs. Well, we'd need a doctor on our team, I said. Perhaps we could work together. We brainstormed about plans, and I jotted down his phone number in Paris, saying I would call him that summer.

Day 35

"TELL THEM WE'RE EVEN MORE HELLBENT TO REACH THE POLE THAN WE WERE THE LAST TIME YOU SAW US."

The plane arrived at 11:00 A.M. sharp. Karl circled our camp twice and then off to the southeast. From his aerial perspective he spotted a better ice strip than we had, and landed a mile away, hidden from our view by pressure ridges. With several of the twenty-one outbound dogs harnessed to the *Gaile,* and the rest on short bits of discarded rope fashioned into leashes, we hurried toward the billowing cloud of snow that had been kicked up by his engines. Five people, including our base manager, Jim Gasperini, Karl and his copilot, and two media representatives, *National Geographic* photographer Jim Brandenburg and his colleague Lynn Peterson, greeted us with warm hugs. Gasperini pulled Paul and me aside and asked in a hushed tone, "Now tell me, how are you guys really doing?" His sympathetic look reflected the skepticism that was mounting back home.

"Tell them we're even more hellbent to reach the Pole than we were the last time you saw us," Paul responded with firm confidence.

"We're going to make it, Jim. Don't worry," I added.

He nodded, knowing that somehow he'd have to sell that sense of assurance to the media crew in Resolute. He went on to report a litany of business matters: more problems with various media contracts, conflicts over the cost-sharing plan for additional flights, and logistic difficulties in returning the outbound dogs to their homes. More headaches and more debts were what all this meant to Paul and me. We scrambled for a solution to each problem. The business side and the trail side of the expedition were two different worlds, and we had to think for both.

Meanwhile, Karl transferred fuel from two fifty-five-gallon drums into his plane's tanks while our teammates loaded the sled and tied dogs in place. Excited by the new smells, the famished dogs nipped at everything in sight, hoping to hit upon a morsel of food. One wolfed down a pair of mitts left lying in the snow, while another grabbed Lynn's tape recorder from under a seat on the plane. Tape was scattered across the plane floor like confetti by the time she got to it. After a flurry of photos and handshakes, the plane doors closed and in a flash they were gone.

We returned to camp, where Richard, who had been baby-sitting the other dogs, was waiting, and then held a quick huddle to organize our departure. "I have an idea," said Brent. He suggested we check the two drums Karl had left behind on the ice, to see if there was any fuel left in them.

"Wouldn't that be cheating?" Geoff asked.

"No one would ever know," Brent responded.

"And besides," Richard added, "it's not really a resupply, just something we found on the ice."

Paul glanced at me and asked, "What do you think?"

I was stunned. I knew our fuel shortage had remained a major concern among the team, but I wasn't aware that it had become so grave an issue that they would be willing to break our own rules over it. "Listen," I said, "the goals we set for ourselves are more important than the fuel in those tanks. And besides, I personally don't feel our fuel shortage has reached crisis proportions. As the weather warms, we'll be needing a lot less fuel than you think."

This episode, like the crisis of conscience we underwent following Ann and Mantell's retrieval of additional supplies from Drep Camp on Day 4, tested our commitment to a goal that was to make this North Pole journey unique from others since Peary's: we would rely solely on the supplies we brought with us. And since this rule was self-imposed, the integrity of the expedition had as much to do with how it hung on our consciences in years to come as with how the media portrayed it. If we bent the rules, we would only be defeating ourselves. Furthermore, if we accepted so much as a scrap of paper from outside, doubts might be raised among observers about our adherence to the plan.

The issue came up in subtle ways. For example, when we were having severe problems with a plug on our movie camera a few weeks before, a service technician suggested sending a replacement part out on the first dog-pickup flight. As important as that camera was to us, we declined the offer. We would find a way to fix it ourselves or go without. And during our visits with Jean-Louis, I insisted that we accept not even so much as a cup of coffee from his rations. Paul squeezed a bit of levity out of that edict by playing a practical joke on me. The night Jean-Louis camped with us, Paul's tent crew invited him in for popcorn. Geoff joined the gathering in Paul's tent as well. After Jean-Louis retired, Paul suggested to Geoff that he slip back to his tent and nonchalantly mention to me that the popcorn had been traded for some of Jean-Louis's freeze-dried lobster. Geoff followed through, and I bit. Upon hearing of the alleged swap, I exploded with rage and, pouring out obscenities, was headed toward the door when Geoff caught me and clued me in on the gag.

That day, April 11, was to herald a new phase of the expedition, one that's well-illustrated by the spaceflight analogy. Like a rocketship that has escaped earth's atmosphere, we had now surmounted the worst of the brutally cold weather and the pack ice. By sending out our twenty-one most exhausted dogs, we were, in essence, jettisoning spent booster rockets. Each of our three remaining sleds, the *Bria,* the *Crystal,* and the *O'Donnell,* was now twelve feet long, three-fourths of its original length. Dubbed the "zip ships," they each now carried 600 pounds in payload. Thus we now had a third of the weight and slightly less than half the number of "engines" we had on leaving Drep Camp. The spaceflight analogy ends there, because the remaining twenty-one dogs did not represent "fresh fuel." Though they had been kept on full rations and had just enjoyed a day's rest, their reserves were severely diminished.

Apprehensions mounted as we harnessed up our three seven-dog teams. Because the supplies carried by the *Indre* and the *Gaile* had been redistributed, the remaining sleds now carried 150 additional pounds and would be pulled by smaller teams. The one compensating factor was that two people could now be stationed full-time on each sled. We all hoped that Mantell would take advantage of the seventh slot and go easy on his injured heel.

The lead in front of our campsite now had a coating of fresh ice a few inches thick. Brent, our resident expert on young ice, tiptoed out on it, probing with a harpoon, and gave us the high sign to come forward. We levered the sleds forward and eased them down onto the forty-foot-wide highway. The dogs dug their claws into the velvety brine crust that carpeted the fresh sea ice, and, after we helped them build momentum, pulled the sleds along at a good clip. The lead veered north for a short way, so Brent led us along the edge to take advantage of the easy travel. Then, when it swung east, he searched for a safe spot to cross its weakened center portion. A seam generally forms down the center of refrozen leads, where the ice either overlaps or pulls apart a foot or more from residual motion that comes after the initial shifting that formed the lead subsides. He found a section with an overlap, and we lined up the sleds to shoot them across, one by one. The thin, pliable ice deflected a bit as each sled rumbled over the center. The drivers stepped lightly, distributing most of their weight on the sled, to avoid punching through the ice.

We continued northward on old pans interspersed with eroded ridges. The area was covered in a deep mantle of what we called "freeze-dried corn snow," in which the flakes have been consolidated by the Arctic's cold, dry winds into a latticework of ice crystals. It has the texture of very coarse sand, and is about as difficult as sand to push sleds through. The friction was tremendous. The dogs pulled mightily while we pushed like pistons against the upstanders. As each of the three dog teams started grinding to a halt and dropping to the rear, Paul and I frantically switched team members around, hoping to strike a better distribution of power. Ann, the smallest member of our crew, got bumped three times, replaced by someone who had more bulk to thrust against a stuck sled. Among the array of intense emotions we were all experiencing, she now added anger to her list. Much to her credit, she was determined to be considered an equal player in good times or bad.

We carried on for a few hours, moving only a few hundred yards. Suddenly the handwriting was on the wall: we would never reach the Pole. From the distraught looks on my teammates' faces, I knew they had come to the same horrifying conclusion. We were doomed. Paul and I, grunting along together behind the *Bria,* pondered our situation. We agreed without a doubt that this expedition's only chance for success now lay in trimming back to just a couple of people and our very best dogs, so that the remaining rations could be stretched well into May or possibly June. To us, it seemed the only chance. We had no other options. But how would we break the news to the others? And how would we make the awful decision as to who would go and who would stay? Paul and I assumed the team would find this proposal abhorrent, and we feared serious dissension would break out if we brought it up now. At team meetings in Ely and Frobisher, we had discussed this very scenario. Paul and I had made it clear then that if we hit dire straits, one or more members might be asked to go out. Furthermore, if it came down to choosing just two candidates, he and I reserved the right to fill those slots. They had all acknowledged this months before. But now that they had invested weeks of excruciating work and hardship on the trail, would they still agree to it? Would they let go of their dreams of standing at the Pole, of tasting the fruits of their labor? If the group split in factions over this scheme, the hostilities that would develop in our state of mental strain would doom us more surely than our heavy loads. What if it erupted in a mutiny? What a horrible scene that would be. To end this trip on a note of bitterness would be far worse than failing to reach the Pole.

"The only way they'll accept this proposal," I said to Paul, "is if they come to realize of their own accord that it's the only option."

Paul agreed. "We'd best just carry on for a few days till everyone is utterly fried, and then ask for suggestions," he said.

I looked back. Neither of the other sleds was moving. Geoff was trudging toward us, shrouded in thick frost that had condensed on his clothing from perspiration. "We'd like to have a meeting," he said, panting heavily. "We can't go on like this any longer."

Paul and I nodded. We levered the sleds to an open spot and set up the tents. Then, with long faces and heavy hearts, we all packed tightly into Paul's tent. It felt as though we were attending a wake. We knew that this "summit conference," as we called it, would be a pivotal event; we had both of our pocket tape recorders running.

"The reality hit hard today," Paul said as he opened the meeting. "It's apparent that more of this grind is not going to get us to the Pole. We need an immediate and a long-range plan that will assure that we reach the Pole without resupply."

To Paul's surprise and my own, Brent immediately forwarded the proposal that we had been contemplating. He suggested setting aside enough rations for three people and one dog team to make a final dash. "The way things are shaping up," he said, "we're going to get stuck doing that anyway. We might as well plan for it. Those going out can push themselves into the ground for the next few weeks, and then two or three people can go on with one tent, two sleeping bags, three gallons of gas, and a hundred pounds of pemmican—making a quick pace with ten dogs." Mantell and Geoff nodded in agreement. I glanced at Paul, realizing we had misjudged the team. They had come to the same conclusion we had.

"Let's make the rounds here," Paul said, asking each of us to state what we thought our best bet was for reaching the Pole.

Geoff went first. "Personally, I wouldn't mind getting a resupply if it meant that everyone could get to the Pole. But that's not the consensus of the group. Our best chance is to somehow trim more weight and travel as fast and far as we can. Then, if we start getting close and have only a few supplies left, we send just two people on. I'm willing to be one of the 'retro rockets.' "

"I guess I feel the same way," said Mantell. "Originally the 'unsupported' part was real important to me, because it is the biggest challenge. But when I dig down real deep inside and ask myself whether I would want to get there unsupported or not at all, it's real touchy. But I guess I could live with the fact that I may not get there personally."

Brent was next. "To me, the bottom line is that the expedition has to be successful. If I'm an instrument in making that happen—even if it's just Will crawling on his hands and knees to get there—then I'll be happy."

"What are your thoughts, Richard?" Paul asked.

"It would be pretty hard to go back. I'm here to go to the Pole," he said firmly.

Then it was Ann's turn."I don't know, really, how I feel. I've said from day one that if it meant getting people there, I'd be willing to go out. Each day, though, that gets a little harder to swallow. I feel almost as strongly as Richard does. But on the other hand I agree with Brent. It will do the expedition as a whole no good if someone doesn't make it. No one looks at second best."

"Can I say one more thing?" Richard added. "Deep down inside me, if we don't all get there, I'll feel this wasn't unsupported. To me, pulling people out is using air support backwards, sort of a 'reverse resupply.' Instead of that, let's take some gambles. Let's chuck all of our personal gear, except maybe an extra pair of socks, and drop a tent and get down to cooking on only one stove. We could also eat a lot less and stretch our food further."

The group looked toward me, knowing it was my turn to speak. "The reality of this expedition changed for me today," I said somberly. "I realized that it's impossible to accomplish what we set out to do. Unless we're lucky, we're simply not all going to make it, and that's very hard for me to accept. Though there's a chance we could carry on as planned, I feel that to be safe we have to plan for sending a few people and a certain number of dogs on at the end. We have to figure out the supplies needed for that, set them aside, and then work as a group with what's left." I pointed out that we also had a financial consideration. The only way we could afford an additional flight to send out more dogs and people was to share one of Jean-Louis's resupply charters. His next one was about two weeks away. Whatever plan we came up with would have to be targeted for that date, I said.

"Why don't we figure out what we'd need for this final assault team," said Brent, "and then figure out what we've got left in our sleds."

Ideas now started flying as we sought to forge a plan. Discussion about the makeup of the final assault team was tabled; it was simply too difficult an issue for us to reckon with in our exhausted state. Rather, we focused on more neutral issues—our dogs and sleds. We considered our diet; perhaps we could rely on cheese as our main protein and turn over our own pemmican rations to the dogs. We considered ways of shedding more weight. We felt that with close scrutiny we could find ways to trim weight from the sled loads. Jettisoning a tent and its equipment was one idea; that would save forty pounds. But it would place us at great risk if we encountered a severe blizzard, so we discarded that notion. Another idea concerned our sleeping bags. We all knew they were the silent killers. Some of them now contained more than fifty pounds of ice. We realized we could save a hundred or more pounds if we threw the heaviest ones out. By zipping the others together in pairs, we could sleep three people in two bags. It seemed like an acceptable notion, but we agreed that we would have to test that system for a night before discarding the bags, to see if we could tolerate such tight quarters.

We set a goal: each sled was to be 100 pounds lighter before leaving the campsite. We would give the dogs a day's rest and feed them well. In fact, we agreed to give each dog three pounds of pemmican for the next few nights. That move was a big gamble. It would cut heavily into our remaining supply, but we felt it was the only means of bringing the dogs back up to full steam. We would also shed more than 100 pounds of weight from the sleds. We agreed to do some soul-searching that night and make lists of every item we could possibly jettison. When we assembled again in the morning, we would compare our lists and get to work reorganizing our loads.

We adjourned the summit conference with a sense of relief. Despite the misgivings some team members harbored about the assault-team proposal, our spirits were boosted by this sharing of ideas and the sense that we were now taking firmer control over a desperate situation. The discussion left us with a glimmer of hope that with a bit of luck—a long, northbound frozen lead, perhaps—we could still get all seven people to the Pole. Fate would tell between now and Jean-Louis's next charter flight. In the meantime, it was imperative that we prepare to deploy a final assault team. As disagreeable as that option was, we firmly felt that it still represented our only clear shot at success, and we were pleased that the proposal seemed to have been accepted relatively painlessly by everyone.

A Hunting Memory

Cold and mosquitoes
are torments
that never come together.
I lie down on the ice,
I lie down on the ice and snow
so my jaws chatter.
This is I!
Aja-aja-ja.

Is it memories
of the seasons,
of the seasons,
(mosquitoes swarming)
of the seasons
(ice paralysing)
make the mind swoon,
as I stretch my limbs out
on the ice?
This is I!
Aja-aja-ja.

Aj! But songs
require strength,

and I search
for words. Yes, I!
Aja-aja-ja.

Aj! I raise my head and see
the subject of my song:
the broad-antlered reindeer!

Powerfully I hurled
the spear and throwing-pole,
my weapon tethering the bull
right in the middle of the loin
He trembled, and he fell.
And then lay still.

Aj! But songs
require strength,
and I search
for words.
Here is the song.
Here is the memory.
It's only I who sings.
Aja-aja-haja-haja!

—Ivaluardjuk (Iglulik Eskimo man)

Tale of a Hunter's Daughter

RACHEL A. QITSUALIK (CANADIAN INUIT, 1998)

achel Qitsualik is one of the most eloquent of a new generation of Inuit writers. Daughter of a minister who was also a hunter, Qitsualik, like so many of her generation, was sent away to boarding school at Inuvik at a young age, where she was taught to abandon her native language in favor of English. She has since used her eloquence in English to reclaim her own culture and speak out on its behalf.

Her columns and commentary appear weekly in *Nunatsiaq News,* a prominent voice for the Inuit of the Canadian Arctic (www.nunatsiaq.com). The following column, a story of hunting with her father as a young girl, appeared in September 1998. Although it describes events that occurred some years ago, the essay illustrates the importance of hunting to the culture and families of the Arctic, even in these decades of rapid change in the Far North.

OTTAWA—My father turned to me, saying, "No, you can't come with us. And even if you did, you would not be treated like a girl."

But I knew I was wearing him down. My father was readying for a four-day hunting trip. Throughout his entire preparation, I had badgered him, trying to convince him to take me along.

401

"But I've never gone on a caribou hunt," I argued, "and I'll run along-side the sled. I can run for a long time now and I'll use my own rifle."

"We'll walk fast," he countered, "and not take breaks. It will be too hard for you."

He returned to checking the camp stove, and coiled some extra rope into the grub box. It was my job to help harness the dogs and strap the sleeping gear with ropes onto the sled. My father, as well as another hunter and son, had planned their short trek into the mainland over what was left of the spring snow and patchy ice.

I used my last bit of ammunition, saying "Qilak is going and he's the same age as me."

It worked. "If it's alright with your mother ... you can come along," my father said.

Victory!

The sled was packed very lightly. A few caribou sleeping skins, a small tent, my father's .222 rifle with scope, my new bolt-action .22, binoculars, gas for the camping stove, kettle, box of hardtack biscuits, a pair each of hip waders (we wore short rubber boots lined with duffel sox), and my favorite shades—my only concession to vanity.

Keeping Up with the Men

The first day of travel was very ordinary at first. We moved along the coastline of the mainland, starting off in the early evening when it was cooler and the packed snow firmer. As promised, I ran alongside the dogsled and helped untangle the leads, on the run, whenever neces-sary. It was already very different from a family trip. There were no breaks for tea or to rest the dogs.

So far, I was doing just fine, and I was trying not to be too smug about keeping up, proving to my father that he had underestimated my capabilities.

It looked like it was going to be more of the same steady progress that we had made thus far, but it also looked like we were now leaving the coastline and heading towards rougher terrain. The steel runners of the sled, which were not iced due to the softer snow, began to drag and clump with the softer, deeper snow of the hills we were soon traversing.

The sled began to snag more and more on rocks and the thawed, jutting landscape. Each time, the dogs cooperated less and less well as they were commanded to spring forward. It would not have been as bad if the entire ground had been like this, but the revealed areas were interspersed with areas of good snow, upon which the dog team would suddenly race forward only to hitch to a sudden stop upon another obstacle.

After yanking, backing up, and pulling for what seemed an endless number of times, I began to lose my enthusiasm. I was calling upon all my energy reserves to keep from looking like I was lagging behind. It was too chilly to take off layers of outer clothing, yet somehow still too warm with all the pushing and pulling, and my own sweat was beginning to bother me.

The dogs licked snow and somehow kept trudging, no longer trying to veer around rocks, but instead just crashing right onto them. The sled runners would emit a high-pitched squealing sound each time they ground against the stone, hurting my teeth and adding to my pounding headache.

Tears of Fatigue

I looked longingly towards the melted ice on the coast below, refraining from drinking from the swampy ponds that we crashed through for hours. Besides, they looked buggy. After an extended time of this, I was fighting back tears of fatigue.

With every pause we took, I started falling a few more feet behind. I had hit a wall in my stamina a while back, then caught a second wind, only to fall back again a little more listless, sweating less and less due to being dehydrated. Fueled by stubborn pride, I pushed forward to what now seemed a hypnotic state of gasping for air and lurching one more forced step ever forward.

That evening—or rather, early morning (it was well past 2 A.M.), when we finally made camp, a quickly erected and Spartan tent was set up. Only a thin layer of single skins were laid down, without the rocks being cleared for a sleeping area as would be done for a "family" tent.

Every muscle ached in my body, especially those in my arms and legs. I could barely lie down due to that pain, as well as a rock that stuck exactly in the middle of my back. I was forced to quasi-sleep on my elbows and knees, my head awkwardly resting on my arms.

I suppose that my suffering had not gone unnoticed by my father, who must have felt sorry for me, since upon awakening I was served tea in my sleeping bag, and was treated to a hardboiled swan egg.

Having been utterly dead to the world, I hadn't noticed father going out that morning to bag some breakfast. He showed me how to shell the eggs, salted and peppered half of one, and added to the fare some fresh bannock (which I, understandably, wolfed down). Feeling a little better both physically and spiritually, I went to fetch water for the dogs to drink.

We were inland now. Managing to collect swan eggs should have been a hint. They were very shy of people, and made huge nests in inaccessible places, usually near mud-packed, boggy areas. And unless you hadn't already guessed as much, those were the conditions under which we travelled all that day, having to don our hip waders.

We half pushed, half pulled the sled—and sometimes the dogs themselves—through slushy snow and muddy fields. Though I was not very heavy, I had to crawl onto the sled whenever the mud went past my knees, which would make me sink with a quicksand effect.

By the middle of the day, my father had become hoarse from urging the dogs on. They did not look happy, and increasingly scrapped with each other out of sheer frustration.

It started to rain a very fine mist, not one worth setting up a tent for, but enough to sting and somehow work its way past mitts and into the sleeves of my sweater. I was now wearing my "safari" cap, trying to ignore my annoyingly bedraggled hair that ceaselessly became dislodged, dangling in my face between alternate efforts to slog through the muck and scramble onto the sled whenever it began to move again. My spirit was virtually past caring about anything, and we must have made camp sometime as day and night blurred into one. My next memory was of awakening to a sunny day.

It was day three of our trip. I was a little more lively, not because of the rest, but because this would probably be the day that we would sight caribou. The landscape had changed. Unsurprisingly, the snow was disappearing fast, and the few tiny lakes that dotted the landscape looked dangerously thin and yellowed in spots.

After hitching the dogs, I managed to find time to quickly explore the area we were in, and discovered some old cranberry patches left from the previous year, as well as a few dumbly observing ptarmigan. I had a good arm from my father teaching me to throw stones at targets bobbing in water, and could easily "miluq" (kill with a stone) a bird or two, but I didn't bother since we were in a hurry. Besides, I was more interested in caribou. I raced back, and we continued our journey.

Caribou!

With greater frequency, the hunters began to make short stops to survey the area. At one of these stops, my father spotted four caribou on the other side of a small hill. As was the rule when game was near, everyone communicated using sign language. My father held up four fingers and pointed in the direction of the animals.

Both hunters ran back to the sleds and instructed Qilak and I to watch the dogs while they went to stalk the caribou. My father whispered to me that at no time was I to let the dogs follow him. The dogs knew that any gunshot signalled a hunt, which was irresistible to them. Upon hearing the first shot, they would start running, but I was to remain off the sled, fixing it and the dogs to the ground with the "kisaq," a claw-shaped anchor.

I was overexcited, but managed to quiet the dogs, who were now crouched, ears perked, intently watching my father and the other hunter beginning to stalk the caribou. But the dogs could already tell that a hunt was underway, for as they watched the hunters adopt a partial belly crawl toward the caribou, they took it as a signal that a gunshot would soon follow. The whole team was positioned as though ready to pounce, waiting anxiously as the hunters stalked out of sight.

They didn't have long to wait.

Two shots cracked off simultaneously. As instructed, I leapt to anchor the kisaq, using my body to weigh it down, but the dogs were too strong! The team bolted violently, and I was dragged along in a cloud of flying snow.

My slight form—a little under 90 pounds—was no match for a team of crazed huskies determined not to miss the hunt. I tried to dig in the anchor again, aiming to snag it upon an onrushing oue showed me how k, only to be bounced off of it painfully. At some point, I managed to find my legs, stumbling, falling onto the moving sled, to which I clung for dear life.

I spied Qilak ahead of me, trying to stop his own father's sled, he too being trapped in his own dragging nightmare. We were headed straight for a small, barely frozen lake. I tried steering my sled but once again was too light to gain purchase, and we plowed right over the lake.

Thin Ice

Ice was cracking all around me and the back part of the sled began to sink. The dogs were still hurtling at top speed, so I was powerless by now to slow them down. My eyes locked onto the lake as I stared in horrified fascination at the ice shattering all around me. The dogs were running too quickly to sink, but the sled runners were starting to sag as the front of the sled whipped from side to side. I grasped the ropes as I was dragged across an ice crack, witnessing dark water opening up behind me. Choked with horror, I observed helplessly that the same dragging that opened up the ice also carried me barely ahead of drowning or freezing to death—whichever may have come first. The only power left to me was my singular ability to cling.

I was shaken and numb with exhaustion when we reached my father, Qilak's father, and all four caribou, quite dead, splayed across the tundra. There had seemed, in all the chaos, to have been only two shots fired. I guessed that the other shots might have been fired almost immediately following the first, as the caribou were not far away from each other.

My situation had made me miss it all. I'm not sure that my father and his partner had seen what had happened, for they had been on the other side of the hill, and Qilak and I agreed with our mutual silence that they didn't need to know about it. At least, we hoped they didn't know about it.

After skinning and quartering the caribou, we sat down for a meal of caribou ribs. Mission accomplished. As a bonus, although they were late spring caribou, the skins were in excellent condition, having molted early, so that they were just the right thickness for bedding. They would make good replacements for those used in summer camping, as these new skins would not shed as much hair as our older, well-used ones.

The return trip home was not as taxing. Taking a longer, much easier route through the snaking coastline, it seemed almost anti-climactic.

A couple of days later, I had finally washed the mud out of my hair, nails, mitts and socks. I was feeling a little dejected, not knowing how well—or poorly—I had performed on the trip. I was feeling like a failure over not controlling the dogs. "At least Qilak hadn't either," I told myself; it wasn't only me that had screwed up.

Home.

Unlike his usual, advisory self, my father didn't mention anything one way or another. Normally, when I goofed at something, he would lecture me on what I had done wrong, what I could do to fix it.

Another Trip?

Now, however, he seemed too busy to comment. He was already preparing for his next trip, which was to Hatt Island to retrieve camping gear left behind during a prior season. I was not very cheery when I helped him with the usual preparations. Untangle traces, fill the smaller gas can, spread out the tarp to dry, fetch this fetch that—I was listless through it all.

My father was getting ready to clean his rifles. He told me that while he did so, he would also check the sight on my .22, and clean and oil its barrel for me.

"Go and get my old canvas rifle case," he ordered, "and take this box of shells."

I knew my father owned a brand new sealskin case for his rifle. I watched him set aside some shells, presumably for shooting practice, for which we normally expended many rounds. As he did so, I was puzzled as to why he would want me to fetch his old rifle case, and voiced it: "Why the old rifle case when you already have the new one?"

(I tried not to sound too surly, peering out from under my cap.)

"You'll need it when you come along tomorrow. It's only a short trip but I'll need help watching the dogs on seal hunts along the way."

Did he need to ask twice? I tried not to yell out a whoop. After all, an undisciplined whoop would not befit a hunter's daughter.

Pijariiqpunga.

Delight in Singing

It's wonderful
to make up songs:
but all too many of them fail.

It's wonderful
to have your wishes granted:
but all too often
they slip by.

It's wonderful
to hunt reindeer:
but all too seldom
you succeed,
standing like a bright fire
on the plain.

—Piuvkaq (Utkuhikjalik Eskimo man)

Cold Oceans: By Sea Kayak to Greenland

BY JON TURK (AMERICAN, 1998)

Trained in chemistry but a self-described "wanderer," Jon Turk relinquished a scientist's life in order to undertake epic journeys in the cold regions of the planet, supporting his travels by writing textbooks. In 1980, he attempted to round by sea kayak South America's notoriously storm-battered Cape Horn. A few years later he tried to retrace the Northwest Passage by small boat (completing about one-quarter of it), followed by a dogsled trip on Baffin Island. The fourth and final adventure told in his 1998 book, *Cold Oceans,* was Turk's journey from Canada's Ellesmere Island to Greenland, retracing a famous Inuit migration led by the shaman Qitdlaq in the 1860s.

While Steger and Schurke's account of their expedition is very frank in its descriptions of the emotional state of the team members, Turk takes this one step further and weaves an account of his personal life—and his eventual commitment to a marriage—into the accounts of his journeys. "I want to wander. You want a family," he tells his partner Chris, breaking off the relationship for the third time. But Turk eventually tracks Chris down where she works at an oil survey camp in the Alaskan bush, proposes marriage, and embarks with her on the crossing to Greenland.

This excerpt follows their reconciliation, their encounter with an Inuit hunter who gives advice and help, and a frightening experience with the wind at the very outset of their paddle.

I drove back to Southern Cross and staked the dogs out in front of Chris's cabin. We shared spring skiing and a trip to the desert, and the magic of our romance returned. Chris had a job with a mineral exploration company in Alaska, and I planned to work on a fishing boat again, so we drove north together. During the long drive, Chris told me that she wanted a more stable life: a home and children. I wasn't prepared for this commitment, so when we reached Anchorage we went out to dinner, made love, and broke our relationship for the third time.

I loaded the dogs in the truck and reviewed our conversation as I drove out of town. "I want to wander. You want a family. We don't think we can do both at the same time. I love you, you love me. See ya later, Bye."

Sometimes I understood the reasoning, but sometimes it didn't make sense.

I drove into Talkeetna and walked into a friend's house. I sat down, poured myself some coffee, broke off a chunk of cinnamon roll, and caught up on the news. I was among friends; everything was going to be okay. I sold my dogs and flew to Bristol Bay to fish.

After fishing season, Nathan, Noey, and Reeva flew north, and we all moved to Seldovia, a small town on the Alaskan coast south of Anchorage. Seldovia is cut off from the road system by several glaciers, so it is a virtual island. I bought a small speedboat and started a new textbook. The children and I explored the bay and hiked into the hills.

One day we decided to motor to Homer, a large town across the bay. My fuel pump failed, so we rowed into the harbor. The dealer told me that the new part would arrive in a week. We went to a restaurant, and the children chattered away. I didn't want to spend the money to fly to Seldovia and back by bush plane, I didn't want to row home, and I didn't want to hang out in Homer for a week. I wanted to forget this stupid hassle and go see Chris. We had fought, separated, loved, fought, and separated. Now I wanted to be with her again.

I decided to fly the children back to Seldovia on their own, fly into the interior by myself, find Chris, and ask her to marry me. Then I could return to Homer, install the new fuel pump, and run the boat back to Seldovia.

Chris was working at an isolated camp south of Galena. I could fly from Homer to Galena commercially but would have to hitchhike a ride to the camp. I evaluated my fellow passengers as we boarded the jet in Anchorage. The man with a chain saw as a carry-on looked like a trapper. I guessed that the man with cardboard boxes as luggage was born in Galena and was returning home. Women with children probably wouldn't be much help. But what about that clean-shaven man in spotless blue jeans and a white polo shirt? Midway through the flight I walked down the aisle and tapped him on the shoulder.

"Excuse me, do you work for Anaconda Minerals?"

He looked at me guardedly. "Yes, I'm camp manager, why?"

"I'm Chris Seashore's boyfriend, and I was wondering if I could hitch a ride out to camp with you."

"I didn't know Chris Seashore had a boyfriend."

"She doesn't either, but I'm it."

The man shrugged. "Sure, if there's room in the bush plane, you can come."

After the jet landed in Galena, we boarded a one-engine Cessna and flew south to a rough dirt strip. My benefactor pointed to a substantial plywood building and told me that someone over there would know where to find Chris.

I climbed the steps and entered a spacious room filled with maps, cores, and computers. Three people were hunched over keyboards or drafting tables, and two others were lounging on office chairs. A man told me that Chris was working at a remote site several miles from camp, and I could wait and make myself comfortable. Then one of the loungers announced casually, "I'll take you out there."

I had no idea what type of vehicle he drove, but the journey was becoming almost as much fun as the quest. We walked to a shiny jet ranger helicopter. He motioned me to the front passenger seat, and I climbed in. I fastened my seat belt and placed my headset and walkie-talkie over my ears. The pilot revved up the engine, lifted us a few feet off the ground, tested the chopper's response to the controls, and took off. His voice sounded far away through the headset.

"There'll be a few guys in camp who won't be too happy to see you."

I pushed the talk button. "That's their problem."

We crossed a few ridges and a swamp. He veered wide to avoid scaring a moose, then rose over a high hill.

"I'll put you down right here. Chris is working on a seismic line due north. When you step out of the ship, be sure to latch the door and exit forward. And, oh yeah, make lots of noise. All those gals working on the seismic line carry guns. No one is expecting you. It'd be a pisser if someone thought you were a bear and shot you."

"Thanks for the ride and the warning."

I stepped out, exited forward, and ducked to avoid the wind blast when he took off again. A faint trail led to the seismic line, which was a linear slash across the landscape. I saw no one, and for lack of a better direction, turned east. When I crested a low hill, I saw Chris crouched over some instruments.

I ignored the pilot's warning and walked down quietly. Chris finally looked up when I was a few feet away.

"Jon!"

She stood up and we hugged.

I whispered, "I'm tired of all this bullshit, Chrissy. Let's just get married. We'll work things out somehow."

She pressed against me, and I felt her head nod slowly against my chest. "Okay."

2

That fall, Nathan and Noey flew to California, and Chris, Reeva, and I drove south toward Montana. It was the fourth time I had driven the five-thousand-mile route between Montana and Alaska. The first time I had been alone, haunted and hassled; the second journey was with Dave and seventeen dogs, headed—unprepared—toward a dangerous expedition; the third journey was with Chris, discussing and preparing for our imminent separation. This time we were a family planning a future together.

My fishing season had been successful, and Chris had saved her summer wages, so together we had enough money for the down payment on a house. We talked about building a modern, energy-efficient structure, but Chris argued that we would probably start the project and run off on a series of expeditions, condemning ourselves to a life among piles of insulation and sheetrock. Reeva looked forward to buying any house and moving in, as long as she could paint her room pink.

The taiga flowed past. I suggested that we return to ski the high peaks of the Yukon some spring or summer. Chris seemed to glow, thinking of carving turns through the high cirques.

I had married Elizabeth in the fall of 1967, seventeen years before. Seventeen years in a whirlwind of wives and lovers, interspersed with time alone. Yet in one moment, sitting in the restaurant in Homer, contemplating the logistics of a broken fuel pump, I had decided to marry Chris. Now I felt truly committed.

Chris was sleeping in the seat beside me. Reeva was reading a book about horses. Gravel plinked against the underside of the truck. I chuckled to myself at all the confusions.

3

When Dave and I were seal hunting near Broughton Island, Moosa asked, "How come you guys travel so far from home? Are you like Qitdlaq?"

The others laughed but wouldn't explain the joke.

I asked friends in Broughton and then continued my inquiries in Iqaluit on my way home. Everyone knew portions of the Qitdlaq story, and I gradually pieced the chronicle together from fragments. Much later I researched it in libraries, but that was after I had camped in

Qitdlaq's camps and stored my kayaks on the stone pillars he and his people had built.*

Qitdlaq was born in about 1800 near Cumberland Sound, on the southeast coast of Baffin Island. He became a powerful shaman, an *angakkuq,* who was feared and obeyed by his people. Sometime between 1830 and 1835, while hunting caribou, Qitdlaq crushed a companion's skull with a rock. There is no known motive for the crime. None of the other hunters discussed the murder after they returned to camp, but another *angakkuq* saw it in a dream and ordered several sled dogs to attack Qitdlaq.

Qitdlaq escaped and migrated north with a small group of loyal followers. They settled briefly near Pond Inlet, but fought with a local tribe, lost the battle, and fled again, this time south, down the west coast of Baffin Island.

By 1853 Qitdlaq had moved north of Baffin to Devon Island, where he met British naval commander Edward Inglefield. The two leaders met in the ship's chart room, and Qitdlaq asked about land even farther north. Inglefield spread out a map of Ellesmere Island and western Greenland and explained that Ellesmere was uninhabited but Inuit lived along the Greenland coast. Qitdlaq saw that if he followed the east coast of Ellesmere far enough north, he could cross easily to Greenland.

Qitdlaq's group remained on Devon Island for five years. Generally, the people were prosperous, although Qitdlaq's enemies sent evil spirits to harass them. On one occasion, as the small band traveled across the ice, Qitdlaq saw a long-haired giant on the shore. He cried out, "You, Giant, you are nothing but baleen." Qitdlaq's magic was stronger than that of his enemies, and the giant disappeared. When the

---

*Although written accounts are similar, no two are identical. For consistency, I have relied mainly on a single source. My only deviation from this source is to call the hero Qitdlaq, not Qillaq, to agree with other chronicles and with numerous oral accounts I heard in Greenland. My source is *Qitdlarssuaq: The Story of a Polar Migration,* by Guy Mary-Rousseliere, trans. Alan Cooke (Winnipeg, Man.: Wuerz Publishing, 1991).

Inuit investigated, they found only a whale's jawbone with some baleen attached.

Hounded by invisible *angakkuqs* and restless at heart, Qitdlaq took frequent spirit journeys to the North and returned to tell his people of rich hunting, green grasses, and friendly hunters. Finally, an entire band of forty men, women, and children set out for Greenland, directed only by Qitdlaq's visions and a five-year-old memory of a map in Inglefield's chart room. They probably left in the early spring of 1859, when the sun was returning but the ice was still firm.

They carried all their belongings on ten *komatiks:* furs for winter, tents for summer, and kayaks for hunting in open water. The largest *komatik* was pulled by twenty dogs, an admirable feat of dog handling. The tribe stopped for the summer when the ice broke up in July. Some of the hunters explored inland to hunt caribou while others harpooned seals, narwhals, and walrus from their kayaks. They built stone igloos* and insulated them with sod for a winter camp. During the long dark time, they lived by the light and heat of their blubber lamps. During the full moon, hunters waited patiently by *aglus* to harpoon seals. They set out again in the spring.

Qitdlaq's group reached Smith Sound the following year and gazed across the channel toward Greenland. A warm-water upwelling maintains a permanent open water oasis, called a *polynya,* in Smith Sound. The travelers swung their dog teams north to good ice and crossed to the new land. They found abundant caribou on the shore and hunted walrus, narwhals, and beluga whales in the sound. Millions of birds swarmed the cliffs, and the hunters caught them in nets and gathered eggs. They also found many stone houses, but all were vacant.

The following spring Qitdlaq led his band south until they met people. . .

---

*An igloo is any domed winter home. Permanent igloos were built of stone and moss and covered with hides. Temporary structures on ice were constructed of hardened snow. House-building technology and terminology varied across the Arctic.

4

Qitdlaq was a murderer, a shaman, a leader, and an outcast, but I thought of him mainly as a compulsive wanderer. That day on the ice, watching Dave's fur-clad figure retreat into the whiteness, I realized that if I shared Qitdlaq's wanderlust, perhaps I should share the same ice, the same coastline, and, yes, some of the same hardships.

I could have reached a different conclusion. Even though I still couldn't understand why, Dave and I had retreated, ignominiously, from the dogsled expedition on a beautiful winter day when the wind was still, the sun shone, and we had enough food to reach the next settlement. But the failure had started much earlier. I began the expedition without adequate preparation: I wasn't a good dog handler; my dogs were trained for the forest, not the sea ice; I traveled with a partner whom I didn't like or trust. The Cape Horn and Northwest Passage expeditions also had suffered from poor strategy and execution. A rational person would rethink a lifestyle that had foundered so dramatically and so repeatedly.

But logic conflicted with my dreams. Maybe I was more content on my expeditions than I admitted to myself. Surely I was wily enough to succeed and strong enough to stop whining, even to myself. Could I simply cut through all the bullshit, as I had when I decided to marry Chris? Could it be that easy? And that rewarding?

I decided to follow Qitdlaq across the ice.

Qitdlaq committed his first murder near Pangnirtung and wandered for a few decades before he reached Greenland. I couldn't travel that far in one season and had learned from past mistakes that it is too frustrating to set an unachievable goal. Therefore, I planned to fly to Grise Fiord on the southern coast of Ellesmere Island and follow Qitdlaq's migration along the east coast of Ellesmere and across Smith Sound to Greenland. Greenland is uninhabited in the vicinity of Smith Sound, so I needed to swing south toward civilization. It is about three hundred seventy-five miles between Grise Fiord and Siorapaluk, the first Greenland village. The nearest airport is one hundred seventy-five miles farther, at the U.S. Air Force base in Thule.

All my previous journeys had taken me through remote lands, but the routes had intersected villages and military posts. There were no settlements along the east coast of Ellesmere. The crux of this expedition was that the most difficult passage, the twenty-three-mile crossing to Greenland, was situated late in the journey. If Smith Sound were ice-choked and impassable, I probably wouldn't have enough food to return to Grise Fiord. Failure wasn't an option.

I reasoned that I had accumulated enough Arctic experience to plan and execute an expedition competently. I hoped that I had learned to cope emotionally. Of course, doubts hovered. I recalled a phrase from Stefansson:

I fancy there are few men so sure of a theory that they are free from a bit of nervousness when they come to stake their lives on its holding good.*

But I was too excited to change my mind.

Chris said that she'd like to join me. I was half surprised and half expecting that she would come. In Chris's words:

When Jon decided to row the Northwest Passage in 1982, he was surprised that I wanted to join him. Six years after our first expedition, I longed for magical, high-latitude lighting, the vastness of the Arctic landscape, and the self-imposed time warp created by a long journey. Jon accepted me as an equal partner now and trusted my skill and judgment. In addition I understood Jon a little better.

On an average year, the ice doesn't break up in Grise Fiord until mid-August. If we waited till then, we wouldn't have enough time to complete the journey before winter. So we planned to leave early and drag the boats over the ice. A similar strategy had failed on the Northwest Passage trip, but this time we had two factors in our favor. First, several *polynyas* lie along the east coast of Ellesmere. The *polynyas* guaranteed that we would have ice-free regions to relieve the drudgery of dragging. Second, during the 1980s, light, durable plastic sea kayaks had become

---

*Stefansson, *My Life with the Eskimo*, p. 164.

popular. We thought that these boats would slide over the ice more easily than the cumbersome wherry.

We bought two seventeen-foot-long plastic sea kayaks, about the length of the folding kayak I took on the Cape Horn trip. Although the length was the same, a plastic boat is more streamlined and faster. In addition, the hard plastic is incredibly resistant to abrasion, whereas the flexible rubberized skin of a folding kayak will tear on sharp rocks or wear through if dragged long distances on the ice. Folding kayaks are open in the middle, almost like canoes, and covered with a large cloth spray deck. In contrast, plastic kayaks contain watertight compartments fore and aft and a small central cockpit. A neoprene spray skirt fits around your torso and wraps over the cockpit to provide a watertight seal. If you capsize, you can roll back over with a quick sweep of your paddle. If I had been in a plastic kayak during my disaster at Cape Horn, I wouldn't have flopped out of the cockpit like a rag doll. Our plastic kayaks had rudders controlled by foot pedals to maintain a straight course in waves or currents.

We flew to Grise Fiord on June 22, one day after the solstice. The plane landed on the dirt strip with a clatter of gravel. A few pickup trucks gathered to collect cargo. Most of the other passengers were met by relatives on three-wheeled all-terrain vehicles. The motorcycle-sized engines popped and clattered on the runway and carried their passengers off with a receding roar.

Small towns in New England nestle into the foliage as if they grew there along with the rocks and trees, but there was no foliage to bond Grise Fiord to the landscape. Several dozen brightly colored square houses and a few large metal buildings rose incongruously from the gravel beach and the scattered tundra flowers. We landed late in the afternoon, as the sun finished its flight from east to west and veered north to scribe a flattened circle above the village. Grise Fiord lies at about 77° north latitude. Thus our starting point was four hundred miles farther north than any point on the Northwest Passage trip. We wouldn't see sunset until we returned home. We hitched a ride to town and carried our kayaks down to the beach. I walked out on the white, frozen bay, kicked at the surface, and exposed solid ice hidden beneath a few inches of slushy snow. Light distorted through the translucent crystal as if it were passing through both lenses of a telescope at once, so the ice looked simultaneously wafer thin and thicker than the earth. When I jumped on it, it felt like solid ground.

Chris spoke softly, almost as if to herself. "Let's paddle to Greenland."

A local hunter asssured us that a *polynya* existed to the east and that the floe edge, the boundary between ice and water, was only twenty-five miles away. He pointed to a rocky bluff rendered indistinct by a mirage and announced, "There—water."

We loaded the boats with enough food, fuel, and clothing to last eight weeks. Most of our bulk and weight were carbohydrates: rice, bulgur wheat, and couscous, but we also packed nuts, soup mixes, sugar, and milk. We stuffed in extra warm clothes, a stove and fuel, a few books, and a tent. The waterproof compartments weren't roomy enough to hold everything, so we crammed gear into the cockpits until we could hardly squeeze into the remaining space. Then we loaded more camping gear in waterproof bags, which we lashed on the back deck. I protected my rifle in a waterproof case and lashed it on the front deck where I could reach it quickly if a polar bear attacked.

An older man named Pijimini joined us over coffee in the RCMP office. I outlined our route on the large wall map. Pijimini nodded and walked to the wall hesitatingly, like a schoolboy trying to remember his assignment. He drew a precise line with his finger outward from the bluff beyond Grise Fiord and said, "Ice to here." Then he swept his palm across thousands of square miles of the Arctic Ocean. "Here— ice maybe, water maybe."

He asked to see our kayaks, and we walked to the shore. He carefully inspected the boats, hit the plastic with his fist, sat in the cockpit, and stretched our neoprene spray skirts. Then he led us to a traditional Inuit kayak. The outer skin had been removed, leaving only a skeleton of carefully shaped stems and ribs, tied together with waxed string. Pijimini had carved a flat-bladed paddle from a single board. The paddle was heavier than our paddles but well balanced. Between the handle and the blade, he had cut a delicate curve that looked like an upside-down wave. Pijimini ran his finger along the curve.

"Know what for?" he asked.

"Yes, water from the paddle blade drips off the point and doesn't run onto your hand and up your sleeve."

Pijimini beamed and pointed at me. "Understand him." Then he pointed back and forth at himself and me, saying, "Same, same, kayak-men." He ignored Chris, who stood by silently.

Pijimini assured us we would encounter polar bears, but he shrugged when we asked how dangerous they were.

"Sometimes, maybe yes, sometimes, maybe no."

However, he warned us about walrus. Walrus stalk kayakers, rip their boats apart, and then suck the person's intestines out. They don't eat the rest. I smiled as if Pijimini had told a joke, but he stared unwaveringly to convince me with his gaze.

The RCMP officer admonished, "There is no word for lying in the Inuit language. If he warned you about walrus, believe him."

5

Pijimini insisted on driving us to the open water by snowmachine. After an hour's ride, we reached the floe edge, lifted the kayaks off the *komatik,* and set them on the ice. I thanked Pijimini. He looked across the water and said simply, "Long way to Greenland."

He pulled the cord on his snowmachine, sat on the seat while it idled, and offered one last piece of advice: "You kayak man, you know. Windy, windy—no paddling—stay in tent, drink tea." Then he smiled and drove away.

The sound of his machine drifted off. Southward, across the ice, half a dozen glaciers fell from Devon Island into the frozen sea. Northward, toward Greenland, the gray-green ocean lapped against the ice. We pulled on our spray skirts, lowered into the cockpits, and slid, like alligators, into the water.

The boat felt overloaded and top-heavy. I took a few strokes and stopped. Chris pulled alongside. After all the preparations, the driving, the flights, and the visiting in Grise Fiord, we were alone. Twenty yards of the journey were behind us, with five hundred fifty miles to go.

I had forgotten the feeling of traveling across the Arctic. Normal descriptions of beauty don't work, because the landscape is monotonous, not beautiful; it isn't a picture, but a sensation. In the forest, a person retains scale. You are bigger than a mushroom and smaller than a tree. But in the Arctic you may feel bigger than a glacier yet smaller than a seagull flying overhead. Once you lose scale, you lose the concept of strength or weakness. At one moment I felt that the empty space could crush me. A moment later I took a spirit journey to Smith Sound. The ice was clear. Chris and I were strong, a team now. We wouldn't need the rescue that might be impossible. I followed Qitdlaq as he descended through an *aglu,* and we danced with the walrus at the bottom of the sea.

"You okay, Chrissy?"

"I think so. I'm nervous."

"Take a moment and feel the boat."

A person balances a kayak with thighs and knees rather than with shoulders and paddle, and thus a kayak becomes an extension of the body, more like a ski than a rowboat. I pressed my thighs against the underside of the deck and gently rocked the kayak to feel the balance point and edge. Then I held my paddle in the air, reached behind, and pressed it against the back of my neck to stretch.

Chris followed a similar routine and nodded. "Let's paddle across this bay and make camp early. It's too much to take in all at once."

I had wanted to push further the first day, but I was also glad to stop. The final planning of the expedition was hectic and confusing: arranging gear and escaping from publishers and their irritating last-minute details. Now I had to shift my mental attitude, become calm and alert, pick pleasure and danger out of a long, slow-moving day.

We crossed the bay in an hour, but ice had collected in the inter-tidal zone to form a six-foot-high cliff, called an *ice foot.* We paddled to within a few feet of the beach but couldn't land. The tide was low, so we paddled for an additional few hours until the rising tide lifted us over the ice. We pitched the tent, went for a walk, and cooked dinner. Pijimini had given us some caribou and seal, and we made a rich, fatty stew.

We crawled into our sleeping bags at ten o'clock in the evening, our normal bedtime. I looked up at the tent ceiling and stared at seal-blubber stains from the dogsled trip. We heard shots as Inuit from Grise Fiord hunted ducks and seal. Living in a land with continuous sunlight for three and a half months and continuous darkness for an equal amount of time, they had little regard for clocks or schedules. But during our Northwest Passage trip we had functioned most efficiently on a conventional nine-to-five work schedule. Chris cuddled against me, and I thought about the tremendous difference between her warmth and the aloofness that had separated Dave and me. It wasn't just the body contact, but the feeling that we would work together. The sharp crack of the seal hunter's rifle and the dull thud of a shotgun were the last sounds of humans as we drifted off to sleep.

6

The next day, an onshore wind stacked ice against the beach and threw a cold spray into the air. I argued that if we battled through the bad ice and paddled around the point, we would be protected and could paddle ten or twenty miles for the day. Chris didn't want to take chances so early in the trip and suggested that we wait until conditions improved. I reflected on my shipwreck in Chile and on all of our arguments on the Northwest Passage trip. Chris and I could pull against each other or work together, but the land would define this expedition. I had struggled—and failed—on the past three expeditions. Maybe this time we would move faster by waiting.

We went for a walk and talked about all the unfinished business we had left back home in the Montana forest. We should have painted the deck, finished the instructor's manual for my most recent book, recharged the battery on the old pickup. But we hadn't done any of those things. Now none of that mattered. A flock of black and white diving ducks, called *guillemots,* took off with a winged whir.

The wind dropped by early afternoon, so we broke camp and launched. After a few hours, the wind intensified and veered until it blew directly offshore. We decided to pull in, but the tide was low again and the ice foot blocked us. The wind picked up, and I thought that in an emergency I could stand in the cockpit, grab the top of the ice foot, and pull myself over. But even if I succeeded, I couldn't lift the loaded boats. Consequently, we elected to stay close to the shore, using the ice as a wind shield, and to continue until either the tide rose again or we found an opening. For the next half hour the wind slowly increased, and our worry level rose with it.

In most environments, wind shakes the vegetation or forms ripples on the water, so you can watch it approach. But here the cold air dropped invisibly off the bare mountainside. Rocks don't sway, and we were so close to shore that the water surface gave no indication of air movement. One moment, the wind freshened against my face, and a few seconds later it hit with a blast, jerking one end of my paddle over my head and forcing the other end into the water, under the kayak. The boat sideslipped and ran over the down-dipped blade. Caught between the wind and the paddle shaft, the kayak tipped dangerously, burying the leeward edge. I steadied the boat with a snap of my hips, freed the paddle, and then held the blade low to brace against the water. I glanced across and saw that Chris had also survived the unexpected on-slaught, but the storm washed both of us out to sea. The wind lifted the tops off the waves and blew the water horizontally across the surface. Water rolled over the deck and buried us to our armpits.

As I drifted out to sea, I thought my luck might have run out, and I imagined floating alone in a stormy ocean with only a lingering memory of a second boat drifting out of sight. Fear closed off any sense of tragedy. I viewed the image abstractly because I didn't seem to be involved.

When we were a quarter mile from shore, the wind subsided enough so that I could lift my paddle without being blown over. I turned the boat toward shore and paddled a few feet before another gust drove me backward again. Then the wind slacked off again and I battled forward. Chris had been close by but now fell behind. I was afraid to turn my head because the motion might alter my balance, so I screamed into the wind, "Chris, where are you?"

I heard a faint reply. "Jon, I'm losing ground! I'm being blown out to sea!"

I turned my boat around and yelled, "I'll get a line on you!" Another gust caught me broadside and swept me out of control. Bracing into the waves to avoid capsizing, I washed past her. I couldn't take one hand off my paddle to throw her a line, and anyway, she couldn't catch it and tie it to her bow.

We were only a few yards apart, but the water in the air softened her face and made her seem ghostlike and untouchable. A wisp of hair was plastered against one cheek and sheets of water streaked off her forehead and chin. Even though I was moving and she was nearly stationary, it seemed like she was falling past me. In my imagination, I reached out and touched her parka but couldn't grasp it. Then the wind swirled me ninety degrees and I lost sight of her.

By the time I regained control and swung my bow back into the wind, I was fifty yards farther out to sea. I watched Chris's back and arms as she strained for shore. We both made progress. I pulled close to her again.

"I think the tide is coming up, and I see a break in the ice cliff inside that bay! Can you make it?"

"Maybe!"

The wind howled in the space between us. We were both paddling hard, but I didn't know whether we were moving forward or sliding backward.

"*Maybe* isn't good enough!"

"Okay!"

I forged ahead and again lost sight of her. The windblown spray felt like hailstones against my face. My muscles were near failure, but I felt I would make it. Then I thought about Chris, behind me. Had she lost the will and was she, right now, blowing out to sea? Should I look? I could swing back to try and help her again, but we would both tip over if I tried to tie a line on her bow. Should I turn back to cheer her on and assure myself that I wasn't abandoning her? No, I had to save myself. But she was my wife; I loved her. However, I had the ELT (emergency locator transmitter) and could direct rescue from shore. No, maybe we'd be safer if we rafted off to sea together and transmitted our position precisely from the middle of Baffin Bay. I should turn back and share her fate, whatever it might be. No, this was all foolishness; she persevered through the storm on the Northwest Passage and she'd be right behind me.

A stream had melted a crevasse in the ice just large enough for a kayak. I reached it, jumped out, pulled my boat in, and turned toward the sea. Chris was only a few yards away, and I shouted and waved my arms. A gust pushed her back; then it slacked off and she advanced. Another gust hit. I ran into the water, grabbed her bow, and yanked her onto the shore. She sat in her boat for a moment and didn't move; then I helped her out.

We crouched in still air behind a rock. Chris and I had been lovers for eight years, married for four. We had been through all those painful separations and joyous reconciliations. Now she was close, not drifting behind me in a chaotic sea.

We feared that the wind would rip our tent apart, so we collected rocks to build a wind break. I worked with the same frantic energy that had propelled me to shore but then realized that we didn't need to hurry. Even though I was wet from my lunge into the sea to grab Chris's boat, I wasn't hypothermic.

"Look here, Chris!" I shouted into the wind. "When I lift a rock I don't disturb a single worm, ant, beetle, snake, or lizard. There is nothing out here, not even bugs. We're alone." She came over and brushed against me as she bent down. The faraway feeling in the kayak receded into memory.

Several curious piles of rocks were scattered about the small coastal plain. I lifted a rock off one pile, but Chris touched my arm and motioned me to replace it. The pile was too orderly to be natural.

We stepped back, looked, and realized that it was an ancient fox trap. We explored further and found numerous tent rings, stone igloos, fox traps, and food caches. We had stopped in one of Qitd-laq's camps.

I tried to forget the screaming wind, the nearly lifeless landscape bounded by glaciers on land and ice at sea, and instead imagined a small tribe, isolated from the rest of the world. I saw hunters going out every day, teenagers falling in love, young mothers with little babies. Thinking about the long journey ahead, I felt heartened to realize how much strength is genetically engineered into all of us.

Greeting to Day

To be spoken from bed, in the early morning, before anybody has risen.

I will rise from sleep
with the swiftness of the raven's wingbeat.
I will rise to meet the day.
Wa-wa.

My face turns
from the darkness,
my eyes turn to meet
the dawn, whitening the sky.

—Orpingalik (Netsilik Eskimo man)

Sun and Shadow: Waiting for Sunrise in the Greenlandic Night

BY GRETEL EHRLICH (AMERICAN, 1997)

Gretel Ehrlich is an essayist and non-fiction writer who is drawn to remote places and people, and the human spirit in the face of extremity. She has written about subjects as diverse as her life on a Wyoming ranch, her long and difficult recovery from a lightning strike, and her numerous trips to Greenland over the course of several years. She made one of those trips in the dead of a Greenlandic winter in order to experience the Arctic night.

The following excerpt is from an account of that long night, and the release brought by the first sunrise of the year. Originally appearing in *Harper's* magazine, Ehrlich's essay gives a vivid account of the despair and listlessness that can set in during the endless darkness, and the social problems they can cause. For her, the darkness becomes not simply the absence of light, but a tangible substance, "a kind of cosmic chocolate," while the sun represents an eye. "Its [the sun's] coming means that the boulder rolls away from in front of the cave," she writes, "and we are set free."

Qilaq taatuq. The sky is dark. *Seqineq.* The sun. *Siku.* Ice. *Tarraq.* Shadow. *Aput.* Snow. *Tartoq.* Darkness. *Kisimiippunga.* I am alone.

That's my vocabulary lesson for the day from a mimeographed Green-landic-English dictionary used by Allied troops during World War II, with words about bombs, warships, torpedoes, and German-speaking people. In reading the expedition notes of Knud Rasmussen, I learn that words used in seances are different from secular words, so that the shamanic word for sea is *aqitsoq* (the soft one), rather than the usual *imaq*.

By the time I walk home from the sled maker's shop, the skim of ice is gone and the pathway out to the annual ice used for drinking water has gone to liquid.

At my house I read about dark nebulae—immense clouds composed of the detritus of dying stars. Their function is unclear, but their effect in the universe is to "produce visual extinction." Yet the nebulae themselves are detectable because of "the obscuration they cause." I look up at the sky. The dark patches between constellations are not blanks but dense interstellar obstructions through which light from distant suns cannot pass. They are known variously as the Snake, the Horse-head, the Coalsack. Darkness is not an absence but a rich and dense presence, a kind of cosmic chocolate, a forest of stellar events whose existence is known only by its invisibility.

Polar days are almost the same as polar nights, and anyway, the streetlights in town are always on. I try to keep to a schedule—coffee in the morning, dinner at night, then sleep—but the schedule slides into the body's own understanding of constant dark. I sleep when I should eat and eat in the middle of the night. A recent study suggests that the eye may have its own biological clock, separate from the one in the brain. Now it's possible to think of eyes as circadian timepieces with resettable daily rhythms in the retina that orchestrate the ebb and flow of the hormone melatonin. In the dark and near-dark, I wonder what dances my eye rhythms are making and if, upon reentering the world of all-day sun, I will be blind.

Ann Andreasen is a Faroe Islander who followed a boyfriend to Greenland and decided to stay. Her house is next door to the Chil-dren's House she runs for children whose own homes have been marred by domestic violence or drugs. In the middle of the night a little girl is brought in. She has just witnessed the beating of her mother. The policeman who went to the scene is a friend of the family's, and, as in all Greenland towns, there is no bureaucratic tangle and no prison, just a firm suggestion that the child spend the night elsewhere.

Ann has left her own child, who is sick with the flu, to attend to the newcomer. Badly shaken, the girl is given hot chocolate and cookies, a fresh nightgown and toothbrush, then put to bed. The Children's House is modern, spotless, and cheerful with a capacious kitchen, living and arts area, computers and paints and traditional crafts for the kids. But the stories Ann can tell are a litany of tragedies—the inevitable consequences of a fiercely self-sufficient people meeting up with modern European life, despite or maybe because of Denmark's altruistic socialism.

My daily walk has been the one constant. Down the stairs from my perched green house, I stroll along the rocky edge of town, past the inlet where yesterday a wave generated by a calving glacier washed fifteen anchored boats onto the road. The Danes were so busy trying to save their pleasure boats that they forgot about the dogs tied up at the shore. The dogs drowned.

A week later. Now it's mid-January. A distant sound of thunder jolts me: a glacier calves, and waves made from the iceberg's birth undulate toward shore. Then something catches my eye: low down, from between two white cliffs, a full moon begins to rise—almost too enormous for the mountains that flank it. I stand mesmerized on the edge of the island. For some time the moon rises so slowly I'm afraid it will drop back down. But moons are not betrayed by gravity. Soon it tops the icy towers at the head of the fjord and brightens, suddenly rubescent, as if it had just been cut from ice and thrown up in the air—the absent sun's pale twin.

Morning. I'm not living on earth or ice but on rock and the sharp tooth of Uummannaq Mountain. At eleven the peak catches light like the poisoned tip of an arrow, and the cliffs that gave birth to the moon last night are pink, crimson, and gold. At noon there is a bit of light in the sky, but not enough to read by.

Later, maybe 2:00 A.M. Against the dogs' constant conversation about social hierarchy—urgent matters of food, sex, and rank, and the general angst of being chained on dirty patches of rock and snow—I lie alone in my bed. The moon is down. Unable to sleep, I drink a cheap bottle of blanc de noir—the white of the black, the foam of the night, the light hidden within dark grapes and made to sparkle. But how do they get white from black? How do they separate the two?

When all the blanc is gone there is only noir, *obscurum per obscuris,* a dark path leading through darkness. The Inuit never made much of beginnings, and now I know why. Because no matter what you do in winter, no matter how deep you dive, there is still no daylight and none of the comprehension that comes with light. Endings are everywhere, visible within the invisible, and the timeless days and nights tick by.

I am invited to dinner at a local painter's house with Ann and her husband, Ole Jorgen. Ole Jorgen arrives first to drop off a bottle of wine, and an ashtray almost hits him in the head. The artist—S.—and his wife are fighting. S. has been drunk for days. But they insist we come in. S. has recently suffered a stroke and can't walk. Holding court in his unkempt house, on a low daybed amid empty beer bottles, he looks like a doomed, deposed king, but his conversation is bright.

S.'s Greenlandic wife sets dinner down on the coffee table. It's a traditional soup made with seal meat and potatoes, accompanied by a shrimp and cabbage salad. (Lettuce doesn't survive the trip from Denmark to Greenland.) As the evening wears on, S.'s talk is reduced to expletives and non sequiturs. He adopts a British accent and says "I caun't" over and over, inserting it nonsensically between anyone's words. It's funny at first, but once I realize there will be no end to it I grow bored.

The wine has turned to vinegar; in the middle of the meal S.'s wife vomits in the kitchen sink. As we try to finish dinner fire engines roar by toward Ann's house, and we race outside after them. They pass her house and continue up the hill. My intention is to keep going, but Ole Jorgen says, "You're the guest of honor!"

I talk to S. about his paintings, and he gives me some sketches he's made of the harbor, white cliffs, and icebergs. The man can draw.

When the evening finally ends, I thank him for the gifts. Alone in my green house, I bundle myself up in my made-to-order Feathered Friends sleeping bag and sit by the window. The tranquility of perpetual night is like starch in my brain.

In winter, light sources are reversed. Snow-covered earth is a light, and the sky is a blotter that soaks up everything visible. There is no sun, but there's a moon that lives on borrowed time and borrowed light. Home late from hunting, two men pull a sledge laden with freshly killed seals up a hill, dripping a trail of blood in the snow. As I doze off, I dream that the paths are all red and the sky is ice and the water is coal. I take a handful of water and draw with it: in the frozen sky, I draw a black sun.

Later I can't sleep. The half-moon's slow rising seems like a form of exhaustion, with night trying to hold the moon's head down underwater. It bobs up anyway, and I, its captive audience, catch the illuminated glacial cliffs on the surface of my eyes. The moon's light is reflected light, but from what source? The sun is a flood that blinds us, a sun we can't see.

January 27. The glaciers are rivers, the sky is struck solid, the water is ink, the mountains are lights that go on and off. Sometimes I lie under my sleeping bag on the couch and recite a line from a Robert Lowell poem: "Any clear thing that blinds us with surprise."

I sleep by a cold window that I've opened a crack. Frigid air streams up the rock hill and smells like minerals. In sleep I hear the cracking sound that krill make underwater. Earlier in the day the chunk of glacier ice I dumped into a glass of water made the same sound.

The ice came from the top of a long tongue that spills out at the head of this fjord, as if it were the bump of a tastebud that had been sliced off, or a part of speech. Now it has melted and looks floury, like an unnecessary word that adds confusion to insight. But when I drink it down, its flavor is bright, almost peppery, bespeaking a clarity of mind I rarely taste but toward which I aspire.

When I lie back in the dark, the pupils of my eyes open.

My Uummannaq friends and I have started a countdown until the day the sun appears. After all, there's nothing else to do. Days pass. I try to distinguish the shadowed path from the shadowed world but fail. Then it's February.

The real is fragile and inconstant. The unreal is ice that won't melt in the sun. I walk partway up Uummannaq Mountain and look south. The sun's first appearance of the year will occur in three days, but for now the light is fish-colored—a pale, silvery gray, like the pallor between night and day. I try to remember the feel of sun on my face, but the dark mass, the rock body of Nuussuaq Peninsula, drives the sensation away.

In the night there is none of the old terror of the sun going down and never coming up again, the terror that heart patients feel, because the sun is already gone, and I'm alive, and the darkness is a cloak that shelters me. As I walk down the mountain to the town dump, patches of frostbite, like tiny suns, glow on my cheeks. They burn like lamps, and I wonder if, later, they will cast enough light to read by, if they will help me to see.

Later I walk around the room trying to lift the dark cover of night with a flashlight in my hand, as if its fading beam were a shovel. I'm trying to understand how one proceeds from blindness to seeing, from seeing to vision.

In Greenland's early days a young shaman would come to the old *angakkoq* and say, *Takorusuppara.* "I come to you because I desire to see." After purifying himself by fasting and suffering cold and solitude, he would sit on a pair of polar-bear pants beside the old man, hidden from the villagers by a curtain of skin, and in time would receive *qaamaneq*—a light suddenly felt in his body, an inexplicable searchlight that enabled him to see in the dark.

One young shaman told Knud Rasmussen that his first experience of "enlightenment" was a feeling of rising up—literally, up into the air so that he could see through mountains, could see things far away, even blades of grass, and on that great plain he could locate all lost souls.

The next day. I don't know where I am. Wind comes through the walls. Maybe the walls have fallen away and merged with the walls of the galaxy. In this place it seems that there are only undefined distances that grow wider. I pick up a two-week-old *New York Times* science section brought from America, and it confirms this notion. "Space Telescope Reveals 40 Billion More Galaxies," the headline reads. Following the repair of the Hubble Space Telescope, which gives detailed portraits of galaxies far out in space and far back in time, astronomers learned that the universe is at least five times as vast as they had thought and is still expanding. Because of the telescope's power, many fainter galaxies are now being counted for the first time.

From the window I look into indigo space, and indigo space, like an eyeless eye, looks back at me. The thirteenth-century Zen teacher Dogen wrote, "To say that the world is resting on the wheel of space or on the wheel of wind is not the truth of the self or the truth of others. Such a statement is based on a small view. People speak this way because they think that it must be impossible to exist without having a place on which to rest."

In the harbor, we walk on crystal. Night is a transparency, and ice is the cataract over the eye that won't see. Only the fin-like keels of fishing boats touch water under ice, and the fish look up through their cold lenses at our awkward boots. Beyond the harbor there is still-open water and the fjord is a wrinkled sheath of ink that has lost the word "ice."

Later. Twilight gone to dark. I lie naked, careless, not quite destitute under a full moon on a polar night. Greenlanders thought that the moon and sun were sister and brother who had unknowingly slept together. After they discovered their incest they sailed up to the sky holding torches, and lived in separate houses from then on. In summer only sun, the sister, came out of her house, and in winter only the brother moon came out. Sometimes, though, he had to go away to get animals for the people to eat, which is why, when the new moon came, the people were thankful for the return of its light.

I light two candles and open a bottle of Fitou, a red table wine from a French village I once visited. Strange that I can get it here. The biweekly helicopter from Upernavik, a town 100 miles to the north, comes and goes, its pale headlights wedging a channel of light in dark air: should I run to the heliport and escape, or give up and stay here forever? In the dark there is no middle ground.

Sitting by the window, I must look like a character from an Edward Hopper painting—almost unmoving but not unmoved. Stuck here on this Arctic Alcatraz, I don't know what I'm moved to, except too much drink, and low-fever rage.

I write and drink by candlelight. No leaf, no shadow, no used-up senses finally coming to rest, no lover's post-orgasmic sleep. Only this: a cold room where snow fallen from my boots does not melt and the toilet in the unheated entry of the house stinks because it has not been emptied for days. It occurs to me that the only shadow I've noticed since last autumn is the wavering one a candle makes, casting its uncertainty upon the wall.

Later in the evening the wind stops and a skin of ice hardens over the water. Groups of villagers come down to the harbor to watch and wait. An old woman standing next to me looks far out over the ice and water and says, "If people go out, they will die. They will fall through the ice and go down to where the sea goddess lives. No one knows about ice anymore."

February 3. Jorge Luis Borges reprimands us for thinking that blind people live in a dark world. Behind his blind eyes, he says, there were always colors. In *Paradise Lost,* Milton, also blind, writes of burning lakes, of inward conflagrations. I tell Ludwig, Ole Jorgen's son, the story of Ulysses and the Cyclops, how in order to escape from the Cyclops, Ulysses and his men sharpened a stick and drove it through the giant's eye, then clung to the underbellies of sheep and were carried out of the cave right past their blinded captor.

The sun is an eye. Its coming means that the boulder rolls away from in front of the cave and we are set free. Yet I'm still night-foundered, still blind so much of the time. I read John Muir's book *Travels in Alaska.* He writes of a summer day, crossing a glacier: "July 19th. Nearly blind. The light is intolerable and I fear I may be long unfitted for work. I have been lying on my back all day with a snow poultice bound over my eyes. Every object I try to look at seems double."

I'm done with daylight. It reeks of carbonous toast crumbs left behind after breakfast, of the kind of bright decor that hides a congenital blindness to what is real. Today in my house, with no lights, no water, only a view of the darkness outside from the darkness within, from the unlighted room of the mind and the unheated room of the heart, I know that what is real comes together only in darkness, under the proscenium of night's gaunt hood.

It also occurs to me that the real and the imagined have long since fused here, that it's not the content of experience that is important but the structure of our knowing.

In the next days there is more daylight, three or four hours at least, but not enough to read by—that's become my measuring stick. Tomorrow the sun will peep over the ridge, then disappear. Now I don't want it. I've grown accustomed to the privacy and waywardness of night. In daylight all recognitions turn out to be misconceptions. During one of my many naps I dream that I can hear the sun beating behind the rocky peninsula like an expectant heart.

February 4. Sun Day, Sonntag, Sunday, Solfest. At ten in the morning light heaves up. It's seventeen below zero and the sky over the Nuussuaq Peninsula is a pink lip trembling. The wind is sharp. Ann and Ole Jorgen spread a yellow cloth on the diningroom table for our post-sun feast. In northern Greenland it is still dark. Solfest will not reach Thule for another three weeks.

Here in Uummannaq it is nearly time. Panic sets in. Do the children have mittens, caps, boots on? Gitte, a neighbor, comes by in her pickup to take us all to the topmost viewpoint on the island—her house. Ole Jorgen, Ann, Pipaloq (their two-year-old daughter), Ludwig, and I jump in. At the top we run to the edge of a cliff that looks across roiling fjord waters south toward the mountains. There's a moment of utter breathlessness, then a pale light begins to move into the sky and smears itself from the sharp point of the heart-shaped mountain down into the village. Every object of Arctic clutter momentarily goes from shade to gloss—sleds, harnesses, dogs, drying racks, clotheslines, drying animal skins, cars, baby carriages, empty bottles, gravestones. House by house, the dead windows come alive. The sled dogs stand up and stretch in the sun, shaking all the secrets of winter from their coats.

Eleven forty-seven A.M. Ole Jorgen counts down: five, four, three, two . . . A spray of cloud lifts, lit from below and fired to the color of salmon. From behind the upside-down arch of rock, incandescent daggers spike the sky. In the square notch between two peaks, a tiny crescent of sun appears, throwing flames onto the forehead of morning.

"Look, I can see my shadow!" Ole Jorgen says. His son runs to the wall of the house, affectionately touching the elongated body of his father. "That's you, papa!" he says.

Do shadows prove existence? *"Sono io,"* Gitte yells out across the valley as if yodeling. "I am."

For six minutes the sun burns inside the notch like a flame. When it scuttles behind the ridge again, our shadows dwindle to nothingness. I am not I.

Everyone goes inside to eat and drink: *kaffe,* tea, *mitaq* (whale skin with a quarter inch of fat), rye bread, cheese, smoked salmon, and a dark Dansk liqueur that tastes like night. Outside, the sky is still bright and sun pushes west behind the mountain as if behind the back of a giant, almost appearing again in a crack, then going blank again.

We toast Knud Rasmussen, polar explorer and ethnographer extraordinaire; we toast the return of the sun. After all, we're still alive despite our various bouts of cancer, tooth loss, divorce, marriage, childbearing, barrenness, and, in my case, lightning. As I drink down my liqueur, it occurs to me that there are all kinds of blindness and all kinds of seeing, that a dark world is not emblematic of death but of a feral clarity. And so I must wonder: in this sudden flood of sun, have I seen anything?

Afternoon. The pink light is going, not down but up, a rising curtain lifting light across the face of the village, up the long tooth of Uummannaq Mountain, leaving in its wake the old darkness. The diesel-powered lights of town come on as we stumble home. Dogs are fed.

An old man chips away at an iceberg, carrying a chunk in his pail to melt for drinking water. The world has returned to its dark normalcy.

Walking back to my perched house, I see that out in the bay a collapsed iceberg holds a tiny lake in its center, a turquoise eye glancing upward. The moon comes up in the east as if it were a sun, and for the second time in one day, the mountains go bright.

Today winter was a burning lake and I watched it catch fire.

Epilogue

An Old Woman's Song

Alas, I draw breath heavily,
my lungs breathe heavily,
as I call for my song.

When the news arrived
of far-off friends,
starving for winter game,
I wanted to sing:
to invoke the words from above,
the music from above.
Hajaja!

I forget the fire in my chest,
and the wheeze of the lungs
while I sing,
and I remember the old times
when I was strong.

These were times
when no-one rivalled me
at flensing seal;
when all alone, I boned and cut
the lean flesh
of three great reindeer-bulls
for drying!

Look: delicious slices
spread out on the mountain-stones,
while the sun rides up the sky
in the cool morning,
in the cool morning!

—Akjartoq (Caribou Eskimo woman)

$\mathcal{C}$ontributors

Roald Amundsen, was a Norwegian whose hard training and intelligent approach to Polar exploration made him the most successful Polar explorer of his time—some would say of all time. Between 1903 and 1906, he navigated the small, forty-seven-ton sloop *Gjoa* east to west across the Canadian Arctic, and became the first to complete the Northwest Passage by water. He was planning a drift across the North Pole in 1909 when he heard that Peary had reached it, and shifted his plans south to Antarctica, reaching it by dogsled on December 14, 1911, just weeks ahead of the ill-fated British expedition led by Robert Falcon Scott. He continued his Polar explorations with an air attempt at the North Pole in 1926, in company with the American Lincoln Ellsworth and an air crossing with Ellsworth and the Italian Umberto Nobile. Amundsen died in 1928 when his plane went down in the Arctic Ocean en route to search for Nobile, whose own dirigible had crashed on the ice.

Comock was an Inuit who lived around the turn of the century near Cape Wolstenholme in the northeast part of Hudson's Bay. In 1912 Comock and thirteen Inuit adults and children were intercepted by Robert Flaherty, a Canadian mining engineer and filmmaker, who was on a hunting trip. Comock told Flaherty the story of their drift. Flaherty was deeply struck by the story and recited it years later during a broadcast on BBC radio. It was preserved in book form by Edmund Carpenter as *The Story of Comock the Eskimo*.

Frederick A. Cook served as surgeon on Robert Peary's first Arctic expedition in 1891, worked as ship's doctor aboard the Belgian Anarctic Expedition, and spent several years exploring Mount McKinley in Alaska. He spent two years with Inuit companions on a marathon expedition up Ellesmere Island, during which he claimed to have made a successful bid for the North Pole in 1908, a year earlier than Peary's try. Because Cook spent a year holed up on Ellesmere, both he and Peary returned from their attempts in spring 1909, and Peary immediately attacked Cook's claim. Neither man, it turned out, had very strong evidence for the claim of being first to the Pole. Cook's early claims to have climbed Mount McKinley then came under attack. In the 1920s, he served a six-year prison term for stock fraud, but was granted a presidential pardon in 1940.

Gontran de Poncins, a French nobleman, abandoned careers in the arts and business to become a roving journalist. 1n 1939, he set out for the remotest area of the Central Canadian Arctic on a fifteen-month journey that he hoped would provide him a spiritual escape from Parisian life. His account of that experience, *Kabloona,* written in collaboration with Lewis Galantiere, is one of the most insightful and literary accounts of a Southerner confronting Inuit life.

Gretel Ehrlich spent many years of her adult life on a ranch in Wyoming, which she chronicled in her book *The Solace of Open Spaces.* It was in Wyoming that she was struck by lightning, a harrowing ordeal described in her book *A Match to the Heart.* In recent years Ehrlich has made many trips to Greenland's Arctic; she is writing a book about her experiences there.

Sir John Franklin is perhaps the most famous, and ill-fated, of the mid-nineteenth-century Arctic explorers. Like Samuel Hearne, Franklin went to sea at a tender age with the Royal Navy and fought the French in the Napoleonic Wars (and lost part of his hearing during the Battle of Trafalgar). At the war's end, he took up Arctic exploration. His attempt in 1845 to find the Northwest Passage resulted in the wholesale disappearance of his two ships and 128 men, whose fate was not learned until some ten years and forty or more search expeditions later.

Minnie Aodla Freeman, a Canadian Inuit, was born on the Cape Hope Islands of James Bay and attended an Anglican mission school at Fort George, where she learned English. In 1957 she took a job with the Canadian government to help with the tremendous numbers of Inuit who, in the 1950s, had contracted tuberculosis. She eventually moved south to Ottawa to work as an interpreter for the government's medical social services program. Her memoir is titled *Life Among the Qallunaat*—"Qallunaat" is the Inuit word for Southerners.

Adolphus W. Greely served with valor in the Civil War, and though he had no previous Arctic experience, took part in an expedition that the U.S. Army organized after the war in search of the North Pole. He was given a crash course in the Arctic when, during the 1881 expedition, he and his crew were marooned on Ellesmere Island for almost two years.

Despite questions that lingered over the circumstances of the tragedy and evidence of cannibalism on the part of someone in the party, Greely went on to become a brigadier general, author of many books, and one of the founders of the American Geographical Society.

Isaac I. Hayes, who was trained in medicine, signed on as ship's doctor on Elisha Kent Kane's *Advance.* Funded by New York financier Henry Grinnell, Kane was supposedly looking for Franklin, but more likely he was making an attempt at the North Pole. The ship froze in the ice off Northern Greenland in 1853 and failed to melt out the following year, prompting Hayes and several other crew members to try to make an escape to the south by small boat and dogsled. This ill-starred and at times hilariously inept attempt is the subject of his *Arctic Boat Journey.*

Samuel Hearne went to sea at age eleven, served with the Royal Navy in battle with the French, and then joined the Hudson's Bay Company. In 1769, at age twenty-four, he set out on foot across the Barren Lands west of Hudson Bay in search of the fabled Coppermine River with the hope that, as rumored, it contained fabulous mineral wealth. He didn't find gold, but he did explore tens of thousands of square miles of territory never before seen by Europeans and wrote a perceptive and eloquent account of his travels.

Marie Herbert was a young Irish actress who'd spent much of her childhood in the tropics of Ceylon. Her husband, Wally, a polar explorer, made a traversing of the North Pole by dogsled in 1969. A few years later, he decided to return to the Polar Inuit of North Greenland to make a film about their way of life. Accompanying him during this year-long stay was his young wife and their two-year-old daughter, Kari. Marie's account of her life in the Arctic can be found in her memoir of that year, *The Snow People.*

Barry Lopez is one of America's foremost writers about the natural world. His work spans non-fiction and fiction, essays and book-length works, among them *Desert Notes: Reflections in the Eye of a Raven; Giving Birth to Thunder; Sleeping with his Father: Coyote Builds North America; Of Wolves and Men; River Notes; Arctic Dreams; The Dance of Herons;* and a collection of short stories, *Winter Count.*

Finn Lynge has been a long-time advocate of the rights of native peoples and a representative of the people of Greenland. Born of a Greenlandic father and Danish mother, he has served as a Catholic priest, as Greenland's representative in the European Parliament, and as a consultant in Greenland affairs for the Danish Foreign Ministry in Copenhagen.

Jean Malaurie first went to the Arctic to study the erosion process on stones. Once there, he became interested in the social dynamics of the

Polar Inuit. He spent a year living among them in 1950 when he was twenty-six, just as the United States was constructing a huge Cold War–inspired airbase in Polar Inuit territory. He has since become one of the foremost ethnographers of the Inuit, and his book following his time among the Inuit, *The Last Kings of Thule,* has been translated into twenty-two languages.

Johan August Miertsching was a German-born Moravian missionary who learned the Inuit language while serving in Labrador. In 1859 he was recruited to serve as interpreter aboard the *Investigator,* one of the many British ships sent in search of Franklin. The *Investigator* never found Franklin, but after four years trapped in the Arctic, Miertsching and the other crew members made it home to England. Once home, Miertsching pledged in his diary never to cross the Arctic Circle again.

Minik, spelled a variety of ways, is the English translation of the name of a young Inuit boy who, in 1887, was brought back from Northern Greenland to New York, along with his father and four other Inuit, by the Arctic explorer Robert Peary. Housed in the basement of the American Museum of Natural History, four of the six Inuit, including Minik's father, quickly died of pneumonia. The museum staged a mock burial of Minik's father, but young Minik discovered the ruse and spent years trying to recover his father's body from the museum's collections and return to Greenland. He did eventually make it back to Greenland, later returned to the United States, and died of influenza in a logging camp in 1918.

Fridtjof Nansen, the Norwegian explorer, is one of the few giants of Arctic exploration whose reputation has continued untainted to this day. In 1893 he set forth in the *Fram* to try to lock the ship into the Arctic ice and drift on the currents across the North Pole. The ship set a new record for "farthest north," but drifted short of the Pole itself. Nansen went on to a distinguished career as an oceanographer and in humanitarian work with refugees. He won the Nobel Peace Prize in 1922.

Richard K. Nelson, an American anthropologist, has spent many years living in Alaska and writing about the people of the Far North. His book *Shadow of a Hunter* is an account of a year in the life of the Inupiat people, an Inuit group who live in far northern Alaska. Nelson is also the author of a memoir of his life in the North, *The Island Within.*

Umberto Nobile, an Italian aeronautical engineer, was one of the pioneers of Arctic aviation. A general in the Italian Air Force as well as a professor of aeronautical engineering, he attempted a series of flights into the Arctic and to the North Pole including his own expedition in the *Italia.* The airship reached the Pole on one flight, but encountered bad headwinds on its return, and crashed on the Arctic ice. The flight had been highly politicized from the start and tied to Mussolini's Italian nationalism. When Nobile and the seven survivors were finally rescued, an inquiry found Nobile responsible and he resigned from his commission. After World War II and the collapse of the Fascist government, the report was discredited and he returned to service in the air force and his teaching of aeronautics. He died in 1978.

Duncan Pryde, born in Scotland and raised an orphan. He joined the merchant navy at fifteen and, after an eye injury forced him to resign, worked in a sewing machine factory. At the age of eighteen, he saw an ad posted by the Hudson's Bay Company calling for fur traders in the Far North. Pryde signed up for what turned out to be a thirteen-year-long stint in the Canadian North, ten years of it spent among the Inuit in the Arctic. A colorful writer, Pryde's account of those years is titled *Nunaga*.

Rachel A. Qitsualik is one of the most eloquent of a new generation of Inuit writers. Her father, a minister and a hunter who practiced the traditional ways of life, sent her to government boarding school at a young age where it was expected she would assume Southern ways. She has been an outspoken critic of misdirected government and educational policies toward the Inuit, and is a sharp-eyed chronicler of modern Inuit life. Her columns appear regularly in *Nunatsiaq News,* the Inuit newspaper of the Far North. The paper's Web site is located at www.nunatsiaq.com, which has a link to Rachel Qitsualik's own Web site.

John Rae, physician and explorer, was one of the first Europeans to adopt Inuit methods of travel and the first European to learn the fate of Sir John Franklin's lost expedition. In 1846, he embarked on a series of overland expeditions to the Canadian Arctic and mapped large stretches of new terrain and coastlines. He took part or led several expeditions in search of Franklin over a three-year stretch from 1848 to 1851, but it wasn't until 1853, while on a surveying expedition, that he heard Franklin's story from the Inuit.

Knud Rasmussen, part Danish and part Greenlandic Inuit, was one of the greatest ethnologists of the Inuit culture. Rasmussen spent several years living among the Polar Inuit of Northern Greenland. In 1921, he set out from Greenland by dogsled on an epic, three-year crossing of the American Arctic all the way to Alaska. With several companions and researchers, he visited every major Inuit tribe along the way, recorded their legends, poetry, and customs, and published a many-volumed set of the finding, titled *Report of the Fifth Thule Expedition,* as well as a popular account, *Across Arctic America*. He died in Denmark in 1933.

Vilhjalmur Stefansson, a Canadian of Icelandic descent, spent five years (1913–1918) exploring by dogsled a huge section of the Canadian Arctic and mapping its last large unknown lands. Stefansson spent a year among the Inuit to learn their language and their techniques for traveling and hunting, and conducted zoological and ethnographic studies as well. Stefansson wrote extensively about his travels in the Arctic. He went on to teach and consult at Dartmouth College, and the Stefansson Collection that he left there is one of the world's great libraries of Arctic exploration literature.

Will Steger and Paul Schurke, both residents of Northern Minnesota with a lifelong love of the outdoors, embarked in 1986 on an attempt to recreate a journey by dogsled to the North Pole. They vowed to make the journey without the support of aircraft, which no one had done since 1909 when Peary claimed to have succeeded in attaining the Pole. Their account of the incredible difficulties in first arranging the journey and then pulling it off are described in their book *North to the Pole.*

Georg Wilhelm Steller, a German-trained scientist, accompanied the Arctic explorer Vitus Bering on his 1741 crossing of the North Pacific from Siberia to coastal Alaska, commissioned by the czar of Russia to find the northwest coast of North America. Bering and many of the other sailors perished during the voyage, but Steller, playing an instrumental role in saving the remaining members, lived to write the expedition's story and record his scientific findings.

Jon Turk, an American writer and adventurer, was trained in chemistry but gave up a scientist's life for that of traveler and freelance writer. In 1980, he attempted to round by sea kayak South America's notoriously storm-battered Cape Horn. A few years later he tried to retrace the Northwest Passage by small boat, then made a long dogsled trip on Baffin Island. These adventures, along with Turk's sea kayak journey with his wife tracing an old migration route from Canada to Greenland, are told in his book *Cold Oceans.*

George E. Tyson, a whaling captain, was selected to accompany the American Arctic expedition of Charles Francis Hall in 1871 during the race for "farthest north." As a young sailor aboard an American whaling ship in Baffin Bay, Tyson and his buddies discovered the *Resolute,* one of several ships that had been abandoned in the ice by the British Royal Navy during the search for Franklin. It was years later on his expedition with Hall that Tyson ended up on his own remarkable drift out of the Arctic, spending five months on a shrinking ice floe.